Models of Growth and Distribution for Brazil

LANCE TAYLOR
EDMAR L. BACHA
ELIANA A. CARDOSO
FRANK J. LYSY

A WORLD BANK RESEARCH PUBLICATION
Published for the World Bank
Oxford University Press

Oxford University Press

NEW YORK OXFORD LONDON GLASGOW
TORONTO MELBOURNE WELLINGTON HONG KONG
TOKYO KUALA LUMPUR SINGAPORE JAKARTA
DELHI BOMBAY CALCUTTA MADRAS KARACHI
NAIROBI DAR ES SALAAM CAPE TOWN

The views and interpretations in this book are the authors' and should not be attributed to the World Bank, to its affiliated organizations, or to any individual acting in their behalf.

Library of Congress Cataloging in Publication Data
Main entry under title:

Models of growth and distribution for Brazil.

(A World Bank research publication)
Includes bibliographies and index.
1. Brazil—Economic conditions—1945– —Addresses, essays, lectures. 2. Income distribution—Brazil—Addresses, essays, lectures. 3. Brazil—Economic policy—Addresses, essays, lectures. I. Taylor, Lance. II. International Bank for Reconstruction and Development. III. Series: World Bank research publication.
HC187.M584 330.981'063 80-13786
ISBN 0-19-520206-6
ISBN 0-19-520207-4 (pbk.)

Contents

Figures

Tables

Preface

THE RELATION BETWEEN GROWTH and the distribution of its benefits has become a major concern of economists and policymakers in recent years. Simon Kuznets was the first to observe from cross-country data that the distribution of income shows an initial tendency to worsen among countries with increasing income, but subsequently to improve at still higher income levels. This empirical finding has been confirmed by later writers, although there is much variation among individual countries.

The World Bank has conducted research studies and supported others (of which the present volume is an example) to investigate the extent to which observed changes in the distribution of income during the process of growth can be attributed to the policy regime in the country concerned, as opposed to being an inevitable consequence of growth. Such studies have required the development of new tools of economic analysis, specifically the endogenous-price multisectoral model, or computable general equilibrium model. Such a model is described and used in this volume, which contributes as much to the methodology of economic analysis as to the understanding of the distributional consequences of rapid economic growth in Brazil.

A major finding of this work by Professors Taylor, Bacha, Cardoso, and Lysy is that public policy contributed to the deterioration in the distribution of income over the period studied. Wage policy (and particularly holding down the level of the minimum wage) and the concentration of educational expenditures at the tertiary level are highlighted. This finding stands in contrast to the conclusion drawn by Irma Adelman and Sherman Robinson in their study of Korea (*Income Distribution Policy in the Developing Countries* [Stanford, Calif.: Stanford University Press, 1977]), which was also supported by the World Bank as part of its program of research on growth and distribution. Adelman and Robinson concluded that the overall size distribution of income was not greatly affected by particular policy interventions, nor even by combinations of policies.

The extent to which these differences in main findings are due to variations in the country background, in the extent and intensity of policy interventions postulated, or in modeling approaches is not yet clear. Korea, in contrast to Brazil, is a small country with a relatively egalitarian distribution of income, so that the scope for further policy intervention may be limited. The macroeconomic specification of the model employed for the two countries also is different. The Adelman-Robinson study employed an essentially neoclassical model, whereas Taylor and his co-workers experimented with what have become known as different closing rules. They demonstrate that how macroeconomic equilibrium is obtained between supply and demand, whether with neoclassical or neo-Keynesian closing rules, can lead to profound differences in the macroeconomic story.

The objectives of the present study and the broad approach taken were discussed at a conference in Bellagio in 1973, as part of an overall assessment of the Bank's program of research on distribution and country modeling. The execution of the study and the conclusions drawn from it, however, were the responsibility of the authors. The volume makes an important contribution both to the practice of macroeconomic modeling and to the understanding of the evolution of the Brazilian economy over a period of rapid economic growth.

JOHN H. DULOY
Director, Development Research Center
The World Bank

Acknowledgments

THIS BOOK HAD ITS ORIGINS in a collaborative research project begun in the early 1970s to investigate prospects for growth and income distribution in Brazil through the use of computable planning models and political economic analysis. In addition to the four authors listed on the title page, Francisco Lopes, Dioisio Carneiro, and Pedro Malan made substantial contributions to the research. Sympathetic commentary over the years by Hollis Chenery, Albert Fishlow, Roger Norton, Jack Duloy, Peter Clark, and Rudolfo Hoffman is gratefully acknowledged. Most of the results described herein were complete by 1977, but various delays postponed publication of the book until 1980.

The work was undertaken at several places, mostly the University of Brasilia, Harvard University, Massachusetts Institute of Technology, Stanford University, and the World Bank. We are grateful to all these institutions for their support, and especially to the Bank for providing the bulk of the finance necessary.

Jane Carroll edited the manuscript for publication. Raphael Blow prepared the charts, Brian J. Svikhart supervised production of the book, and Ralph Ward and James Silvan indexed the text.

LANCE TAYLOR

Models of Growth and Distribution for Brazil

1 Introduction

Lance Taylor

THE EXPERIENCE OF BRAZIL in the last fifteen or twenty years provides a classic case for the study of economic change. Following several years of economic stagnation and political unrest, the military coup of 1964 inaugurated first a period of rigorous economic stabilization and then almost a decade of very rapid growth, accompanied by a marked increase in income inequality. Rapid expansion in exports and in the openness of the economy occurred simultaneously with increases in the depth and sophistication of financial intermediation. The functional income distribution apparently shifted toward capital, and at the same time the role of state enterprises increased enormously. An unprecedented marriage of private capitalism and state intervention produced a growth spurt unmatched in recent Latin American history. Regrettably, the pattern of income distribution was such that much of the population did not benefit from this growth.

The papers in this volume explore the Brazilian experience from the point of view of political economy, using computable general equilibrium income distribution models. The investigation has focused on the interactions of growth and income distribution, though the length of the ongoing research project, which began in 1972, has allowed time for both intellectual enrichment and change. The purpose of this volume is to put together the authors' current (early 1978) ideas about the Brazilian economic model[1] and to point to fruitful lines of future research. This chapter provides an outline of the book to ease the reader's task in following our own evolving ideas about economic change in Brazil.

Political Economy

Our observations on political economy are concentrated in chapters 2 and 10. The first of these is an interpretative review of aggregate Brazilian growth since 1964. Chapter 10 covers the extensive debate about the causes of the deterioration in Brazilian income equity that has been observed since 1960. The results of models discussed in other chapters and new statistical evidence are used to weigh the merits of the various explanations of distributional change that have been proposed.

The major points made in the second chapter are:

• The 1968–74 boom in Brazil was not an economic "miracle" but conformed rather closely to the cyclical growth pattern of the economy since World War II.

• The success of inflation control policies since 1964 can be attributed to the massive wage squeeze applied after 1964, especially during the first year of the military regime. Simulations with a macroeconomic model in chapter 4 show quite clearly that while more rapid growth of the money wage would have added to inflation, it would also have improved the functional income distribution.

• Foreign capital played an important dynamic role in the economic upsurge of the late 1960s but also was responsible for some of the most pressing problems of the period.

• Government intervention in the economy increased, though the "inflationary" cash deficit declined. Recent research by Cardoso (1978) shows that wage control was a key factor in permitting this more positive fiscal role.

• The balance of payments during the 1968–73 upswing was not sound. In effect, the 1974 international oil crisis only hastened the time when Brazil could not maintain the potential

1. Other research results following directly from the project are reported by Bacha (1976, 1978, and 1979), Cardoso (1977 and 1978), Cardoso and Taylor (1979), Taylor and Bacha (1976), and Taylor and Lysy (1979).

growth rate of its gross domestic product (GDP) without substantial balance of payments disequilibrium. Probable magnitudes of payments gaps are quantified in chapters 2 and 5.

• When domestic capacity limits and balance of payments constraints started to bind after 1972, economic policy seesawed, as rapid growth became increasingly incompatible with balance of payments stability and inflation control.

• In the immediate future a rigid import diet needs to be imposed to limit net external indebtedness of the country, and there appears to be little room to maneuver foreign trade policy.[2] Economic growth may slow down and inflation may accelerate.

Many of these same themes are taken up again in chapter 10, which focuses on income distribution. There, six sets of explanatory hypotheses about Brazilian distributional trends are analyzed. In brief, the hypotheses and our conclusions about them are:

• An idea often drawn from a paper by Kuznets (1955) is that changes in the structure of employment accompanying the intermediate stages of economic growth can lead to increases in income inequality. Such "Kuznets effects" have been proposed by economists associated with the Brazilian government as a cause of increasing income concentration. Statistical evidence summarized in chapter 10, however, strongly suggests that the change in income inequality resulting from sectoral, regional, and educational employment shifts is of uncertain sign and small.

• A closely related explanation is that excess demand for highly skilled workers widened the wage gap between different levels of skill and led to equity deterioration. Again, both statistical evidence and results from a multilevel-of-skill general equilibrium model of the Brazilian economy described in chapters 6 through 9 suggest that this explanation has little force. In fact, the supply of highly educated (and presumably skilled) workers has grown fast since the early 1960s. Under such circumstances, it would take extremely high rates of biased growth in demand for skills to cause a widening of wage differentials under any sort of competitive labor market assumptions. Simulation results in chapter 9 further show that government policy favoring the expansion of university education over elementary and other lower-

2. The current foreign trade perspective is discussed more fully in Bacha (1978 and 1979).

level education may have led to slower growth because of the high cost of training university graduates.

• Other papers, written by Americans but widely circulated by official agencies in Brazil, argue that on relevant welfare scales income distribution may in fact have *improved* during the 1960s. It is shown that these approaches misinterpret the available data.

• Our own view, already mentioned, is that wage control played a substantial role in income concentration, and this perspective is argued more fully in chapter 10.

• The wage squeeze hypothesis also fits naturally with the idea that institutional factors, including a more complex hierarchical structure in management and rapid expansion of government employment in "supergrades" contributed to the spread in wages. Real wages at the bottom of the earnings scale may have been held down by surplus labor, while in a rapidly growing economy the lid was off at the top. Institutional evidence supporting this explanation is provided.

• The last two hypotheses complement the macroeconomic observation that "forced saving"—shifts of the income distribution away from low-saving classes during periods of accelerating investment and economic growth—must have played a role in shaping Brazilian income distribution during the boom. The processes of forced saving are built into the formal models described in this book, and they may partially explain the Brazilian experience, as discussed in the following sections.

Forced Saving and Growth

In any economy, saving must equal investment in terms of current prices for macroeconomic equilibrium to exist. The question at hand is, What adjustments within the system permit this identity to be observed? Sen (1963) was perhaps the first to point out explicitly that expected patterns of growth and distribution may depend essentially on how a descriptive model of the economy is made algebraically determinate, or closed. Following Sen and others, we can distinguish two closure rules that have been important in the literature: the neoclassical and the neo-Keynesian.

The main neoclassical assumption is that something approximating full employment of factors of production is maintained by freely varying prices. Real wages or rents paid to factors are determined by their marginal productivity, so that with full employment all earnings flows are determined from the side of supply. With earnings given, the total amount saved is determined by behavioral parameters, and investment is assumed to adjust to saving. Expressed with more brevity, the neoclassical position is that "productivity and thrift" determine income distribution and investment in the short run, and the growth pattern of the economy in the long run.

According to the neo-Keynesian position, investment is determined by expectations, nonmarket considerations, and possibly the rate of interest. It is certainly not affected by the supply of saving generated by marginally determined wages and profit rates in the short run. Rather, factor payments and employment levels adjust to permit the supply of saving to equal investment demand. In particular, if real investment rises, the income distribution will shift toward economic agents with higher savings propensities to permit the necessary finance to appear. The extra saving is in some sense unintended and is called "forced" for that reason.

As already mentioned, processes of forced saving are built into our Brazilian models in various ways. A verbal example of the process will illustrate what happens.[3]

Consider an economy in which labor and capital can substitute freely along a well-behaved production function and in which raw material imports are also required to support production. The cost of imports and the money wage are assumed to be fixed, and some labor is unemployed. If investment demand rises, output will go up as more workers find jobs. If exports are fixed in the short run, the balance of payments deficit will become larger, since a higher production level requires more raw material imports. The rate of profit (marginal product of capital) will increase since there are decreasing returns to the existing stock of capital in the short run. The real wage, however, will fall, since higher profits will be passed along in a higher price of output and the money wage is fixed.

Now look at what occurs in terms of saving and investment. Real investment demand has gone up, and the current value of investment has gone up even more because of the price increases. The extra saving comes from increases in real profits that are partly hoarded and from the increased balance of payments

3. The following example is worked out in algebraic form in Taylor and Lysy (1979).

deficit, or "foreign saving." But real wages have fallen, and the real wage bill could have gone either up or down, depending on the elasticity of substitution. The income distribution has shifted to favor national profit recipients and foreigners over workers. Forced saving at the expense of labor has occurred.

Forced Saving in the Models for Brazil

The macroeconomics of the computable models for Brazil described in chapters 3 through 9 can be interpreted along the saving-investment lines just sketched out. The first three of these chapters deal with a one-sector model designed to fit available Brazilian national accounts information, while chapters 6 through 9 describe a much more ambitious multisectoral simulation. In the second exercise, the macro effects of forced saving are complemented by microeconomic stories involving shifts in resource allocation and consumption demand among different producing sectors and economic groups.

The macroeconomic model is based on national income accounting identities, with variant specifications closing them along neoclassical and neo-Keynesian lines similar (but not identical) to those described above. In the neoclassical closure, investment varies to meet available saving, the sum of the government current surplus, the balance of payments deficit, and savings flows from capital and labor incomes. These are determined by factor supplies and by profit and wage rates that follow from standard conditions of marginal productivity. In the neo-Keynesian closure, investment is taken as exogenous, and the marginal productivity conditions are dropped so that the relative returns of labor and capital can vary freely to permit forced saving to equal investment. In both closures, the money wage rate and labor employment are set exogenously (though varied parametrically), and the price level is determined from the sum of costs of labor, capital, and raw material imports.[4]

4. The growth of money supply is determined within the model by the government deficit and foreign trade surplus, and there is a weak feedback from varying prices to consumer demand through the interest rate. Prices are mainly determined by costs, however, and not by the money market. This treatment corresponds to most diagnoses of Brazilian inflation in the 1960s (see chapter 2), and its implicit assumption of endogenicity or passivity of monetary policy is supported by the econometric causality tests reported by Cardoso (1977).

The one-sector model is used to simulate Brazilian historical experience in the 1960s (chapter 4) and to make conditional forecasts for the 1970s (chapter 5). The first main conclusion in chapter 4 is that with plausible values for elasticities of substitution and other parameters, the neoclassically closed model cannot be made to fit Brazilian 1960–70 data,[5] largely because the volume of real investment generated endogenously by the model is far too low. In part because its investment levels are set exogenously, the Keynesian model can be used to replicate the past. In this closure, it is shown that the fall in the real legal minimum wage had a major role in shifting the income distribution away from labor and in slowing inflation. Similarly, rapid export growth may have led to deterioration in the functional income distribution by demanding more extreme savings efforts via inflation and a fall in real wages.

Chapter 5 extends these results to conditional forecasts for the 1970s. In both versions of the model more rapid growth of the money wage would lead to greater inflation, a higher labor share, and possibly higher output growth as well. The appropriate tradeoffs are also mapped out. The distributional effects of import substitution and export promotion policies are then analyzed, and it is shown that in the neo-Keynesian model there is a very costly tradeoff between improvements in the balance of payments and the labor share. This problem disappears in the neoclassical model, where substitution of domestic resources for imports permits accelerated depreciation of the cruzeiro to close the payments gap. Which model more accurately captures the present situation is a matter of judgment, but our own is that the neoclassical substitution assumptions are probably far too optimistic.

Chapters 6 through 9 present a much more detailed approximation to the Brazilian economy in the form of a multisector, multilevel-of-skill general equilibrium model of the functional income distribution. The theoretical structure is described in chapters 6 and 7, the data base in chapter 8, and a number of simulation exercises in chapter 9.[6]

5. The simulations for the 1960s are based on an old set of Brazilian national accounts which have since been superseded. The results for the 1970s are based on the new accounts.

6. In more detail, the model has twenty-five input-output sectors and distinguishes six levels of labor skills, largely by level of education. Capital stocks

Given the complexity of the model, it is useful to think about its solutions at two levels. When the model is solved under variations in parameters or exogenous variables, there is first a macroeconomic adjustment to bring saving in line with investment (or, what amounts to the same thing, to make aggregate supply equal aggregate demand). The mechanism is based on changes in the values of saving and investment resulting from movements both in relative prices and in the overall price level in relation to payments fixed in nominal terms—the exchange rate, certain government taxes and transfers, and remunerations of proprietors or entrepreneurs associated with production in certain sectors (especially small owner-operators in agriculture and the services). When aggregate demand falls, for example, all prices fall, and the income distribution shifts in favor of the proprietors and recipients of transfer payments. Government nominal expenditures decline (its purchases are fixed in real terms), but so do tax revenues and certain subsidies; the impact of price deflation on government saving is complex and of uncertain sign. The balance of payments deficit in domestic currency may also respond either negatively or positively, depending on import changes and relative price variation. Finally, with a fall in prices the value of a given real investment demand vector will fall, and the sum of saving from all sources must adjust accordingly. The usual result is that deflation improves the income distribution, calculated from all payments to labor (four to six skill types in each sector), capital income recipients by sector, and proprietors.

This macro savings-investment adjustment is accompanied by numerous microeconomic changes in the equilibrium solu-

---

are fixed in the short run in each sector, so that in addition to labor payments by skill types and sector, twenty-five quasi-rent flows are distinguished in the functional distribution. Payments to and employment of both labor and capital are determined by marginal productivity rules, assuming constant elasticity of substitution production functions in the sectors. The 120-odd income flows in the model are treated separately in calculating income distribution, but they are aggregated to four household classes by income and sector specialization in arriving at final consumer demand patterns via direct addilog complete expenditure systems. The model is completely closed with respect to saving and investment, with the former coming from the government surplus, balance of payments deficit, corporate retained earnings, depreciation allowances, and households. The specification is relatively complex, but of a type becoming more common in the literature. For other examples, see Adelman and Robinson (1977) and McCarthy and Taylor (1980).

tion—that is, shifts in employment levels by sector and consumer class, in costs and prices of particular sectors, in profit rates, tax revenues, and so on. A large number of such results are presented in chapter 9. The more interesting ones follow:

- In sensitivity analyses, it appears that the elasticity of labor supply from sectors such as agriculture and tertiary activities with surplus labor strongly affects economic equilibrium. More inelastic labor demand curves in these sectors lead to reduced growth and shift the income distribution toward capital. Among consumers, more diverse income elasticities of demand (a strong taste for luxuries by the rich, for example) lead to greater income inequality. Both results are consistent with the "structuralist" diagnosis of Latin American development problems and with the focus of formal development models such as that of Taylor and Bacha (1976).
- Under the model's pricing assumptions, changes in labor costs are passed along into higher prices, and the wage structure is kept stable by assumed high elasticities of substitution among skill types. Under such circumstances, increases in employment taxes in certain sectors, for example, are largely passed along into higher market prices and do not affect employment through neoclassical factor substitution. The employment shifts that are observed really come from consumer responsiveness to higher prices in the taxed sectors and are not large. Increases in profit taxes, on the other hand, are borne by recipients of profit incomes and improve the income distribution.
- Redirection of transfer payments from richer to poorer segments of the population does not affect relative prices unfavorably and thus is equalizing. Resulting changes in consumer demand from income effects substantially modify the mix of sectoral outputs, suggesting once again that divergence in demand patterns between rich and poor plays a major role in conditioning income inequality.
- Upgrading the educational attainment of any group in the labor force is equalizing, since it leads to an increase in aggregate supply, which is spread toward poorer people. Because of the high elasticities of substitution among types of labor skill, upgrading does not lead to large shifts in relative wages, but the shares of the affected groups in national income change markedly. Expanded education of low-skill workers would be both more equalizing and less costly in terms of gross national product (GNP) than would an expansion of the higher educational system.

• For all skill types, employment elasticities with respect to overall export increases are about 0.1. Low-skill groups benefit more from expansion of agricultural or food exports, however, while those with high skills benefit from export of the relatively high-technology products that the government has favored.

In general, the summary measures of income inequality such as the Gini coefficient do not show large improvements—a few percentage points at most—as a result of equalizing policies such as those described above. A combination of policies, however, would in part be additive and might lead to fairly noticeable improvements. At least according to the model, income inequality *can* be lessened by policy. The problem is that many Brazilian governmental actions seem to have taken the other direction.

Toward More Egalitarian Policies?

The general view we arrive at from the numerical results, the available data, and less easily formalized considerations of political economy, is that the "model" of growth adopted by Brazilian economic technocrats under the military regime has led to deterioration in relative income equity. The income distribution *could* be made more equal through a variety of policies. Specifically, we can draw on the results just summarized above to make several observations.

• From the one-sector model, it appears that a decline in money wages reduces the labor share and favors profit incomes; it may even retard the rate of economic growth. Less rigorous control of money wages might therefore benefit poorer classes, though at the cost of a higher rate of inflation. The crucial government policy variable here is the *minimum* wage, but it is argued on institutional and econometric grounds in chapter 10 that the entire wage structure is sensitive to the minimum, so that the government does have the ability through wage policy to help or harm a substantial proportion of the working population.

• Within the multisectoral framework, it appears that reduction of structural divergences in the economy (such as bottlenecks in the labor supply or highly diverse income elasticities of demand for different products) would lead to increased income equality. One obvious policy (though it does not fit neatly with the neoclassical production and consumption economics of the general equilibrium model) would be control of the expansion of sales of "modern" or "luxury" commodities by multinational and other firms operating in Brazil. Some of the political and institutional difficulties implicit in such a strategy are discussed in chapter 2.

- Well-designed tax and transfer policies could substantially improve the income distribution. Results from both the small and large models suggest that reductions in taxes on wages would not act as any particular spur to employment, but that shifting from taxes on wages to taxes on profits would lead to increased income equality (with the proviso that real investment is maintained). Redirection of transfer payments toward poorer segments of the population would clearly reduce inequality and shift production patterns away from luxury commodities and employment patterns away from the household-servant sector. Whether such shifts would be institutionally feasible given existing patterns of control of Brazilian industry is a moot point.
- Redistribution of assets toward poor people (for example, in agriculture) would improve their income position, and general equilibrium secondary effects would be neutral or equalizing in distributional terms. Again, the pattern of consumer demand would shift away from luxuries and toward wage goods.
- Stimulation of investment to break bottlenecks in sectors producing capital goods and intermediate goods would help equalize relative price shifts, so long as the general equilibrium model's competitive pricing assumptions are broadly applicable to Brazil.
- As mentioned above, education to develop labor skills would lead to more rapid growth of output and income equalization. But both growth and equity would benefit more from educational programs directed toward the illiterate and people with low educational attainments than from support of universities and other institutions training the highly skilled.
- Consideration of the employment-generating effects of exports from different sectors suggests that policies stimulating sales abroad of relatively high-technology goods may be misplaced.

On the basis of the model, a collection of policies of this type would lead to observable but not radical improvements in distributional equality, but such limited results are in the nature of the analysis conducted here. General equilibrium economic computations may provide rough guidelines for taking small but visible equalizing steps. They say very little about the design of larger political and economic changes in Brazil.

The relevant political question is, of course, whether the ruling Brazilian model would permit policy measures to bring about even a small amount of economic equalization. In chapters 2 and 10 it is argued that the dominant forces in the post-1964 regime—large government enterprise and multinational management, the bureaucracy, and the 10 to 20 percent of the Brazilian population that has reaped the fruits of the boom—had scant interest in income redistribution. It may be that this coalition is weakening, and more active redistribution policies will be possible. But this is a topic of investigation beyond the scope of the present volume.

Toward Better Models?

Has anything been learned that can help future model builders? It seems clear from the results here and in Adelman and Robinson (1977) that some sort of forced saving mechanism holds the key to macro adjustment in general equilibrium models in which saving must equal investment and in which output responds to aggregate demand. Income gainers and losers under any policy change can be traced by asking how the payments flows they receive will adjust to an assumed savings-investment disequilibrium.

Two sets of considerations constrain these responses. First, how well can specific groups maintain the real value of their payments flows as prices change? Such a question leads into issues of economic power and coercion which economists have ignored for decades. Second, insofar as relative income gainers and losers are determined by differences in small and hard-to-estimate parameters such as savings rates and Engel elasticities, detailed projections of the effects of policy changes on the functional distribution are beyond the realm of feasibility. A purely macro analysis with a model based on available data can, however, give substantial insight, as the results from chapters 3 through 5 demonstrate.

Under the circumstances, my own judgment is that a large model such as that in chapters 6 through 9 adds little to what one can learn from macro analysis based on a relevant class-based categorization of the functional income distribution, and from detailed partial equilibrium analysis of important areas of the economy such as education.[7] Useful research programs could be built around applied studies in that direction. Other efforts could be devoted to socioeconomic processes that cumulate to lead to large distributional shifts over time. The Taylor and Bacha (1976) model of Belindia is a first step along such lines, but there are undoubtedly many other roads for alert, politically observant economists to explore.

References

Adelman, Irma, and Sherman Robinson. 1977. *Income distribution policies in developing countries: A case study of Korea.* Stanford: Stanford University Press.

Bacha, Edmar L. 1976. *Os mitos de uma década: Ensaios de economia brasileira.* Rio de Janeiro: Paz e Terra.

———. 1978. Brazil's balance of payments before and after the oil crisis. Paper prepared for the UNCTAD/UNDP project on the balance of payments adjustment process in developing countries, July 1976. Brasília: University of Brasília; processed.

———. 1979. Notes on the Brazilian experience with minidevaluations, 1968–76. Paper presented at the Ford Foundation/Central Bank of Barbados seminar on developing countries and the international financial system, Barbados, January 11–14, 1978. *Journal of development economics* 6(December):463–82.

Cardoso, Eliana A. 1977. Moeda, renda e inflação: Algumas evidências da economia brasileira. *Pesquisa e planejamento econômico* 7(2):423–34.

———. 1978. Growth and real wages: Modelling the Brazilian economic miracle. Cambridge: Massachusetts Institute of Technology, Department of Economics; processed.

7. For example, the results on shifts in taxes and transfer payments in the large Brazilian general equilibrium model depend essentially on its macroeconomic specifications, and the direction of the results is certainly not affected by sectoral detail. In contrast, the results on the equalizing effects of education do not have to be formally derived in a general equilibrium framework, though they should be interpreted in light of macro balance.

Cardoso, Eliana A., and Lance Taylor. 1979. Identity-based planning of prices and quantities: Cambridge and neoclassical models for Brazil. *Journal of policy modelling* 1(January):83–111.

Kuznets, Simon S. 1955. Economic growth and income inequality. *American economic review* 45(March):1–28.

McCarthy, F. Desmond, and Lance Taylor. 1980. Macro food policy planning: A general equilibrium model for Pakistan. *Review of economics and statistics* 62(February):107–21.

Sen, Amartya K. 1963. Neoclassical and neo-Keynesian theories of distribution. *Economic record* 39:53–64.

Taylor, Lance, and Edmar L. Bacha. 1976. The unequalizing spiral: A first growth model for Belindia. *Quarterly journal of economics* 90:197–218.

Taylor, Lance, and Frank J. Lysy. 1979. Vanishing income redistribution: Keynesian clues about model surprises in the short run. *Journal of development economics* 6(March):11–30.

2

Selected Issues in Post-1964 Brazilian Economic Growth

Edmar L. Bacha

THIS CHAPTER ADDRESSES SELECTED ISSUES of Brazilian economic growth under the post-1964 military regime.[1] The aggregate growth record is summarized in the first section, using the concepts of potential GDP and GDP gap. Inflation control policies are also discussed in this section, with emphasis on the roles of the wage control program, monetary policy, and mechanisms for monetary correction. After a review of the role played by foreign capital, the pattern of state intervention in the economy is analyzed. A discussion of the balance of payments situation follows, with stress on the import-intensive nature of the post-1964 growth pattern. The section on macroeconomic policymaking since the oil crisis shows the difficulties that Brazilian policymakers felt in trying to satisfy multiple objectives in a context where the limits of the economically possible became much nar-

1. Parts of this chapter are drawn from Bacha (1977 and 1978). Readers not familiar with the economy of Brazil may benefit from reading Furtado (1963) and Baer (1965) for historical background; and Fishlow (1973 and 1974), Baer (1973), and Malan and Bonelli (1977) for complementary views on post-1964 Brazilian economic growth. A discussion of income distribution issues is postponed to chapter 10.

rower than before. Factors affecting the short- and medium-term perspectives for the economy are summarized in the last section.

Growth Record

The available figures for real aggregate output in Brazil provide a picture of an economy vigorously expanding at an average 7.5 percent potential growth rate in the post–World War II period.[2] Actual growth follows a cyclical pattern, with 1952–56, 1961–67, and the period from 1974 on characterized by a slowdown of growth rates and 1947–52, 1956–61, and 1967–74 characterized by rapid economic upswings. The cycles peak in 1952, 1961, and 1974. Following a common procedure, we obtain a potential output path by connecting the peak output levels with an exponential growth rate line (see table 2-1 and figure 2-1).

The growth rates of potential output accelerate slightly: they are 7.2, 7.4, and 7.7 percent a year, respectively, in 1947–52, 1952–64, and 1964–74. This pattern is in line with a historical trend of accelerating growth rates in the Brazilian economy since the beginning of the century.[3]

In this framework, the recent growth experience is best described as a vigorous economic recovery rather than an economic miracle. Its duration and the high growth rates attained can be explained by the broad gap between actual and potential growth since 1962. The economy was able to grow at an average 11.2 percent rate for seven years from 1967 to 1974 (which compares favorably with the 8.6 percent average growth rate maintained for

2. The output series for 1949 through 1976 was constructed by the economics department of Brazil's Central Bank, by interpolating between the "old" (1947 through 1972) and the "new" (1949, 1959, and 1965–76) GDP estimates of the Vargas Foundation. The values for 1947 and 1948 were obtained by applying to the Central Bank's 1949 value the same growth rates as in the "old" Vargas Foundation estimates. The value for 1977 is from *Conjuntura Econômica*, February 1978.

3. Haddad (1977) estimates the following yearly growth rates for aggregate output since 1900:

1900–02 to 1910–12:	3.96 percent
1910–12 to 1920–22:	3.97 percent
1920–22 to 1930–32:	4.04 percent
1930–32 to 1940–42:	4.71 percent
1940–42 to 1945–47:	5.49 percent.

Table 2-1. Gap between Potential and Actual Output, 1947–77
(1970 actual output = 100)

Year	Potential output (1)	Actual output (2)	Gap [(1) – (2)] / (1)
1947	22.4	22.4	0.000
1948	24.0	24.0	0.000
1949	25.7	25.6	0.004
1950	27.6	27.3	0.011
1951	29.6	29.0	0.021
1952	31.7	31.7	0.000
1953	34.1	32.6	0.046
1954	36.6	36.0	0.017
1955	39.3	38.6	0.018
1956	42.2	40.0	0.055
1957	45.4	43.4	0.046
1958	48.7	46.9	0.038
1959	52.3	49.7	0.052
1960	56.2	54.6	0.029
1961	60.4	60.4	0.000
1962	65.0	63.8	0.019
1963	70.1	65.0	0.078
1964	75.5	67.1	0.125
1965	81.3	69.1	0.177
1966	87.6	71.7	0.222
1967	94.3	75.2	0.254
1968	101.5	83.6	0.214
1969	109.4	91.9	0.190
1970	117.8	100.0	0.178
1971	126.8	113.3	0.119
1972	136.6	126.6	0.079
1973	147.1	144.2	0.020
1974	158.3	158.3	0.000
1975	170.6	167.3	0.020
1976	183.7	182.7	0.005
1977	197.9	191.3	0.035

Source: Economics department of the Central Bank of Brazil, based on the Vargas Foundation national accounts.

five years from 1956 to 1961), because during the six previous years, from 1961 to 1967, on average it had grown at only 3.7 percent a year (which compares unfavorably with the 6.0 percent yearly average experienced for four years in the previous downswing, from 1952 to 1956). Such statistical considerations suggest that the basic structural parameters limiting the country's

Figure 2-1. Gap between Potential and Actual Output, 1947-77 (1970 actual output = 100)

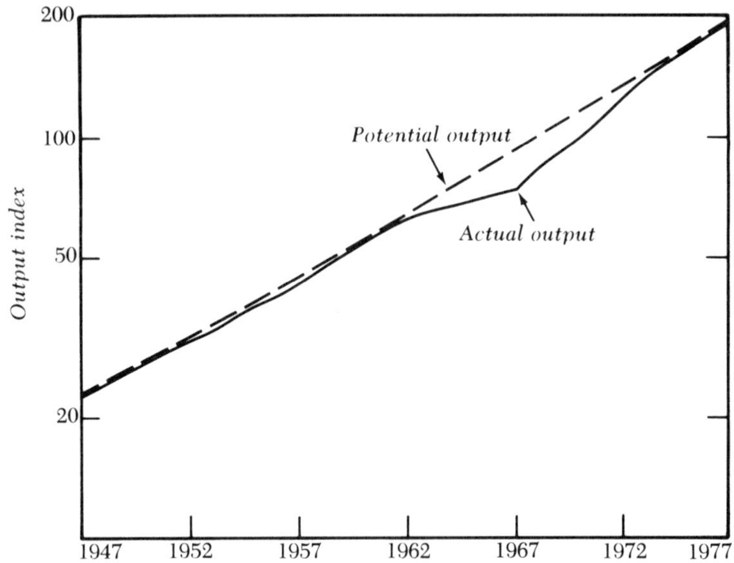

Source: Table 2-1.

potential growth rate have changed only slightly in the past few years, and that the interruption of the 11 percent growth path in 1974 had to do as much with the limitations of domestic capacity as with the international oil crisis.

The above description is supported by a recent study of Suzigan and others (1974), in which a potential output series is constructed for the industrial sector in 1955–72. This is done by applying cumulated investments to the 1961 peak industrial output–capital ratio. The quotient between actual and potential output, which has the value 1.0 in 1961, reaches a low figure of 0.79 in 1965, increases to 0.84 in 1966, and recedes to 0.80 in 1967. Thereafter, it starts a continuous upward trend, climaxing with a value of 0.98 in 1972, the last year in their series. The cyclical nature of the 1967–74 experience is confirmed by the behavior of the quarterly Vargas Foundation capacity utilization

Table 2-2. Vargas Foundation Capacity Utilization Indexes for Manufacturing Industry, 1968–77

Year	*January*	*April*	*July*	*October*
1968	n.a.	n.a.	n.a.	0.83
1969	n.a.	0.85	0.83	0.86
1970	0.86	0.85	0.87	0.86
1971	0.86	0.86	0.87	0.87
1972	0.87	0.86	0.87	0.89
1973	0.89	0.90	0.90	0.90
1974	0.90	0.89	0.89	0.87
1975	0.87	0.87	0.87	0.87
1976	0.89	0.89	0.89	0.87
1977	0.87	0.86	n.a.	0.82

n.a. Not available.
Source: Conjuntura Econômica, various issues.

index in the manufacturing sector (table 2-2). The initial value for this indicator is 0.83 in the fourth quarter of 1968; the following numbers show an uninterrupted upward trend, until a maximum value of 0.90 is attained, kept constant from the second quarter of 1973 to the first quarter of 1974.

The successful economic recovery after 1967 was generated by conventional expansionist monetary and fiscal policies. Roberto Campos, the economic czar in government from 1964 through 1967, meant to save Brazilian capitalism from inflationary mentality by squeezing aggregate demand. His successor, Antonio Delfim Netto, among other "bizarre structuralist ideas" (as Campos has put it in Simonsen and Campos 1974, p. 66), interpreted Brazilian inflation in 1966–67 as cost determined.[4] Acting on this diagnosis, Delfim Netto introduced direct price controls and, keeping a tight rein on wage deals, promoted active credit expansion for firms, consumers, and government.[5]

Expansion started with consumer durables and government expenditures, reached private investment subsequently, but left the wage goods sectors dependent on the behavior of export outlets since domestic markets did not recover significantly. Suzigan and others (1974) suggest that recovery proceeded in two

4. See Delfim Netto and others (1967).

5. The shift in government emphasis and economic philosophy is well documented by Fishlow (1973), and by Simonsen in Simonsen and Campos (1974, chap. 5).

stages: the first, from 1966 through 1969, was commanded by the expansion of consumer durables; and the second, from 1970 through 1973, centered on the dynamism of the capital goods industry.

An unusual characteristic of the post-1964 period was that inflation was successfully kept under control until 1972, despite the pressure of increasing demand, after having been significantly reduced from 87 percent a year in 1964 to 24 percent in 1967. A tight incomes policy seems to have been the main factor for this success. From January 1964 through February 1965 the Rio de Janeiro cost of living index went up by 91 percent, but the government in March 1965 allowed a minimum wage increase of only 57 percent from the levels established in February 1964. From February 1965 to February 1966 the cost of living went up by 44 percent, but the minimum wage was readjusted in March 1966 by only 27 percent. In March 1967 the minimum wage went up by 25 percent when the cost of living increased by as much as 37 percent from February 1966 to February 1967. After 1967 the wage squeeze was reduced, but only in the 1974–76 period did legal minimum wage readjustments consistently surpass observed cost of living increases (see table 2-3).

The lag of wages behind price increases under declining rates of inflation was made possible after the substitution of a military-backed regime for an elected government in April 1964. Previously, during the populist Goulart government, competitive bidding for popular support had led to a mobilization of the urban proletariat, with a multiplication of strikes and an acceleration of inflation rates. The 1964 regime brought about an immediate change in policy toward labor associations. Labor leaders were arrested and charters of some unions revoked. Usually, an intervener from the Labor Ministry was appointed, with control later turned over to "loyal" union members. The 1967 constitution prohibited strikes in essential activities, which are left undefined in the legal text. Strikes also were supressed under the provisions of the 1967 national security law. Free bargaining between labor unions and employers' associations was suspended, and all wage agreements were to be regulated by a wage formula dictated by the government. The formula was made up of three components. The first was designed to compensate for past inflation, reestablishing the average real wage observed in the preceding twenty-four months. The second anticipated future inflation, attempting to maintain during the following twelve months the same average

Table 2-3. Minimum Wages and Cost of Living in Rio de Janeiro, 1963–77

	Minimum wage		*Cost of living*	
Date	*Cruzeiros*	*Percentage change*	*Index (1965–67 = 100)*	*Percentage change*
January 1964			31.5	—
February 1964	42.00	—		
February 1965			60.3	91.4
March 1965	66.00	57.1		
February 1966			86.8	43.9
March 1966	84.00	27.2		
February 1967			119	37.1
March 1967	105.00	25.0		
February 1968			145	21.8
March 1968	129.60	23.4		
April 1969			185	27.6
May 1969	156.00	20.4		
April 1970			226	22.2
May 1970	187.20	20.0		
April 1971			274	21.2
May 1971	225.60	20.5		
April 1972			325	18.6
May 1972	268.80	19.1		
April 1973			368	13.2
May 1973	312.00	16.1		
April 1974			461	25.3
May 1974	376.80	20.8		
April 1975			580	25.8
May 1975	532.80	41.4		
April 1976			817	40.9
May 1976	768.00	44.1		
April 1977			1,180	44.4
May 1977	1,106.40	44.1		

Note: The cruzeiro was devalued steadily over this period.
Source: Conjuntura Econômica, various issues.

real wage as in the preceding period. A productivity adjustment factor was the third component of the formula. In theory, these rules not only guaranteed the purchasing power of wages but also maintained constant the wage share in output. In practice, expected future inflation was consistently underestimated until the late 1960s, whereas the allowance for productivity increases was much smaller than the observed growth of GDP per capita through the mid-1970s. (For details, see Carvalho 1973, and Fishlow 1974).

During Campos's term as economic minister, the wage policy was supplemented by an orthodox monetary policy in an attempt to reduce the inflation rate faster. The negative effects of this policy on real output promoted Delfim Netto to adopt an alternative approach to monetary policy, which, in the words of Mario Simonsen,

> started to be passively conducted in accordance with the principle that real output growth should not be affected by liquidity crises ... This resulted in an expansion of the means of payment at rates above what would normally be accepted by a believer in the quantity theory of money ... Actually, this passive monetary policy was compatible with inflation control only because the Government started to adopt an intense policy of price controls.[6]

Inflation control through a rigid incomes policy with monetary policy following the purely passive role of providing for the "needs of trade" was baptized "gradualism" by Brazilian technocrats. Structuralist economists from the United Nations Economic Commission for Latin America (ECLA), however, had warned since the early 1950s that shock treatment stabilization policies, as recommended by the International Monetary Fund (IMF), would result in sharp output losses with meager gains in combating inflation. They also stressed that inflation should be fought by the eradication of structural cost pressures rather than by demand management (Grunwald 1961). Given the populist ideological underpinnings of their doctrines, structuralist economists did not acknowledge that authoritarian regimes could succeed in substantially reducing inflationary pressures without impairing growth prospects by rigidly controlling wage earners' claims to higher nominal incomes. Hence, gradualism can be

6. See Simonsen and Campos (1974, pp. 85, 86, 114). "Passiveness" of monetary policy is hardly a novelty in modern Brazilian economic history. Using quarterly data for 1954–69, Cardoso (1977) has shown that the econometric evidence for a "needs of trade" causation sequence running from nominal GNP to money stock is at least as strong as the evidence for the reverse sequence of most macroeconomic models, running from money stock to nominal income. The conclusion that the money supply is passive is strengthened when the causation tests proposed by Sims (1972) are performed using quarterly series of inflation rates and growth rates of money stock for the 1946–74 period.

viewed as a belated, though twisted, admission of the correctness of ECLA economists' criticisms of the IMF brand of monetarism as a means of fighting inflation in Latin America. The success of gradualism also promoted orthodox Brazilian economists to review their macroeconomic models. For example, the inflation model of Simonsen (1970) is embedded in a demand-constrained output-determination process and stresses cost determination of price levels through a feedback mechanism which is only moderately qualified by the pressure of demand on capacity.[7]

The inflation control policy was accompanied by extensive reforms in the financial sector, the tax system, and the exchange rate regime, giving them more flexibility and increasing overall saving and the availability of foreign exchange. With wages under control, exchange rates, interest rates, tax collections, and public enterprise tariffs and prices could be raised without impairing private sector profit rates. The costs were borne by the public at large through a "corrective inflation" that fed only partially into legally determined wage levels.

The principle of monetary correction—of nominal interest rates or the value of debt instruments for expected or actual inflation—was first introduced for government bills in 1965. The extension of monetary correction to other financial instruments eventually allowed a considerable expansion of financial intermediation in the country, which previously was constrained by rigid ceilings on interest rates (Fishlow 1974).

The crawling peg as a system of exchange rate adjustment was introduced in August 1968, following the lead of Chile and Colombia (Bacha 1979). Previously, the exchange rate was devalued at long intervals and in large steps to keep up with a steadily growing domestic price level. Consequently, there were large fluctuations in the real exchange rate, which favored speculative activities and forced the government to adopt strict foreign exchange controls. These hindered export activities and made medium-term financial transactions more difficult. Under the crawling peg, the cruzeiro is devalued in small steps at fre-

7. Cavallo (1977) vindicates the structuralist model for Argentina, showing that for industrial goods the short-run contractionary effect of credit restriction is stronger on supply than on demand. Consequently, in the short run, credit restriction *increases* excess demand and aggravates inflationary pressures. Cavallo's theoretical model may help explain the stagflationary consequences of the Campos economic policies in Brazil. For more detailed empirical evaluations of these policies, see Morley (1971) and Fishlow (1973).

quent but uncertain intervals. The incentive to speculate in foreign exchange is minimized, and risk-averse entrepreneurs can be attracted to export activities as foreign exchange restrictions are lessened. The consistent pattern of minidevaluations decreased the probability of financial losses arising from unpredictable large devaluations. Hence, this policy also helped local entrepreneurs gain access to international financial markets.

Under the Geisel government, after 1974, wage readjustments were put in line with observed inflation rates. This policy decision closed the main escape valve of the monetary correction system (including the crawling peg) and consequently made the Brazilian inflation rate extremely vulnerable to the oil crisis of late 1973. This crisis occurred at the peak of a domestic cyclical expansion, when the high growth rates of the "miracle" period started catching up with available input capacity. Scarcities of raw materials and manpower became apparent in Brazil's main urban centers in 1972–73 (Singer 1977). This coincided with an exhaustion of surplus capacity in the industrial sector, as indicated both by the behavior of the Vargas Foundation index of capacity utilization (table 2-2) and by the proportion of industrialists considering demand to be "strong" rather than "normal" or "weak" in the Vargas Foundation quarterly industrial survey. Overheating of the economy is clearly indicated by this index. In October 1973, 60 percent of the respondents considered demand to be "strong," as compared with an average of 22 percent of the respondents in the final quarter of the four previous years.[8]

Excess demand in output and factor markets together with the increase in the prices of oil and other tradable products resonated with the monetary correction system and nearly tripled the rate of inflation between 1972 and 1976. The next to the last section below analyzes in more detail the post-1973 macroeconomic problems of the country.

Foreign Capital

The outward-looking economic strategy followed after 1964 relied heavily on the domestic expansion of multinational corporations (MNCs) for its dynamism. As reported in Suzigan and

8. See *Conjuntura Econômica*, various issues. The relevant data are collected in Bacha (1978).

others (1974), leading sectors of industrial growth in the post-1966 period were transport equipment, electrical machinery and appliances, mechanical industry, rubber, chemicals, and nonmetallic mineral products. Foreign capital has a dominant influence in the first four sectors, as shown in table 2-4. Chemicals grew under the impulse of Petrobrás, the state petroleum company, and nonmetallic minerals benefited from the boom in construction activity initially promoted by the National Housing Bank

Table 2-4. Patterns of Asset Ownership of the 5,113 Largest Nonfinancial Enterprises, 1974

Sector	Total net assets (millions of cruzeiros)	Percentage share: Public enterprises	Percentage share: Foreign enterprises	Percentage share: National private enterprises
Mining	9,637	62	12	26
Manufacturing	161,571	20	29	51
Nonmetallic	7,551	2	35	64
Metallic	27,711	34	12	54
Mechanical	8,293	1	46	53
Electrical	6,476	0	61	39
Transport equipment	15,155	4	63	33
Wood	8,782	0	9	91
Furniture	577	0	0	100
Rubber	1,834	6	61	33
Leather	685	0	11	89
Chemicals	40,162	55	23	22
Textiles	12,411	0	13	87
Food	16,910	1	31	68
Beverages	3,571	0	14	86
Tobacco	2,095	0	99	1
Printing	2,143	0	2	98
Miscellaneous	8,211	0	47	53
Agriculture, forestry	4,825	1	3	96
Construction	18,317	15	3	82
Public utilities	97,836	88	7	6
Transport	19,052	78	1	21
Other	78,784	90	8	2
Commerce	30,735	1	5	95
Services	84,656	27	4	69
Total	407,557	37	15	48

Note: Percentages may not add to 100 because of rounding.
Source: "Quem é Quem na Economia Brasileira," *Visão*, August 31, 1975, p. 29.

and later financed by low-interest loans from the Eurodollar market.[9]

Foreign capital also has a monopoly in the tobacco industry and participates heavily in the modern sectors of food and other manufacturing activities. The overall participation of foreign firms in the total value of Brazilian fixed assets is not large. The "Who's Who" data on 5,113 nonfinancial firms published by *Visão*, a Brazilian business magazine (see table 2-4), estimate the foreign share of fixed assets to be 15 percent. At issue, however, are bigness, technological dynamism, access to credit sources, asset concentration, and market dominance. Being in control of new technological developments in industrial processes and products, the subsidiaries of MNCs can condition the milieu in which they operate. This occurs especially when domestic firms expand passively in response to the growth of their market, and the government "pragmatically" adapts its policies, infrastructure investment, and the country savings potential to the growth needs of the leading privately controlled sectors.[10] This seems to have happened in post-1964 Brazilian experience. For example, the extraordinary growth of the foreign-owned car industry stimulated the expansion of private Brazilian and foreign firms producing spare parts and metallic products; determined the rhythm of oil imports, refinery construction, and road building; conditioned the style of urban planning; and channeled a large share of private saving to finance the purchase of cars. The car industry in its multiple ramifications epitomizes the premature affluent society brought to Brazil by the confluence of interests associated with the MNCs.

According to Furtado (1972), the Brazilian experience also illustrates another fundamental distortion stemming from an uncontrolled expansion of MNCs' activities. This relates to the consequences of adapting the pattern of domestic final demand to the expansion needs of the MNCs. The products sold by these firms conform to the market needs in industrial countries, where per capita incomes are five to ten times higher than in Brazil. To

9. The interrelationship between "dynamism" and foreign ownership comes up even more clearly when only the largest 318 industrial firms are taken into account, as in Von Doellinger, Faria, and Cavalcanti (1974). In their sample of big firms, the share of total assets owned by foreign enterprises in mining and manufacturing is 40 percent rather than the 29 percent that can be calculated from the data in table 2-4.

10. This theme is further explored in Bacha (1976, Essay no. 1.3).

produce an attractive market for these firms in Brazil, income must be highly concentrated on the top and, for a given family income, demand needs to be twisted toward international goods. At a minimum, this conclusion is not negated by the fact that in a sample of twenty-one countries from all continents Brazil has the largest share of income going to the top 20 percent of the population (Atkinson 1975). More broadly based international comparisons of income distributions in Chenery and others (1974) also find Brazil among the countries with the highest levels of income inequality.

The demand twist toward foreign-controlled goods has been referred to in the literature as the "international demonstration effect." It is stressed by Wells (1976), whose criticism of the Furtado thesis is based on data showing that ownership of consumer durables is widespread among urban groups in the country, rather than concentrated in the top 5 or 10 percent of urban families. Wells's point (which should be viewed as a complement to rather than a substitute for Furtado's hypothesis) is supported by the results of consumer budget surveys conducted in São Paulo in 1958 and 1970. They show a distinctly higher share of expenditures on consumer durables in workers' family budgets (and a correspondingly lower share of expenditures on food items) in 1970, in spite of slightly lower real family incomes (DIEESE 1974). In a subsequent paper, Wells (1977) criticizes these survey results and apparently changes his mind on the empirical importance of the demand twist toward durables. A definite empirical judgment on these questions is made difficult by the paucity of hard data.

Role of the State

As a result of the political impasse of the early 1960s, both Presidents Janio Quadros (1961) and João Goulart (1962–63) failed to enlarge the revenue base for the expansion of state economic activities. Public sector expenditures rose from 20 percent of GDP in 1955 to 27 percent in 1962, and gross investment of the public sector (including state enterprises) represented 39 percent of total capital formation in 1962, up from 25 percent in 1955 (Silva 1971). Nonetheless, the tax base was inelastic and the fiscal machinery outdated. Exporters benefited from the establishment of a single exchange rate in 1961, but with the extinction of the multiple exchange rate system the government lost a revenue source that in 1960 had generated income equal to 15 percent of its regular tax collections. The acquisition of the surplus over exports of bumper coffee crops from 1958 to 1960 also imposed severe financial strains on the government. As a consequence, deficits soared. As a proportion of GDP, the federal government budget deficit increased from less than 1 percent in 1955 to nearly 5 percent in 1962 (Ministry of Planning 1964). Concurrently, government agency or public enterprise programs for road building, oil exploration and refining, electricity supply, communications, and iron ore mining and steel production, among others, lagged behind planned levels as strictly enforced price controls undermined the financial capabilities of these agencies.

The 1964 regime, by doing away with the participation of the urban working class in the power structure, resolved the political impasse in clearly defined ways. The state was made solvent at the new high levels of expenditure with the costs being borne by the public at large through the mechanism of corrective inflation. The 1964–67 wage crunch was the crucial element of this operation. At a more explicit level, a substantial tax reform was implemented, the fiscal machinery streamlined, and a "realistic" price policy initiated for the output of public services and government firms.

The success of the reforms allowed federal government expenditures to grow at a faster rate than GDP since the mid-1960s. The government share in output averaged 9.5 percent in 1966–70. This increased to 10.1 percent in 1971–75 and to 10.5 percent in 1976–77. Federal government revenues expanded at an even faster rate. Budget deficits became increasingly smaller after 1967, and equilibrium was achieved in 1973. From 1974 onward, a small budget surplus was generated. Throughout the period, except for 1968 and 1977, net sales of government bonds and bills either more than compensated for the deficits or else added to the surpluses. Consequently, a continuous downward pressure on the money stock was exerted by the operations of the monetary authorities with the federal Treasury.[11]

The emphasis on administrative decentralization, efficiency, and profit making resulted in a significant expansion and diversification of the activities of public enterprises, as well as in new mechanisms of financial coordination through holding compa-

11. The relevant data are in *Conjuntura Econômica*, various issues. Derived statistics are compiled in Bacha (1978).

nies such as Eletrobrás, Telebrás, Siderbrás, and Portobrás at the national level, and Fepasa, Sabesp, and Telesp at the level of the state of São Paulo. As of 1974, nineteen of the twenty largest, and forty-five of the hundred largest Brazilian corporations were state-owned. Only eleven of those forty-five are not in public utilities. The growth rate of state corporations has been sufficiently high, however, to increase their share in the total profits of the hundred largest corporations from 54 percent in 1968 to 63 percent in 1974. The proportion of net assets of the same hundred largest corporations belonging to state enterprises went up from 67 to 74 percent between 1970 and 1974. Thus, despite a lower profit rate, the state enterprises, through their access to earmarked taxes, compulsory loans, and general government funds, apparently managed to grow at a faster pace than their private counterparts.[12]

This complex growth pattern of public capital goes beyond federal activities. State and local governments have been seized by a *desenvolvimentista* (developmentalist) mentality that may eventually cause them to assert the position of their own firms in the marketplace, even in the face of opposition from private interests.[13] In spite of eventual conflicts, it can be argued that public investments were meant to play only a supporting role in the expansion of private initiative, particularly that of foreign origin. According to Tavares and Serra (1973), the crucial element guaranteeing the economic dynamism of the period was the high level of "organic solidarity" achieved by the productive activities of the state and the MNCs.[14] Together, they formed "an integrated nucleus of expansion," by dividing the tasks between them. The state supplied the domestic market with basic inputs and external economies at low cost, which the MNCs used to expand in both the domestic and export markets.[15]

12. The average profit rate for state enterprises was 9 percent over the 1968–74 period, as compared with average profit rates over the same period of 12.5 and 15.8 percent, respectively, for the private national and foreign firms included in the hundred largest Brazilian corporations. See *Visão*, August 31, 1975.

13. A good case in point is the state of Minas Gerais, which has recently moved toward industrialization with its own public corporations, such as Camig, Casemg, Cemig, Frimisa, and Usiminas.

14. The "organic solidarity" between the state and the MNCs is illustrated by the industrial incentives policy of Minas Gerais, which succeeded in attracting to this mineral-rich region subsidiaries of Fiat, Krupp, Peugeot, and Terex (a division of General Motors), among others.

15. Additional information on the role of the state in the economy can be found in Baer (1973), Baer, Kerstenetzky, and Villela (1973), Maneschi (1972), and Silva

The state enterprises need not necessarily follow the logic of *dependência*, however, as their importance in the economy grows, their internal linkages strengthen, and the country's growth needs in a changing international environment lead them into conflict with the MNCs. To put it more specifically, at least since the First National Development Plan (1971), there have been some attempts within the government to strengthen the industrial basis of the country through import substitution in heavy industries. Nonetheless, the external financing conditions in this period were so favorable that the alternative of furthering growth with external inputs imposed itself rather naturally. Domestic and international conditions after 1974, however, have led the government to favor a program of import substitution in capital goods and basic industrial inputs (such as ferrous and nonferrous metals, fertilizers, petrochemicals, and pulp and paper) based on expanded domestic sources of energy. The same conditions imposed restrictions on further growth of import-intensive consumer durables, such as automobiles, which were on center stage in the 1968–73 economic boom. As a consequence, state enterprise activities became more important for the economy, whereas foreign corporations based in the domestic market started playing a less relevant role than before.

Before discussing the changing economic roles of state enterprises and MNCs in post-1974 Brazil, the evolution of the payments balance needs to be considered and economic policy-making in the country since the oil crisis analyzed.

Balance of Payments

A battery of tax and credit incentives coupled with the system of minidevaluations proved very successful in promoting Brazilian exports of both nontraditional primary products and manufac-

(1972). In view of the recent revision of Brazilian national accounts, it should be pointed out that the estimates presented in these sources for the share of government-related activities in GDP are considerably overestimated for the more recent years. For example, Baer, Kerstenetzky, and Villela assert that the share of government and public enterprises in gross fixed investment was 60.7 percent in 1969, whereas *Conjuntura Econômica*, vol. 29, no. 6 (1975), p. 83, estimates this share as 43.4 percent in 1970. According to the latter source, the share of public expenditures (excluding state enterprises) in GDP was 22.4 percent in 1970, whereas Baer, Kerstenetzky, and Villela estimated this share as 34 percent in 1969.

tured goods. Revised and friendly legislation on foreign capital welcomed immense inflows of Eurodollar loans and renewed inflows of direct investment and official loans that had come to a standstill in 1963.[16]

The outward-looking post-1964 growth pattern is better characterized by its import intensity than by export promotion policies or access to international financial markets. This is vividly illustrated in table 2-5 and figure 2-2, where the proportional resource deficit (equal to the ratio to exports of the difference between imports and exports of goods and commercial services) is plotted for the 1959–77 period. A distinction is made between the current deficit (with exports and imports measured in current dollars) and the basic deficit (with exports and imports calculated in constant 1970 dollars). The current deficit is influenced by terms of trade movements, whereas the basic deficit maintains the terms of trade constant at its 1970 value.[17]

The cyclical movement of both resource deficits replicates the behavior of the GDP gap in figure 2-1 except that a trough is reached in 1965 rather than in 1967, and the 1974 peak is much higher than the value observed in 1962. The large difference in the 1974 peak value of the current deficit can be attributed to the oil crisis, since the deficits in 1970–73 are not much larger than those observed in the 1959–62 period. The values for the basic deficit indicate a balance of payments performance in the early 1970s worse than in the late 1950s and early 1960s. Under constant terms of trade, a trendless resource surplus of about 7.5 percent of exports is observed in 1959–62, whereas a rapidly growing deficit averaging 10 percent of exports is indicated for 1970–73.

Projecting forward the average growth rate in 1965–73 of the ratio of imports to exports in constant 1970 prices, we conclude that a gap of the magnitude observed in 1974, under current dollar prices, would occur in 1977 or 1978, under constant 1970

16. These trends are reviewed in detail by Von Doellinger, Faria, and Cavalcanti (1974).

17. The choice of 1970 as base year would seem inadequate, as the terms of trade in this year are the highest value in the series, except for 1973, 1976, and 1977—the first being the best year in memory for Brazilian commodity exports, and the last two being heavily affected by a temporary but sharp shortage of world coffee. In the 1960s, however, the terms of trade were negatively affected by a worldwide excess supply of coffee. Barring such events, in the 1980s Brazil might be able to maintain terms of trade with average values similar to those observed in 1970, which is the reason this year was chosen as a base for the index.

Table 2-5. Ratio to Exports of C.i.f.-Trade Deficits, 1959–77
(imports and exports in millions of U.S. dollars)

Year	*Exports of goods and commercial services (X)*	*Imports of goods and commercial services (M)*	*Current deficit ([M – X]/X)*	*Exports of goods and commercial services in 1970 prices (X*)*	*Imports of goods and commercial services in 1970 prices (M*)*	*Basic deficit ([M* – X*]/X*)*	*Terms of trade (1970=100)*
1959	1,324	1,348	0.018	1,568	1,456	−0.071	90.9
1960	1,320	1,428	0.082	1,593	1,582	−0.072	91.5
1961	1,458	1,428	−0.021	1,679	1,555	−0.074	94.4
1962	1,264	1,437	0.137	1,658	1,552	−0.064	81.8
1963	1,459	1,447	−0.008	1,921	1,526	−0.216	79.5
1964	1,482	1,211	−0.183	1,641	1,319	−0.196	98.4
1965	1,646	1,034	−0.372	1,813	1,111	−0.387	98.0
1966	1,806	1,420	−0.214	2,060	1,493	−0.275	91.9
1967	1,731	1,576	−0.090	1,976	1,623	−0.179	89.8
1968	1,980	2,006	0.013	2,286	2,026	−0.114	86.0
1969	2,445	2,273	−0.070	2,748	2,317	−0.157	90.2
1970	2,908	2,874	−0.012	2,908	2,874	−0.012	100.0
1971	3,074	3,686	0.199	3,172	3,543	0.117	92.8
1972	4,177	4,772	0.142	3,829	4,299	0.123	98.2
1973	6,455	7,084	0.097	4,317	5,097	0.181	107.9
1974	8,292	14,060	0.696	4,372	6,593	0.508	88.3
1975	9,083	13,482	0.484	4,604	6,215	0.350	90.5
1976	10,530	13,631	0.294	4,601	6,230	0.354	104.8
1977	12,689	13,421	0.058	4,614	5,797	0.256	118.8

Source: Central Bank of Brazil, *Boletim Mensal*.

Figure 2-2. Ratio to Exports of C.i.f.-Trade Deficits, 1959-77

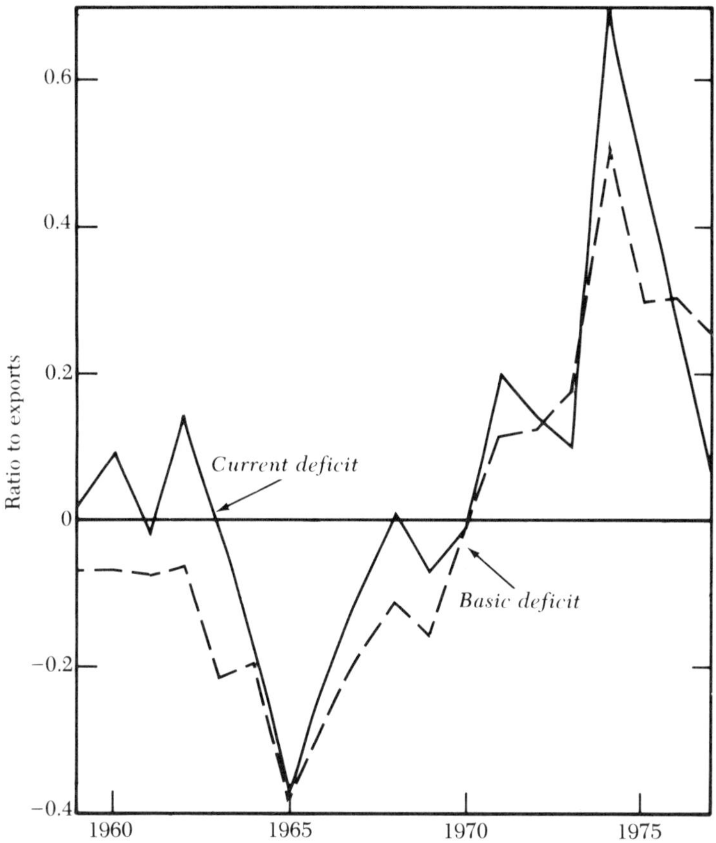

Source: Table 2-5.

prices. This result stresses the import-biased nature of post-1964 growth. It suggests that the oil crisis only anticipated in time a c.i.f.-trade deficit that would occur a few years hence, even under the unusually high 1970 terms of trade.

The pre-1974 growth pattern could be maintained without serious balance of payments dislocations, once the 1965 import slack was absorbed, only because the terms of trade improved signifi-

Table 2-6. Foreign Capital: Demand and Supply, 1970–77
(millions of U.S. dollars)

Item	*1970*	*1971*	*1972*	*1973*	*1974*	*1975*	*1976*	*1977*
Foreign capital demand	1,234	2,157	2,691	3,361	9,043	8,873	9,022	8,385
Debt service plus profit remittances	1,025	1,270	1,722	2,385	2,821	3,818	5,026	6,800
Resource gap	209	887	969	976	6,222	5,055	3,996	1,585
Foreign capital supply	1,779	2,687	5,130	5,539	8,106	7,923	10,214	8,845
Direct investment (net)	132	168	318	940	887	895	1,010	800
Loans and financing	1,433	2,037	4,299	4,495	6,891	6,530	7,921	8,345
Short-term capital (including errors and omissions)	214	482	513	104	328	498	1,283	300
Additions to foreign reserves	+545	+530	+2,439	+2,178	−937	−950	+1,192	+460

Sources: Central Bank of Brazil, *Boletim Mensal*; and *Conjuntura Econômica*, February 1978.

cantly between 1968 and 1973. This means that to maintain a high GDP growth rate in the future, Brazil needs to reduce the income elasticity of its import demand, because it cannot hope to increase continuously the ratio of exports to GDP. This is in line with the results of the simulations in chapter 5, according to which a less import-intensive strategy is a precondition for a high steady rate of GDP growth in the near future. The growth perspectives for the near term are more troublesome because of the balance of payments burden of the large foreign debt that has accumulated since the oil crisis.

In table 2-6 the trends in Brazil's balance of payments can be followed since 1970, when the country began to experience a consistent resource gap. This table reshuffles the external accounts to indicate the balancing of foreign capital supply and demand. Capital demand is divided in two components: the resource gap (that is, the c.i.f.-trade deficit plus tourism and governmental and other nonfactor services) and debt service plus profit remittances. Capital supply has three sources: net direct investment, loans and financing, and short-term capital. The movement of foreign reserves is the balancing item between foreign capital supply and demand.

Two periods can be distinguished in this table, 1970–73 and 1974–77. During the first period, capital demand increased at a rate of nearly 40 percent a year, but capital supply more than matched this growth rate.[18] As a result, foreign reserves soared from US$1.2 billion to US$6.4 billion between December 1970 and December 1973 (table 2-7).

In 1974, as a result of a US$6.2 billion gap in the resource account, foreign capital demand increased by 170 percent with respect to its value in 1973. In both 1974 and 1975 foreign reserves declined nearly US$1 billion. Subsequently, the resource gap declined significantly as a result of import controls, high coffee prices, and expanded manufactured exports. Nevertheless, under the pressure of rapidly increasing debt service, capital demand was kept at a very high level of more than US$8.0 billion

18. Foreign capital demand would have reached US$9.2 billion in 1977, had it continued to grow at the rate of 40 percent a year after 1973. This is slightly higher than the observed value of capital demand in 1974 and confirms the results of the forecasting exercise above, according to which the oil crisis merely anticipated by three years the deficit that Brazil would have experienced in 1977. (Note that "billion" is used throughout this book to mean "thousand million.")

Table 2-7. External Indebtedness and International Reserves, 1969–77
(millions of U.S. dollars at year end)

Year	*Total foreign debt*	*Governmental*[a]	*International institutions*[b]	*Private suppliers' credits*	*Currency loans*[c]	*Other*[d]	*International reserves*
1969	4,403	1,104	364	447	1,605	879	656
1970	5,295	1,246	456	611	2,285	698	1,187
1971	6,622	1,403	576	845	3,193	604	1,723
1972	9,521	1,504	762	1,136	5,528	591	4,183
1973	12,572	1,687	972	1,442	7,849	621	6,416
1974	17,166	2,151	1,388	1,812	11,211	603	5,269
1975	21,171	2,430	1,655	1,980	14,561	546	4,041
1976	25,985	2,756	1,993	2,414	18,194	628	6,544
1977	32,037	2,864	2,355	3,773	21,528	1,517	7,256

a. Includes U.S. Agency for International Development (AID), Export-Import Bank, U.S. Public Law 480, Canadian Wheat Board, and others.
b. Includes World Bank, Inter-American Development Bank, and International Finance Corporation.
c. Federative Republic of Brazil, Resolution 63, Law 4131, and Instruction 289.
d. Includes compensatory loans plus foreign debt generated by the acquisition of foreign assets in the field of electricity and telecommunications plus consolidated public debt plus bonds.
Sources: Central Bank of Brazil, *Boletim Mensal*; and *Conjuntura Econômica*.

a year, and capital supply more than met the increased requirements. Consequently, by December 1976 foreign reserves reached their previous peak and continued to grow to US$7.3 billion in December 1977.

Loans and financing were by far the most important source of capital supply during the entire period. According to table 2-7, in 1970 official debt (that is, that owed to governments and international institutions) was 32 percent of total Brazilian foreign debt. In the same year, private sources (that is, private suppliers' credits plus currency loans) represented 55 percent of total debt. In 1976–77 official sources were only 10 percent of the additions to foreign debt, while private credits and currency loans represented 80 percent of the total.

The size of foreign debt increased substantially from US$5.3 billion in 1970 to US$17.2 billion in 1974 and then to US$32 billion in 1977. The rate of expansion of net debt (gross debt minus international reserves) was equally pronounced: it rose from US$4.1 billion in 1970 to US$11.9 billion in 1974 and then to US$24.8 billion in 1977.

As a proportion both of exports and of GDP, net debt doubled in value between 1973 and 1977, when it was twice as large as exports and equal to 15 percent of GDP. Until 1974 the ratio of net debt service to exports was reasonably stable at an average value of 0.35. After 1974 debt services started growing very rapidly to reach 52 percent of exports in 1977.[19]

Between 1974 and 1977 strict import controls were applied, and the quantum of imports declined by nearly 13 percent, while real GDP increased by slightly more than 20 percent. This is a surprising result in view of the strong upward trend of the import coefficient during the "economic miracle." The excessive level of imports in 1974 seems to have been one factor contributing to this result. When the average income elasticities of imports observed in the 1965–72 period were applied to the real output growth in 1974, "excess" 1974 imports were estimated at more than US$1 billion, or nearly 10 percent of the import bill (Bacha 1978). This excess is shown in the national accounts by a change in inventories amounting to 7.5 percent of GDP (in constant 1970 cruzeiros). The largest previous figure in the series is 4.3 percent in 1973. In no other year since 1966 did inventory changes

19. The figures in this paragraph are derived from official sources in Bacha (1978).

amount to more than 2.8 percent of GDP. The conclusion is that a part of the increase in imports in 1974 was additions to inventories made in anticipation of import restrictions after the oil price increase.

A second reason for the success of import controls was a decline in the rate of fixed investment from 25 to 22 percent of GDP between 1974–75 and 1977. This was accompanied by a shift toward domestically produced components in the investment projects approved by CACEX, the foreign trade department of the Central Bank of Brazil, allowing capital goods imports in 1977 to be 34 percent lower than in 1974.[20]

The decline in imports under conditions of an increasing rate of domestic absorption also was accompanied by a rekindling of inflation rates. For these reasons, observers agree that imports will have to start growing again if GDP growth is to be maintained with declining rates of domestic inflation. Government spokespersons have suggested that ongoing projects of import substitution will significantly reduce the income elasticity of import demand. Two recent independent forecasts are more cautious about likely patterns of the demand for imports.

For the 1978–82 period Banco Garantia (1978) and Wharton (1978) anticipate growth rates of output in the neighborhood of 7 percent a year.[21] They both assume income elasticities of import demand equal to 1.44. (Observed elasticities were 2.02 between 1965 and 1972, and 1.68 between 1968 and 1972.) Exports are projected to grow at a rate of 11.6 percent a year by Wharton and at 10.4 percent a year by Garantia. (Past growth rates of real exports were 10.1 and 12.1 percent a year, respectively, in 1965–72 and 1968–72.) In both cases foreign reserves are assumed to be kept constant at their December 1977 levels.

Banco Garantia and Wharton forecasts for net external debt and significant debt ratios are shown in table 2-8. In their scenarios, net debt continues to grow at relatively fast rates, with the ratio of net debt to exports and the debt service rate tending to sta-

20. CACEX promotes agreements between importers and local suppliers of capital goods to ensure an "adequate" participation of domestic industry in investment projects benefiting from fiscal incentives. The dollar share of national firms in these investment agreements increased from 58 to 77 percent between 1974 and 1977.

21. Actually, 6.7 percent in the case of Garantia, and 7.1 percent in the Wharton forecasts. In both cases GDP growth rates start in the range of 5–6 percent and then converge to 7–8 percent a year.

Table 2-8. Wharton and Banco Garantia Forecasts for Net External Debt and Significant Debt Ratios

Item	1978	1979	1980	1981	1982
Wharton					
Net debt[a]					
(billions of U.S. dollars)	27.7	32.5	37.5	42.3	47.0
Net debt/exports	2.2	2.4	2.4	2.3	2.3
Net debt service/exports	0.59	0.60	0.66	0.66	0.65
Banco Garantia					
Net debt[a]					
(billions of U.S. dollars)	27.9	31.3	35.3	39.6	44.4
Net debt/exports	2.3	2.2	2.3	2.3	2.3
Net debt service/exports[b]	0.64	0.58	0.63	0.63	0.65

a. Gross debt = net debt + US$7.3 billion.

b. Values calculated by the author, assuming the same ratio of net debt services at year t to net debt at end of year $t-1$ as estimated by Wharton.

Sources: Wharton (1978); Banco Garantia (1978).

bilize at levels not yet experienced in recent Brazilian history. Notice, particularly, that net debt services will tend to absorb 65 percent of exports during the period. (In the recent past, the highest previous rate was 52 percent, observed in 1977.)

In summary, moderately high GDP growth rates in the near future are likely to cause considerable balance of payments dislocations. The external finance may be available as a counterpart to the surpluses of the oil-producing countries, and its deployment in the Brazilian economy may be a good investment in the long run. But it is not clear that the international banking community will have the nerve to sit still while Brazil's debt service increases continuously until reaching the all-time ratio of 65 percent of total exports. On the basis of recent trends, which are discussed in the next section, it is more likely that Brazilian policymakers will see fit to reduce the growth rate of domestic absorption rather than face the external economic and political costs of a rapidly expanding foreign debt.

Economic Policymaking after the Oil Crisis

Since 1974 the macroeconomic policies of the federal government have followed a stop-and-go pattern, indicative of the difficulties of meeting policy objectives when the options were more narrowly limited than before. The planning document of the government published in 1974 effectively ignored the constraints imposed on the economy by the emergence of domestic capacity limitations and the quadrupling of oil prices in 1973. It forecast growth rates of output of 10 percent a year for the 1975–80 period, assuming that inflation rates would decline and that the balance of payments would be kept in equilibrium (Federative Republic of Brazil, 1974).[22]

The projections of the planning document notwithstanding, monetary and fiscal policy followed a cautious path in 1974. Partly as a result of international reserve losses, the money supply in real terms expanded by only 5.7 percent on the average between 1973 and 1974. Federal government outlays increased modestly by 5.5 percent in real terms during the same period. Prices appeared to respond perversely to the deceleration of demand growth. Under the previous government, some critical prices had been frozen to hide real inflation rates. Dislodging this "inflation backlog" when the full impact of higher oil prices was being felt meant that prices increased faster in 1974 than in 1973. The GDP price deflator went up by 20.5 percent in 1973 and by 31.5 percent in 1974.

Fiscal and monetary restraints under conditions of autonomously rising prices and a higher propensity to import soon showed in the behavior of manufacturing output. In relation to the same period in 1973, growth of industrial consumption of electricity in Rio de Janeiro and São Paulo decelerated continuously from 16.6 to 4.0 percent from the first to the fourth quarter of 1974. When this growth rate of consumption declined further to 1.3 percent a year in the first quarter of 1975, the government decided that it could not stand an economic recession on top of the political problems it was facing as a consequence of the victories of the opposition party in the senatorial elections of November 1974.

The decisions were made to expand aggregate demand, as a means of stimulating industrial production, and to fight the bal-

22. Contemporaneous macrosimulation exercises by Cardoso and Taylor (see Cardoso 1975, and chapter 5 of this book) pointed out the internal inconsistencies of the plan targets. Later on, the minister of planning (Velloso 1975) offered the following argument in defense of his growth forecasts: "If, in August 1974, a target growth rate of 4–6 percent had been established for 1975, despair would have been total. And this lower growth rate would have materialized not in 1975 but in 1974 itself."

ance of payments deficit in the short run by means of rigid import controls and, in the medium run, by programs of export promotion and import substitution emphasizing self-sufficiency in so-called basic inputs (steel, petrochemicals, nonmetallic minerals, fertilizers, and pulp and paper). These decisions are reflected in the behavior of the money base and of government expenditures. In spite of international reserve losses, the money base grew by 47 percent between June 1975 and June 1976, while federal government expenditures in the first half of 1976 were 81 percent higher than in the first half of 1975. (In June 1976 wholesale prices were 39 percent above those of June 1975.) Industrial output responded swiftly to the demand expansion, growing by 10.8 percent between 1975 and 1976. Inflation rates responded both to the demand pressure and to the cost tensions arising from the import control program. After increasing slowly from 31.5 to 32.7 percent between 1974 and 1975, the implicit price deflator rose by 41.3 percent in 1976.

At the end of 1976 the government concluded that reheating of the economy had gone too far. The rekindling of inflation rates was imputed to the excessiveness of the demand expansion, although independent cost-push pressures seem to have been equally important. For example, Munhoz (1978) suggests that the cost increases brought about by the import control program added 8.9 percentage points to the rate of inflation in 1976, which is about the difference in the rate of increase of the GDP price deflator between 1975 and 1976.[23]

Interpretation of the causes of inflation may be disputed, but the recent events made policymakers aware of the necessity to revise downward the ambitious investment program outlined in 1974. The government proclaimed a new policy alternative, the strategy of progressive deceleration, which, according to a diagram in Velloso (1977, p. 122), contemplated a period of GDP growth in the neighborhood of 5 percent a year extending through 1980.

23. Munhoz calculates the expenditure increases that were due to higher mark-ups on oil sales to domestic consumers, higher tax rates on oil and fuel, additional import taxes, the creation of the import deposit, and the freeing of interest rates. These represented a Cr$90 billion cost increase in 1976, or 129 percent more than the value of these expenditures in 1975. Multiplying this figure by the share of such expenditures in GDP in 1975 (6.9 percent), we arrive at the 8.9 percentage points mentioned in the text.

Perspectives

Brazilian political scientists have noted that, lacking popular support, the post-1964 authoritarian regime tried to legitimize itself through its economic performance (Lafer 1975; Soares 1978). From 1967 to 1972 this task was facilitated by the existence of unused industrial capacity, an initial trade surplus, and the strongest boom in world trade and international capital markets since World War II. Not having to worry about labor union movements, Brazilian policymakers had an easy life collecting the dividends of an expansionary policy after inflation reached manageable levels in 1967.

When the "narrow limits of the possible" (Taylor 1974) made their presence felt after 1972, Brazilian economic policymaking seesawed in a frustrating attempt to make high GDP growth rates compatible with declining inflation rates and balance of payments equilibrium. Future scenarios were difficult to visualize because the economic troubles came at a time of political unrest. The extent of public dissatisfaction was made obvious in the November 1974 elections when the poorly organized opposition party easily won in sixteen out of twenty-one senatorial races. On another political front, at the same time as the House of Representatives, at the request of the opposition party, was carrying on an investigation of the "extravagant" role of MNCs in Brazil, the most prestigious Brazilian newspaper and newsmagazines launched a fierce campaign against the "excessive" state intervention in the economy. In the background of this dispute stands the question of under whose command the large import substitution and export promotion projects now under consideration are going to be executed.

In the development of the Northeast petrochemical complex an ingenious formula was found to combine the interests at stake. As reported by Araujo and Dick (1974), nearly all firms are jointly owned by a national group, a foreign group, and Petroquisa (a Petrobrás subsidiary). The foreign group always holds a minority interest, and its share is not larger than that of Petroquisa. U.S. and German firms balked at the deal, but adventurous Japanese capital signed up for the job. The government, however, is only reluctantly coming to realize that a new growth phase will not get under way without a new division of tasks between state enterprises and foreign firms.

Lacking balanced economic growth as a legitimization device, the government will also have to come to grips with the issues of political liberalization and popular participation to enable the country to go through the difficult transition period without political turmoil. The sharp tradeoffs between GDP growth, balance of payments equilibrium, and inflation rates, the power balance between state enterprises and multinational corporations, and the institutionalization of the political regime are problems inherited from the previous growth phase. From their solution will derive the pattern of Brazil's development in the 1980s.

References

Araujo, J. T., and V. Dick. 1974. Governo, empresas multinacionais e empresas nacionais: O caso da indústria petroquímica. *Pesquisa e planejamento econômico* 4(3):629–54.

Atkinson, A. B. 1975. *The economics of inequality*. Oxford: Clarendon Press.

Bacha, Edmar L. 1976. *Os mitos de uma década: Ensaios de economia brasileira*. Rio de Janeiro: Paz e Terra.

———. 1977. Issues and evidence on recent Brazilian economic growth. *World development* 5(1–2):47–67.

———. 1978. Brazil's balance of payments before and after the oil crisis. Paper prepared for the UNCTAD/UNDP project on the balance of payments adjustment process in developing countries, July 1976. Brasília: University of Brasília; processed.

———. 1979. Notes on the Brazilian experience with minidevaluations, 1968–76. Paper presented at the Ford Foundation/Central Bank of Barbados seminar on developing countries and the international financial system, Barbados, January 11–14, 1978. *Journal of development economics* 6(December):463–82.

Baer, Werner. 1965. *Industrialization and economic development of Brazil*. Homewood, Ill.: Irwin. Published in Portuguese as: A industrialização e o desenvolvimento econômico do Brasil. Rio de Janeiro: Vargas Foundation, 1975.

———. 1973. The Brazilian boom, 1968–72: An explanation and interpretation. *World development* 1(8):1–16.

Baer, Werner, Isaac Kerstenetzky, and Annibal V. Villela. 1973. The changing role of the state in the Brazilian economy. *World development* 1(11):23–34.

Banco Garantia. 1978. *Carta mensal* (São Paulo, June).

Cardoso, Eliana A. 1975. 1982: Algumas projecões condicionais para o Brasil. M.A. thesis, University of Brasília.

———. 1977. Moeda, renda e inflação: Algumas evidências da economia brasileira. *Pesquisa e planejamento econômico* 7(2):423–34.

Carvalho, L. 1973. *Princípios e aplicação da política salarial pós-1964*. Ensaios para discussão no. 8. Brasília: University of Brasília, Department of Economics.

Cavallo, D. 1977. *Stagflationary effects of monetarist stabilization policies*. Ph.D. dissertation, Harvard University.

Chenery, Hollis, and others. 1974. *Redistribution with growth*. London: Oxford University Press.

Delfim Netto, Antonio, and others. 1967. Análise do comportamento recente da economia brasileira. Working paper of the Joint Advisory Group to the Ministries of Finance and Planning. Partly reproduced as an appendix to Ministry of Planning, *Diretrizes do governo: Programa estratégico de desenvolvimento*. Rio de Janeiro: Departamento de Imprensa Nacional, 1967.

DIEESE (Departamento Intersindical de Estatística e Estudos Sócio-Econômicas). 1974. Família assalariada: Padrão e custo de vida. *Estudos sócio-econômicos* 2 (January).

Federative Republic of Brazil. 1974. *Projeto do II plano nacional de desenvolvimento (1975–1979)* [Second national development plan]. Rio de Janeiro: Serviço Gráfico, Instituto Brasileiro de Geografia e Estatística (IBGE).

Fishlow, Albert. 1973. "Some reflections on post-1964 Brazilian economic policy. In A. Stepan, ed. *Authoritarian Brazil*. New Haven: Yale University Press.

———. 1974. Indexing Brazilian style: Inflation without tears? *Brookings papers on economic activity* 1:261–82.

Furtado, Celso. 1963. *The economic growth of Brazil*. Berkeley: University of California Press.

———. 1972. *Análise do 'modelo' brasileiro*. Rio de Janeiro: Civilização Brasileira.

Grunwald, Joseph. 1961. The "structuralist" school on price stability and development: The Chilean case. In A. Hirschmann, ed. *Latin American issues: Essays and comments*. New York: Twentieth Century Fund, pp. 95–123.

Haddad, Claudio. 1977. Crescimento do produto real brasileiro, 1900–1947. In F. R. Versiani and J. R. M. de Barros, eds. *Formação econômica do Brasil: A experiência da industrialização*. São Paulo: Edição Saraiva.

Lafer, C. 1975. O sistema político brasileiro. São Paulo: Editora Perspectiva.

Malan, Pedro, and Regis Bonelli. 1977. The Brazilian economy in the seventies: Old and new developments. *World Development* 5(1–2):19–46.

Maneschi, Andrea. 1972. The Brazilian public sector. In Riordan Roett, ed. *Brazil in the sixties*. Nashville, Tenn.: Vanderbilt University Press.

Ministry of Planning. 1964. *Programa de ação econômica do governo, 1964–1966*. Rio de Janeiro: Serviço Gráfico, Instituto Brasileiro de Geografia e Estatística (IBGE).

Morley, Samuel A. 1971. Inflation and stagnation in Brazil. *Economic development and cultural change* 19 (January).

Munhoz, Dercio. 1978. Inflação: Impulsos de custos reversíveis e não reversíveis e a taxa de inflação de equilíbrio. Brasília: University of Brasília, Department of Economics; processed.

Simonsen, Mario Henrique. 1970. *Inflação: Gradualismo versus tratamento de choque*. Rio de Janeiro: Apec Editora.

Simonsen, Mario Henrique, and Roberto Campos. 1974. *A nova economia brasileira*. Rio de Janeiro: José Olympio.

Silva, F. R. 1971. A evolução das funções do governo e a expansão do setor público brasileiro. *Pesquisa e planejamento econômico* 1(2):235–82.

———. 1972. *Avaliação do setor público na economia brasileira*. Relatório de Pesquisa no. 13. Rio de Janeiro: Instituto de Planejamento Econômico e Social / Instituto de Pesquisas (IPEA / INPES).

Sims, Christopher A. 1972. Money, income, and causality. *American economic review* 62(4):540–52.

Singer, Paul. 1977. As contradições do milagre. In *A crise do "milagre."* Rio de Janeiro: Paz e Terra.

Soares, G. 1978. After the miracle. *Luso-Brazilian review* 15(2).

Suzigan, W., and others. 1974. *Crescimento industrial no Brasil: Incentivos e desempenho recente*. Relatório de Pesquisa no. 26. Rio de Janeiro: Instituto de Planejamento Econômica e Social (IPEA).

Tavares, Maria Conceição, and José Serra. 1973. Beyond stagnation: A discussion on the nature of recent development in Brazil. In J. Petras, ed. *Latin America: From dependence to revolution.* New York: John Wiley.

Taylor, Lance. 1974. Short-term policy in open semi-industrial economies: The narrow limits of the possible. *Journal of development economics* 1:85–104.

Velloso, J. P. 1975. Atualidade do II PND. Rio de Janeiro: Centro de Serviço Gráfico, Instituto Brasileiro de Geografia e Estatística (IBGE).

———. 1977. *Brasil: A solução positiva.* São Paulo: Abril-Tec Editora.

Von Doellinger, Carlos, Hugo Barros de Castro Faria, and Leonardo Caserta Cavalcanti. 1974. *A política brasileira de comercio exterior e seus efeitos: 1967–73.* Relatório de pesquisas no. 22. Rio de Janeiro: Instituto de Planejamento Econômico e Social / Instituto de Pesquisas (IPEA / INPES).

Wells, John. 1976. Underconsumption, market size and expenditure patterns in Brazil. *Bulletin of the Society for Latin American Studies* (University of Liverpool) no. 4, pp. 23–58.

———. 1977. The standard of living of the São Paulo working class during the 1960s. Cambridge, England: Cambridge University, Faculty of Economics; processed.

Wharton Econometric Forecasting Associates, Inc. Wharton EFA Brazilian econometric model, January 1978 postmeeting forecast: Economic developments in 1977 and forecasting review. Philadelphia.

3

Theoretical Framework for Identity-Based Planning

Eliana A. Cardoso and Lance Taylor

THIS AND THE FOLLOWING TWO CHAPTERS describe a family of macroeconomic models put together to analyze Brazil's recent growth experience and prospects for the future. The models are constructed around the same skeleton of accounting identities that supports the national accounts—hence the generic name given to them. Our approach has been first to exploit the accounting identities as far as possible in setting up models, only then adding enough additional assumptions to make their solutions determinate. The theoretical basis for identity-based planning is described in this chapter, and in the following two chapters we apply the models empirically to analyze Brazilian growth and distribution during the 1960s and likely tradeoffs during the later 1970s.

The identities come close to giving a unique description of the economy, but they must be supplemented by a few main assumptions. Two particular sets of axioms that can be used to close the model have been widely discussed in recent years. One, usually associated with economists from Cambridge, England, stresses the impact of patterns of demand for investment and consumption goods on growth and distribution. The other set of closure assumptions is associated with neoclassical economists from

Cambridge, Massachusetts, and elsewhere, and emphasizes productivity and thrift. The two sets of assumptions can lead to widely differing interpretations of the same set of data. By and large, the Cambridge, England, version seems to fit better for Brazil.

The rest of this chapter is devoted to setting out the identity-based forecasting technique in detail. We use two examples, beginning in the next section with a simple model to define terms and set the scene. In the following section we then describe the more complex set of equations actually used for Brazil. Each set of models is solved in two stages, starting from an initial base year with data satisfying the identities. The first is the calculation of growth rates of a set of endogenous variables from growth rates of exogenous variables, in a differential version of the basic identities and model closure equations. The second stage uses approximations of the values of all variables in the level form of the model (calculated from the growth rates) as the starting point for an algorithm to generate a fully consistent set of macroeconomic accounts for some subsequent year. That year in turn serves as a base for another step forward in time. The first stage in practice may be sufficiently accurate to be acceptable as a medium-term forecast by itself; it also helps illustrate the interdependency of growth of many variables in one economy. The second stage provides a technique for analyzing long-term growth.[1]

A Simple Model

Consider an economy in which only one good ("GNP") is produced. Variables and equations describing the system appear in tables 3-1, 3-2, and 3-3.

The first two equations in table 3-2 are the usual national income identities for expenditure and factor payments. To provide a basis for forecasting rates of inflation, prices are included ex-

1. Planning techniques similar to the one described here do not figure much in the academic literature, although they are used in practice. At the aggregate level, the best example is given by Cauas (1972). At the disaggregated level, the work of Johansen (1974) is of course relevant. Input-output consistency plans resemble our identity-based projections, although less emphasis is placed on prices. For descriptions, see Lewis (1966), Clark (1975), and the references the latter cites.

Table 3-1. Symbols in the GNP Model

Symbol	*Definition*
X	Output
C	Consumption
I	Investment
G	Real government expenditure
L	Employment
K	Capital stock
P	Price level
w	Wage
r	Rate of profit after taxes
t	Profit tax rate
H^*	Change in the money base (equals government deficit)
α_L	Labor share
α_K	Capital share
ξ_C, ξ_I, ξ_G	Shares of consumption, investment, and government in total spending
γ_L, γ_K	Shares of labor and capital income which are consumed
g	Growth rate of the capital stock
ϵ	Rate of technical progress in Hicks-neutral form

plicitly in equations in (3.1.1) and (3.1.2). On the quantity side the aggregate capital stock K appears in the definition of factor payments, despite the well-known theoretical demonstrations of its nonexistence. We work with aggregate "capital" in recognition of the extreme difficulty of estimating in any other way the contribution of investment to growth of productive capacity.

Equation (3.1.2) also implies that capital gains on the existing stock accrue to recipients of profit incomes, that is, after-tax profits are rPK, and these increase with the price level P, even when the after-tax rate of profit r and capital K are constant. In this illustrative model, the corporate tax rate t is the only fiscal policy instrument. The tax incides on profits in the usual way,

$$(PX - wL)\,(1 - t) = \alpha_K PX(1 - t) = rPK,$$

Table 3-2. Level Form of the GNP Model

$PX = PC + PI + PG$	(3.1.1)
$PX = wL + rPK/(1 - t)$	(3.1.2)
$\alpha_L = wL/PX$	(3.1.3)
$\alpha_K = rPK/[(1 - t)\,PX]$	(3.1.4)
$PC = \gamma_L wL + \gamma_K rPK$	(3.1.5)
$PG = H^* + trPK/(1 - t)$	(3.1.6)
$I = gK$	(3.1.7)

Table 3-3. Log-Change Form of the GNP Model

$X' = \xi_C C' + \xi_I I' + \xi_G G'$	(3.1.1′)
$X' = \alpha_L L' + \alpha_K K' + \epsilon$	(3.1.2p′)
$P' = \alpha_L w' + \alpha_K \left(r' + P' + \dfrac{t}{1-t} t'\right) - \epsilon$	(3.1.2c′)
$L' = \alpha_L' + P' + X' - w'$	(3.1.3′)
$K' = \alpha_K' + X' + P' - \left(r' + P' + \dfrac{t}{1-t} t'\right)$	(3.1.4′)
$P' + C' = (1/\xi_C)\,[\gamma_L \alpha_L (w' + L') + \gamma_K \alpha_K (1 - t)$ $(r' + P' + K')]$	(3.1.5′)
$P' + G' = \dfrac{trPK/(1-t)}{PG}\,[t'/(1 - t) + r' + P' + K'] + \dfrac{H^*}{PG}(H^*)'$	(3.1.6′)
$I' = g' + K'$	(3.1.7′)

and equation (3.1.2) follows directly. In the discussion below of implications of different ways of closing the model, we give examples by varying t and observing how other variables respond.

Equations (3.1.3) and (3.1.4) respectively define labor and capital shares in product and will prove useful in setting up neoclassical specifications below. Equation (3.1.5) is based on the usual simplifying assumption that propensities to consume from labor and profit incomes are constant (at levels γ_L and γ_K respectively). Equation (3.1.6) sets the government deficit equal to H^*. The simplest assumption is that the deficit is financed by borrowing from the Central Bank, adding the amount H^* to the money base (or stock of "high-powered" money). For the moment, we assume that the interest rate varies enough to permit monetary emissions to be absorbed.[2] Obviously the increase in money stock will have some medium-term feedback on inflation, but its consideration is deferred to the next section.

Finally, equation (3.1.7) defines investment as the rate of growth of capital stock. Evidently the capital growth rate g is

2. The actual money stock, however defined, will be related to the money base H through well-known multiplier formulas that possibly respond to the interest rate and that are based on institutional characteristics of the banking system. We are consolidating the banks with the rest of the private sector and thereby avoiding the need to use credit multipliers. This approach follows Christ (1968), who pointed out the importance of constraints like (3.1.6). For an analysis which takes the banking structure into account, see Hansen (1973).

determined by I and K at any point in time, but as the I/K ratio shifts in response to variations either in investors' anticipations or in available savings, g will shift as well. Behavioral assumptions underlying the change in g are discussed in some detail below.[3]

If one eliminates PX from (3.1.1) and (3.1.2) and applies (3.1.5) and (3.1.6), it follows that

$$PI + H^* = (1 - \gamma_L)\, wL + (1 - \gamma_K)\,(1 - t)\, \alpha_K PX \qquad (3.1.8)$$
$$= (1 - \gamma_L)\, wL + (1 - \gamma_K)\, rPK$$

so that private saving (on the right-hand side) equals investment minus government saving, which is equal to $-H^*$. This savings-investment identity represents Walras's law in the GNP model and is consistent with national income accounting conventions. It is also the most basic identity of all, and we rely on it heavily in interpreting our empirical results.

Log-Differential Form of the Model

Since economists like to think in growth terms, it is useful to throw the table 3-2 equations into logarithmic differential form. So expressed, the model gives growth rates of endogenous variables consistent with the growth of exogenous variables, specified from the outside. The log-differential equation system is of course linear in all growth rates, and it is easy to see how the variables interact in it, as exemplified below. In applications, it also seems to give fairly precise forecasts of endogenous variables in the level form (calculated by applying the consistent set of growth rates from the log-linear system to base-year levels) for a period of two or three years.[4] In a later section we discuss how such forecasts can in turn be fed into an equation-solving computer algorithm to get a full solution to the identities in the

3. Variables such as g appear in the planning model literature under the name of "stock-flow conversion factors" (see Manne 1963) and are usually assumed to be determined technologically. As mentioned in the text, we prefer to treat the macroeconomic g as behavioral, determined by availability of saving in Cambridge, Massachusetts, models and by investors' "animal spirits" in the Cambridge, England, variety.

4. This was the period used by Johansen (1974) in one pioneering exercise in forecasting based on log-changes. We found it appropriate in our own work, in the sense that three-year forecasts of variables were still quite close to level solutions of the full model. Accuracy seemed to deteriorate fairly rapidly for periods longer than three years.

forecast year. For the moment, however, we concentrate on seeing how the log-differential version of the GNP model operates. Table 3-3 gives the relevant equations, in the form of growth rates of the variables, that is, X' is the rate of growth of X or $(dX/dt)/X$.

Equation (3.1.1′) is the result of differentiating (3.1.1) after the price P has been canceled out. This equation implies that $dX = dC + dI + dG$, and this is transformed to (3.1.1′).

To get to (3.1.2c′) and (3.1.2p′) note that the log-differential version of equation (3.1.2) can be written after a bit of manipulation as

$$P' - \alpha_L w' - \alpha_K \left(r' + P' + \frac{t}{1-t} t' \right) + \epsilon = \alpha_L L' + \alpha_K K' - X' + \epsilon$$

where the shift variable ϵ can be added to both sides without upsetting the exhaustion-of-product identity. When set to zero, the left side of this equation is a natural expression for a cost-based Laspeyre index of the price level, with cost-decreasing technical progress ϵ included. This is equation (3.1.2c′). But then the right side must also be set to zero to maintain product exhaustion, and the resulting equation (3.1.2p′) is equivalent, at least in the first order log-differential approximation, to a neoclassical aggregate production function with Hicks-neutral technical change. Double-entry bookkeeping in the price-equals-cost identity (3.1.2) assures that if weighted log-changes in costs are constrained to sum to the log-change in the price level, then weighted log-changes in inputs will just exhaust the output change. Log-differential cost and production functions are born as twins from the same accounting identity.

In the rest of table 3-3, (3.1.3′) and (3.1.4′) are merely the log-differential versions of the corresponding equations in table 3-2. Equation (3.1.5′) also follows readily from (3.1.5) when one observes that

$$\frac{wL}{PC} = \frac{wL/PX}{PC/PX} = \alpha_L / \xi_C$$

and similarly for the profit recipients' share in total consumption. The last equations, (3.1.6′) and (3.1.7′), follow from their level-form counterparts in straightforward fashion.

The table 3-3 system comprises eight independent linear equations with fifteen variables. In principle, seven additional restrictions are required to close the system, either via specification of exogenous variables or incorporation of extra equations. In addition, the model structure itself limits the possible ways it can be closed. For example, with exogenous specification of the rate of technical change ϵ, equation (3.1.2p′) shows that only two of the model's three quantity-side log-changes—L', K', and X'—can be fixed independently.[5] A similar observation holds regarding cost and price changes and equation (3.1.2c′). Finally, factor shares cannot vary independently, as can be shown by multiplying (3.1.3′) and (3.1.4′) respectively by α_L and α_K, summing, and applying (3.1.2c′) and (3.1.2p′). This manipulation gives

$$\alpha_L\,(\alpha_L)' + \alpha_K\,(\alpha_K)' = 0, \qquad (3.1.9')$$

that is, the adding-up properties of the model constrain differential changes in the factor shares to sum to zero. In effect, only one factor-share change can be specified exogenously, or at least if both are constrained they must satisfy the adding-up condition. As we will see, neoclassical factor demand equations automatically require factor-share changes to satisfy (3.1.9′).

To illustrate other characteristics of the model, we must introduce more detail. The following subsection is devoted to this task, using log-changes in the profit tax rate t' to "drive" the model under our two sets of rules for closing it.[6]

Closing the Log-Differential Model

Assume that the level of investment I is fixed at any point in time. Then with the historically given level of capital stock and our assumption of full capacity utilization, the capital growth rate K' is predetermined by definition: $K' = I/K$. For simplicity in medium-term forecasting, we also assume that the rate of growth of employment L' and the technical progress rate ϵ are fixed exogenously (although if desired the identity approach could easily be extended to include endogenous determination of these

5. There is an implicit assumption that neither unintended stock accumulation nor changes in capacity utilization are important. In short-term forecasting this could be remedied by adding an explicit variable (perhaps with a corresponding behavioral equation) for stock changes, or else by incorporating variations in capacity utilization into the residual ϵ.

6. For a somewhat similar analysis, see Asimakopulos and Burbidge (1974).

growth rates by appropriate supply functions). From (3.1.2p′), the output growth rate X' then becomes an endogenous variable. To save symbols in the manipulations which follow, we set ϵ equal to zero for the moment, and normalize prices by making P' equal to zero as well.

To close the model, three additional restrictions are required. After the Cambridge, England, economists Keynes, Kalecki, and Kaldor, we call a K specification (KS) one in which two of the three government policy variables G', t', and $H^{*\prime}$ *and* the log-change in the capital stock growth rate g' are set exogenously. These assumptions boil down to stating that the government respects its budget constraint (3.1.6′), and that at any moment entrepreneurs (or the planner) are modifying the rate at which they accumulate capital in line with changes in expectations and investors' "animal spirits." Together with the predetermined value of K', specification of g' makes the growth rate of investment I' endogenous from (3.1.7′). Also, if we let $H^{*\prime}$ be endogenous, we can insert equation (3.1.5′) for the consumption growth rate C' into (3.1.1′), use the production function (3.1.2p′), and come up with an equation in which the "factor price" growth rates w' and r' depend on the already determined variables I', G', L', and K'. The log-differential cost function (3.1.2c′) gives another equation for the same two variables. Solving for r' and substituting the result into (3.1.4′) finally gives

$$\alpha_K{}' = \frac{1}{\alpha_K\,[\gamma_L - (1-t)\,\gamma_K]}\Big\{\,\xi_I I' + \xi_G G' - \gamma_K\,\alpha_K t t' - [1 - \gamma_L\,\alpha_L - \gamma_K\,\alpha_K\,(1-t)]\,X'\Big\}.$$

This equation shows that an increase in the investment growth rate I' is associated with growth in the profit rate and capital share. Growth in the profit tax rate t' reduces these variables. If, however, the immediate tax proceeds are respent by the government (so that $dG = \alpha_K PXtt'$), then the capital share will *increase* with this sort of balanced-budget expansion of government activity.

These are standard results for a KS model, arising from its "widow's cruse" specification in which wage recipients save less than those who receive profits, so that the denominator of the fraction outside the braces in the above equation is positive. With the investment growth rate predetermined, even if a tax increase takes income away from capitalists initially, the profit rate then has to rise to keep up saving. By the same sort of reasoning, the capital share falls if the output growth rate X' is higher—with more total output becoming available, a smaller share has to be diverted to high savers via high incomes for them.

Another fiscal effect is that profits do fall if dG is enough smaller than dt. Contrary to most KS models this can occur because from (3.1.6) decreases in monetary emissions H^* must accompany tax revenue increases if government spending does not change. This government saving (or decrease in growth of private money stocks) can in principle support investment as effectively as private saving. How it is made available to investors is a financial market question, which we do not go into here.

The alternative way of closing the model is to adopt the neoclassical N specification (NS), in which factor shares are supposed to change in regular, predictable fashion as factor prices shift. Postponing until next section consideration of how technical change affects derived demands for labor and capital, we assume as in cost-minimizing textbook production theory that the labor-output ratio, for example, depends only on the real wage, $L/X = f(w/P)$. In addition, if there is smooth substitution between capital and labor at a predictable rate σ, then the log-change version of this equation becomes $L' - X' = -\sigma(w' - P')$, and the tradeoff parameter σ can be interpreted as the elasticity of factor substitution, defined in the usual way.

If $w' - P'$ is added to both sides, this expression becomes

$$\alpha_L' = (1 - \sigma)(w' - P'). \qquad (3.1.10')$$

The corresponding equation for the capital share is

$$\alpha_K' = (1 - \sigma)\left(r' + \frac{t}{1-t}t'\right). \qquad (3.1.11')$$

(Note that P' does not appear here, since both output and the existing capital stock are assumed to have the same price.)

Adding (3.1.10′) and (3.1.11′) to the equations of table 3-3 gives an NS model. To save algebra, we adopt the often-applied special case in which $\sigma = 1$ and factor shares stay constant—we are saying either that there is an aggregate Cobb-Douglas production function or that we expect factor shares will not be shifting significantly in any case.

In the Cobb-Douglas (or any other neoclassical) case, it is easy to verify from (3.1.10′) and (3.1.11′) that factor-share growth rates satisfy the adding-up condition (3.1.9′). Hence, only one of the two factor demand growth rate equations is really independent. This additional restriction forces some K-specification exogenous variable to become endogenous—the usual candidate is the log-change of the growth rate of capital g'.[7]

Now we can examine the impact of raising the profit tax and thus set $t' > 0$. Equation (3.1.4′) and the Cobb-Douglas assumptions show immediately that the profit rate r *falls* as the tax rate increases, regardless of whether the government respends the revenue. The balanced-budget theory of an increasing profit share does not hold in an NS model. The reason is that factor payments (and therefore consumption) are fixed by marginal productivity assumptions, and investment is endogenous. A tax increase raises government saving, and this leads in part to an *increase* in investment, in part to a fall in "required" private saving and thus in the profit rate.

The increment in investment is surprising and bears closer study. In the Cobb-Douglas N specification, wage and profit growth rates from (3.1.3′) and (3.1.4′) are $w' = X' - L'$ and $r' = X' - K' - [t/(1-t)]\,t'$. Substituting these expressions into (3.1.5′) gives

$$C' = (1/\xi_C)\left\{-\gamma_K \alpha_K t t' + [\gamma_L \alpha_L + \gamma_K \alpha_K (1-t)]\,X'\right\},$$

so that consumption growth *declines* as the tax rate increases. Since output growth X' has been determined from the "production function" (3.1.2p′), the growth rate of investment I' must *increase* from (3.1.1′). An increase in the profit tax leads to a decrease in the profit rate, a decrease in consumption, and, paradoxically, to higher investment. Such a perverse investment response is no less disquieting than the widow's cruse in KS models. It is a standard feature of full-employment NS models (see Sen 1965) and illustrates once again how important are hidden implications of seemingly innocuous model-closing assumptions.

Finally, note that in both forms of the model discussed so far, output growth X' is fixed in the short run by predetermined variables in equation (3.1.2p′). However, the log-change of capital stock growth g' is exogenous in the K specification but

7. Again we abstract from unintended stock changes. One *can* have neoclassical production specifications, exogenous capital formation, and endogenous unplanned inventory accumulation all together in a model, but the latter is a very small vessel in which to accumulate all the flows resulting from changes in the other variables, especially in the medium run.

endogenous (determined by "productivity and thrift") in the N specification. Over time, therefore, growth in output can differ between the two models because they determine rates of capital accumulation in different ways. As we shall see in the empirical analysis of Brazil in the following chapters, this potential divergence in medium-term output growth rates can prove to be highly significant in practice.

Calculation of a New Level-Form Solution

The foregoing discussion shows that, at least in its growth rate version, when the identity model is closed in different ways it can produce responses to tax changes of opposite sign, and other surprises. Since neither set of hypotheses on closure is exactly well founded, a certain humility in recommending policy is suggested, particularly since we will verify that similar problems occur in level-form solutions of the models as well. We now describe briefly how these can be computed.

To get levels of variables in an N specification, some parametric form for an aggregate cost or production function has to be used. The simplest is the standard constant elasticity of substitution (CES) function, derived on the assumption that the parameter we label σ stays constant even for large relative price changes. The level form of the labor demand equation becomes $L/X = \xi(w/P)^{-\sigma}$ where ξ is a constant of integration (usually called a distribution parameter). There is a similar equation for capital demand, and the corresponding production and cost functions themselves are well known.

One way to solve the level model is to take the value of w calculated from the log-differential version as an initial guess in an iterative scheme. The above equation for L/X then gives a guess at X and the capital demand equation gives r (both these calculations depend on the exogenously specified growth of labor L and capital K). One can then test if the price-equals-cost identity (3.1.2) is satisfied to an acceptable degree of precision; if not, the guess at w can be modified until the identity holds. For the NS version of the Brazil model discussed in the next section, three-year projections of price and output changes from the log-differential equations of table 3-6 satisfied the price-equals-cost identity in the forecast year to within about 1 percent.

In the KS model, price and quantity projections are not tied together by marginal productivity conditions as in the labor demand equation given above, giving rise to potential inconsistency when both (3.1.2p′) and (3.1.2c′) are applied with arbitrary finite changes of exogenous variables but with factor shares unchanged from their base-year values.[8] One way to finesse this problem is to treat either the price projection from (3.1.2c′) or the output projection from (3.1.2p′) as exact and to calculate the other variable from identities holding in the forecast year. We chose to get a forecast of X from the integration of (3.1.2p′) over time with constant factor shares. Then a guess at w from the other log-change equations gives a new value for α_L from (3.1.3), and α_K becomes $1 - \alpha_L$. We calculate r from (3.1.4) and C from (3.1.5). Investment I comes from (3.1.7), and we can now determine whether the output demand-supply balance is satisfied. If not, w must be modified accordingly. As we see in more detail below, higher investment demand leads to a lower real wage via "forced saving," which is in the spirit of KS models. In the Brazil exercise, a few iterations of the type just described were usually necessary to compute new price levels, since the projections over a three-year period from the log-differential model were usually between 10 and 20 percent different from the final values of prices in the level solutions.

A Model for Brazil

The identities in the preceding section can be extended to more elaborate descriptions of the economy, although bookkeeping complexity and implicit behavioral assumptions increase apace as this is done. In this section we discuss a model put together to make medium-term forecasts for Brazil. The model still has only one production sector, but detail regarding balance of payments and tax structures makes it too cumbersome for algebraic solu-

8. That is, the factor shares turn out to be weights in a first-order approximation to changes in the exhaustion-of-product identity (3.1.2). For finite changes of prices and quantities, this approximation will of course be in error, as the factor shares themselves will vary. One major difference between the KS and NS models is that the latter restricts price and quantity changes in such a way as to make factor-share changes vanish to second order in equations such as (3.1.2c′) and (3.1.2p′). (For a straightforward demonstration in a model similar to ours, see Jones 1965.) This goes far toward explaining the difference in accuracy of forecasts over three years of the two log-differential specifications, as discussed in the text.

tion. For that reason, numerical simulations are used to analyze its characteristics in the following two chapters.

Variables and level-form equations are listed in tables 3-4 and 3-5. We begin by summarizing the most important extensions beyond the GNP model, and later discuss the log-differential version of the Brazil model and how it is closed.

Equation (3.2.1) is analagous to (3.1.1), except that three more demand categories are included: exports net of competitive imports,[9] government demands for investment goods, and depreciation of the stock of domestically produced capital goods. The coefficient δ_X in equation (3.2.1) refers to *physical* depreciation, but we assume in (3.2.4) that it is also the legal depreciation rate used in calculating the user cost of capital. In general, the two concepts need not be the same. As before, we omit consideration of stock changes for simplicity in medium-term forecasting, but otherwise equation (3.2.1) corresponds to the usual GNP accounting conventions.

Equation (3.2.2) is the balance of payments written in world prices, scaled in terms of the domestic currency by the exchange rate ρ. Movements in import and export prices can of course affect the model projections through this equation, along with quantum changes. It is convenient to treat Brazilian imports as noncompetitive (see note 9). Because their demand-generation mechanisms are different we distinguish three types—complementary imports of intermediates (M), capital goods for new investment (I_F), and consumption goods (C_F). Along with a depreciation term for existing imported investment goods, these appear (multiplied by their corresponding world prices) on the right of (3.2.2). The remaining term F represents capital inflows in the simplest possible balance of payments definition, the "foreign savings gap." Both here and below in the money supply equation, we omit exogenous reserve changes, debt service charges, and a host of other financial market complexities. Full treatment of financial flows, although easy to include in the identity framework in principle, would greatly complicate an already messy model. We shunned the additional effort for this reason.

9. In the Brazilian case, competitive importation is in principle illegal because of legislation—summed up as the "law of similars"—intended to prohibit the import of products similar to national ones. In practice, the laws are not followed rigorously, but in what follows we in fact treat all imports as noncompetitive.

Table 3-4. Symbols in the Brazil Model

Symbol	*Definition*
X	Domestic production
C_X, C_F	Consumption demands for domestic and noncompetitive imported goods
I_X, I_F	Demands for domestic goods and noncompetitive imports for capital formation
δ_X, δ_F	Depreciation rates of domestic and imported capital stocks
K_X, K_F	Stocks of domestic and imported capital goods
E	Exports less competitive imports of domestic goods
C_G, I_G	Government purchases of domestic goods for consumption and investment
P	Domestic price level
ρ	Exchange rate
M	Volume of noncompetitive intermediate imports
$\pi_E, \pi_M, \pi_C, \pi_F$	World prices of E, M, C_F, and K_F or I_F
P_M, P_C, P_K	Domestic prices of M, C_F, and K_F or I_F
F	Capital inflow (balance of payments deficit in world prices)
V	Value added (net of taxes) per unit output
t_V, t_L, t_K	Tax rates on value added, payments to labor, and profits
w	Wage rate
r	After-tax profit rate
$\theta_X, \theta_F, \theta_L$	User costs of the two types of capital and labor
$\alpha_M, \alpha_L, \alpha_X, \alpha_F$	Shares of noncompetitive imports, labor, domestic capital goods, and imported capital goods in value added net of taxes
L, L_G	Employment levels in production activity and in government service
Y_L, Y_K	Labor and profit incomes
Z	Total value of capital stocks
D_L, D_K	Direct taxes on labor and capital incomes
S_{DL}, S_{DK}	Elasticities of direct taxes with respect to labor and capital incomes
ξ_L, ξ_K	Constant terms in tax functions
Q	Transfers from government to labor income recipients
S_{CR}, S_{Ci}	Elasticities of consumption with respect to wealth and the "real" interest rate
ξ_C	Constant term in the consumption function
B	Outstanding stock of government price-indexed bonds
R	Total wealth in base-year prices
C	Value of total consumption
ϕ_X, ϕ_F	Shares of domestic output and noncompetitive imports in consumption
γ_L, γ_K	Propensities to consume from labor and capital incomes
g_X, g_F	Rates of growth of domestic and imported capital stocks
G	Total government expenditure
T	Government tax revenue
H^*, B^*	New emissions of high-powered money and of bonds
H	Stock of high-powered money (the money base)

Symbol	*Definition*
S_{HX}, S_{Hi}	Elasticities of money demand with respect to real output and the interest rate
ξ_H	Constant term in the money demand function
i	Rate of interest
ϵ	Rate of technical progress in Hicks-neutral form
A	Anticipated rate of inflation

Table 3-5. Level Form of the Brazil Model

$$PX = PC_X + PI_X + P\delta_X K_X + PE + PC_G + PI_G \tag{3.2.1}$$

$$\rho\pi_E E + \rho F = \rho\pi_M M + \rho\pi_C C_F + \rho\pi_F (I_F + \delta_F K_F) \tag{3.2.2}$$

$$\theta_L = w(1 + t_L) \tag{3.2.3}$$

$$\theta_X = \left(\frac{r}{1 - t_K} + \delta_X\right) P \tag{3.2.4}$$

$$\theta_F = \left(\frac{r}{1 - t_K} + \delta_F\right) P_K \tag{3.2.5}$$

$$VX = P_M M + \theta_L L + \theta_X K_X + \theta_F K_F \tag{3.2.6}$$

$$P = (1 + t_V) V \tag{3.2.7}$$

$$\alpha_M VX = P_M M \tag{3.2.8}$$

$$\alpha_L VX = \theta_L L \tag{3.2.9}$$

$$\alpha_X VX = \theta_X K_X \tag{3.2.10}$$

$$\alpha_F VX = \theta_F K_F \tag{3.2.11}$$

$$Y_L = w(L + L_G) \tag{3.2.12}$$

$$Z = PK_X + P_K K_F \tag{3.2.13}$$

$$Y_K = rZ + PB \tag{3.2.14}$$

$$D_L = \xi_L Y_L^{S_{DL}} \tag{3.2.15}$$

$$D_K = \xi_K Y_K^{S_{DK}} \tag{3.2.16}$$

$$R = K_X + K_F + (H/P) + (B/i) \tag{3.2.17}$$

$$C = [\gamma_L (Y_L - D_L + Q) + \gamma_K (Y_K - D_K)]\ \xi_C R^{S_{CR}} (i/A)^{S_{Ci}} \tag{3.2.18}$$

$$\phi_X C = PC_X \tag{3.2.19}$$

$$\phi_F C = P_C C_F \tag{3.2.20}$$

$$\phi_X + \phi_F = 1 \tag{3.2.21}$$

$$I_X + I_G = g_X K_X \tag{3.2.22}$$

$$I_F = g_F K_F \tag{3.2.23}$$

$$G = (1+t_L)\, wL_G + PC_G + PB + (P = \rho\pi_E)\, E + PI_G + Q \tag{3.2.24}$$

$$T = t_V VX + t_L w(L+L_G) + \frac{t_K rZ}{1 - t_K} + (P_M - \rho\pi_M)\, M + (P_C - \rho\pi_C)\, C_F + (P_K - \rho\pi_K)(I_F + \delta_F K_F) + D_L + D_K \tag{3.2.25}$$

$$G - T = H^* + (PB^*/i) + \rho F \tag{3.2.26}$$

$$H = \xi_H PX^{S_{HX}} i^{S_{Hi}} \tag{3.2.27}$$

Equations (3.2.3) to (3.2.7) are analagous to (3.1.2), setting value added at factor cost equal to the total value of inputs.[10] The first three equations are simply definitions of user costs of labor and nationally produced and imported capital goods. Labor cost includes a social security tax on wages (responsible for about 20 percent of total tax revenue in Brazil), while capital costs are determined by the rate of profit, the profit tax, and depreciation charges. Along with intermediate imports (valued at a within-country cost P_M, which can differ from the world cost $\rho\pi_M$ because of tariffs), these inputs exhaust total value added in (3.2.6). Final output price P is determined by an indirect tax markup on the price of value added V in (3.2.7).

Equations (3.2.8) through (3.2.11) define the shares of the inputs in value added, as do (3.1.3) and (3.1.4) in the simple model. In the N specification of the Brazil model, these equations in log-change form are used to set up derived demand relationships such as (3.1.10′). Details of the specification appear in the section below on "Price-Sensitive Production Responses in an N Specification."

Equations (3.2.12) through (3.2.18) link factor payments to the total value of consumption C. Labor and capital incomes are defined by the three equations beginning with (3.2.12). Capital incomes are assumed to include interest payments on government bonds, which can be issued along with money to cover fiscal deficits. Because indexation is widely applied in Brazil, the bonds are treated as inflation-corrected consuls, each paying the *real* equivalent of one cruzeiro a year in base-year prices. Because of the escalator, total income from bonds is PB, that is, the stock of bonds multiplied by the price index. These government interest payments show up in chapter 5 as important determinants of saving in the NS Brazil model. Their importance is emphasized by Blinder and Solow (1974).

Equations (3.2.15) and (3.2.16) describe in convenient constant elasticity form the relationship between direct tax revenues and incomes. Here as elsewhere the distinction between capital and labor incomes is supposed to approximate the personal income

10. Our usage is slightly nonstandard, since we include the cost of raw material imports in "value added." This simply reflects reality in an underdeveloped country, where production is strongly constrained by import requirements. Our subsequent assumption of substitutability between imports and other inputs perhaps understates the importance of this constraint.

distribution—the constant ξ_L is smaller than ξ_K in a crude representation of a progressive direct tax system.

The next equation (3.2.17) defines total wealth R (in base-year prices); along with the nominal rate of interest deflated by the anticipated rate of inflation, i/A, this is supposed to have some influence on the *value* of consumption C in (3.2.18). We assume that the elasticities of C with respect to wealth and the real interest rate are constant.[11]

The three equations beginning with (3.2.19) define shares of consumption of national and noncompetitively imported goods in the total budget and require that they sum to one. To complete specification of consumer demand responses, an additional equation is required to determine one of the two budget shares. Details of how this can be done in a convenient log-differential specification appear in the section on "Consumer Demand Responses."

After the capital growth rate definitions (3.2.22) and (3.2.23), equations (3.2.24) through (3.2.26) give the government accounts. The total value of government expenditure G comprises government consumption and investment, bond interest payments, the total subsidies paid to exporters (based on the difference between the domestic price P and the domestic value of export receipts $\rho\pi_E$), government transfer payments, and wages and employment taxes for government employees. These are also included in total tax receipts T, along with value added and profit taxes, direct taxes, and tariffs based on the difference between world and domestic prices of imports.[12] Equation (3.2.26) shows that the difference between government expenditures and tax receipts is met by monetary emissions H^*, new bond issues with value PB^*/i, and capital inflows ρF, which in the first round after entry into the country pass through the Central Bank.

Equation (3.2.27) closes the model, setting the stock of high-powered money H equal to its demand. As written, this equation

11. The nonstandard specification of interest rate deflation by anticipated inflation, i/A instead of $i - A$, allows this to be done easily.

12. In formal terms one can set $P_i = \rho(1 + \tau_i)\pi_i$, where i indexes traded goods and τ_i is an ad valorem tariff. Unchanging tariffs imply that $P_i' = \rho' + \pi_i'$, which can be used in specifying price changes in the log-differential model. Such relationships are used informally in the K specification of the present model (since they will turn out to contain only exogenous log-changes), but are treated as explicit restrictions in the N specification (where both ρ' and the P_i' are endogenous).

makes the demand for "real balances" (H/P) depend in constant elasticity form on real output and the nominal interest rate. In effect, it determines the interest rate, which then feeds back weakly into consumer demand and private saving. This feedback aside, (3.2.27) serves mainly as a check on consistency of monetary policy, with the real configuration of the economy determined by other parts of the model.

The savings-investment identity in the present model is

$$(Y_L - D_L + Q) + (Y_K - D_K) - C = PI_X + P_K I_F + H^* + (PB^*/i),$$

so that private saving (not including depreciation) equals net capital formation plus that part of the current government deficit financed from within the country. Another version of the same identity is

$$\begin{aligned} PI_X + P_K I_F = {} & [(Y_L - D_L + Q) + (Y_K - D_K) - C] \\ & + (T - G) + \rho F. \end{aligned}$$

This sets capital formation equal to the sum of private net saving, government saving, and capital inflows. We rely heavily on this equation in interpreting our numerical results in the next two chapters.

The Log-Change Version of the Model and a K Specification

Table 3-6 sets out the growth rate version of the Brazil model—the equations at first glance resemble so much hen scratching, but in fact are merely more complicated variants of their counterparts of table 3-3. The dual log-differential approximations to cost and production functions appear as (3.2.6c′) and (3.2.6p′). These equations follow from the growth rate version of the exhaustion of product equation (3.2.6), under the same assumptions which gave us (3.1.2c′) and (3.1.2p′). Overall accounting consistency requires that differential changes in the factor shares sum to zero,

$$\alpha_L \alpha_L' + \alpha_M \alpha_M' + \alpha_X \alpha_X' + \alpha_F \alpha_F' = 0. \qquad (3.2.28')$$

Any specification of exogenous variables must satisfy this restriction, even if it is not independent of the rest of the model.

In table 3-4 there are fifty-seven variables; in the log-change version with its twenty-eight equations (both the dual cost and production functions are included) twenty-nine additional restrictions are required. For KS closure, these take the form of

Table 3-6. Log-Change Form of the Brazil Model

$$PXX' = PC_XC_X' + PI_XI_X' + P\delta_XK_XK_X' + PEE' + PC_GG_G' + PI_GI_G' \tag{3.2.1'}$$

$$\begin{aligned}\rho\pi_E E(\pi_E' + E') + \rho FF' &= \rho\pi_M M\,(\pi_M' + M') + \rho\pi_C C_F\,(\pi_C' + C_F') \\ &\quad + \rho\pi_F I_F I_F' + \rho\pi_F \delta_F K_F K_F' + \rho\pi_F\,(I_F + \delta_F K_F)\,\pi_F'\end{aligned} \tag{3.2.2'}$$

$$\theta_L' = w' + \frac{t_L}{1+t_L}\,t_L' \tag{3.2.3'}$$

$$\theta_X' = P' + \frac{r/(1-t_K)}{\delta_X + r/(1-t_K)}\left(r' + \frac{t_K}{1-t_K}\,t_K'\right) \tag{3.2.4'}$$

$$\theta_F' = P_K' + \frac{r/(1-t_K)}{\delta_F + r/(1-t_K)}\left(r' + \frac{t_K}{1-t_K}\,t_K'\right). \tag{3.2.5'}$$

$$V' = -\epsilon + \alpha_M P_M' + \alpha_L\theta_L' + \alpha_X\theta_X' + \alpha_F\theta_F' \tag{3.2.6c'}$$

$$X' = \epsilon + \alpha_M M' + \alpha_L L' + \alpha_X K_X' + \alpha_F K_F' \tag{3.2.6p'}$$

$$P' = V' + \frac{t_V}{1+t_V}\,t_V' \tag{3.2.7'}$$

$$\alpha_M' = P_M' + M' - V' - X' \tag{3.2.8'}$$

$$\alpha_L' = \theta_L' + L' - V' - X' \tag{3.2.9'}$$

$$\alpha_X' = \theta_X' + K_X' - V' - X' \tag{3.2.10'}$$

$$\alpha_F' = \theta_F' + K_F' - V' - X' \tag{3.2.11'}$$

$$Y_L' = w' + \frac{L}{L+L_G}L' + \frac{L_G}{L+L_G}L_G' \tag{3.2.12'}$$

$$ZZ' = PK_X\,(P' + K_X') + P_K K_F\,(P_K' + K_F') \tag{3.2.13'}$$

$$Y_K Y_K' = rZ\,(r' + Z') + PB\,(P' + B') \tag{3.2.14'}$$

$$D_L' = S_{DL}Y_L' \tag{3.2.15'}$$

$$D_K' = S_{DK}Y_K' \tag{3.2.16'}$$

$$RR' = K_XK_X' + K_FK_F' + (H/P)(H' - P') + (B/i)(B' - i') \tag{3.2.17'}$$

$$\begin{aligned}C' &= [\gamma_L\,(Y_L - D_L + Q) + \gamma_K\,(Y_K - D_K)]^{-1}\,[\gamma_L Y_L Y_L' - \gamma_L D_L D_L' \\ &\quad + \gamma_L QQ' + \gamma_K Y_K Y_K' - \gamma_K D_K D_K'] + S_{CR}R' + S_{Ci}\,(i' - A')\end{aligned} \tag{3.2.18'}$$

$$\phi_X' = P' + C_X' - C' \tag{3.2.19'}$$

$$\phi_F' = P_C' + C_F' - C' \tag{3.2.20'}$$

$$\phi_X\phi_X' + \phi_F\phi_F' = 0 \tag{3.2.21'}$$

$$\frac{I_G}{I_X+I_G}I_G' + \frac{I_X}{I_X+I_G}I_X' = g_X' + K_X' \tag{3.2.22'}$$

$$I_F' = g_F' + K_F' \tag{3.2.23'}$$

$$\begin{aligned}GG' &= (1 + t_L)\,wL_G\left(\frac{t_L}{1+t_L}\,t_L' + w' + L_G'\right) + P(C_G + E + B \\ &\quad + I_G)\,P' + PI_GI_G' + PC_GC_G' + PBB' + (P - \rho\pi_E E)\,E' \\ &\quad - \rho\pi_E E\,(\rho' + \pi_E') + QQ'\end{aligned} \tag{3.2.24'}$$

$$\begin{aligned}TT' &= t_V VX\,(t_V' + V' + X') + t_L w\,(L + L_G) \\ &\quad \left(w' + t_L' + \frac{L}{L+L_G}L' + \frac{L_G}{L+L_G}L_G'\right) + \frac{t_K rZ}{1-t_K}\left(\frac{1}{1-t_K}\,t_K'\right. \\ &\quad \left. + r' + Z'\right) + (P_M - \rho\pi_M)\,MM' + P_M MP_M' - \rho\pi_M M\pi_M' \\ &\quad + (P_C - \rho\pi_C)\,C_FC_F' + P_CC_FP_C' - \rho\pi_C C_F\pi_C' + P_K\,(I_F \\ &\quad + \delta_F K_F)\,P_K' + (P_K - \rho\pi_K)\,(I_F + \delta_F K_F)\left(\frac{I_F}{I_F + \delta_F K_F}I_F'\right. \\ &\quad \left. + \frac{\delta_F K_F}{I_F + \delta_F K_F}K_F'\right) - \rho\pi_F\,(I_F + \delta_F K_F)\,\pi_F' - \rho[\pi_M M + \pi_C C_F \\ &\quad + \pi_F\,(I_F + \delta_F K_F)]\,\rho' + D_LD_L' + D_KD_K'\end{aligned} \tag{3.2.25'}$$

$$GG' = TT' + H^*\,(H^*)' + (PB^*/i)[(B^*)' + P' - i'] + \rho F\,(\rho' + F') \tag{3.2.26'}$$

$$H' = P' + S_{HX}X' + S_{Hi}i' \tag{3.2.27'}$$

exogenous specification of variables. It is convenient to group the "obvious" exogenous growth rates as follows:

"Naturally exogenous" variables (6): π_E', π_M' π_C', π_K', ϵ, A'
Tax and expenditure variables (10): I_G', C_G', P_M', P_C', P_K', t_V', t_L', t_K', Q', L_G'
Log-changes determined by stock-flow relationships at the initial time point (4): K_X', K_F', H', B'.

These make up a total of twenty variables. Addition of either Φ_X' or a system of demand equations (details in the section on "Consumer Demand Responses") and of a numeraire price change (it is convenient for Brazil to work with the money wage increase w') brings the total to twenty-two.

Selection of the seven remaining exogenous variables is in part affected by the way the model is to be closed. To begin, observe that although current rates of growth of money emissions $H^{*\prime}$ and new bond placements $B^{*\prime}$ are given at any point in time, their values can be changed arbitrarily, subject only to the log-differential version of the government budget constraint, equation (3.2.26′). In most contexts, it is appropriate to assume that the government focuses on monetary policy and chooses a value of $H^{*\prime}$ at the beginning of any forecast period, to be maintained until the next period. The growth rate of bond emissions $B^{*\prime}$ then becomes endogenous, determined jointly by money expansion and fiscal variables.[13]

The balance of payments involves another pair of related variables—the log-changes in the exchange rate ρ' and the level of capital inflow F'. As we shall see, imposition of the cost-equals-marginal-product restrictions in a fully neoclassical specification requires that ρ' be treated as endogenous, forcing F' to be exogenous. By contrast, in a KS model (essentially given by the equations in table 3-6 plus equation [3.2.37′]), ρ enters only as a scaling variable and has to be determined exogenously, with F' endogenous. In either case, it is realistic to treat quantity export growth E' as being determined by a multitude of microeconomic factors and as exogenous to the macroeconomic system.

13. In effect, we permit discrete jumps in the money growth rate, which means that smoothly differentiable stock-flow equations of the form (3.2.22) cannot be used to relate the flow of money emissions H^* to the money stock H. This has some implications for computation of a completely new level solution to the model in some future year, discussed below in note 18.

Four exogenous log-changes remain. In a K specification these are easily chosen. Growth in investment is determined by some interaction of animal spirits, government policy, and other variables, so that g_X' and g_F' are exogenous.[14] Finally, two of the three variables, X', L', and M', entering the production function (3.2.6p′) must be specified. In practice, it is simplest to treat L' as exogenous (subject to sensitivity analysis) and to relate M' to X' by a constant multiplier—the elasticity of noncompetitive imports with respect to output. This parameter can be modified in practice to reflect government plans (or hopes) regarding future possibilities for import substitution.

We conclude that appropriate KS exogenous variables are as follows:

Other exogenous variables (9): ϕ_x' (determined by equation [3.2.37′]), w', ρ', $H^{*\prime}$, E', g_X', g_F', L', M'.

As mentioned above, the choice of exogenous variables in an N specification depends on marginal productivity relationships. These are set out in the following subsection.

Price-Sensitive Production Responses in an N Specification

The natural way to extend the two-factor derived demand equations (3.1.10′) and (3.1.11′) to many inputs is to assume that the latter enter separably into the production function. Separability assumptions drastically reduce the number of parameters to be specified, and permit the assumed structure of production to be tailored to whatever econometric evidence on the relationship of factor demands to cost changes happens to be available. At best, in a country like Brazil, one may have a few estimates of elasticities of substitution between aggregate capital and labor, and just possibly some investigation as to how demands for inputs within these two broad groupings respond to relative cost changes. Rarely, if ever, will studies of substitution possibilities between such things as unskilled labor and earth-moving machinery be available.

In the present model, it is convenient to separate the inputs into two groups. At an upper level, noncompetitive imports, labor, and a capital aggregate are all supposed to substitute with

14. Given greater knowledge of investment demand functions, we would make g_X' and g_F' functions of growth rates of interest and profit rates, without changing the basic logic of the K specification.

one another according to an elasticity σ_X.[15] And at a lower level, the two types of capital substitute in making up the aggregate with an elasticity σ_K.

To specify production tradeoffs formally, we can apply the user cost expressions (3.2.3′) to (3.2.5′), plus one additional equation for the log-change θ' of the cost of the capital aggregate,

$$\theta' = (\alpha_X + \alpha_F)^{-1} (\alpha_X \theta_X' + \alpha_F \theta_F'). \qquad (3.2.29')$$

This equation is based on the usual principle that summing log-changes of the components of an aggregate weighted by their base-period shares is the way to get the log-change of the aggregate.

We are almost ready to write down factor demand equations, but one problem remains—how to treat the residual ϵ introduced in equations (3.2.6c′) and (3.2.6p′). As discussed above, technical change can be viewed either as reducing costs or as increasing the productivity of inputs. But which costs and inputs? Conventionally, technical progress is often viewed as labor-augmenting, which means that labor-output ratios tend to fall over time, while capital-output and import-output ratios remain fairly constant (or respond only to price changes). Accepting this hypothesis, we can assign the whole impact of ϵ to reducing the derived demand for labor. In analogy to (3.1.10′) the appropriate equation for the change in the labor share is

$$\alpha_L' = (1 - \sigma_X) \left(\theta_L' - V' - \frac{\epsilon}{\alpha_L} \right). \qquad (3.2.30')$$

The last term on the right side rescales the technical progress term ϵ into labor terms by dividing it by α_L, and shows that it affects the labor share in the same way as an increase in the cost of value added V' or a decrease in labor costs θ_L'.

Demand for noncompetitive imports is not affected by technical change and so takes the simpler form

$$\alpha_M' = (1 - \sigma_X)(P_M' - V'). \qquad (3.2.31')$$

15. Capital-labor substitution is an ancient article of faith, but economists are often doubtful that imports can substitute for other inputs and thus tend to treat noncompetitive imported intermediates M and output X as proportional. A priori, this may not be realistic; for example, acceleration of the development of hydroelectric capacity in place of increased oil imports is always a possibility. To assume that imports, labor, and capital all substitute with the same elasticity goes well beyond this, but in the absence of contrary evidence the hypothesis is perhaps permissible.

Demand for the capital aggregate (call it K) can be described in the same way, except that it must be broken down into demands for national capital K_X and imported capital K_F. The first step in doing this is to note that the neoclassical way of relating the log-change in the aggregate capital-output ratio to cost changes is

$$K' - X' = -\sigma_X (\theta' - V') .$$

If the two types of capital substitute with elasticity σ_K, then the change in the domestic capital–capital aggregate ratio is

$$K_X' - K' = -\sigma_K (\theta_X' - \theta') ,$$

and similarly for imported capital. It is easy to substitute the K' terms out of these equations and change them to factor-share form to get

$$\alpha_X' = (1 - \sigma_X)(\theta' - V') + (1 - \sigma_K)(\theta_X' - \theta') \quad (3.2.32')$$

and

$$\alpha_F' = (1 - \sigma_X)(\theta' - V') + (1 - \sigma_K)(\theta_F' - \theta') . \quad (3.2.33')$$

The log-changes in factor shares from (3.2.30′) through (3.2.33′) can be shown to satisfy the adding-up condition (3.2.28′).[16]

In (3.2.29′) through (3.2.33′) we have added five equations and only one variable, θ'. Already we see that some of the variables set exogenously in the K specification must be made endogenous. Actually, the situation is more complicated yet, for another set of restrictions exists on the prices of traded goods. As indicated in note 12, world and domestic prices for traded goods are related as $P_i = \rho(1+\tau_i)\,\pi_i$ where τ_i is the tariff on traded good i. In growth rate form, such equations become

$$P_M' = \rho' + \pi_M' + \frac{\tau_M}{1 + \tau_M}\tau_M' \quad (3.2.34')$$

$$P_K' = \rho' + \pi_K' + \frac{\tau_K}{1 + \tau_K}\tau_K' \quad (3.2.35')$$

$$P_C' = \rho' + \pi_C' + \frac{\tau_C}{1 + \tau_C}\tau_C' . \quad (3.2.36')$$

In a K specification the variables in these growth-rate identities are all exogenous, and therefore they need not be treated as explicit restrictions. Such is not the case in the NS version (ρ' and

16. When the foregoing analysis is put in level and not log-change form, it becomes a two-level CES production function. See Sato (1967) for the details.

the P_i' are endogenous), and (3.2.34′) through (3.2.36′) become equations within the model.

Though they contain many variables, the implicit links among the foregoing derived demand equations virtually dictate which ones can be treated as exogenous and which as endogenous—another example of the rigidity of neoclassical hypotheses. If we treat all tax growth rates, world price changes, and so on as exogenous, the structure of variable dependence is as follows:

For reasons already discussed we treat L' and w' as exogenous. Therefore, (3.2.30′) plus equation (3.2.9′) for the labor share log-change α_L' together make X' a function of P'.

From (3.2.4′) and (3.2.5′), the growth rates determining the cost of capital are those of prices P', the profit rate r', and the cost of imported capital goods P_K'. By the trade arbitrage equation (3.2.35′), P_K' is determined by the growth rate in the exchange rate ρ'. After appropriate substitutions, (3.2.32′) and (3.2.33′) and the corresponding definitional equations for α_X' and α_F' reduce to a system of two equations in $X', P', K_X', K_F', r', \rho'$, and various tax rate log-changes. Evidently, r' and ρ' are determined by the other variables in the system.

By the adding-up condition (3.2.28′), the growth rate of the import share α_M' has now been determined. The other variables appearing in (3.2.28′) make the import growth rate M' a function of X' and P', since the growth rate of import costs P_M' is determined by ρ' from (3.2.34′).

From (3.2.6p′) we get another equation involving only X' and P' by substituting out M'. This can be solved with the relationship mentioned above for these two variables. By the accounting built into neoclassical algebra, the inflation rate generated from the cost side by (3.2.6c′) and (3.2.7′) will be consistent with these jointly determined values of X' and P' through the adding-up condition (3.2.28′). The actual numbers which emerge from the derived demand equations will of course depend on growth rates of labor, capital, taxes, and technical progress. But the logic of the solution procedure must go as indicated: X' and P' are determined jointly, and everything else follows from them.

Finally, note that g_X', the log-change in the growth rate of nationally produced capital goods, must be endogenous for the reasons already given above in the discussion of the simple model. We have in effect specified all terms in the national demand-supply balance (3.2.1′) except investment, so the latter is determined as well. Similarly, the balance of payments (3.2.2′) reduces to an equation linking F' and g_F'. To make KS and NS simulations comparable, we set the trade gap growth rate F' in the neoclassical model equal to values generated by the Keynes-Kaldor version, and thus determine g_F' endogenously as well.

The final exogenous growth rates in the N specification thus become:

"Naturally exogenous" variables (6): π_E' π_M', π_K', π_C', ϵ, A'
Tax and expenditure variables (10): I_G', C_G', t_V', t_L', t_K', Q', L_G', τ_M', τ_K', τ_C'
Log-changes determined by stock-flow relationships at the initial time point (4): K_X', K_F', H', B'
Other exogenous variables (6): ϕ_X' (determined by [3.2.37′]), w', F', $H^{*\prime}$, E', L'.

Consumer Demand Responses

The next topic is how to determine ϕ_X' and ϕ_F' as prices and the value of total consumption change, for use in both versions of the model. In developing countries one usually has some idea of the shares in the total consumption budget of various classes of goods in the economy, plus some hazy notion of income elasticities. Brazil is no exception to the rule. The consequence is that fairly strong hypotheses about consumer behavior must be imposed in advance to produce usable demand forecasts.

Begin by observing that income elasticities in principle describe demand log-changes in response to log-changes in an index of *real income*, $C' - \phi_X P' - \phi_F P_C'$. Let η_X denote the income elasticity of demand for X and η_{XX} and η_{XF} denote compensated price elasticities (with real income constant); the log-change in consumption of good X is

$$C_X' = \eta_X\,(C' - \phi_X P' - \phi_F P_C') + \eta_{XX} P' + \eta_{XF} P_C' + \beta_X$$

where β_X is an exogenous shift term. There is a similar equation for C_F'.

A fair amount of international evidence (summarized by Sato 1972, for example) suggests that quantities such as η_X and η_{XX} are related as $\eta_{XX} = -\sigma_C \eta_X$, where σ_C has a value around one-half. If we impose this relationship and (3.2.21′) on the demand equations we find that after a bit of algebra they can be written as

$$\phi_X' = (\eta_X - 1)\,C' + (1 - \eta_X \phi_X - \eta_X \sigma_C)\,P'$$

$$+ \phi_F \left(\frac{\eta_F \sigma_C}{\phi_X} - \eta_X\right) P_C' + \beta_X , \qquad (3.2.37')$$

and similarly for ϕ_F'. Implicit are the following restrictions on parameters:

$$\phi_X \eta_X + \phi_F \eta_F = 1$$

$$\phi_X \beta_X + \phi_F \beta_F = 0$$

$$\eta_{XF} = \phi_F \sigma_C \eta_F / \phi_X$$

$$\eta_{FX} = \phi_X \sigma_C \eta_X / \phi_F.$$

The first of these conditions is called Engel aggregation in the consumer demand literature; it assures that the budget constraint will be satisfied after income changes. The second condition does the same with regard to taste shifts. The third and fourth conditions define the cross-price elasticities in terms of the parameter σ_C.

Equations (3.2.37′) and (3.2.19′) through (3.2.21′) form a consistent demand system. Alternatively, one could use (3.2.37′), the similar equation for ϕ_F', and (3.2.19′) and (3.2.20′). In either case, the demand specification amounts to making the ϕ_i' price dependent in a plausible way which also satisfies the adding-up condition (3.2.21′). As always, the basic identities remain in force.[17]

Solution Techniques for the Level Form

Although they are complex algebraically, both versions of the Brazil model were solved in their level form by the methods sketched in the section "Calculation of a New Level-Form Solution." Basically, we used the guess at the price level P coming from the log-change model to generate values of all other variables, and then iterated until the product demand-supply balance (3.2.1) in the K specification or the exhaustion-of-product equation (3.2.6) in the N specification was satisfied. We began these procedures with a completely specified base year (1960 in

17. The method for specifying demand elasticities described here is from Frisch (1959) in its essentials, although he gives an explicit derivation in terms of utility functions. If one assumes that own-price elasticities stay constant over time, then one can update estimates of the Frisch parameter σ_C as the demand basket changes by letting it satisfy $-\sigma_C = \eta_{XX}\phi_X + \eta_{FF}\phi_F$. Updating income elasticities according to the rule $\eta_i = -\sigma_C \eta_{ii}$ then assures that Engel aggregation is satisfied. This procedure can be justified in terms of the direct addilog utility function (Sato 1972).

chapter 4 and 1970 in chapter 5), and took three-year time steps to generate forecasts for the subsequent decade. In each of these years, we also generated multiplier matrices showing responses of endogenous growth rates to exogenous ones, which proved quite useful in calibrating the model.[18]

References

Asimakopulos A., and J. B. Burbidge. 1974. The short-period incidence of taxation. *Economic journal* 84:267–88.

Blinder, Alan S., and Robert M. Solow. 1974. Analytical foundations of fiscal policy. In A. S. Blinder and others. *The economics of public finance.* Washington, D. C.: Brookings Institution.

Cauas, Jorge. 1972. Short-term economic theory and policy: The Chilean case, 1964–70. World Bank, Development Research Center, restricted circulation document.

Christ, Carl F. 1968. A simple macroeconomic model with a government budget restraint. *Journal of political economy* 76(1):53–67.

18. Two additional points should perhaps be made here. First, as mentioned above, we set $H^{*\prime}$, the growth rate of money emissions, exogenously at the beginning of each forecast period. If emissions at the beginning of the period are $H_0{}^*$, then at the end of the period the level of emissions and money stocks $H_T{}^*$ is

$$H_T{}^* = H_0{}^* \exp (H^{*\prime}\, T)$$

where $\exp (H^{*\prime}\, T)$ denotes the exponential function and T is the length of the forecast period. Straightforward integration shows that the money stock H_T is given by

$$H_T = \frac{1}{H^{*\prime}} (H_T{}^* - H_0{}^*) + H_0$$

where H_0 is the initial money stock.

Second in the NS model, we used two-level CES cost, production, and derived demand equations in calculating the level solutions. These are all well known, though it is worth noting explicitly that labor demand is given by

$$\bar{L}/X = (\xi_{XL} V / \theta_L)^{\sigma_x}$$

where $\bar{L}$ is the effective labor force, that is, the employed population multiplied by the increase in labor productivity cumulated over the forecast period, and ξ_{XL} is a scaling factor increasing at a rate ϵ/α_L over time from an initial value calculated from the base-year labor share.

Clark, Peter B. 1975. Intersectoral consistency and macroeconomic planning. In Charles R. Blitzer, Peter B. Clark, and Lance Taylor, eds. *Economy-wide models and development planning*. New York and London: Oxford University Press.

Frisch, Ragnar. 1959. A complete scheme for computing all direct and cross demand elasticities in a model with many sectors. *Econometrica* 27:177–96.

Hansen, Bent. 1973. On the effects of fiscal and monetary policy: A taxonomic discussion. *American economic review* 63: 546–71.

Johansen, Leif. 1974. *A multi-sectoral study of economic growth*. 2nd ed. Amsterdam: North-Holland.

Jones, Ronald W. 1965. The structure of simple general equilibrium models. *Journal of political economy* 73:557–72.

Lewis, W. Arthur. 1966. *Development planning: The essentials of economic policy*. New York: Harper and Row.

Manne, Alan S. 1963. Key sectors of the Mexican economy, 1960–70. In A. S. Manne and H. M. Markowitz, eds. *Studies in process analysis*. New York: John Wiley.

Sato, Kazuo. 1967. A two-level constant elasticity-of-substitution production function. *Review of economic studies* 34:201–18.

———. 1972. Additive utility functions for double-log consumer demand functions. *Journal of political economy* 80:102–24.

Sen, Amartya K. 1965. The money rate of interest in the pure theory of growth. In F. H. Hahn and F. P. R. Brechling, eds. *The theory of interest rates*. London: Macmillan and St. Martin's Press.

4

Brazilian Growth and Distribution in the 1960s: An Identity-Based Postmortem

Eliana A. Cardoso

BRAZILIAN ECONOMIC DEVELOPMENT during the 1960s is the subject of a vast literature. Economists agree that this period contained three distinct phases: (1) in the years before 1962 industrialization based on vigorous import substitution had its finale, accompanied by rampant inflation; (2) from 1963 to 1967 was a period of reduced capital formation and slowdown in industrial expansion with sharply declining inflation rates; and (3) from 1968 onward there was a sustained recovery of output growth accompanied by low inflationary pressure that lasted until 1974. There is, however, strong disagreement on the interpretation of these events. Was growth disequalizing or not? Was worsening in Brazilian income distribution the result of government's wage policy and stabilization? Was the structure of income distribution related to stagnation in the middle 1960s, and was the wage squeeze a necessary condition for the post-1968 economic recovery?

Our identity-based model can scarcely put an end to a seemingly unending polemic and counterpolemic on these questions, but the results given below suggest that: (1) wage repression may well have worsened the income distribution; (2) reductions in labor costs may be a very inefficient policy to induce employment growth; and (3) growth of exports may also have been accompanied by distributional shifts against the poor.

It should be stressed that these findings rely both on the specific formulation of the identity model and on the vagaries of the Brazilian national accounts. The latter have very great shortcomings not dealt with here but which should be kept in mind. There can be no statistics unless someone has first done the counting. In Brazil, however, often nobody has done that, and in such cases there are only informed estimates or more or less wild guesses. No one can cook a gourmet dinner out of a few rotten potatoes, but if nothing else is available, the cook will have to make do.

In 1974 the Vargas Foundation revised its figures for the national accounts at current prices, raising its previous GDP estimates by 4.4 percent in 1959 and 18.3 percent in 1970. New figures are not available for the intervening years which are the subject of this chapter.

In addition, as indicated in chapter 3, there are at least two possible ways of closing national accounting identities to make a complete model. If the Brazilian experience in the 1960s must be forced into one of these alternative Procrustean beds of economic theory, the one built up from Kaldor-Kalecki (KS) hypotheses is far less deforming. Even with a wildly implausible parameterization, the neoclassical (NS) model cannot reproduce Brazilian experience as recorded by the official statistics. This last point is discussed in appendix B to this chapter, where the actual data are compared with the simulated data obtained from the Kaldorian and neoclassical solutions. Appendix A describes how data were put together for the base year (1960) in a manner which satisfies the particular set of accounting identities used here.

The main part of this chapter is organized as follows: in the second section basic KS growth paths are discussed. Effects of wage reduction (third section) and of tax reduction (fourth section) on growth, employment, and labor share are then considered. In the fifth section the relation of exports to recent Brazilian economic performance is briefly analyzed. Conclusions are summarized in the last section.

Kaldorian Base Growth Paths

In this section two Kaldorian base growth paths are presented, and one is chosen for comparison in the following sections.

A complete listing of the assumed values of the exogenous growth rates for the base paths is shown in table 4-6 of appendix B, and table 4-1 in this section contains results for the key variables from the KS model. The first four columns represent base path A, and the first three combined with the fifth represent path B. The only difference between A and B is that the growth rate of money wages (w') in 1966–69 is equal to 0.23 in A and 0.30 in B.

To begin with path A, as can be seen in table 4-6, employment growth is nil in the first two periods, which correspond to the phase of slow growth, and in 1966–69 it is set at 0.046 a year. The residual ϵ is set at 0.020 in 1960–63, 0.005 in 1963–66, and 0.012 in 1966–69. Low values for ϵ were chosen because of the existence of excess capacity in 1963–66. The growth rates of domestic and imported capital stock are respectively 0.079 and 0.024 in 1960–63, 0.068 and 0.024 in 1963–66, and 0.068 and 0.024 in 1966–69. The elasticity of noncompetitive imports, M, with respect to output is 1.0 and wages grow at 0.45 per year between 1960–63 and 1963–66 and 0.23 per year in 1966–69.

Table 4-1. Values of Key Variables in Kaldorian (KS) Base Solutions

KS model	*Base paths A and B* 1960	1963	1966	*Path A* 1969	*Path B* 1969
1. Output (X)[a]	2.675	3.016	3.343	4.063	4.063
2. Output growth rate (X')	—[b]	0.040	0.034	0.065	0.065
3. Inflation rate (P')	—[b]	0.443	0.442	0.259	0.296
4. Profit rate (r)	0.175	0.165	0.153	0.172	0.160
5. Labor share (α_L)	0.540	0.489	0.473	0.431	0.476
6. Private savings share	0.104	0.121	0.125	0.141	0.136
7. Government savings share	−0.037	−0.046	−0.031	−0.048	−0.049
8. Capital inflow (F)	0.328	0.107	−0.017	0.169	0.362
9. Exchange rate (ρ)	0.110	0.573	2.209	4.062	4.062
10. Capital inflow/export value	0.225	0.063	−0.008	0.062	0.143
11. Interest rate (i)	0.060	0.113	0.147	0.126	0.141
12. Government interest payments (PB)	0.004	0.408	1.781	4.369	4.881

Note: The data in the tables in this chapter refer to year-end values in the stated years.

a. In billions of cruzeiros.

b. The base year is 1960 for figuring subsequent rates of output growth and inflation.

These assumptions generate output growth rates of 0.040 (1960–63), 0.034 (1963–66), and 0.065 (1966–69), as can be seen in the second line of table 4-1. In the third line we see that the inflation rate drops off abruptly from 0.443 a year in the first two periods to 0.259 in the last one.

Failure to implement a satisfactory anti-inflationary policy had been haunting Brazilian governments since the early 1950s. Inflation in both 1959 and 1960 was in excess of 30 percent. In 1963 an acceleration of inflation and a decline of output growth occurred simultaneously. After 1964 minimum wage changes were maintained at a rhythm markedly inferior to the price level, curbing inflation but clearly not rooting out inflationary expectations as had been predicted by policymakers. From 1967 onward, however, inflation did stabilize at around 20 percent a year and output grew rapidly.

The fourth line of table 4-1 exhibits a falling rate of profit between 1960 and 1966 and then a recovery in 1969. The labor share declines throughout the period, establishing an impressive difference between the 1969 and the 1960 values. The cause of this development appears in the next line in the shape of a steady increase in the proportion of private saving, not including depreciation, in the value of domestic output. (Such proportions are called savings shares in the tables.) As is well known, movements in private saving are mediated in Kaldorian models by shifts in the functional income distribution.

The increase in the proportion of private saving corresponds to the official data until 1966. According to Baer (1965), the private sector was the principal source of saving in the economy during the early 1960s. He presents data showing that the proportion of private saving in the product increases from 6.6 percent in 1960 to 12.4 percent in 1963 and 14.1 percent in 1965. From 1965 on, this proportion declines.

Private saving increased to compensate for declining capital inflows between 1960 and 1966, as can be seen in line 8, and to compensate for growing government dissaving in 1960–63 and 1966–69. (Similar estimates of government dissaving can be found in Fishlow 1973.) To understand the evolution of government saving it is necessary to know how tax revenue and public expenditure shifted over time.

On the tax side, the elasticity of total revenue with respect to the value of output exceeds unity, so that taxes divided by *PX* rise from 0.197 in 1960 to 0.26 in 1969. Once again, this is consistent with the data presented by Baer (1965). According to his estimates, direct plus indirect taxes divided by gross output rose from 0.20 in 1960 to 0.267 in 1968.

This behavior in the tax system comes from growing tax rates on both labor payments and value added. The rate on payments to labor grows from 0.046 in 1960 to 0.113 in 1969 and on value added from 0.157 in 1960 to 0.20 in 1969. Estimates of taxes on labor payments can be found in Bacha and others (1972), and the estimated values for the value added tax are consistent with an appropriate average of Brazilian sales taxes and are related to the government fiscal reforms of the 1960s. The tax increases are also caused by the form of the income tax equations where the elasticities of direct taxes with respect to labor and capital income were set equal to 1.1.

Not only did the tax share increase during this period but also government activity expanded. Government dissaving increases in 1960–63, falls until 1966, and increases again after 1967. This can be seen in line 7.

On the financial side, money emissions H^* grow at 0.55 in 1960–63, 0.40 in 1963–66, and 0.30 in 1966–69. Line 11 of table 4-1 shows that this implies a growing interest rate. Government bonds, unimportant in 1960, grow in significance from 1966 onward, and nominal payments to bondholders increase, as can be seen in the last line of table 4-1. The increase in the public debt is a response to government and foreign trade deficits and results from the interactions among expenditures and monetary and exchange rate policies.

The exchange rate ρ is assumed to increase at 0.55 in 1960–63, 0.47 in 1963–66, and 0.203 in 1966–69. These trends do not represent real devaluation. On the contrary, ρ rises much less than the difference between world and domestic prices, so that it really appreciates in the period.

Consider now the base Kaldorian path B represented by columns 1, 2, 3, and 5 in table 4-1. All exogenous rates of growth are the same as before except for the rate of growth of money wages (w') in 1966–69, which is set equal to 0.3. From Bacha and others (1972), the growth rate of money wages in manufacturing was somewhere between 0.23 and 0.30 in 1966–69. The advantage of using a bigger rate in our model is that it generates an increase in the average real wage rate, which in fact occurred, as the data indicate.[1]

The main difference between the solution labeled B and path A concerns the labor share in GNP. It falls markedly between 1966 and 1969 in path A, but in path B it remains constant after 1966 because total saving adjusts to growth in investment by an increased deficit in the balance of payments (line 8), and hence there is less private saving than before.

The evidence seems to point to a noticeable rise in the ratio of profits to wages and salaries in the urban sector between 1960 and 1968, consistent with both paths.[2] But if one also believes that the gap broadened in 1965–66 as a consequence of stabilization policies and that thereafter it did not increase markedly, path B should be preferred.[3]

Effects of Wage Reduction on Growth, Inflation, and Labor Share

As shown by Fishlow (1973), after 1964 the Brazilian government prevented the minimum wage from growing at the rate prices and productivity were increasing. To implement wage restriction, an estimate of the expected inflation during the following twelve months was required. This so-called inflationary residual was consistently and deliberately underestimated so that real minimum wages fell by 20 percent between 1964 and 1967.[4] In addition, between 1960 and 1969 the disparity between managers' and employees' wages increased considerably. Accordingly, the average real wage in path B increased at a rate well below the growth rate of output.

Nobody denies that the draconian wage control imposed by the Brazilian government served well the purpose of stabilization. It

1. Again from Bacha and others (1972), the average real wage in manufacturing grew at 0.02 a year from 1966 to 1969. More information on wage behavior during this period can be found in Fishlow (1973), who refers to unpublished data. Data on real wage rates in other sectors appear in chapter 10.

2. Comparisons between macro variables underlying table 4-1 and actual statistics are presented in appendix B to this chapter.

3. This position is advanced by Fishlow, in a revision of his 1973 work, who quotes a study by Wells (1974).

4. A more detailed discussion of the mechanisms of government wage policy that induced a deterioration of the real minimum wage can be found in chapter 10.

Figure 4-1. Inflation Rate and the Labor Share

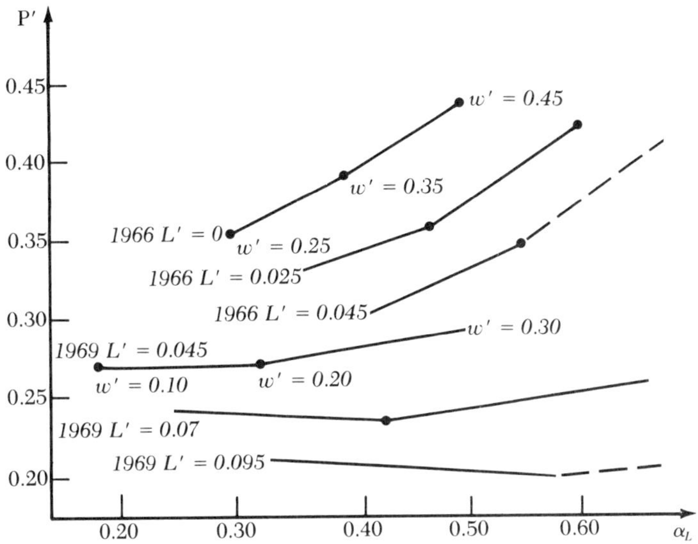

Source: Table 4-2.

is the effect of such policy on growth, employment, and income distribution that has been the focus of spreading debate. The following exercises suggest that Brazilian wage policy cannot be justified on the ground that increased labor absorption induced by lower real wages helped the underemployed poor, as maintained by Morley and Williamson (1975). Nor can it be argued that money wage repression served the purposes of accumulation, because the deterioration of income distribution in Brazil was not counterbalanced by a greater volume of aggregate national saving.[5] As suggested by Oliveira (1972), however, it can be maintained that the reduction of wage costs kept profits high and permitted an increase in private saving (this can be seen in line 6, table 4-1).

Figure 4-1 demonstrates the tradeoffs between labor share and price stabilization in a K specification. Each curve shows how, for

5. This second point has already been made by Fishlow (1974).

Table 4-2. Inflation Rate and Labor Share for Different Employment and Wage Growth

Wage growth	Employment growth								
	1963 $L' = 0$	1966 $L' = 0$	1969 $L' = 0.045$	1963 $L' = 0.015$	1966 $L' = 0.025$	1969 $L' = 0.07$	1963 $L' = 0.045$	1966 $L' = 0.045$	1969 $L' = 0.095$
1963 $w' = 0.45$	$P' = 0.443$ $\alpha_L = 0.489$			$P' = 0.425$ $\alpha_L = 0.536$			—		
1966 $w' = 0.45$		$P' = 0.442$ $\alpha_L = 0.473$			$P' = 0.422$ $\alpha_L = 0.575$			—	
1969 $w' = 0.30$			$P' = 0.296$ $\alpha_L = 0.476$			$P' = 0.261$ $\alpha_L = 0.664$			—
1963 $w' = 0.35$	$P' = 0.374$ $\alpha_L = 0.446$			$P' = 0.356$ $\alpha_L = 0.489$			$P' = 0.341$ $\alpha_L = 0.526$		
1966 $w' = 0.35$		$P' = 0.390$ $\alpha_L = 0.371$			$P' = 0.368$ $\alpha_L = 0.456$			$P' = 0.351$ $\alpha_L = 0.533$	
1969 $w' = 0.20$			$P' = 0.267$ $\alpha_L = 0.302$			$P' = 0.234$ $\alpha_L = 0.427$			$P' = 0.201$ $\alpha_L = 0.568$
1963 $w' = 0.25$	$P' = 0.309$ $\alpha_L = 0.401$			$P' = 0.289$ $\alpha_L = 0.443$			$P' = 0.274$ $\alpha_L = 0.477$		
1966 $w' = 0.25$		$P' = 0.359$ $\alpha_L = 0.271$			$P' = 0.335$ $\alpha_L = 0.336$			$P' = 0.316$ $\alpha_L = 0.398$	
1969 $w' = 0.10$			$P' = 0.271$ $\alpha_L = 0.161$			$P' = 0.241$ $\alpha_L = 0.231$			$P' = 0.210$ $\alpha_L = 0.312$

—Unreasonable results.

the same employment growth rate, the variation of the nominal wage growth rate affects the labor share and the inflation rate. The numbers underlying figure 4-1 are presented in table 4-2. They suggest the following:

- Reading down the columns, we see that at a constant employment growth rate, slower nominal wage growth leads to declining inflation but also to a fall in real wages and the labor share. Labor loses because the price level does not decrease as rapidly as the money wage.
- Reading across the rows, we see that for constant nominal wage growth, the rate of inflation drops as the employment growth rate increases. Inflation is lower because higher rates of employment mean more rapid output growth. With more goods available and the same exogenous changes in investment, exports, and government expenditures, private consumption can be more easily supplied, with smaller changes in prices. Lower inflation rates mean higher real wage increases. Combined with higher employment growth, these give an increased labor share.
- When both the above results are combined for the same year, a decrease in the money wage together with an employment increase produces less inflation and a smaller labor share.

More precisely, table 4-3 presents three different paths for the KS model, showing year-end values in three columns under each year. The first corresponds to the already familiar path B where wage growth rate is 0.45 a year in 1960–66 and 0.30 a year in 1966–69. In the second column (C) wage growth rate is set equal to 0.35 a year in 1960–66 and to 0.20 a year in 1966–69. The last hypothesis (path D) combines the decline in the growth of the wage rate with an increase in the employment growth rate to 0.025 in the periods where it was nil and 0.07 in the last period where it was 0.045. This results in 6.089 million more jobs in 1969, a full 25 percent increase in the total labor force estimated by hypothesis B.

The immediate impact of the wage decrease is deflationary, as can be verified from the third line of table 4-3. The decline of prices, however, is not enough to compensate the decline of nominal wages, so that real wages decline not only in comparison with the base path, but also along the same path for the whole period, as can be seen in line 6.

Table 4-3. *Effects of Wage Reduction on Growth, Inflation, and Labor Share*

KS model	1963 Path B $w' = 0.45$ $L' = 0$	1963 Path C $w' = 0.35$ $L' = 0$	1963 Path D $w' = 0.35$ $L' = 0.025$	1966 Path B $w' = 0.45$ $L' = 0$	1966 Path C $w' = 0.35$ $L' = 0$	1966 Path D $w' = 0.35$ $L' = 0.025$	1969 Path B $w' = 0.30$ $L' = 0.045$	1969 Path C $w' = 0.20$ $L' = 0.045$	1969 Path D $w' = 0.20$ $L' = 0.07$
1. Output (X)[a]	3.016	3.016	3.126	3.343	3.360	3.587	4.063	4.082	4.489
2. Output growth rate (X')	0.040	0.040	0.052	0.034	0.036	0.046	0.065	0.065	0.075
3. Inflation rate (P')	0.443	0.374	0.356	0.442	0.390	0.368	0.296	0.267	0.234
4. Profit rate (r)	0.165	0.171	0.159	0.153	0.171	0.148	0.160	0.203	0.167
5. Labor share (α_L)	0.489	0.446	0.489	0.473	0.371	0.456	0.476	0.302	0.427
6. Real wage (w/P)[a]	0.057	0.052	0.055	0.058	0.046	0.052	0.059	0.038	0.047
7. Real labor income (Y_L/P)[a]	1.296	1.180	1.337	1.325	1.045	1.359	1.537	0.979	1.506
8. Private savings share	0.121	0.121	0.109	0.125	0.129	0.104	0.136	0.154	0.116
9. Government savings share	−0.046	−0.035	−0.027	−0.031	−0.012	0.006	−0.049	−0.040	−0.010
10. Capital inflow (F)	0.107	−0.055	−0.025	−0.017	−0.316	−0.264	0.362	−0.275	−0.197
11. Employment level in the productive sector (L)[b]	21.289	21.289	22.947	21.289	21.289	24.734	24.425	24.425	30.514

a. In billions of cruzeiros.
b. In millions of jobs.

Lines 4 and 5 show that in the KS solution with slow wage growth the rate of profit increases and the wage share decreases in comparison with the base solution. Since real output in the second hypothesis (path C) is maintained roughly constant as compared with the base path, the main impact of wage decreases is on distribution. In the third hypothesis (path D), where a decrease in the wage is combined with an increase in employment, the real wage declines by 18 percent from 1960 to 1969. Even if this loss is compensated by a huge increase in employment, the gap between the share of profits and wages still increases in an impressive way. By comparing paths B and D for 1969, it can be verified that for an implicit elasticity of employment with respect to real wages equal to 1,[6] the labor share decreases from 0.476 in hypothesis B to 0.427 in hypothesis D. In 1966, when a real wage decrease of 15 percent is compensated by an 11 percent increase in employment, the labor share still falls. In 1963 an increase of 7.5 percent in employment against a decrease of 3.5 percent in real wages results in a constant labor share. Even if a wage squeeze results in a huge increase in employment the functional income distribution becomes markedly more unequal.

Our results differ from Morley and Williamson's because our model is closed with respect to saving. Like them, we show that an increase in aggregate demand leads to more employment, which may well benefit the poor. The increased demand, however, has to be "financed" by more saving, and in any kind of widow's cruse model this shifts the income distribution toward

6. An employment elasticity with respect to real wages equal to 1 is an overestimation of its real value. On this see Bacha and others (1972). The elasticity estimates were obtained as follows:

$$\eta = \frac{\dfrac{\text{Increase in employment between path B and D}}{\text{(Employment in B + employment in D) /2}}}{\dfrac{\text{Decrease in real wage between paths B and D}}{\text{(Real wage in B + real wage in D) /2}}}$$

$$\text{In 1969:}\quad \frac{(30.514 - 24.425)/27.4695}{(0.047 - 0.059)/0.053} = 1$$

$$\text{In 1966:}\quad \frac{(24.734 - 21.289)\ /\ 23.0115}{(0.052 - 0.058)\ /\ 0.055} = 1.37$$

$$\text{In 1963:}\quad \frac{(22.947 - 21.289)\ /\ 22.118}{(0.055 - 0.057)\ /\ 0.056} = 2.1.$$

the rich. This effect occurs in the identity model and not in that of Morley-Williamson. Their results are optimistic because they have conveniently left out the nonfavorable distribution mechanisms. Wage repression combined with stimulation of effective demand is not the sort of policy that shifts incomes away from rentiers and other high-saving classes. The poor almost always pay for rapid economic growth, and Brazilian policy in the 1960s (hypothesis B) made their burden more onerous.

Effects of Labor Tax Reduction on Growth and Labor Share

Bacha and others (1972) suggested that a favorable impact on employment would result from reduction of labor taxes. Since they analyzed the effect of a tax reduction in terms of intersectoral employment shifts, their conclusions cannot be tested here, but some related macroeconomic results can be studied. Because of the difference in tax rates across sectors, we set our "average" t_L equal to 0.046 in 1960 and 0.113 in 1969, instead of the figures 0.18 and 0.34 that apply in Brazilian manufacturing industry and appear in Bacha and others (1972).

Table 4-4 supplies the results from three runs. The base KS

Table 4-4. Effects of Labor Tax Reductions on Growth and Labor Share

	1966			*1969*		
KS model	*Path B*	$t_L' = 0$	$t_L' = 0$, $L' = 0.01$	*Path B*	$t_L' = 0$	$t_L' = 0$, $L' = 0.05$
1. Output (X)[a]	3.343	3.343	3.394	4.063	4.068	4.151
2. Output growth rate (X')	0.034	0.034	0.039	0.065	0.065	0.067
3. Inflation rate (P')	0.442	0.450	0.442	0.296	0.309	0.303
4. Profit rate (r)	0.153	0.163	0.157	0.160	0.183	0.174
5. Labor share (α_L)	0.473	0.450	0.469	0.476	0.418	0.448
6. Real wage (w/P)[a]	0.058	0.057	0.058	0.059	0.055	0.058
7. Real labor income (Y_L/P)[a]	1.325	1.292	1.365	1.537	1.440	1.569
8. Private savings share	0.125	0.131	0.126	0.136	0.153	0.145
9. Government savings share	−0.031	−0.039	−0.036	−0.049	−0.070	−0.064
10. Capital inflow (F)	−0.017	0.009	0.031	−0.362	0.494	−0.525
11. Employment level in the productive sector (L)[b]	21.289	21.289	21.937	29.425	24.425	25.488

a. In billions of cruzeiros.
b. In millions of jobs.

solution (B) is in the first column, where the labor tax rate is supposed to have been growing as actually observed. The second column gives results for solutions where labor taxes are supposed not to have changed during the period ($t_L{}' = 0$). In the third column it is assumed that a reduction in labor taxes could affect employment favorably.

As can be seen on line 9, the first impact of tax reduction is to decrease government saving (or increase government dissaving). To maintain real investment, the model operates in the following ways: first there is a more rapid rate of inflation; with rates of employment constant (or even growing) this reduces the labor share. In contrast to the solution without tax reduction, increased profit rates work in the same way as the drop in the labor share to increase private saving. Foreign saving also increases as a counterpart to the increase in imports of consumption goods resulting from a fall in their price in relation to home goods. These shifts in saving work against labor income so that the functional distribution in the KS model worsens even when the rate of employment growth is increased. Constant employment results can be predicted on widow's cruse grounds as indicated in chapter 3, but the employment growth results depend on parameters. In column 3 the labor tax rate is assumed to be 83 percent less than in the base path. This implies a reduction in labor costs of 0.067. Real wages also decline by 0.017 percent in the last hypothesis when compared with the base path. If employment responds to the 8.4 percent decrease in costs with an elasticity of 0.5 as suggested by Bacha and others (1972), the labor share still declines as can be seen in line 5 of table 4-4. As is shown in chapter 9, these distributional responses to a tax change carry over in a multisectoral model as well.

Exports and Growth

One current interpretation of recent Brazilian growth is that it was made possible only by post-1964 trade policy. This point of view is expressed by Von Doellinger, Faria, and Cavalcanti (1974). They also suggest that the incentives and subsidies given to exports may have led to distributional deterioration since those mechanisms benefit the proprietors of scarce resources, especially capital, while trying to achieve a greater supply of such resources in the future. The exercise below suggests that even in

Table 4-5. Effects of Export Reduction on Growth and Labor Share

	1963			1966			1969		
KS model	*Path B*	$E' = 0$	$E' = 0$ $L' = -0.003$	*Path B*	$E' = 0$	$E' = 0$ $L' = -0.002$	*Path B*	$E' = 0$	$E' = 0$ $L' = 0.039$
1. Output (X)[a]	3.016	3.016	3.016	3.343	3.328	3.316	4.063	4.035	3.981
2. Output growth rate (X')	0.040	0.040	0.040	0.034	0.033	0.032	0.065	0.064	0.061
3. Inflation rate (P')	0.443	0.428	0.426	0.442	0.435	0.437	0.296	0.271	0.278
4. Profit rate (r)	0.165	0.155	0.155	0.153	0.138	0.140	0.160	0.127	0.134
5. Labor share (α_L)	0.489	0.511	0.509	0.473	0.507	0.501	0.476	0.550	0.527
6. Private savings share	0.121	0.114	0.114	0.125	0.112	0.114	0.136	0.111	0.117
7. Government savings share	−0.046	−0.050	−0.050	−0.031	−0.038	−0.039	−0.049	−0.056	−0.060
8. Capital inflow (F)	0.107	0.326	0.321	−0.017	0.404	0.394	0.362	1.334	1.300

a. In billions of cruzeiros.

the absence of subsidies, export growth could have led to deterioration in the functional income distribution.

Table 4-5 presents results of the base path B compared with two different paths. The second column corresponds to the hypothesis of export stagnation: export growth rates which were equal to 0.05 in 1960–63, 0.035 in 1963–66, and 0.03 in 1966–69 are set equal to zero in path B for the whole period. In the third column employment response to exports is overestimated, and the elasticity of employment with respect to exports is set equal to the export share in output. When exports stagnate, employment and output decrease: employment growth rate becomes negative in 1960–66 and falls to 0.039 in 1966–69. Even so, the labor share in the third hypothesis still increases when compared with the base path where there are greater exports and employment. These results can be interpreted as follows: lower exports mean more product available domestically and less need for extreme savings efforts via inflation and a fall in real wage to meet investment targets.

Conclusions

In this chapter the identity-based model developed in chapter 3 was applied to the Brazilian experience in the 1960s. First a base path was developed to track the observed behavior of main macroeconomic variables in the period. Since it was impossible to develop a reasonably close approximation to the observed economic behavior with a neoclassical closure (see appendix B), we chose to simulate the model only for the Kaldorian variant.

The main exercise was estimation of the effects of alternative wage paths in the economy. It was concluded that under reasonable assumptions about employment response, wage reductions make income distribution markedly more unequal. Because our model is closed with respect to saving it was possible to show that the burden of economic growth during the 1960s was made even more onerous to the workers by Brazilian wage policy.

After an exercise with alternative export paths, we concluded that export growth probably led to deterioration in the functional income distribution by demanding more extreme savings efforts via inflation and a fall in real wages. These results seem to imply that recent Brazilian growth has been disequalizing and that government wage policy and export promotion may well have contributed to deterioration of the income distribution.

Appendix A: Data and Sources

In this appendix are described the sources of the data used to set up the identities of the model in table 3-5 for the 1960 base year.

Equation (3.2.1) is the accounting definition of total product and expenditure in our system. The values of the variables come directly from the national accounts with the minor modifications, including:

- The value of X in 1960 cruzeiros (Cr\$2.675 billion) differs from the value of GNP in the accounts (Cr\$2.756 billion) because there are two differences in definition between X and GNP. First, the value of intermediate imports is included in X but not in GNP, and second, government wage payments are excluded from the value of output PX but are included in GNP.
- Since 1960 is our base year, we set price level P to unity.
- The value of consumption of goods produced within Brazil (C_X = Cr\$1.811 billion) differs from personal consumption in the national accounts (Cr\$1.913 billion) because consumption imports are excluded from the former.
- The value of gross fixed capital formation by firms in the national accounts is Cr\$0.336 billion. To find investment in nationally produced goods we subtract Cr\$0.056 billion, which corresponds to imports of capital goods. The remaining investment is split into two parcels—net capital formation and depreciation of nationally produced capital stock. Since this stock includes all construction, we assume a relatively low depreciation rate ($\delta_X = 0.02$).
- Our value for government consumption (C_G = Cr\$0.287 billion) is lower than the corresponding item in the national accounts (Cr\$0.366 billion) because it does not contain government wage payments ($w[1 + t_L] L_G$ = Cr\$0.079 billion).
- The values of E and I_G are equal to the corresponding entries in the accounts.

Equation (3.2.2) is basically a "trade gap" statement of the balance of payments. It appears in domestic prices since all terms are multiplied by the exchange rate ρ. We set this equal to an annual average for 1960, with a value of Cr\$0.11 to the dollar.

The dollar values of intermediate imports $\pi_M M$ and imports of capital goods π_F $(I_F + \delta_F + \delta_F K_F)$ in 1960 were respectively US\$0.400 billion and US\$0.492 billion according to the *Boletim* of the Central Bank of Brazil (vol. 3, no. 5). Our dollar value for imports of consumption goods (US$0.893 billion) differs from that of the *Boletim* by including nonfinancial services. Finally, the value of F in equation (3.2.2) was calculated as a residual and represents only a trade gap.

Equation (3.2.6) is a breakdown of value added into its component costs. Value added itself (VX = Cr$2.312 billion) is the estimate of national income at factor cost from the accounts plus depreciation on nationally produced and imported capital goods ($\delta_X K_X + \delta_F K_F$) plus intermediate imports at post-tariff prices ($P_M M$) minus government wage payments.

We used depreciation rates $\delta_X = 0.02$ and $\delta_F = 0.05$ for the two types of capital stock. The total stock itself ($K_X + K_F$ = Cr$4.926 billion) was estimated by deflating the values in Langoni (1974).

Our employment estimates (L = 21.289 million, L_F = 1.362 million) are from Hoffman (1972). The labor tax rate of 0.046 is calculated from estimates of incidence of this tax in manufacturing by Bacha and others (1972). The 0.18 percent incidence estimate from this source was corrected by the share of the labor force (0.25) covered by IMPS, the national insurance scheme.

The tax rate on value added ($t_V = 0.157$) was calculated from the difference between value added at factor cost and the value of output.

The shares of inputs in equations (3.2.8) through (3.2.11) follow directly from (3.2.6).

In equation (3.2.14) capital income includes payments received for holding government bonds. The total expenditure of the government for bond payments in 1960 was negligible and will become significant only after 1965.

Equations (3.2.15) and (3.2.16) define personal income taxes. Total revenue of Cr$62 million comes from the statement of the Brazilian Treasury (*Boletim* of the Central Bank, 1965). Our breakdown between taxes on labor and on capital incomes was done in view of tax schedules and the overall income distribution.

The money base (H = Cr$0.374 billion) appearing in equation (3.2.17) and elsewhere is from the 1965 issue of the *Boletim* of the Central Bank. Pastore (1973) provides econometric justification for our value of 30 percent for the expected inflation rate in 1960.

In equation (3.2.18) private consumption C is set to the corresponding value in the national accounts. Transfer payments (Q = Cr$0.119 billion) also come from the accounts. We follow Kaldor

(1966) and Brazilian evidence in setting γ_L, the propensity to consume from labor income, equal to 0.99. The propensity to consume from capital income ($\gamma_K = 0.675$) follows as a residual. Elasticities of consumption with respect to wealth ($S_{CR} = 0.05$) and the deflated interest rate ($S_{Ci} = -0.05$) are from Christ (1968). We set the income elasticity of demand for domestic goods, η_X, to 0.98. By Engel aggregation the elasticity for imports, η_F, becomes 1.7674. The substitution parameter for consumption, σ_C, was set equal to 0.5. Equations (3.2.19) through (3.2.23) define consumption shares and capital stock growth rates, all of which follow directly from estimates already made. Equations (3.2.24) to (3.2.26) then set out the government accounts.

Total tax receipts (T = Cr\$0.527 billion) differ from the total of government revenue in the national accounts because of some nontax items (Cr\$0.086 billion). The largest receipts come from value added taxes ($t_V VX$ = Cr\$0.364 billion). Tariffs are other indirect taxes with revenues calculated from equations of the form $(P_C - \rho\pi_C)\, C_F$ where all values were previously known. After using independent estimates of income taxes $(D_L + D_K)$ from the national accounts and of employment taxes $(t_L\, w[L + L_G])$, we find total profit taxes and the profit tax rate ($t_K = 0.04$) as residuals.

In equation (3.2.25) all government expenditure items come from the national accounts as discussed above. The difference between expenditures and receipts is covered by expansion of the money base H^* and by new bond emissions PB^*/i. Our estimate of Cr\$572.4 million for the money base comes from the *Boletim*, 1965, and new bond emissions are calculated as a residual.

The final equation (3.2.27) enforces equilibrium in the money market. The income elasticity ($S_{HX} = 0.7$) is from Pastore (1973), and the interest elasticity ($S_{Hi} = 1.0$) is from Christ (1968).

Appendix B: Failure of the Neoclassical Specification

A complete relation of the assumed values of the exogenous growth rates for our base paths is shown in table 4-6.

Table 4-7 provides end-of-year comparisons of the state of the Brazilian economy in 1963, 1966, and 1969. The estimates are from the national accounts scorekeepers of the Vargas Founda-

Table 4-6. Values of Exogenous Growth Rates in the Base Solutions: Kaldorian Path A and Neoclassical Path α

Kaldorian solution (KS), path A	*1960–63*	*1963–66*	*1966–69*	*Neoclassical solution (NS), path α*	*1960–63*	*1963–66*	*1966–69*
1. L'	0.000	0.000	0.046	L'	0.000	0.000	0.046
2. w'	0.450	0.450	0.230	w'	0.450	0.450	0.230
3. π_E'	0.000	0.030	0.004	π_E'	0.000	0.030	0.004
4. π_M'	0.000	0.019	0.000	π_M'	0.000	0.019	0.000
5. π_C'	0.008	0.012	0.033	π_C'	0.008	0.012	0.033
6. π_K'	0.000	−0.015	0.031	π_K'	0.000	−0.015	0.031
7. ϵ	0.020	0.005	0.012	ϵ	0.020	0.005	0.012
8. A'	0.120	0.000	−0.200	A'	0.120	0.000	−0.200
9. e'	0.550	0.450	0.203	F'	−0.500	−5.000	0.000
10. L_G'	0.000	0.000	0.040	L_G'	0.000	0.000	0.040
11. I_G'	0.010	0.030	0.180	I_G'	0.010	0.030	0.180
12. C_G'	0.065	0.040	0.070	C_G'	0.065	0.040	0.070
13. P_M'	0.550	0.470	0.203	t_M'	0.000	0.000	0.000
14. P_C'	0.558	0.462	0.236	t_C'	0.000	0.000	0.000
15. P_K'	0.550	0.435	0.234	t_K'	0.000	0.000	0.000
16. t_V'	0.000	0.050	0.030	t_V'	0.000	0.050	0.030
17. t_L'	0.000	0.150	0.150	t_L'	0.000	0.150	0.150
18. t_K'	0.000	0.000	0.000	t_K'	0.000	0.000	0.000
19. Q'	0.499	0.610	0.402	Q'	0.499	0.610	0.402
20. E'	0.050	0.035	0.090	E'	0.050	0.035	0.090
21. $(H^*)'$	0.550	0.400	0.300	$(H^*)'$	0.550	0.400	0.300
22. β_X	0.000	0.000	0.000	β_X	0.000	0.000	0.000
23. g_X'	−0.050	0.000	0.050				
24. g_F'	0.000	0.000	0.100				
25. r_{MX}	1.000	1.000	1.000				

Note: r_{MX} = elasticity of imports in relation to output. β_X and r_{MX} are not rates of growth but have been included to complete the values exogenously specified.

tion and the base solutions of the KS model and NS model where the elasticity of substitution σ_X is assumed to be 1.8.

The value of output generated by neoclassical solutions and the same exogenous rates of growth used for the Kaldorian path A vary according to different values ascribed to the elasticity of substitution σ_X. As σ_X increases, both prices P and real output X increase, providing the following results for 1969:

σ_x	*0.3*	*0.6*	*0.8*	*0.9*	*1.2*	*1.5*	*1.8*
PX (billions of cruzeiros)	97.524	98.135	99.084	99.503	101.797	104.192	104.745

Since "actual" *PX* was approximately Cr$130 billion, as the values assumed for σ_X grow, better adjustments of the NS simulations to the official data are obtained. That is why we choose σ_X

Table 4-7. Comparison of Observed Macrovariables and Model Results: Kaldorian Path A and Neoclassical Path α

	1963			1966			1969		
Macrovariables	*Observed value*	*KS model*	*NS model*	*Observed value*	*KS model*	*NS model*	*Observed value*	*KS model*	*NS model*
1. Output growth rate (X')	0.050	0.040	0.040	0.034	0.034	0.023	0.070	0.065	0.060
2. Inflation rate (P')	0.434	0.443	0.420	0.470	0.442	0.447	0.230	0.259	0.230
3. GNP ($PX - P_M M + w[1 + t_L] L_G$)	11.929	11.269	10.547	53.724	48.334	46.898	133.100	128.148	105.678
4. Private consumption (C)	8.154	8.108	7.830	38.837	33.216	32.129	95.600	84.727	77.158
5. Private gross fixed capital formation ($P[I_X + \delta_X K_X] + P_K[I_F + \delta_F K_F]$)	1.611	1.763	1.144	6.059	6.516	4.300	14.517	17.079	7.769
6. Government gross fixed capital formation (PI_G)	0.488	0.510	0.475	2.140	2.094	1.975	7.432	7.840	6.785
7. Government consumption ($PC_G + w[1 + t_L] L_G$)	1.592	1.626	1.535	6.251	6.814	6.741	15.468	17.870	15.846
8. Government interest payments (PB)	n.a.	0.408	0.379	0.148	1.781	2.056	4.149	4.369	5.793
9. Transfer payments (Q)	0.534	0.534	0.534	3.417	3.417	3.417	11.418	11.418	11.418
10. Government tax revenue (T)	2.147	2.311	2.152	12.960	11.158	10.325	37.197	33.061	27.686
11. Direct taxes ($D_L + D_K$)	0.260	0.339	0.309	1.339	1.598	1.463	3.598	4.790	3.739
12. Exchange rate (ρ)	0.577	0.573	0.417	2.216	2.209	1.845	4.071	4.062	3.389
13. Export value in dollars ($\pi_E E$)	1.525	1.697	1.197	1.868	2.058	2.058	2.522	2.735	2.735
14. Imports of goods and nonfinancial services in dollars ($\pi_M M + \pi_C C_F + \pi_K [I_F + \delta_F K_F]$)	1.567	1.796	1.767	1.699	2.040	2.060	2.526	2.897	2.733

n.a. Not available.

Note: Value figures (cruzeiros unless specified dollars) are in billions.

= 1.8 to simulate the NS path. Such a value seems to be high when compared with the available empirical evidence. Estimates for the elasticity of substitution in manufacturing industries in Brazil suggest values around 0.5.[7] Our higher value could be justified on the basis that it represents the elasticity of substitution for the whole economy, since agricultural and service sectors, where capital substitutes more easily for labor than in industry, represent an important share of GNP in Brazil. There is no evidence to determine an appropriate elasticity of substitution, but the data for other countries indicate that the assumed value of 1.8 for σ_X would be a prime reason to take the NS results with a grain of salt.

This caveat should be kept in mind when examining the comparisons in table 4-7. For the output growth rates (on the first line of the table) the Kaldorian specification shows a better fit in 1966 and 1969. On prices, however, a small advantage appears to lie with the neoclassical specification.

The shares of consumption in GNP according to the three sets are:

	Vargas data	*KS model*	*NS model*
1963	0.684	0.719	0.742
1966	0.723	0.687	0.685
1969	0.718	0.661	0.730

Except for 1963, the K specification underestimates the share of consumption, but the relative differences are not large, particularly since the official estimates include inventory changes in the data for consumption. In contrast, the N specification overestimates the share of consumption in GNP, except for 1966.

The investment estimates of the KS model agree well with the accounts in 1963 and 1966 but are higher than the official estimates in 1969. The relatively higher KS rate of inflation for this last period derives from distributional shifts required to generate saving to meet the higher investment levels. This is one reason the labor share in the K specification turns out to be smaller and consumption lower than in the N specification. (Results for the Kaldorian base solutions in table 4-1 can be compared with the neoclassical base solutions presented in table 4-8.)

The N specification generates lower rates of investment than

7. Estimates of σ_X can be inferred from Bacha and others (1972).

Table 4-8. Values of Key Variables in NS Base Solutions

NS model (paths α and β)	*1960*	*1963*	*1966*	*1969 (path α)*	*1969 (path β)*
1. Output (X)[a]	2.676	3.023	3.256	3.885	3.892
2. Output growth rate (X')	—[b]	0.040	0.023	0.060	0.060
3. Inflation rate (P')	—[b]	0.419	0.447	0.230	0.300
4. Profit rate (r)	0.175	0.163	0.151	0.152	0.151
5. Labor share (α_L)	0.540	0.524	0.514	0.520	0.521
6. Private savings share	0.104	0.113	0.120	0.124	0.132
7. Government savings share	−0.037	−0.070	−0.062	−0.099	−0.078
8. Capital inflow (F)	0.327	0.073	0.0	0.0	0.0
9. Exchange rate (ρ)	0.110	0.417	1.845	3.389	4.181
10. Capital inflow/ export value	0.224	0.043	0.0	0.0	0.0
11. Interest rate (i)	0.060	0.106	0.136	0.106	0.131
12. Government interest payments (PB)	0.004	0.380	2.056	5.793	7.146

a. In billions of cruzeiros.
b. The base year is 1960 for figuring subsequent rates of output growth and inflation.

its rival and the official estimates. The following figures refer to national net saving in both KS and NS models:

	1960	*1963*	*1966*	*1969*
KS model (path A)	0.08	0.08	0.093	0.098
NS model (path α)	0.08	0.046	0.058	0.025

The savings shares[8] generated in the NS model from 1963 on are much smaller than in the KS model and incompatible with the observed behavior of the economy.

The reason the savings share behaves differently in our models is as follows. In the KS model investment was generated exogenously, and the labor share shifted to obtain enough saving to maintain investment. In the marginalist world the labor share cannot move as freely as that. Observe on line 5 of table 4-8, where details for the NS model are presented, that the labor share declines from 0.54 in 1960 to 0.52 in 1963 and is then maintained roughly constant around this figure. Values for government revenue, however, are lower in the NS model (this can be observed

8. NS saving rises with σ_X, and the estimates shown in the text refer to the run where σ_X was made equal to 1.8.

on line 10 of table 4-7). Low tax receipts come from a smaller base (price times output) for the value added tax. Since government expenditures are exogenous and maintained at the values assumed for the Kaldorian simulations, government dissavings will be increasing in the NS model, as can be seen in line 7 of table 4-8. In consequence, national saving will be lacking in relation to the KS model: investment and growth will be smaller.

One final reason for mistrusting the simulations called A and α for the period 1966–69 is that they yield a decline in the real wage rate which, as pointed out above, did not actually occur. To solve this problem we run another simulation set using exactly the same exogenous growth rates as in table 4-6 except for the growth rate of money wages (w') in 1966–69, which we make equal to 0.30 instead of 0.23. In this case (paths B and β), the results for 1969 will diverge from the previous analysis and assume the values in table 4-9.

Table 4-9. Comparison of Observed Macrovariables in 1966–69 and Model Results When Growth Rate of Money Wages (w') = 0.3

Macrovariables	*Observed value*	*KS model (path B)*	*NS model (path β)*
1. Output growth rate (X')	0.070	0.065	0.060
2. Inflation rate (P')	0.230	0.296	0.300
3. GNP ($P_X - P_M M + w[1 + t_L] L_G$)	133.100	141.665	130.537
4. Private consumption (C)	95.600	94.691	91.326
5. Private gross fixed capital formation ($P[I_X + \delta_X K_X] + P_K[I_F + \delta_F K_F]$)	14.517	21.228	13.467
6. Government gross fixed capital formation (PI_G)	7.432	8.759	8.370
7. Government consumption ($PC_G + w[1 + t_L] L_G$)	15.468	20.293	19.549
8. Government interest payments (PB)	4.140	4.881	7.146
9. Transfer payments (Q)	11.418	11.418	11.413
10. Government tax revenue (T)	37.197	37.127	34.252
11. Direct taxes ($D_L + D_K$)	3.598	5.182	4.711
12. Exchange rate (ρ)	4.071	4.062	4.181
13. Export value in dollars ($\pi_E E$)	2.522	2.734	2.734
14. Imports of goods and nonfinancial services in dollars ($\pi_M M + \pi_C C_F + \pi_K[I_F + \delta_F K_F]$)	2.256	3.091	2.730

Note: Value figures (cruzeiros unless specified dollars) are in billions.

The main trouble with this new set of figures is a larger difference between the model and the official estimates for the inflation rate. For the remaining variables the adjustment is good. In the K specification, the share of private capital formation in GNP is of the same magnitude as in the previous simulation (0.14). Imports now are bigger because of a shift in consumer demand toward them as prices of domestic goods accelerate.

References

Bacha, Edmar L., and others. 1972. *Encargos trabalhistas e absorçao de mão-de-obra.* Rio de Janeiro: Instituto de Planejamento Econômico e Social/Instituto de Pesquisas (IPEA/INPES).

Baer, Werner. 1965. *Industrialization and economic development of Brazil.* Homewood, Ill.: Irwin. Published in Portuguese as: A industrialização e o desenvolvimento econômico do Brasil. Rio de Janeiro: Vargas Foundation, 1975.

Christ, Carl F. 1968. A simple macroeconomic model with a government budget restraint. *Journal of political economy* 76(1):53–67.

Fishlow, Albert. 1973. Brazilian income size distribution: Another look. Berkeley: University of California, Department of Economics; processed. Published in Portuguese as: Distribuição da renda no Brasil: Um novo exame. *Dados* 11(1973):10–80. (Published by Instituto Universitario de Pesquisas, Rio de Janeiro.)

———. 1974. Indexing Brazilian style: Inflation without tears? *Brookings papers on economic activity* 1:261–82.

Hoffman, Helga. 1972. *Desemprego e subemprego no Brasil.* Brasília: University of Brasília, Department of Economics; processed.

Kaldor, Nicholas. 1966. Marginal productivity and the macroeconomic theories of distribution. *Review of economic studies,* 33:309–19.

Langoni, Carlos Geraldo. 1974. *As causas do crescimento econômico do Brasil.* Rio de Janeiro: Apec Editora.

Morley, Samuel A., and Jeffrey G. Williamson. 1975. Growth, wage policy and inequality: Brazil in the 1960s. SSRI Workshop Series no. 7519. Madison, Wis.: University of Wisconsin; processed.

Oliveira, Francisco. 1972. A economia brasileira: Critica a razao dualistica. *Estudos Cebrap* 2:3–82 (São Paulo).

Pastore, Affonso Celso. 1973. *Observacoes sobre a politica monetaria no programa brasileira de estabilização.* São Paulo: University of São Paulo, Instituto de Pesquisas Econômicas; processed.

Von Doellinger, Carlos, Hugo Baros de Castro Faria, and Leonardo Caserta Cavalcanti. 1974. *A política brasileira de comércio exterior e seus efeitos: 1967–73.* Relatório de pesquisas no. 22. Rio de Janeiro: Instituto de Planejamento Econômico e Social/Instituto de Pesquisas (IPEA/INPES).

Wells. John. 1974. Distribution of earnings, growth and the structure of demand in Brazil during the 1960s. *World development* 2(1). Published in Portuguese in R. Tolipan and A. C. Tinelli. *A controversia sobre distribuição da renda e desenvolvimento.* Rio de Janeiro: Zahar Editores, 1975.

5

Planned and Possible Growth in the Late 1970s: Some Identity-Based Complications for Brazil

Eliana A. Cardoso and Lance Taylor

WITH THE SLOWING DOWN OF BRAZILIAN economic growth in the mid-1970s, debate regarding economic policy took up two interrelated problems. One is how the economy might adjust to a radically changed foreign trade position, while still maintaining the rapid growth rates that may be necessary to the political survival of the present regime. The other is how an easing of wage control and other anti-egalitarian incomes policies might affect overall economic performance. In this chapter the identity-planning technique of chapter 3 is used in an attempt to shed some light on these issues.

We first develop base solutions for the 1970–82 period for both KS and NS variants of the chapter 3 model. This procedure is necessary because there are no historical data for the 1970s that can be used as a standard of comparison, as in the analysis of the 1960s in chapter 4. Moreover, in 1975 when the work for this chapter was done there were separate sets of national accounts for the 1960s and 1970s in Brazil, and we therefore had to develop a data base independent of that of chapter 4. Details of our procedures and comparisons of the two base solutions with the known 1970–73 statistics appear in the appendix to this chapter. After discussion of the base solutions in the first two sections, we take up the effects of wage policy and the problems of foreign trade. The chapter concludes with a critique of the current national development plan and our own assessment of likely prospects for future growth.

A K-Specification Growth Path

Table 5-1 summarizes three solutions to the model—one based on the Kalecki-Kaldor specification, and two neoclassical variants in which the elasticity of substitution σ_X is set respectively at values of one-third and two-thirds. These projections for the 1970s are more or less plausible, but in no sense should they be interpreted as *the* identity-based forecast for Brazil. At best, they represent reference growth paths around which changes in policy variables can be rung to indicate possible tradeoffs.

The top part of table 5-1 gives results from a KS model in which employment growth is set at 3 percent a year, hence the label A(0.03) attached to the solution. The residual ϵ is set at 2 percent after 1973 (slightly below its apparent value during recent years), and the growth rates of domestic and foreign capital stock are respectively 9.6 and 9.1 percent throughout the forecast period. The elasticity of noncompetitive imports M with respect to output is 1.5, and wages grow at 23 percent a year. The second line for the KS model shows that these assumptions generate output growth rates a bit below 9 percent from 1973 on, well within the range discussed in Brazil. The inflation rate drops off gradually from 20 to 16 percent, so that the real wage increases.

The fourth and fifth lines demonstrate a falling profit rate (r) and a rising labor share (α_L) over the 1973–82 period. The cause of these developments shows up in the next line of the table in the guise of a steady decrease in the proportion of private saving (not including depreciation) to the value of domestic output. As described in chapters 3 and 4, movements in private saving are mediated in KS models by shifts in the functional income distribution. Here, r falls because less private saving overall—and thus mainly from capital—is required.

A projected falling profit rate in Brazil is dubious—one of several reasons the table 5-1 forecasts are not definitive. But, like

Table 5-1. Values of Key Variables in Base Solutions with 3 Percent Annual Employment Growth

Base solution and variable	*1970*	*1973*	*1976*	*1979*	*1982*
KS model, solution A(0.03)					
1. Output (X)	204.1	279.7	363.4	474.7	619.0
2. Output growth rate (X')	—	0.105	0.087	0.089	0.088
3. Inflation rate (P')	—	0.208	0.191	0.164	0.160
4. Profit rate (r)	0.184	0.217	0.215	0.196	0.171
5. Labor share (α_L)	0.507	0.432	0.409	0.418	0.437
6. Private savings share	0.149	0.169	0.148	0.123	0.093
7. Government savings share	−0.023	−0.041	−0.024	−0.004	0.020
8. Foreign savings share	0.004	0.005	0.017	0.026	0.039
9. Capital inflow (F)	0.189	0.407	2.411	6.106	13.974
10. Exchange rate (ρ)	4.59	6.12	8.26	11.16	15.06
11. Capital inflow/export value	0.069	0.062	0.203	0.283	0.355
12. Interest rate (i)	0.240	0.262	0.235	0.226	0.225
13. Government interest payments (PB)	8.8	42.2	84.3	123.1	112.9
NS model ($\sigma_X = 1/3$), solution $\alpha(0.03)$					
1. Output (X)	204.1	276.4	345.3	417.3	499.7
2. Output growth rate (X')	—	0.105	0.074	0.063	0.060
3. Inflation rate (P')	—	0.171	0.179	0.211	0.223
4. Profit rate (r)	0.184	0.196	0.193	0.211	0.240
5. Labor share (α_L)	0.507	0.489	0.499	0.479	0.446
6. Private savings share	0.149	0.153	0.127	0.131	0.146

7. Government savings share	−0.023	−0.059	−0.081	−0.109	−0.154
8. Foreign savings share	0.004	0.005	0.014	0.020	0.026
9. Capital inflow (F)	0.189	0.405	2.399	6.081	13.919
10. Exchange rate (ρ)	4.59	5.45	5.86	7.54	9.88
11. Capital inflow/export value	0.069	0.062	0.202	0.282	0.354
12. Interest rate (i)	0.240	0.232	0.196	0.205	0.235
13. Government interest payments (PB)	8.8	37.8	81.1	208.4	645.5
NS model ($\sigma_X = 2/3$)					
1. Output (X)	204.1	277.1	343.6	414.5	490.4
2. Output growth rate (X')	—	0.105	0.072	0.062	0.056
3. Inflation rate (P')	—	0.161	0.187	0.201	0.211
4. Profit rate (r)	0.184	0.191	0.192	0.204	0.224
5. Labor share (α_L)	0.507	0.503	0.504	0.499	0.489
6. Private savings share	0.149	0.148	0.126	0.124	0.133
7. Government savings share	−0.023	−0.062	−0.085	−0.119	−0.180
8. Foreign savings share	0.004	0.005	0.014	0.021	0.027
9. Capital inflow (F)	0.189	0.405	2.399	6.081	13.919
10. Exchange rate (ρ)	4.59	5.27	5.83	7.27	9.13
11. Capital inflow/export value	0.069	0.062	0.202	0.282	0.354
12. Interest rate (i)	0.240	0.226	0.194	0.197	0.216
13. Government interest payments (PB)	8.8	36.7	81.9	206.8	631.8

Note: Value figures in billions of 1970 cruzeiros.

many oil importers, the nation will almost certainly have balance of payments deficits in the medium term. Since trade deficits represent foreign saving, national saving will in general have to decline as a share of output during the next few years, unless investment grows very rapidly. The magnitude of this shift in sources of saving is documented by lines 8 and 11 of the KS model, respectively showing the share of foreign saving in output and the value of capital inflow divided by exports. The latter indicates that foreign saving may rise from 7 to 35 percent of export value in world prices.[1]

National saving can adjust to an increased balance of payments deficit through decreases in either private or government saving. As indicated, a decrease in private saving leads to decreased profit rates and an improved labor share. The evolution of government saving is determined by tax revenue and public expenditure shifts over time. On the tax side, the elasticity of total revenue with respect to the value of output exceeds unity, so that taxes divided by PX rise from 0.245 in 1970 to 0.260 in 1982. This responsiveness in the tax system comes from the form of equations (3.2.15) and (3.2.16) in table 3-5 for income taxes. The elasticities S_{DL} and S_{DK} are each set at 1.15 and generate rapidly rising direct tax receipts.

An increasing tax share is probably realistic, but the assumed growth rates of government activity are not quite sufficient to offset it, so that the government shifts from dissaving to saving over the period.[2] Again, this can be accommodated only by a reduction in private saving.

Money emissions H^* grow at 20 percent a year, maintaining the interest rate stable (line 12). Throughout the period, the government ends up buying bonds to such an extent that even its nominal payments to bondholders decline (line 13). Such avoidance

1. The A(0.03) solution is built on the assumption that export volume grows at 10 percent a year after 1973, with export prices increasing at the same rate. World prices for all types of imports are likewise assumed to increase at 10 percent from 1973 on, but at 12 percent during 1970–73. The hypothesis that there will be no further terms-of-trade shifts against Brazil is optimistic.

2. Government employment and the value of transfer payments are assumed to grow respectively at 3 and 30 percent a year throughout the period. Government purchases of goods for consumption and investment grow at 7 percent between 1973 and 1976, and 9 percent thereafter.

of debt on the part of government is difficult in the NS model, with correspondingly unfavorable effects on its saving and overall growth.

The decrease in public debt in the K specification is a response to increasing government surpluses and the foreign trade deficit. The course of bond sales could be modified by changes in expenditure policy, money emissions, or the exchange rate. For the 1973–82 period the exchange rate is assumed in KS models to increase at 10 percent a year. This trend represents real devaluation (that is, ρ rises substantially faster than the difference between world and domestic prices) and makes capital inflow an even more important source of saving than the dollar valuations would indicate.

An N-Specification Growth Path

By latter-day Brazilian standards, the NS forecasts are dismal indeed. Details appear in table 5-1 for values of the elasticity of substitution σ_X, which probably bracket the "true" parameter, if one exists.[3]

The key to understanding the NS results lies once again in the savings-investment balance, except that as pointed out in chapter 3 causality now runs from the side of thrift. In a marginalist world, growth in labor, capital, and productivity generates not only output increase but also the configuration of relative prices and factor shares. Savings decisions and the availability of goods then determine investment. If saving under given production and institutional assumptions is lacking, then the economy invests little and grows slowly. This is roughly what happens in the NS simulations in table 5-1.

To understand the details of the difference between the KS and NS forecasts, observe that in 1973 both output and inflation are lower in the NS version, even though wage increases and growth in inputs from 1970 are the same in both. This shortfall has two causes: (1) output growth in the marginalist model for the same

3. For a sample of regression equations from which estimates of σ_X can be inferred, see Bacha and others (1972) and Macedo (1974). Following Sato (1967) we set σ_K equal to 2.

growth in inputs will be smaller because, when integrated over time in the KS forecast, the log-change "production function" (3.2.6p′) of table 3-6 contains a hidden assumption that the marginal product of a production input does not fall off as its (relative) availability increases. The difference over three years is small but, as the 1973 column of the table shows, noticeable. (2) The 1973 price level is higher in the KS version because the income distribution shifts through an increase in the profit rate and an inflation-induced decrease in the labor share to maintain high investment. Similar inflation and forced saving are precluded in the N specification by the marginal productivity relationships tying together output and price changes.

These differences assure that saving in 1973 is smaller in the NS simulations. Private saving is lower because the profit rate and labor share cannot move as freely in a marginalist world. The government's saving is lower because the yield on the value added tax—its major revenue source—depends on the product of real output and the price level. These savings deficiencies translate into lower real investment and increased reliance on bond sales by the public sector to cover its deficit.

Over time, these processes cumulate so that growth is slower in the NS models—real output in 1982 is one-sixth lower than in the K specification. In addition, government saving is increasingly negative as the burden of meeting payments on its indexed bonds increases—the last lines for both NS simulations show how this expenditure item grows. All in all, prospects in the NS forecasts are rather bleak.

With appropriate massage of policy, performance of the NS model could be improved—we shall see how reduction of the public deficit is a means to increase growth. Nonetheless, such tricks are only palliative—savings responses in neoclassical models *are* less flexible than in their KS analogues. The NS functional income distribution cannot change without limit, so that savings shortfalls always get translated in part into reductions in investment and growth, in part into increases in the profit rate. In the model runs reported here, we avoided pushing the NS results via policy modification into either rapid growth or major distributional shifts. Unless otherwise stated, all policies are the same in KS and NS simulations. For comparison with the A(0.03) solution of the KS model in table 5-1, we chose the NS solution $\alpha(0.03)$, with the elasticity of substitution σ_X set at one-third, since its results are slightly more optimistic.

Wages and Inflation

Two aspects of wage change since the military coup of 1964 have been widely discussed in Brazil. The first is the relationship between the apparent success of anti-inflationary policy and wage repression, based on the liquidation of labor unions with the consequent cancellation of the power of workers as a class to fight for higher wages (see chapter 2). The second noteworthy feature has been the progressive widening of the Brazilian wage structure—on the one hand, the minimum wage fell by 35 percent between 1964 and 1970; on the other, the overall wage share remained more or less constant. The obvious deduction is that the wage structure has spread, with lower-income groups losing out to their better-paid peers.

Wage and income spreading may be inevitable in the course of development of an avowedly capitalist country such as Brazil, but it does not fit well into the model framework sketched here. What does fit, however, is the shift in the distribution of profits and wages under different hypotheses about how the overall wage level might evolve. In particular, one might ask what would be the effects of a less draconian wage policy on distribution and growth. Table 5-2 provides some answers by comparing the base solutions of the model with growth paths in which nominal wage growth is increased from 23 to 30 percent a year.

The immediate impact of the wage increases is inflationary, as can be verified from the fourth line of the K specification. (Compare the columns headed $L'=0.03$ and "constant tariffs.") Inflation decreases over time, however, and the real wage and real labor income (lines 5 and 8) grow noticeably. Lines 6 and 7 show that in the KS solution with rapid wage growth the rate of profit decreases and the wage share increases in comparison with the base solution.

A troublesome aspect of more rapid wage growth is the increase it generates in the foreign deficit (line 9). This can be traced to a shift in consumer demand as prices of domestic goods accelerate, so that consumption of imports increases from the base solution (line 10). We countered this demand response in the "shifting tariffs" solution by increasing tariffs on consumer imports at rates of 37 percent a year for 1973–76, 13.7 percent for 1976–79, and 11 percent for 1979–82. These changes sufficed to bring capital inflows back down to levels comparable to those of the A(0.03) solution.

Table 5-2. Model Responses to Different Wage Growth Rates

Model and variable	1976			1979			1982		
	$L'=0.03$ $w'=0.23$	*Constant tariffs* $w'=0.30$	*Shifting tariffs* $w'=0.30$	$L'=0.03$ $w'=0.23$	*Constant tariffs* $w'=0.30$	*Shifting tariffs* $w'=0.30$	$L=0.03$ $w=0.23$	*Constant tariffs* $w'=0.30$	*Shifting tariffs* $w'=0.30$
K specification									
1. Output (X)	363.4	363.4	363.4	474.7	470.9	470.8	6[illegible]9.0	604.7	604.4
2. Output growth rate (X')	0.087	0.087	0.087	0.089	0.086	0.086	0.088	0.083	0.083
3. Price level (P)	3.311	3.740	3.733	5.417	7.106	7.083	8.649	13.478	13.428
4. Inflation rate (P')	0.191	0.232	0.231	0.164	0.214	0.213	0.160	0.213	0.213
5. Real wage (w/P)	3.481	3.802	3.810	4.233	4.922	4.938	5.298	6.383	6.407
6. Profit rate (r)	0.215	0.204	0.204	0.196	0.179	0.178	0.171	0.149	0.147
7. Labor share (α_L)	0.409	0.447	0.448	0.418	0.489	0.490	0.437	0.540	0.542
8. Real labor income (Y_L/P)	123.9	135.3	135.6	165.2	191.7	192.3	225.7	272.0	273.0
9. Capital inflow (F)	2.411	2.929	2.016	6.106	8.227	5.051	13.974	20.271	11.151
10. Import consumption (C_F)	8.9	10.1	8.0	13.2	17.0	11.7	13.8	27.6	16.4
11. Private savings share	0.148	0.145	0.145	0.123	0.119	0.119	0.093	0.092	0.091
12. Government savings share	−0.024	−0.025	−0.019	−0.004	−0.005	0.006	0.020	0.018	0.036
13. Foreign savings share	0.016	0.018	0.012	0.026	0.027	0.017	0.039	0.037	0.021

N specification

1. Output (X)	345.3	345.4	345.4	417.3	429.7	430.1	499.7	537.6	538.3
2. Output growth rate (X')	0.074	0.074	0.074	0.063	0.073	0.073	0.060	0.075	0.075
3. Price level (P)	2.854	3.523	3.523	5.375	7.492	7.475	10.501	15.612	15.519
4. Inflation rate (P')	0.179	0.249	0.249	0.211	0.252	0.251	0.223	0.245	0.244
5. Real wage (w/P)	4.036	4.037	4.037	4.278	4.669	4.679	4.363	5.511	5.544
6. Profit rate (r)	0.193	0.193	0.193	0.211	0.192	0.191	0.240	0.185	0.184
7. Labor share (α_L)	0.499	0.499	0.499	0.479	0.508	0.509	0.466	0.524	0.526
8. Real labor income (Y_L/P)	143.7	143.7	143.7	166.5	181.8	182.2	185.9	234.8	236.2
9. Capital inflow (F)	2.399	2.929	2.016	6.081	8.226	5.049	13.919	20.270	11.148
10. Import consumption (C_F)	11.6	11.0	8.7	18.5	18.1	12.5	29.6	29.9	17.9
11. Private savings share	0.127	0.137	0.137	0.131	0.134	0.133	0.146	0.129	0.128
12. Government savings share	−0.081	−0.059	−0.053	−0.109	−0.060	−0.048	−0.154	−0.062	−0.043
13. Foreign savings share	0.014	0.017	0.012	0.020	0.026	0.016	0.026	0.035	0.019

Note: Value figures in billions of 1970 cruzeiros.

Since real output growth is maintained roughly constant in the KS solutions (the shifts observable in line 1 come from an increased share for relatively slow-growing employment in the solutions with faster wage growth), the main impact of wage changes is on distribution. Line 7 of the N specification shows that the labor share also increases in the marginalist model, but the more interesting result in lines 1 and 2 is that output growth accelerates. If the results of this fixed-employment model are taken seriously, wage repression in Brazil may have slowed the growth rate—a major policy target! In the simple world of the model, it is easy to see how a wage inflation generates more rapid growth. In the first instance, government dissaving decreases because the price-times-quantity base of the value added tax increases with higher prices. The increased saving gets translated into higher real output and incomes, which generate more private saving and still more output. Whether such processes would cumulate in the real Brazilian economy as opposed to the model is another question, but one that deserves further investigation.[4]

Growth, Distribution, and the Trade Gap

Both versions of the identity model arrive at broadly similar results when wage inflation is considered—the overall rate of inflation will increase, the labor share will rise, and there may even be some favorable effects on output. Such agreement is less apparent when the two specifications are applied to another problem of interest in Brazil—the probable evolution of the balance of payments. In this section we examine how aggregate commercial policy—devaluation, import substitution, export promotion, and the like—affects forecasts from the two versions.

Figure 5-1 demonstrates tradeoffs between employment growth and the trade deficit in the K specification. The A(0.02) and A(0.03) solutions assume no import substitution—the elasticity of intermediate imports with respect to output is set at 1.5,

4. This result parallels that of chapter 4. Similarly, when labor taxes are cut in a KS model for the 1970s, the labor share goes down because government saving falls as the tax decreases, and private saving must take up the slack. In an N specification, both the labor share and output growth decrease, with the exact combination of evils depending on parameters, notably the elasticity of substitution σ_X.

Figure 5-1. The Tradeoff between Trade Deficit and Employment Levels in the K Specification

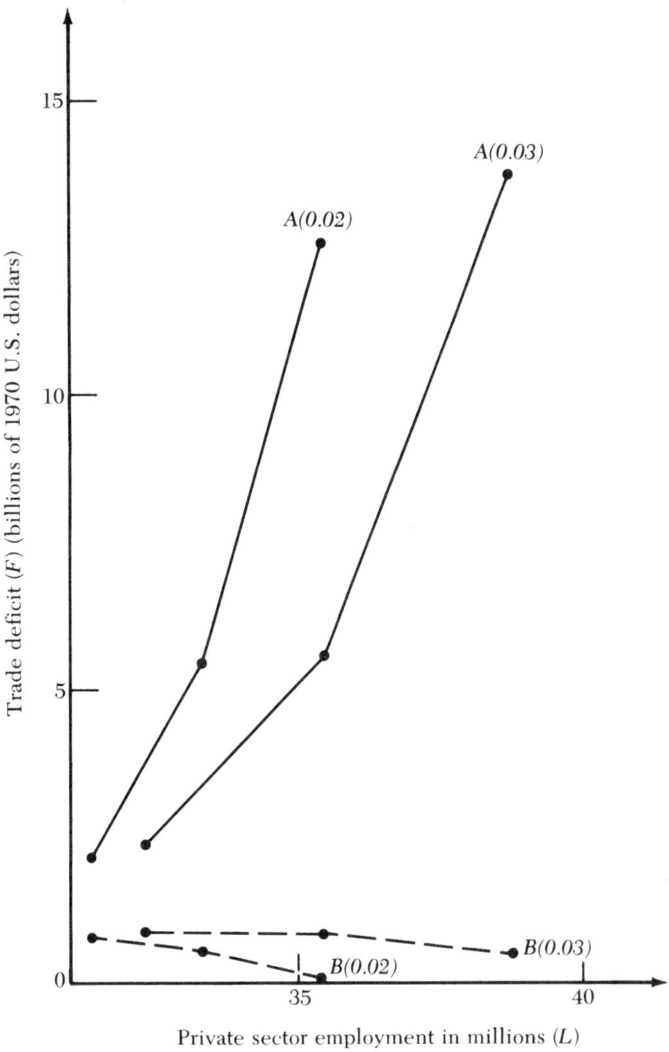

Note: Paths A(0.02) and A(0.03) are without import substitution policies; paths B(0.02) and B(0.03) reflect import substitution as described in the text.

tariffs are not changed, and historical growth rates of nationally produced and imported capital stocks are maintained at 9.6 and 9.1 percent respectively. On these assumptions, the growth in the trade gap is staggering and probably not feasible in reality. At 3 percent employment growth in the A(0.03) solution the trade deficit rises to almost US$14 billion in 1982. Even with the 2 percent employment growth of the A(0.02) solution (more than 3 million less jobs in 1982) the deficit is still almost US$13 billion. Clearly, more favorable alternatives must be sought.

The B solutions are based on the gamut of import substitution policies. Beginning in 1973, the elasticity of intermediate imports with respect to output is set to unity (instead of 1.5), domestically produced capital goods are assumed to be able to substitute for imports at approximately a one-to-one ratio (with volumes measured in 1970 cruzeiros), and consumer imports are held more or less at their A-solution levels by tariff increases of 9.5 percent a year in 1973–76, 7.9 percent in 1976–79, and 6.7 percent in 1979–82. On these hypotheses, the trade gap is driven down to US$0.5 billion in 1982, when employment grows at 3 percent. Again, 2 percent employment growth gives a balance of payments improvement of only US$0.5 billion.

In the "real" future, the alternatives will probably lie somewhere between these two cases. The assumption of proportionality between intermediate imports and output of the B solution is a traditional one, but is unrealistic when the extreme dependence of the Brazilian economy on imported energy is taken into account. Similarly, national capital goods cannot trade off at even terms with imported ones—the step from simple lathes to 1,000-megawatt steam turbines is not trivial. The B projections tend to fatuity in many ways.[5]

We conclude that with favorable conditions under which the nation could find finance for US$3 billion to US$7 billion a year in foreign exchange, the denouement would lie somewhere between cases A and B. An imposed smaller trade gap would lead to enough economic disruption to peril the regime. A larger gap

5. Apart from excessive optimism about import substitution, there are other means of conjuring away the problems raised by the A solutions. For example, a growth rate of exports (in volume) of 12 instead of 10 percent gives an expansion path midway between the A and B solutions of figure 5-1. The trade gap is elegantly obliterated by increased exports (at current subsidy rates); only one question is left open—to whom will they be sold?

probably could not be financed. One still has to ask what would be the distributional implications of a middle course. From the extremes of high and low import substitution at 3 percent employment growth, table 5-3 sheds some light on this question.

In the KS models along the top of the table, import substitution reduces foreign saving, increases required private saving, and causes the profit rate to rise and the labor share to fall (all as usual). The major policy question is how far α_L can drop before political disruption ensues; in such terms the labor share of 0.336 in 1982 under an import-substitution policy seems very low indeed. Of course, a US$14 billion trade deficit with no import substitution but a decent labor share may not be feasible either. We observe the rapidly approaching horns of a gigantic policy dilemma.

Within its drab projection of the future, the NS model reacts less violently than the KS model to the trade crisis. A decrease in foreign saving comparable to that in the KS model with import substitution is accommodated in the marginalist version via accelerated exchange rate devaluation; this reduces imports uniformly and makes remaining foreign saving more valuable domestically. Exact estimates of the required devaluation of the cruzeiro would again be sensitive to parameters, but in the solutions here they are moderate. Without import substitution, the exchange rate rises in 1976–79 and 1979–82 at 8.3 percent and 9.0 percent a year respectively. These rates increase to 11.2 percent and 12.3 percent in the $\beta(0.03)$ solution with import substitution.

Income distribution gets slightly worse in the NS runs as more private saving is generated. And as usual, reduced foreign saving also forces down the rate of growth. The effect is fairly small, however, since foreign saving is initially a small share of the total. The reduction in output in 1982 would be only a bit more than 1 percent, which is acceptable.

In effect, we arrive at two views of how the economy might adjust to its future trade problems. The KS model stresses limited adjustment possibilities and their resulting unfavorable effects on employment and the functional distribution of income. The NS model points to the conclusion that import substitution is possible (via some appropriate policy of devaluation of the cruzeiro) and in fact will lead to only modest reduction in the growth of real output. Our own opinion is that neoclassical optimism is misguided and that the K specification gives a more realistic view of what is in store for Brazil, but we could be

Table 5-3. Model Responses to Enforced Import Substitution with 3 Percent Annual Employment Growth

Model and variable	1976		1979		1982	
	A(0.03)	B(0.03)	A(0.03)	B(0.03)	A(0.03)	B(0.03)
K specification						
1. Output (X)	363.4	361.7	474.7	474.7	619.0	631.4
2. Price level (P)	3.311	3.564	5.417	6.382	8.649	11.036
3. Profit rate (r)	0.215	0.233	0.196	0.238	0.171	0.238
4. Labor share (α_L)	0.409	0.382	0.418	0.355	0.437	0.336
5. Private savings share	0.148	0.161	0.123	0.155	0.093	0.145
6. Government savings share	−0.024	−0.023	−0.004	−0.001	0.020	0.028
7. Foreign savings share	0.017	0.006	0.026	0.003	0.039	0.001
8. Capital inflow (F)	2.411	0.916	6.106	0.869	13.974	0.550
9. Exchange rate (ρ)	8.26	8.26	11.16	11.16	15.06	15.06
10. National investment (I_X)	44.2	47.7	59.2	70.4	79.3	105.9
11. Imported investment (I_F)	5.7	4.2	7.5	3.8	9.8	3.3
12. Intermediate imports (M)	16.4	14.3	24.5	18.8	36.5	25.0
13. Import consumption (C_F)	8.9	8.9	13.2	13.4	18.8	19.7

	1976		1979		1982	
	$\alpha(0.03)$	$\beta(0.03)$	$\alpha(0.03)$	$\beta(0.03)$	$\alpha(0.03)$	$\beta(0.03)$
N specification						
1. Output (X)	345.3	345.3	417.3	413.9	499.7	490.5
2. Price level (P)	2.854	2.859	5.372	5.506	10.501	11.154
3. Profit rate (r)	0.193	0.193	0.211	0.214	0.240	0.247
4. Labor share (α_L)	0.499	0.499	0.479	0.471	0.446	0.428
5. Private savings share	0.127	0.127	0.131	0.135	0.146	0.159
6. Government savings share	−0.081	−0.080	−0.109	−0.105	−0.154	−0.152
7. Foreign savings share	0.014	0.005	0.020	0.003	0.026	0.001
8. Capital inflow (F)	2.399	0.910	6.081	0.863	13.919	0.547
9. Exchange rate (ρ)	5.863	5.873	7.544	8.216	9.877	11.908
10. National investment (I_X)	13.7	13.8	7.9	8.0	−2.5	−3.3
11. Imported investment (I_F)	7.7	4.9	11.2	6.2	15.1	8.4
12. Intermediate imports (M)	10.4	10.4	12.9	12.5	16.0	15.0
13. Import consumption (C_F)	11.6	11.1	18.5	15.8	29.6	22.2

Note: A and α solutions are without import substitution; B and β solutions have substitution. Value figures in billions of 1970 cruzeiros.

wrong. We hope so, or the Brazilian miracle may be in for very serious trials indeed.

The Second National Development Plan

By way of summarizing our empirical results, we draw some comparisons between the model projections and forecasts of Brazilian growth which can be gleaned from the 1974 second Plano Nacional de Desenvolvimento (National Development Plan, or II PND). Like many national planning documents, this one is quite verbose. It does, however, point out four economic "pillars" that will support Brazilian development. They are accelerated growth, combat of inflation, equilibrium in the balance of payments, and improvement of the income distribution. In the final part of the plan document, table 3 gives a set of social and economic indicators, which can be used to assess the strength of these pillars. The following growth rates are easily derived:

	Annual growth rate, 1970–80 (percent)
GNP	9.9
GNP per capita	7.2
Personal consumption	9.5
Gross investment	11.7
Economically active population	2.9

Even when compared with our more optimistic projections, these rates look high. For example, we find output growth varying between 6.8 and 8.9 percent in KS solutions and 4.2 and 7.5 percent in NS solutions, well below the 9.9 percent of the II PND. Realistically, even in the more optimistic K specification, it is hard to see how more than, say, 7 percent growth is feasible within probable limits on payments deficits and shifts in the income distribution.[6]

As for distribution itself, the II PND recognizes explicitly that

6. These numbers should be compared with those for the latter part of the 1960s in chapter 4—in a K specification potential growth rates for Brazil appear to be unequivocally lower now than they were a decade ago. The analysis in chapter 2 of course corroborates this finding.

overall inequality in Brazil is high and is unlikely to be improved by growth alone. For this reason the plan document proposes, at least rhetorically, that real income will improve noticeably for all classes. The policy instruments which are supposed to bring about income equalization affect both employment and wage levels. The authors of the plan document seem to hope for employment growth upward of 3.5 percent a year and promise wage readjustment incorporating 4 percent annual productivity growth (well below the plan's own estimate of the growth of consumption per capita).

In our KS projections, with real wages growing at 6 percent and the private savings share dropping off, we observe some small improvement in the functional income distribution by the end of the forecast period (see line 4 of the K specification of table 5-3). Slower growth in real wages, say, 4 percent annually, would surely lead to a decrease in the labor share. (To see this, merely reverse the analysis underlying table 5-2, where accelerated growth in wages increased the labor share.)

In the neoclassical projections, real wage growth over 5 percent annually would also improve the wage share. But in the most optimistic NS simulation, the share of investment in GNP is less than 20 percent and rises to 22 percent only in the KS version. By contrast, the II PND proposes a 25 percent investment share. If the functional distribution works the same way in the Brazilian economy as in our models, income equalization along with such a high investment rate is improbable.

Similar contradictions show up in the plan's balance of payments forecasts. The II PND foresees that the proportion between the balance of payments deficit and gross investment will remain below 20 percent. To make comparisons, we have to correct our "trade gap" definition of the payments deficit for debt service charges. If these grow from their 1973 level at the relatively modest rate of 20 percent a year, the current account deficit becomes US$18 billion in 1982 in the A(0.03) projection. At our postulated value of the exchange rate ρ, this deficit amounts to 22 percent of the value of gross fixed capital formation. In the N specification with its lower investment, this proportion is still higher.

Of course, massive import substitution in the K specification B(0.03) solution of figure 5-1 reduces the foreign savings share to almost nil, but with an extremely unfavorable effect on the income distribution. By contrast, the labor share is almost unaffected in the neoclassical $\beta(0.03)$ solution with import substitution, but capital formation is negligible in 1982.

In summary, the II PND confronts serious dilemmas. On the N specification of our model, growth as rapid as foreseen in the plan is simply out of the question, although the functional income distribution deteriorates only gradually and import substitution for balance of payments equilibration can be achieved via modest exchange rate devaluation. Moreover, table 5-2 shows that more rapid wage growth would increase both the output growth rate and the wage share, at the cost of accelerating price inflation.

In the K specification there are limited possibilities for the economy to adjust to balance of payments deficits—serious import substitution leads to an impossibly low labor share in the table 5-3 forecast for 1982. And as in the NS model, more rapid wage growth improves the income distribution but also causes notably more rapid inflation and a falling rate of profit.

Surpassing ingenuity would seem to be required of any macroeconomic architect hoping to design a development strategy supported by the four pillars of the II PND.

Appendix: Data and Sources

In this appendix we discuss the sources of the data used to set up the identities of the model in table 3-5 for the 1970 base year, and also compare our "forecasts" of 1973 with the official description of the economy that year, given in the new national accounts from the Vargas Foundation (1974).

Sources of Data for 1970

Equation (3.2.1) in table 3-5 is the accounting definition of total product and expenditure in our system. The values of the variables come directly from the national accounts with minor modifications, including:

- The value of X in 1970 cruzeiros (Cr$204.121 billion) differs from the value of GNP in the accounts (Cr$206.5647 billion) because there are two differences in definition between X and GNP. First, the value of intermediate imports is included in X but not in GNP, and second, government wage payments are excluded from the value of output PX but are included in GNP.

- Since 1970 is our base year, we set the price level P to unity.
- The value of consumption of goods produced within Brazil (C_X = Cr$139.807 billion) differs from personal consumption in the national accounts (Cr$143.4274 billion) because consumption imports are excluded from the former.
- The value of gross fixed capital formation by firms in the national accounts is Cr$35.1683 billion. To find investment in nationally produced goods we subtract Cr$4.9292 billion, which corresponds to imports of capital goods. The remaining investment is split into two parcels—net capital formation and depreciation of nationally produced capital stock. Since this stock includes all construction, we assume a relatively low depreciation rate ($\delta_X = 0.02$).
- Our value for government consumption (C_G = Cr$12.165 billion) is lower than the corresponding item in the national accounts (Cr$20.512 billion) because it does not contain government wage payments ($w[1+t_L]\ L_G$ = Cr$8.347 billion). Our estimate of the latter is less than that appearing in the national income table of the national accounts. Part of the difference is due to the fact that we include payments in kind (such as military uniforms and food for officials) in C_G. More important, personnel expenditures in the accounts seems to include payments to people no longer working actively for the government (such as pensioneers), which we exclude.
- The values of E and I_G are equal to the corresponding entries in the accounts.

Equation (3.2.2) is basically a "trade gap" statement of the balance of payments. It appears in domestic prices since all terms are multiplied by the exchange rate ρ. We set this equal to an annual average for 1970, with a value of Cr$4.59 to the dollar.[7]

The dollar values of intermediate imports $\pi_M M$ and imports of capital goods $\pi_F(I_F + \delta_F K_F)$ in 1970 were respectively US$1.1512 billion and US$1.0739 billion, according to the November 1971 issue of the *Boletim* of the Central Bank of Brazil. Our dollar value for imports of consumption goods (US$688.7 million) differs from that of the *Boletim* by including nonfinancial services. Finally, the value of F in equation (3.2.2) was calculated as a residual and, as mentioned above, represents only a trade gap.

7. See *Conjuntura Econômica*, vol. 28 (May 1974), p. 152.

It differs from the usual current account balance by not including debt service charges and other factor payment flows abroad, and differs from the overall balance by not including movements of capital. These corrections could be added to our figures for F to adjust it to conform with other concepts of the balance of payments.

Equation (3.2.6) is a breakdown of value added into its component costs. Value added itself (VX = Cr\$172.924 billion) is the estimate of national income at factor cost from the accounts plus depreciation on nationally produced and imported capital goods ($\delta_X K_X + \delta_F K_F$) plus intermediate imports at post-tariff prices ($P_M M$) minus government wage payments.

We used depreciation rates $\delta_X = 0.02$ and $\delta_F = 0.05$ for the two types of capital stock. The total stock itself ($K_X + K_F$ = Cr\$369.536 billion) was estimated by multiplying the national accounts estimate of GNP by 1.9, a number around which most estimates of the capital-output ratio cluster.[8] From the study of Langoni (1974) one can calculate that the participation of imported capital goods in the total stock of machinery and equipment in Brazil was around 30 percent in 1969 and 27 percent in 1970, and that the share of imports in total capital stock (including construction) was about 10 percent. From this we get values of Cr\$332.582 billion for K_X and CR\$36.954 billion for K_F.

Profits after depreciation can be derived from equation (3.2.6) when other payments have been subtracted from value added. After calculation of the profit tax rate (see below) we find the rate of profit r. Our value of 0.184 is similar to estimates derived from balance sheet data for large firms in Brazil.

The cost of labor in (3.2.6) comes from a mimeographed document ("Brasil—Agregados Macroeconomicos") circulated by the Vargas Foundation as background for the new national accounts. Our estimate of Cr\$87.969 billion is the Vargas estimate less government wage payments. Our employment estimates (L = 27 million, L_G = 2.57 million) are from Hoffman (1972). The labor tax rate of 0.12 is calculated from estimates of incidence of this tax in manufacturing by Bacha and others (1972). The 42.7 percent incidence estimate from this source was corrected for the extra payment, or "thirteenth salary," that some workers receive at Christmas in Brazil and by the share of the labor force (34.8 percent) covered by INPS, the national insurance scheme.

8. For example, see Suzigan and others (1971).

The tax rate on value added ($t_V = 0.18$) was calculated from the difference between value added at factor cost and the value of output. The rate estimated this way is compatible with an appropriate average of the two Brazilian sales taxes, the ICM and IPI.

The shares of inputs in equations (3.2.8) through (3.2.11) follow directly from (3.2.6). The following three equations, (3.2.12) through (3.2.14), define incomes of labor and capital. The wage rate in (3.2.12) and other equations ($w =$ Cr\$2,900 a year) was calculated from the total wage bill and employment figures in (3.2.6). It is somewhat higher than income per capita, which was Cr\$2,226 for 1970.

In equation (3.2.14) capital income includes payments received for holding government bonds. The type of government title most common in 1970, the ORTN with one-year duration, paid an interest rate of 4 percent plus a monetary correction, giving a nominal return of around 24 percent. The total expenditure of the government for bond payments in 1970 was Cr\$8.848 billion (Central Bank of Brazil, *Relatorio*, vol. 8, p. 106, table VI.3). In the model, we treat government bonds as inflation-corrected consuls. PB is the nominal payment of the bond, and the market value of the bond stock is PB/i. The real value of the stock is $(PB/i)/P$, or B/i. This enters in equation (3.2.17) defining total wealth.

Equations (3.2.15) and (3.2.16) define personal income taxes. Total revenue of Cr\$4.6 billion comes from the statement of the Brazilian Treasury (Central Bank of Brazil, *Relatorio*, vol. 8, p. 94, table V.2). Our breakdown between taxes on labor and on capital incomes was done in view of tax schedules and the overall income distribution.

The money base ($H =$ Cr\$17.731 billion) appearing in equation (3.2.17) and elsewhere is from Pastore (1973). The same source also provides econometric justification for our value of 20 percent for the expected inflation rate in 1970.

In equation (3.2.18) private consumption C is set to the corresponding value in the national accounts. Transfer payments Q also come from the accounts, corrected for government interest payments PB which appear in (3.2.14). We follow Kaldor (1966) in setting γ_L, the propensity to consume from labor income, equal to 0.03. The propensity to consume from capital income ($\gamma_K = 0.628$) follows as a residual. Elasticities of consumption with respect to wealth ($S_{CR} = 0.05$) and the deflated interest rate ($S_{Ci} = -0.05$) are from Christ (1968). We set the income elasticity

Table 5-4. Comparison of Observed 1973 Macrovariables and Model Results

Macrovariables	*Observed value*	*KS model*	*NS model*
1. Output growth rate, 1970–73 (X')	0.110	0.105	0.101
2. Inflation rate, 1970–73 (P')	0.186	0.208	0.171
3. GNP ($PX - P_M M + w\,[1 + t_L]\,L_G$)	477.163	521.336	448.141
4. Private consumption (C)	327.060	372.034	347.623
5. Private gross fixed capital formation ($P[I_X + \delta_X K_X] + P_K[I_F + \delta_F K_F]$)	89.993	90.829	38.333
6. Government gross fixed capital formation (PI_G)	18.060	18.771	16.780
7. Government consumption ($PC_G + w\,[1 + t_L]\,L_G$)	46.190	46.528	43.644
8. Government interest payments (PB)	41.763	42.183	37.766
9. Transfer payments (Q)	44.767	44.297	44.231
10. Government tax revenue (T)	128.655	130.425	115.595
11. Increase in the money base (H^*)	13.052	12.611	12.611
12. Exchange rate (ρ)	6.126	6.122	5.446
13. Export value in dollars ($\pi_E E$)	6.767	6.513	6.513
14. Imports of goods and nonfinancial services in dollars ($\pi_M M + \pi_C C_F + \pi_K[I_F + \delta_F K_F]$)	7.431	6.912	6.908

Note: Value figures (cruzeiros unless specified dollars) are in billions.

of demand for domestic goods, η_X, to 0.98. By Engel aggregation the elasticity for imports, η_F, becomes 1.7674. The substitution parameter for consumption, σ_C, was set equal to 0.5. Equations (3.2.19) through (3.2.23) define consumption shares and capital stock growth rates, all of which follow directly from estimates already made. Equations (3.2.24) to (3.2.26) then set out the government accounts.

Total tax receipts (T = Cr$49.968 billion) differ from the total of government revenue in the national accounts (Cr$50.965 billion) by some minor nontax items. The largest receipts come from value added taxes ($t_V VX$ = Cr$31.127 billion). Tariffs are the other major indirect tax, with revenues of CR$1.105 billion (taken from *Anuario Econômico Fiscal* for 1971 from the Ministry of Finance). After using independent estimates of income taxes ($D_L + D_K$) from the national accounts and of employment taxes ($t_L w[L + L_G]$), we find total profit taxes and the profit tax rate ($t_K = 0.04$) as residuals.

In equation (3.2.25) all government expenditure items come from the national accounts as discussed above. The difference between expenditures and receipts is covered by expansion of the money base H^* and by new bond emissions PB^*/i. Our estimate of CR$2.988 billion for the money base comes from Pastore (1973), and new bond emissions are calculated as a residual but have a value near that given by Pastore in his discussion of Brazilian money supply.

The final equation (3.2.27) enforces equilibrium in the money market. The income elasticity ($S_{HX} = 0.7$) is from Pastore (1973), and the interest elasticity ($S_{Hi} = -1.0$) is from Christ (1968).

Comparisons in 1973

Table 5-4 gives comparisons of the state of the Brazilian economy in 1973 as estimated by the national accounts scorekeepers of the Vargas Foundation and in our KS and NS models (solutions A[0.03] and α[0.03]). These assessments are all relatively close, although they illustrate some apparent bias of the national accountants in favor of a K specification.

Beginning with 1970–73 output growth rates, we observe fair agreement among all three sources, with the models being slightly lower. On prices, however, the models bracket the officially postulated rate of inflation over the three-year period. Here the advantage appears to lie with the K specification, for the rate of inflation was, if anything, officially underestimated in 1973 and perhaps before.

For reasons discussed above, the N specification generates 1973 rates of investment far lower than its competitor—saving from both government and persons is lower and this means less capital formation.[9] The KS model investment estimate agrees well with the accounts because it was made to do so. As we saw in analyzing table 5-3, the relatively high KS rate of inflation comes from distributional shifts required to generate saving to meet this investment. Although official estimates are not available on such changes, one wonders if their importance has not been underestimated.

For most of the remaining variables, agreement among the three sets of figures is quite close. The main exceptions are low values for government revenue and the exchange rate in the NS model. As discussed earlier, low tax receipts come from a smaller base (price times output) for the value added tax in the NS projection. The low exchange rate is the result of interaction between fairly high foreign saving and a gentle tradeoff between foreign and domestic resources in the NS production and consumption functions. Even with an elasticity of substitution as low as one-third, it may be that this model overestimates substitution possibilities in the short run.

References

Bacha, Edmar L., and others. 1972. *Encargos trabalhistas e absorçao de mão-de-obra*. Rio de Janeiro: Instituto de Planejamento Econômico e Social/Instituto de Pesquisas (IPEA/INPES).

Christ, Carl F. 1968. A simple macroeconomic model with a government budget restraint. *Journal of political economy* 76(1):53–67.

Hoffman, Helga. 1972. *Desemprego e subemprego no Brasil*. Brasília: University of Brasília, Department of Economics; processed.

Kaldor, Nicholas. 1966. Marginal productivity and the macro-

9. On the consumption side of the ledger, the shares of *C* in GNP according to the three 1973 sets of accounts are: official, 0.685; KS, 0.714; NS, 0.776. The relative difference between NS and the other two is fairly large.

economic theories of distribution. *Review of economic studies* 33:309–19.

Langoni, Carlos Geraldo. 1974. *As causas do crescimento econômico do Brasil*. Rio de Janeiro: Apec Editora.

Macedo, Roberto Bras Matos. 1974. Models of the demand for labor and the problem of labor absorption in the Brazilian manufacturing sector. Ph.D. dissertation, Harvard University.

Pastore, Affonso Celso. 1973. *Observacoes sobre a politica monetaria no programa brasileira de estabilização*. São Paulo: University of São Paulo, Instituto de Pesquisas Econômicas; processed.

Sato, Kazuo. 1967. A two-level constant elasticity-of-substitution production function. *Review of economic studies* 34:201–18.

Suzigan, W., and others. 1971. *Crescimento industrial no Brasil*. Rio de Janeiro: Instituto de Planejamento Econômico e Social/ Instituto de Pesquisas (IPEA/INPES).

Vargas Foundation. 1972. *Contas nacionais do Brasil. Conceitos e metodologia*. Rio de Janeiro.

———. 1974. *Sistema de contas nacionais: Novas estimativas*. Rio de Janeiro; processed.

6

The General Equilibrium Income Distribution Model

Frank J. Lysy and Lance Taylor

IF CONVENTIONAL GENERAL EQUILIBRIUM theory says anything at all about income inequality, it certainly must do so through analysis of factors influencing the functional distribution or the pattern of rewards received by rather large aggregates of economic actors. These may be the traditional urban capitalists and workers, or lords and peasants in the countryside, or the highly educated and illiterate everywhere. In all cases, functional distribution models boil down to a set of rules for assigning payments to different economic groups and necessarily focus on income inequalities between them. Myriad other factors which influence within-group inequality (such as age, location, sex, color, and a host of other ascriptive characteristics) are left out of the picture.

The model described in this and the three following chapters follows this tradition. We are perhaps a bit more ambitious than most authors in attempting to deal with around a dozen different types of income recipients spread across twenty-five sectors (giving a total of 130 recipient classes in all), but even so to remain at a high level of aggregation. For this reason, the model is built up using the standard tools of aggregate theory—sectorwide production functions, assumed homogeneous behavior on the part of large groups of consumers, different savings propensities from functional income flows such as wages and profits, and so on.

As will be clear shortly, the details of specifying all these relationships are complex, but roughly speaking the model operates on two levels. In macro terms the general equilibrium model resembles the identity model of chapters 3 through 5 in that its results are strongly influenced by the saving-equals-investment constraint. For empirical reasons, the wage structure is made rigid, so that distributional shifts often take the form of labor movements among sectors. These are mediated by changes in real factor payments resulting from inflation or deflation of the general price level in relation to payments fixed in money terms. The changes in the general price level "force" current-price saving to equal investment, just as in the identity formulation.

Against this macro backdrop, the general equilibrium model also presents many microeconomic stories about workers of a certain type moving from one sector to another in response to wage differences, profits dropping off in response to excessive investment in a sector, import levels changing as the cruzeiro devalues, and so on. The intrinsic interest of these stories varies with the different questions asked of the model, as shown in detail in chapter 9. But in all cases our parables are spun out in terms of the parameters of thoroughly neoclassical specifications regarding sectoral production functions and marginal productivity relationship on the supply side, and consumer responses to price and income changes in demand. Though of dubious validity, the neoclassical apparatus is used without apology, because there is little other theory that has been mathematized sufficiently to support numerical work.

In this chapter, we mainly discuss a one-sector version of the general equilibrium model to elucidate its macroeconomic properties and overall structure (see table 6-1 for a list of the symbols used). Chapter 7 takes up the description of the model, and an appendix thereafter goes into detail about how we solved it on the computer.

A One-Sector Version

Assume that output X in a one-sector economy is produced using labor, a capital good made up of some quantity of X invested in the past, and the services of proprietors or entrepreneurs who

Table 6-1. Symbols in the One-Sector Model

Symbol	Definition
Levels of economic variables	
V, X	Value added and total output
L, K, L^E	Levels of wage labor, capital, and the self-employed
Y^L, Y^K, Y^E	Incomes of labor, capital, and the self-employed
Q	Real aggregate consumption
D	Real net fixed capital formation
G	Real government expenditure on goods
T	Nominal government transfer payments
Prices	
P	Price of output
P^V	Price of value added
P^L	Price of labor services
P^K	Price of capital services
P^E	Price of entrepreneurial services
w	Wage rate
r	Profit rate (after tax)
Parameters	
v	Ratio of value added to output
e	Ratio of entrepreneurial services to output
b	Ratio of capital to value added
c	Ratio of labor to value added
σ	Capital-labor elasticity of substitution
α_L, α_K	Labor and capital distribution parameters in the CES function
t^L, t^K	Tax rates on labor and capital
d	Legal and real rates of depreciation
g	Growth rate of capital
$\gamma^L, \gamma^K, \gamma^E$	Consumption propensities out of labor, capital, and self-employment incomes
γ	Average consumption propensity out of labor and capital incomes

receive income independent of that generated by the two classic factors of production. Separating payments to proprietors in the accounting amounts to a crude representation of the large number of self-employed workers associated with production of goods and services in Brazil (especially in agriculture and the service sectors) and is consistent with the "proprietors' income" category in the distributional data of most countries.

Capital and labor are assumed to combine to produce value added, V, according to some production function. This value added is related to output via the coefficient v in the equation

$$V = vX, \tag{6.1}$$

and the number of active proprietors, L^E, is determined by output through a similar factor of proportionality, e.

If the production function takes the standard CES form, it can be written as

$$V = [\alpha_K K^{(\sigma-1)/\sigma} + \alpha_L L^{(\sigma-1)/\sigma}]^{\sigma/(\sigma-1)} \tag{6.2p}$$

where K and L are the amounts of capital and labor available in any time period, α_K and α_L are distribution parameters in the CES function, and σ is the elasticity of substitution between the two production factors.

If there is perfect competition (which is about the only assumption on market behavior that can be handled easily in a big general equilibrium model), one can work with either a cost function or a production function. The cost function corresponding to (6.2p) is

$$P^V = [(\alpha_K)^\sigma (P^K)^{1-\sigma} + (\alpha_L)^\sigma (P^L)^{1-\sigma}]^{1/(1-\sigma)} \tag{6.2c}$$

Here, P^V is the cost of producing a unit of value added, and P^K and P^L are user costs of capital and labor, discussed below.

Define b and c respectively as the capital/value added and labor/value added ratios in the economy. By a recently popularized result in production theory known as Shephard's lemma (see, for example, Diewert 1971 for a description), these factor input ratios and therefore choice of technique are determined by the equations

$$b = \partial P^V / \partial P^K = (\alpha_K P^V / P^K)^\sigma \tag{6.3}$$

and

$$c = \partial P^V / \partial P^L = (\alpha_L P^V / P^L)^\sigma. \tag{6.4}$$

Under competition, equation (6.2c) can be derived from (6.2p) through the use of (6.3) and (6.4), and (6.2p) can be derived from (6.2c).

Let the average remuneration of proprietors be P^E. Then the output price P is just the sum of the values per unit of the two inputs, value added and proprietors' services,

$$P = vP^V + eP^E. \tag{6.5}$$

The government is assumed to impose taxes at rates t^L and t^K on labor incomes and profits. These enter the user prices of labor and capital as follows:

$$P^L = w(1 + t^L) \tag{6.6}$$

and

$$P^K = \left(\frac{r}{1 - t^K} + d\right) P. \tag{6.7}$$

In equation (6.6) the wage rate is w, and it is blown up by the tax rate t^L to give user cost. In (6.7) r is the after-tax profit rate, and d is the rate of depreciation. In a one-good economy it is assumed that capital, though fixed, is continually revalued in current prices, hence the appearance of the price level P in (6.7).

With this much algebra developed, we can quickly write down expressions for the use of capital, for labor and proprietors, and for their associated incomes Y^K, Y^L, and Y^E:

$$L = cvX \tag{6.8}$$

$$Y^L = wL \tag{6.9}$$

$$K = bvX \tag{6.10}$$

$$Y^K = rPK \tag{6.11}$$

$$L^E = eX \tag{6.12}$$

$$Y^E = P^E L^E. \tag{6.13}$$

Let real consumption be denoted by Q, and assume that propensities to consume from the three types of income are γ^L, γ^K, and γ^E. Then total value of consumption is

$$PQ = \gamma^L (Y^L + T) + \gamma^K Y^K + \gamma^E Y^E \tag{6.14}$$

where T represents government transfer payments to labor. Output itself is distributed among consumption, investment, and government uses. The balance equation is

$$X = Q + D + dK + G. \tag{6.15}$$

The new terms are D, new capital formation; dK, replacement investment; and G, government acquisition of goods and services.

One last independent equation contains a simple accelerator investment theory,

$$D = gK. \tag{6.16}$$

In a planning context g can be interpreted as a planner's desired rate of growth; in a behavioral model it might be animal spirits. In either case it is a variable conveniently treated as exogenous.

Before discussing how the model is solved, we can check the savings-investment balance by equating aggregate demand and supply. On the demand side we have from (6.14) through (6.16) that

$$PX = PQ + P(g + d)K + PG = \gamma^L(Y^L + T) + \gamma^K Y^K + \gamma^E Y^E + P(g + d)K + PG.$$

On the supply side we apply Euler's theorem to break total value added down into its component costs ($P^V V = P^K K + P^L L$) and get

$$\begin{aligned} PX &= P^V vX + P^E eX && \text{from (6.5);} \\ &= P^L L + P^K K + P^E L^E && \text{from Euler's theorem;} \\ &= w(1 + t^L)L + \left(\frac{r}{1 - t^K} + d\right) PK \\ &\quad + P^E L^E && \text{from (6.6) and (6.7);} \\ &= Y^L + t^L wL + Y^K + \frac{t^K r}{1 - t^K} PK \\ &\quad + dPK + Y^E && \text{from (6.9), (6.11), (6.13).} \end{aligned}$$

Equating total demand and supply and simplifying finally gives the savings-investment identity,

$$PgK = (1 - \gamma^L)(Y^L + T) + (1 - \gamma^K)Y^K + (1 - \gamma^E)Y^E + \left[t^L wL + \frac{t^K}{1 - t^K} rPK - PG - T\right]. \qquad (6.17)$$

This sets capital formation equal to the sum of private and government saving. Evidently (6.17) is not independent of the other equations of the model but does indicate, for example, that when investment is determined exogenously there is no room in the accounting for independent determination of all savings sources. In chapter 9 this rather banal statement is shown to provide a skeleton key to understanding the numerical results of the general equilibrium model.

There are twenty-four variables in the first sixteen (independent) equations. To solve the model in any year, we have to set values for eight variables. If for simplicity we assume full employment, then K and L become exogenous. It is reasonable to make the government policy variables t^L, t^K, T, and G exogenous, along with the investment demand variable g. Finally, we have to normalize prices, since the foregoing equation system is homogeneous of degree zero in all prices. It is convenient to treat P^E, the remuneration of proprietors, as the numeraire, so that all prices are measured in relation to this particular level of income per head.

Solving a one-sector model numerically is straightforward; in fact, two ways are sketched here. The first is based on the production function (6.2p), which gives value added V when capital and labor inputs are specified. Output X then follows from (6.1).

To go a bit further, we put (6.4) and (6.8) together to get an expression for the price of labor in terms of the value added cost P^V and the value added/labor ratio (V/L):

$$P^L = \alpha_L P^V (V/L)^{1/\sigma}. \tag{6.18}$$

A similar expression for the user cost of capital P^K is

$$P^K = \alpha_K P^V (V/K)^{1/\sigma}. \tag{6.19}$$

Since V, K, and L have all been determined, these expressions make both P^L and P^K proportional to P^V.

G, D, and dK are specified exogenously, however, and knowing X we can get the level of consumption Q from (6.15). Plugging Q into (6.14) and using (6.6) and (6.7) gives

$$P = \left[Q\left(1 + \gamma^K d\,(1 - t^K)\frac{K}{Q}\right)\right]^{-1} \left[\gamma^L \frac{P^L L}{1 + t^L} + \gamma^L T + \gamma^K P^K (1 - t^K) K + \gamma^E L^E P^E\right]. \tag{6.20}$$

We can now substitute (6.18) and (6.19) into (6.20) to get a linear equation in which P depends only on P^V and P^E. Equation (6.5) has similar form, and the two can be solved together to get P and P^V, given the variables appearing in (6.20). Back substitution then determines the rest of the model.

In the special case in which government taxes and purchases and the depreciation rate are all set at zero, the value of P determined by this procedure is

$$P = \frac{(\gamma^E - \gamma)\, P^E eX + \gamma^L T}{Q - \gamma X} \tag{6.21}$$

where γ is a consumption parameter determined so that

$$\gamma(P^L L + P^K K) = \gamma^L P^L L + \gamma^K P^K K.$$

Evidently P will be positive if $\gamma^E > \gamma$ (the propensity to consume of proprietors exceeds the average consumption share from value added) and/or if transfer payments to workers represent a significantly positive income flow. Either condition is likely to be satisfied in practice.

Furthermore, P increases when total consumption Q falls. From (6.15) with X fixed, this is equivalent to saying that the price level increases when exogenous demand goes up. One can also show that real incomes change even though costs of labor and capital are proportional to P^V from (6.18) and (6.19), and P^V increases when P increases. For example, the real wage is

$$\frac{P^L}{P} = \frac{\alpha_L}{v}\left(\frac{V}{L}\right)^{1/\sigma}\left(1 - \frac{eP^E}{P}\right). \tag{6.22}$$

This formula shows that as exogenous demand rises and the price level P goes up, the real wage rises as well. A similar statement applies to the real return to capital, but the real remuneration of proprietors, P^E/P, falls. The reason, of course, is that the demand increase forces consumption to be curtailed and the income distribution to shift toward those with low consumption (and high savings) propensities. Proprietors with incomes fixed in numeraire terms and workers (insofar as their consumption is supported by nominal transfer payments) are the losers in this process.[1]

In the Brazilian general equilibrium model inflation extracts forced saving of this type not just from proprietors and recipients of transfer income, but from all income flows fixed in nominal terms (foreign transactions denominated with an unchanging exchange rate being the most important additional example). The income distribution also shifts in other ways to favor high savers when aggregate demand is high; for example, increases in the profits share and a widening wage structure benefit high-saving skilled employees. Although the details are complex, the basic logic of the general equilibrium model's macroeconomic behav-

1. Of course, additional distribution stories can be told when transfer payments or proprietors' remunerations go up. An increase in transfers, for example, drives up the price level (since it also represents an increase in effective demand) but doubly benefits workers as opposed to proprietors and capitalists since the transfer is paid to the former group.

ior is similar to that indicated here. So, too, the techniques we use to solve the big model can be illustrated with the help of the foregoing equations.

Sketch of a Solution Algorithm

The basic problem with trying to use production functions in the solution of a model with many sectors is that they provide no obvious means to assign shiftable factors across sectors. Factor prices, however, summarize precisely the information required to generate each sector's derived demands for inputs. Since for realism we assume that capital stocks in each of the general equilibrium model's twenty-five sectors are fixed in the short run, the relevant factor prices are the wages of its six types of labor skill. In the one-sector variant, the logic of the solution algorithm can be illustrated by a series of computational steps beginning with a guess at the wage w and therefore the cost of labor P^L from (6.6). Contingent on the wage guess, one can also guess a level for output X and get value added V from (6.1).

Equation (6.19) then gives an expression for the user cost of capital P^K in terms of the cost of producing a unit of value added P^V and the value added/capital ratio (V/K). We can substitute (6.19) into the cost function (6.2c) and go through some algebra to get the equation

$$P^V = \frac{(\alpha_L)^{\sigma/(1-\sigma)} P^L}{[1 - \alpha_K (V/K)^{(1-\sigma)/\sigma}]^{1/(1-\sigma)}}. \tag{6.23}$$

From this equation and the guessed values of P^L and V we can get P^V. But then back substitution through the rest of the equations gives P from (6.5), P^K from (6.19), r from (6.7), employment and income levels from (6.8) to (6.13), consumption from (6.14), and a new guess at output X from (6.15). This can be used to get a new value of V for use in (6.23), and iterations continue until (6.15) is satisfied to an acceptable degree of precision. This process converges rapidly, except when the bracketed term in the denominator of (6.23) becomes negative, reflecting insufficient capital accumulation in previous periods.

This "inner" iteration on outputs gives production, price, and employment patterns contingent on fixed nominal values of the wage. Holding wage(s) fixed and shifting demand variables such as government expenditure and investment gives rise to one set of experiments with the model. Since there are decreasing returns in the short run and producers are assumed to be on their marginal cost functions, real wage(s) must fall to generate more employment as demand increases. In chapter 9 some general equilibrium model solutions are analyzed in these terms.[2]

In addition to the fixed wage solutions, we analyze results from the model after an "outer" iteration in which the wage is varied in such a way as to bring labor demand(s) in line with prespecified supply(ies), that is, the model specification discussed in the one-sector variant through equation (6.20). The main effect of this iteration is to vary the overall price level to bring saving in line with investment, along the lines already discussed. But it also changes relative wages and has some impact on labor assignments across sectors, as shown below.

Extension to Many Sectors and Income Recipients

The full-blown general equilibrium model has an overall structure very similar to that of its one-sector condensation. Before going into great detail in the next chapter, it is worthwhile to indicate how the equation system of the simple model will be extended. The major complications are:

- The one-sector concepts of output and value added appearing in equation (6.1) are extended to twenty-five sectors, and in addition noncompetitive intermediate imports are treated as a production factor.
- The cost function (6.2c) for value added is generalized to a form built up from separable subfunctions for labor and capital aggregates. The eleven capital goods in the model, ten domestic and one imported, are assumed to enter in fixed proportions into an aggregate in each sector, while the six types of labor trade off with a fairly high elasticity of substitution. (Two types of labor are exclusively agricultural, two more participate in all sectors, and

2. The theory of a two-sector model in which the real wage falls to accommodate increases in demand, production, and employment (with accompanying distributional shifts) is developed in Taylor (1974).

the final two highly educated classes work only in nonagricultural sectors.)

• Because of the foregoing production detail, factor input equations analogous to (6.3) and (6.4) are complex, but still of the same general form.

• Equation (6.5) is also extended to make producers' prices depend on intermediate input costs (of both domestically produced goods and imports) as well as costs of value added and entrepreneurs.

• Wages for each labor type in different sectors are made proportional (though not equal, to reflect the existing intersectoral wage structure). Unlike labor, capital is not considered to be shiftable, hence there is in each sector a separate rate of profit, analogous to r in (6.7).

• Equations (6.8) to (6.13) are generalized to deal with the existence of a separate group of proprietors for each sector and with the distribution of capital incomes to the various classes of workers and proprietors, as well as to "employers" or rentiers. Some profits are not distributed, giving rise to retained earnings, a new source of saving.

• The various classes of income recipients are grouped into four consumer classes with different savings propensities, analogous to the parameters γ^L, γ^K, and γ^E in (6.14). In addition, each class is assumed to have a different set of demand parameters, describing class-wide utility-maximizing consumer choice among the products of the twenty-five sectors plus imports.

• Intermediate demands and exports enter as additional elements on the right side of the twenty-five equation generalization of (6.15). In addition, a balance of payments equation is included, with capital inflows as the equilibrating item (and another source of saving).

• Investment is still exogenous, as in (6.16), but the choice variable g must be extended to vector form to deal with capital formation in each of the sectors.

• The catalog of government policy variables is extended to include a full set of taxes, a vector of purchases from each sector, employment of functionaries, a variety of transfers, power to fix the exchange rate, tariffs, and export subsidies, and other tools.

The following chapter presents the algebra necessary to formalize all these complications.

References

Diewert, W. E. 1971. An application of the Shephard duality theorem: A generalized Leontief production function. *Journal of political economy* 79:481–507.

Taylor, Lance. 1974. Short-term policy in open semi-industrialized economies: The narrow limits of the possible. *Journal of development economics* 1:85–104.

7

Formal Statement of the General Equilibrium Model

Frank J. Lysy and Lance Taylor

As its title indicates, this chapter sets out the formal specification of the general equilibrium model. Since a big model's accounting is sufficiently complex to require many equations, space limitations dictate that their economic interpretation be held to a minimum. For the same reason, the journal literature is invoked for most mathematical derivations.

The model is set up to be solved as a forward simulation from year zero (1959, in actuality) in years Δ, 2Δ, and so on. All the solutions described in this book are based on three-year time intervals, though the sequencing could easily be varied in practice. The time structure of the model implies that all variables in the following equations ought to have a time argument (τ), but this is omitted except where necessary for clarity. There are assumed to be $N + 1$ sectors, numbered from zero to N. Sector zero corresponds to noncompetitive imports of various types; the rest of the sectors produce goods for national use or foreign trade. In practice, we worked with twenty-five of these.

Since each sector produces different kinds of commodities, for some purposes additional distinctions must be drawn among them. In particular, of the domestic sectors 1, 2, ..., N only those with subscripts in the set $\{K\}$ are assumed to produce capital goods.

There are six types of employed labor, denoted by $m = 1, ..., L$, classified on the basis of educational level or occupation for two types of agricultural labor. Except for these rural workers, who are assumed to be tied more or less permanently to the land, people in the labor force can shift freely among sectors. Besides wage recipients, there are also assumed to be N types of self-employed proprietors, one type for each sector. For lack of any better hypothesis, numbers of these entrepreneurs are determined by a fixed coefficient relationship with sector outputs. Finally, we assume that there are four types of employers in the economy, denoted by $z = 1, ..., Z$, receiving capital earnings from various sectors. All of these income recipients are further grouped by patterns of expenditure; that is, workers, proprietors, and employers are supposed to fit into four classes, $u = 1, ..., U$, in which all members have identical income tax liabilities and consumption functions.

The first section in this chapter is devoted to a description of price determination in the model, and the next section shows how employment and income levels are calculated. We then describe consumption behavior and outline our hypotheses about investment functions and capital accumulation. The final sections discuss commodity balances and national accounting conventions and show how the model is closed. An appendix describes the computer strategy we followed in solving the model, and a number of other aspects of its numerical structure. In most equations, the subscripts i and j refer to sectors, k to types of capital goods, m and s to types of labor, g to government, t to trade services, and u to consumer classes (see table 7-1 for a list of the symbols used).

Cost Functions and Input Coefficients

Any multisectoral model of the type considered here requires a mechanism for assigning labor, capital, and foreign exchange to production in different industries. Cost or production functions defined at the sectoral level are about the only means available to do this, despite the grave theoretical doubts which have been raised about them. For reasons of expediency, we adopt thoroughly neoclassical specifications here.

Table 7-1. Symbols in the Multisector Model

Symbol	Definition
Subscripts and their associated maximum values	
i or $j = 1, \ldots, N$	Sector
$m = 1, \ldots, L$	Labor category
$k = 1, \ldots, K$	Capital type
$s = 1, \ldots, S$	Categories of labor by sector, $S = (N+1)L$
$z = 1, \ldots, Z$	Categories of employers
$u = 1, \ldots, U$	Household categories
t	Trade and transport sector
τ	Time period
g	Government sector
Levels of economic variables	
V_i, X_i	Value added and output
L_{mi}, K_{ki}, L_s	Levels of wage labor, capital, and the self-employed
Y^L_{mi}, Y^K_s, Y^L_s	Wage income, distributed profit income, and the wage incomes of the self-employed
Q_i	Real aggregate consumption
D_{ki}	Real net fixed capital formation
I_k	Real replacement investment
G_i	Real government expenditure on goods
E_i	Real exports of goods
L^*_i, K^*_i	Indexes of the labor and capital aggregates
y_s	Income per person
y_u	Income per earner by household type
z_u	Total consumption per earner by household type
q_i^u	Consumption per earner of good *i* by household type *u*
Prices	
P_i	Price of output
P_i^V	Price of value added
P_i^L	Price of labor services
P_i^K	Price of capital services
P_i^E	Price of entrepreneurial services
P_i^U	Consumer price of goods
P^X_0, P^K_0, P^U_0	Domestic price of imported intermediates, investment goods, and consumption goods
$\pi^X_0, \pi^K_0, \pi^Q_0$	World price of imported intermediates, investment goods, and consumption goods
π^E_i	World price of exported goods
w_{mi}	Wage rate
r^K_i	Profit rate (after tax and depreciation)
r^F	Foreign exchange rate (cruzeiro/dollar)

Table 7-1 (Continued)

Symbol	*Definition*
Parameters	
v_i	Ratio of value added to output
e_i	Ratio of entrepreneurial services to output
b_{ki}	Ratio of capital type k to the aggregate capital stock in sector i
b_i	Ratio of aggregate capital to value added
c_{mi}	Ratio of labor type m to the aggregate labor demand in sector i
c_i	Ratio of aggregate labor to value added
a_{ij}	Input-output coefficient
h_{ij}	Element of the $(1 - A)^{-1}$ matrix
σ_i^L, σ_i^V	Elasticity of substitution among labor types and between capital and labor
α_{mi}^L, α_{Ki}, α_{Li}	Distribution parameters of the CES functions
t_{mi}^L, t_i^V, t_i^K	Tax rates on labor, value added, and profits
t_0^Q, t_0^X	Tariffs on consumption goods and intermediates
d_{ki}, δ_{ki}	Legal and real rates of depreciation
g	Expected growth in the economy used in investment plans
F_i	Sectoral factor to modify g for investment plans
R_{ig}	Distribution matrix for profit
γ_i	Rate of technical progress
ϵ_i	Rate of decline in requirement of entrepreneurial input
A_u, B_u	The constant term and the slope in the household tax functions
Φ_u	Household propensity to save
$\psi_i{}^u$	Trade markup for consumption goods
λ_i^u, ρ_i^u, σ_i^u, χ_u	Parameters in the household demand systems
θ_i^u	Average household budget shares

Note: The following principles were generally adhered to:

1. Roman upper-case letters are generally levels.
2. Roman lower-case letters are generally parameters.
3. Greek letters are generally parameters.
4. Subscripts are used to denote a specific variable within a certain narrow category; for example, $t_i{}^V$ is the value added tax rate within sector i.
5. Superscripts are used to denote a specific variable within a fairly broad class; for example, $t_i{}^V$ is the tax on value added, rather than the tax on labor, or capital, or output.
6. A subscript of "0" means an imported quantity, or a parameter referring to an imported quantity.
7. A variable which has a double subscript may sometimes appear with a single subscript. In such cases, the single subscript means a summation or an average has been taken over the excluded subscript. For example, L_m is the total demand for labor type m, where the summation is over sectors ($L_m = \Sigma_i L_{mi}$).

Unfortunately, even in neoclassical economies, additional problems for the numerical modeler arise. For example, all types of capital and labor can in principle substitute for each other, but at least for underdeveloped countries it is impossible to parameterize production tradeoffs with such a degree of generality. The most straightforward simplification of a general cost function is to assume that it is separable. In our case, we assume separate subfunctions for aggregate labor, aggregate capital, entrepreneurial inputs, and intermediate inputs; substitution is allowed among the different types of labor in that aggregate, and between aggregate labor and capital. We further assume that overall constant returns to scale would hold if the capital stock of each sector were allowed to adjust fully. But, as described below, since capital is fixed in each sector in the short run, it will earn a quasi rent which will depend on the scale of output.

Labor

Both because a breakdown of costs is observable and because they make model solution simpler, we work with neoclassical cost (not production) functions. In parametric form, the cost P_i^L of the sector i aggregate labor input L_i^* is postulated to be a CES function of the different labor types, that is,

$$P_i^L = \sum_{m=1}^{L} \left\{ (\alpha_{mi}^L)^{\sigma_i^L} [W_{mi}(1 + t_{mi}^L)]^{1-\sigma_i^L} \right\}^{1/(1-\sigma_i^L)} \quad (i = 1, ..., N) \qquad (7.1)$$

where the α_{mi}^L are distribution parameters in the CES production function for L_i^*, and σ_i^L is the elasticity of substitution among different labor types in sector i.[1] The w_{mi} represent wages received by labor type m in sector i, and the t_{mi}^L are employment taxes (such as for social security). Given the wages, taxes, and parameters of the cost function, it is straightforward to calculate the P_i^L. The same is true of the coefficients c_{mi} relating the use of each type of labor in the sector to the total labor input (c_{mi} =

1. Although it is not used explicitly in the model, the production function for effective total labor L_i^* is

$$L_i^* = \left[\sum_{m=1}^{L} \alpha_{mi}^L (L_{mi})^{(\sigma_i^L - 1)/\sigma_i^L} \right]^{\sigma_i^L/(\sigma_i^L - 1)}.$$

L_{mi}/L_i^*). As discussed in chapter 6, Shephard's lemma implies that

$$c_{mi} = \frac{\partial P_i^L}{\partial[w_{mi}(1+t_{mi}^L)]} = \left[\frac{P_i^L \alpha_{mi}^L}{w_{mi}(1+t_{mi}^L)}\right]^{\sigma_i^L}$$

$$(i = 1,\ldots,N;\ m = 1,\ldots,L). \tag{7.2}$$

For numerical specification of the parameters entering these, equations, data are required on elasticities of substitution among labor types and on the share of each type of labor in total sectoral labor payments in the base year. The elasticities can be estimated cross-sectionally as in Fishlow (1973). The shares are used in connection with equations of the form

$$\frac{(1+t_{mi}^L)w_{mi}L_{mi}}{P_i^L L_i^*} = (\alpha_{mi}^L)^{\sigma_i^L}\left[\frac{(1+t_{mi}^L)w_{mi}}{P_i^L}\right]^{1-\sigma_i^L}$$

which follow from (7.2). The left side here is just the share of labor type m in total labor payments in sector i. If we let this be u_{mi} and let v_{mi} be the quantity

$$[(1+t_{mi}^L)w_{mi}]^{1-\sigma_i^L},$$

the above equation can be thrown into the form

$$u_{mi}B_i = (\alpha_{mi}^L)^{\sigma_i^L} v_{mi},$$

in which

$$B_i = (P_i^L)^{1-\sigma_i^L} = \sum_{m=1}^{L} (\alpha_{mi}^L)^{\sigma_i^L} v_{mi}$$

because of equation (7.1). These equations determine the quantities $(\alpha_{mi}^L)^{\sigma_i^L}$ up to the scaling factor B_i, which can be determined by a normalization. The most convenient one is $P_i^L = 1$ in the base year, in which case $B_i = 1$, and

$$\alpha_{mi}^L = (u_{mi}/v_{mi})^{1/\sigma_i^L}.$$

Capital

We make two nonsubstitution assumptions about capital stocks by sector. First, within each sector fixed proportions are maintained among different capital types; that is, if b_{ki} is the ratio between capital of type k used in sector i, K_{ki}, and the sector's capital aggregate K_i^*, then

$$b_{ki} = \text{constant} \quad (k = 0 \text{ and } k = k\epsilon\{K\};\ i = 1,\ldots,N)$$

where $k = 0$ denotes noncompetitively imported capital goods. We assume that the b_{ki} are normalized to sum to one in each sector.

The second nonsubstitution assumption is that capital cannot be shifted out of a sector once it is installed there. This means that in each sector, even with overall constant returns to scale, the fixed capital stock earns a quasi rent P_i^K in the short run. How this rent is determined and its role in the overall price system are discussed below.

Value Added

Aggregate labor and capital inputs (L_i^* and K_i^*, respectively) combine to produce "value added," which in our usage is the usual concept less payments to proprietors. Our value added can be defined in a reasonable way because of the separability assumptions made about the production function. As with the labor aggregate, we assume that L_i^* and K_i^* combine in sector i according to a CES cost index. The cost of value added, P_i^V, is given by

$$P_i^V = [(\alpha_{Ki})^{\sigma_i^V}(P_i^K)^{1-\sigma_i^V} + (\alpha_{Li})^{\sigma_i^V}(P_i^L)^{1-\sigma_i^V}]^{1/(1-\sigma_i^V)}$$
$$(i = 1,\ldots,N) \tag{7.3}$$

where P_i^K, the cost to the sector of using its aggregate capital stock, is given in equation (7.6) and where α_{Ki} and α_{Li} are distribution parameters calculated in accordance with base-year shares of capital and labor in value added, given the sectoral elasticity of substitution σ_i^V. The formulas for labor- and capital-output ratios, analogous to (7.2), are:

$$c_i = (L_i^*/V_i) = \left[\frac{P_i^V \alpha_{Li}}{P_i^L}\right]^{\sigma_i^V} \quad (i = 1,\ldots,N) \tag{7.4}$$

$$b_i = (K_i^*/V_i) = \left[\frac{P_i^V \alpha_{Ki}}{P_i^K}\right]^{\sigma_i^V} \quad (i = 1,\ldots,N) \tag{7.5}$$

where V_i is value added in sector i.

As stated above, we assume that in any time period K_i^* is fixed in each sector. Making K_i^* exogenous in equation (7.5) gives an expression for the quasi rent P_i^K of sector i capital in terms of the cost of value added and the ratio of value added to capital:

$$P_i^K = \alpha_{Ki} P_i^V (V_i/K_i^*)^{1/\sigma_i^V} \quad (i = 1, \ldots, N). \tag{7.6}$$

Back substitution of this expression into the sector cost function (7.3) gives the value added cost P_i^V in terms of labor cost P_i^L and the sector's value added/capital ratio:

$$P_i^V = \frac{(\alpha_{Li})^{\sigma_i^V/(1-\sigma_i^V)} P_i^L}{\left[1 - \alpha_{Ki}(V_i/K_i^*)^{(1-\sigma_i^V)/\sigma_i^V}\right]^{1/(1-\sigma_i^V)}} \quad (i = 1, \ldots, N). \tag{7.7}$$

Note that as the value added/capital ratio increases, so does P_i^V because of decreasing returns to labor when capital is fixed. Evidently, for given values of P_i^L and V_i/K_i^* we can calculate P_i^V, provided that the latter is not so large that the bracketed term in the denominator of (7.7) becomes negative. With P_i^V given, (7.6) gives the quasi rent P_i^K. As already indicated in chapter 6, iteration on the wages underlying P_i^L and on the value added/capital ratios in each sector is used to solve the model numerically.

Producers' Prices

Once value added prices are known, we can use the input-output table to calculate producers' prices. In the interest of simplicity we assume away the possibility of substitution between intermediate inputs and value added (interpreted in the usual way, including payments to proprietors). Producers' prices of domestically produced goods are given by

$$P_i = \sum_{j=1}^{N} a_{ji} P_j + a_{0i} P_0^X + \frac{1}{1 - t_i^V}(v_i P_i^V + e_i P_i^E) \quad (i = 1, \ldots, N) \tag{7.8}$$

where the $a_{ji}(j = 1, \ldots, N)$ are input-output coefficients for domestically produced intermediate inputs; a_{0i} is the input-output coefficient for noncompetitively imported intermediates in sector i; v_i is the coefficient relating a sector's value added to its output ($v_i = V_i/X_i = 1 - \sum_j a_{ji} - a_0^i - e_i$); e_i is the ratio between E_i, the number of proprietors in sector i, and its output ($e_i = E_i/X_i$); and P_i^E is the average remuneration of a proprietor in the sector. P_0^X is a price index for noncompetitive intermediate inputs, given by

$$P_0^X = r^F \pi_0^X (1 + t_0^X) \tag{7.9}$$

where r^F is the exchange rate, π_0^X is the world price of the intermediate, and t_0^X is its tariff-cum-scarcity premium. The only other terms appearing in (7.8) are the value added tax rates t_i^V.

Technical Progress

Since we want to generate more or less steady growth with the model, it is convenient to assume that technical progress is purely labor augmenting. This is also consistent with the no-substitution specification among capital types, in connection with which it is realistic to assume that capital-output ratios stay constant over time.

If the sector i rate of technical progress is γ_i, its effects are given by the equation

$$\alpha_{Li}(\tau) = \overline{\alpha_{Li}} \exp\left[\frac{\gamma_i(\sigma_i^V - 1)}{\sigma_i^V}\tau\right] \quad (i = 1,\ldots,N) \tag{7.10}$$

where $\exp\left[\frac{\gamma_i(\sigma_i^V - 1)}{\sigma_i^V}\tau\right]$ is the exponential function and $\overline{\alpha_{Li}}$ is the base-year value of the labor distribution parameter for the value added cost function in sector i.

We also assume that the role of independent proprietors will decline in most sectors as the importance of corporations increases. This implies the specification

$$e_i(\tau) = \overline{e_i}\exp(-\epsilon_i\tau) \quad (i = 1,\ldots,N), \tag{7.11}$$

in which $\overline{e_i}$ is the base-year proprietor input coefficient. The rates of decline of proprietor inputs ϵ_i should exceed the γ_i for labor by a substantial margin. Both sets of parameters can be estimated in various ways from time series data on factor inputs and payments.

Interindustry Factor Price Structure

Like data from all other countries, the numbers for Brazil reveal substantial differences in wages for the "same" type of labor across industries. The same is true for average remunerations of proprietors and rates of return to capital. There is no good theoretical explanation for this observation, although the intersectoral differences seem to remain fairly stable over time. For this reason, we simply assume that payments to workers and proprietors in different sectors are related to economywide levels by factors of proportionality:

$$w_{mi}(\tau) = \overline{w_{mi}}(\tau)w_m(\tau) \qquad (i = 1,\ldots,N \text{ and } i = g; \; m = 1,\ldots,L) \tag{7.12}$$

$$P_i^E(\tau) = \overline{P_i^E}(\tau) P^E(\tau) \qquad (i = 1, ..., N). \tag{7.13}$$

The barred terms in these equations are exogenously specified, with w_m and P^E being respectively the economywide wage index for type m labor and the remuneration level of proprietors, both at time τ. The factors of proportionality are given a time index to indicate that there may be shifts in intersectoral payment levels, for example, as observed by Mata and Bacha (1973). Finally, note that the wage level of type m workers in government service would be given by w_{mg} in (7.12).

Price Determination

All the foregoing equations are homogeneous of degree zero in prices, wages, and payments to proprietors. Hence, some sort of price normalization condition must be added to the specification. It is convenient to normalize on proprietors' remunerations, with the condition

$$P^E(\tau) = \text{constant, for all time periods.} \tag{7.14}$$

As discussed in more detail in the appendix, the foregoing equations determine all commodity prices P_i and factor input coefficients as functions of the factor prices w_m, P^E, and r^F, and of the value added/capital ratios (V_i/K_i^*).[2] The next variables to be tied up in equations are the V_i themselves, as the quantity side of the model is closed. Assuming that levels of value added are temporarily given in each sector, we first see how factor incomes are determined, then how these fix consumption levels for several income groups. Along with exogenously specified items of final demand (investment, exports, and government purchases), consumption levels by sector then give an estimate of sector outputs X_i from the usual quantity-side Leontief balance equations, and the X_i give a new estimate of the V_i, as $V_i = v_i X_i$. Iteration on output levels then gives a quantity solution to the model consistent with the given wages w_m. Details appear in the following sections.

2. In practice it is convenient to set the exchange rate r^F as changing exogenously over time, more or less in line with some overall price index. This rules out extraneous devaluation or revaluation of the exchange rate, with consequent (though minor) perturbations in resource allocation.

Employment and Income Levels

This section is devoted to the relationship between output (or value added) levels, and uses of and payments to factors of production. In the following section, we trace these payment flows back around to the demand side to show how they determine the X_i, given factor prices and exogenous final demands.

Employment Levels

The demand for labor type m in sector i is given by

$$L_{mi} = X_i v_i c_i c_{mi} \quad (i = 1, ..., N; m = 1, ..., L). \tag{7.15}$$

We assume that employment of type m labor by the government, L_{mg}, is specified exogenously. In effect, we now have $L(N + 1)$ different employment (and wage) levels specified. Let these be indexed in some convenient order by s, and $S = L(N + 1)$. We can also calculate employment of proprietors, which we define as L_s:

$$L_s = e_i X_i \quad (s = S + i; i = 1, ..., N). \tag{7.16}$$

Labor Incomes

Multiplying by wage or remuneration rates gives labor incomes received by the different groups:

$$Y_{mi}{}^L = w_{mi} L_{mi} \quad (m = 1, ..., L; i = 1, ..., N \text{ and } i = \text{g}) \tag{7.17}$$

and

$$Y_s^L = P_i^E L_s \quad (s = S + i; i = 1, ..., N). \tag{7.18}$$

Capital Incomes

More or less in line with Brazilian demographic census categories, we assume that there are Z types of employers in the economy, who receive only income from capital. Lacking a good theory of what gives rise to the actual number of corporation directors, or *fazendeiros*, we simply assume that these are specified exogenously:

$$L_s(\tau) = \overline{L_s(\tau)} \quad (s = S + N + 1, ..., S + N + Z). \tag{7.19}$$

To calculate capital earnings themselves, we have to break quasi rents $P_i{}^K$ down into depreciation and profit components. This is normally done via a formula such as

$$P_i^K = \sum_{k\epsilon\{K\}} P_k b_{ki} \left(\frac{r_i^K}{1 - t_i^K} + d_{ki} \right) + P_0^K b_{0i} \left(\frac{r_i^K}{1 - t_i^K} + d_{0i} \right)$$
$$(i = 1, \ldots, N)$$

where r_i^K is the after-tax rate of profit in sector i, t_i^K is the rate of capital taxation (corporate profit tax), d_{ki} is the *legal* rate of type k capital depreciation used for tax purposes in sector i, the P_k are producers' prices of capital goods, and P_0^K is the domestic price of a noncompetitively imported capital good,

$$P_0^K = r^F \pi_0^K (1 + t_0^K). \tag{7.20}$$

In this last equation, π_0^K is an index of world prices of capital goods and t_0^K is the tariff (or scarcity premium) for such imports.

The foregoing decomposition for P_i^K presumes that changes in prices of capital goods are immediately reflected by shifts in profit rates and depreciation allowances. Such assumptions are simply stated and are rather common in the literature, but scarcely credible. In any case, we follow tradition by accepting them and rewrite the decomposition to get sectoral profit rates as

$$r_i^K = \frac{(1 - t_i^K) \left(P_i^K - \sum_{k\epsilon\{K\}} P_k b_{ki} d_{ki} - P_0^K b_{0i} d_{0i} \right)}{\sum_{k\epsilon\{K\}} P_K b_{ki} + P_0^K b_{0i}}$$
$$(i = 1, \ldots, N). \tag{7.21}$$

We use these profit rates to get earnings from capital, which are assumed to be distributed from production sectors to the $S + N + Z$ income recipient classes according to coefficients R_{is}, where i as usual denotes sector and s denotes income recipients. Since there are retained earnings in business, the sum $\sum_s R_{is}$ will be less than one for each i. The equation for capital incomes distributed to persons (who can be workers and proprietors as well as capitalists) is

$$Y_s^K = \sum_{i=1}^{N} R_{is} X_i v_i b_i r_i^K \left(\sum_{k\epsilon\{K\}} b_{ki} P_k + b_{0i} P_0^K \right)$$
$$(s = 1, \ldots, S + N + Z). \tag{7.22}$$

In terms of the data, not much is known about the distribution coefficients R_{is}, although it is clear from Fishlow's work that they are related to occupation group, particularly in agriculture. As discussed in chapter 8, we made a heroic series of guesses to quantify these parameters, since changes in the R matrix (through land reform or worker acquisition of assets through the new government savings funds or something similar) prove at least in the world of the general equilibrium model to be a potent redistributive tool.

Incomes per Participant

For use in calculating the overall income distribution, we put all income flows on a per participant basis:

$$y_s = (Y_s^L + Y_s^K)/L_s \quad (s = 1, ..., S + N + Z). \qquad (7.23)$$

Labor incomes Y_s^L for employers are equal to zero here and in equation (7.24) below.

Total Consumption Levels by Class

To make simulation of consumption behavior tractable, we group the $S + N + Z$ types of income recipients into U consumer classes and calculate average incomes for each class:

$$y_u = \left(\sum_{s \in \{S_u\}} Y_s^L + Y_s^K \right) \Big/ \sum_{s \in \{S_u\}} L_s \quad (u = 1, ..., U). \qquad (7.24)$$

Here, the set $\{S_u\}$ is made up of the indexes s of income recipients in consumption class u.

The consumption groups are arranged to include income recipients at more or less the same income level. Hence, it is reasonable to assume that marginal tax rates for all persons within a group are equal. We further assume linear tax functions of the form $A_u + B_u y_u$ where A_u is a constant in the tax function (which in practice is made negative, reflecting income transfers from the government to persons) and B_u is the marginal tax rate on earned income. With the linearity assumption, the formula for z_u, the value of total consumption per participant in group u, is

$$z_u = (1 - \Phi_u)(y_u - A_u - B_u y_u) \quad (u = 1, ..., U) \quad (7.25)$$

where Φ_u is the marginal (and average) propensity to save.

Expenditure Determination

Perhaps it is worth pointing out explicitly once again that the consumption levels z_u are functions only of output levels X_i, given prices and the specification of the tax functions, capital earnings distribution matrix, and so on. Hence, sectoral consumption levels will depend only on output levels as well. The details appear in the next section.

Sectoral Consumption Functions

Although we are assuming that producers' prices of goods have been determined (through fixing the factor prices and output levels in each stage of the solution algorithm), we have to transform these somewhat to find the prices that consumers pay. In addition, we must make assumptions about the utility functions of income recipients to determine their consumption patterns.

Consumers' Prices

Assume that some physical quantity of trade services is associated with the purchase of each consumer good—this quantity may vary by consumption class to reflect such things as different trade margins on food products in rural and urban areas. If the trade markup on good i to consumer class u is Ψ_i^u, the consumer's price P_i^u of commodity i is given by

$$P_i^u = P_i + \Psi_i^u P_t \quad (i \neq t;\, u = 1, ..., U) \tag{7.26}$$

where the P_i are producers' prices of commodities and P_t is the producers' price of trade services (one of the sectors in the model). If there are noncompetitive imports of consumption goods, their price is

$$P_0^u = r^F \pi_0^Q (1 + t_0^Q) + \Psi_0^u P_t \quad (u = 1, ..., U) \tag{7.27}$$

where π_0^Q is the world price of such imports and t_0^Q is their tariff-cum-scarcity premium.

Utility and Expenditure Functions

There are basically only two types of well-tested direct utility functions which are used to derive complete systems of demand equations: the Stone-Geary linear expenditure system and the

Houthakker direct addilog system. Since the latter is based on easily interpreted elasticities, we prefer to work with that. Derivations of most of the formulas stated here are not given, since they appear in the review article by Sato (1972).

For each consumption class u, assume that a representative person has a total consumption expenditure equal to z_u and a utility function which can be represented by

$$\sum_{\substack{i=0 \\ i \neq t}}^{N} \lambda_i^u (q_i^u)^{-\rho_i^u} \quad (u = 1, ..., U)$$

where q_i^u is the quantity of commodity i consumed and λ_i^u and ρ_i^u are parameters interpreted below.

If this function is maximized subject to a budget constraint written in terms of consumers' prices

$$z_u = \sum_{\substack{i=0 \\ i \neq t}}^{N} P_i^u q_i^u \quad (u = 1, ..., \text{U}), \tag{7.28}$$

the following demand functions result:

$$q_i^u = \left(\frac{\lambda_i^u \rho_i^u z_u}{\chi_u P_i^u} \right)^{1/(\rho_i^u + 1)}$$

$$(i = 0, ..., N \text{ and } i \neq t;\ u = 1, ..., U) \tag{7.29}$$

and

$$q_t^u = \sum_{i \neq t} \Psi_i^u q_i^u \quad (u = 1, ..., U). \tag{7.30}$$

The demand functions in (7.29) are not quite in closed form, since we have introduced a new parameter χ_u for each consumer class. This turns out to be equal to the sum

$$\sum_{i \neq t} \rho_i^u (q_i^u)^{-\rho_i^u} \lambda_i^u \quad (u = 1, ..., U),$$

although this fact is not necessary for computing quantities demanded. Rather, all one has to do is iterate on χ_u in the computer until the representative consumer's budget constraint (7.28) is satisfied (for given consumer prices and income) for each consumer class u. Naturally, when the iteration is complete the budget constraint is *not* an equation independent of the demand equations (7.29). Also, given the q_i^u, demands for trade services can easily be calculated from (7.30).

Since the direct addilog function is fundamentally an extension to full parametric form of the Frisch (1959) rules for estimating a complete set of demand elasticities, we can apply Frisch's methods to estimate its parameters. The basic assumption is that own-price *compensated* demand elasticities σ_i^u (with signs reversed) are related to the corresponding income elasticities η_i^u by the equation

$$\sigma_i^u = \sigma^u \eta_i^u (1 - \theta_i^u \eta_i^u),$$

where θ_i^u is the budget share of the ith good in expenditures of the uth class of consumers. For each consumer class, the common proportionality factor σ^u between income and own-price elasticities in general will vary as the expenditure level and budget shares shift. If one knows (or guesses) the value of σ^u at any point in time, however, together with known values of the income elasticities it determines the whole demand system (the key point noted by Frisch, though he preferred to work with the inverse of our σ^u, the well-known Frisch parameter).

The key assumption of the direct addilog demand system is that the compensated price elasticities σ_i^u stay constant over time. In making use of this assumption, it is convenient to work directly not with these elasticities, but with the transformed values

$$\rho_i^u = (1 - \sigma_i^u)/\sigma_i^u$$

appearing in (7.29). Differentiating q_i^u in that equation with respect to price shows directly that the compensated demand elasticity is

$$1/(\rho_i^u + 1) = \sigma_i^u.$$

(Note the analogy between the form of these exponents and those in the CES production function in note 1.) The addilog utility function generalizes the production function to take into account nonunitary income elasticities of demand.

The λ_i^u are analogous to the distribution parameters in a CES function and can be calculated from base-year budget shares, which appear in equation (7.29) rewritten in the form

$$\lambda_i^u = (q_i^u)^{\rho_i^u} \theta_i^u \chi_u / \rho_i^u.$$

Here we simply choose the value of χ_u that satisfies the normalizing condition

$$\sum_{i \neq t} \lambda_i^u = 1$$

(given previously calculated values for the ρ_i^u, base-year consumption levels q_i^u, and budget shares θ_i^u).

Total Consumption Demand

When consumption levels for the representative consumers of each consumption class have been calculated from (7.29) and (7.30) they have to be aggregated to give total flow demand for consumption goods by sector. The equations are:

$$Q_i = \sum_{u=1}^{U} \left(\sum_{s \epsilon \{S_u\}} L_s \right) q_i^u \quad (i = 0, ..., N). \qquad (7.31)$$

Investment Functions

There are no very credible investment theories one can use for developing economies such as that of Brazil. In this section we set out a specification which is easy to manage and leads to fairly steady growth of the economy. The theory adopted is in the tradition of the "stock-flow conversion factors" often used in development planning (for an example, see Johansen 1974, chap. 10) and at least has precedent to back it.

Net Capital Formation

Let D_{ki} be demand in sector i for capital good k, for purposes of net investment. The simplest theory of the D_{ki} is that entrepreneurs in each sector (and national planners) share a forecast g of the expected growth in the economy, but that this is marked up or down by factors F_i in the sectors to account for different expectations, historical growth patterns, or animal spirits. In this case, we have

$$D_{ki}(\tau) = g(\tau)F_i(\tau)K_{ki}(\tau) \quad (i = 1, ..., N;\ k \epsilon \{K\} \text{ and } k = 0).$$

That is, the expected growth rate in the sector is $g(\tau)F_i(\tau)$, and each type of capital used by it is expected to grow at this rate.

Total demand for each type of capital for net investment is given by the sum of D_{ki} across sectors:

$$D_k(\tau) = \sum_{i=1}^{N} D_{ki}(\tau) \qquad (k \epsilon \{K\} \text{ and } k = 0). \tag{7.32}$$

Replacement Investment

The D_{ki} are demands for *net* investment. It is also necessary to take into account demands for replacement of existing stocks. The simplest way to do this is to assume that capital stock demands roughly equaled supplies in the preceding period, and that investors' forecasts as to growth were fulfilled. Then $\overline{K}_{ki}$, the supply of type k capital in sector i, is

$$\overline{K}_{ki}(\tau) = K_{ki}(\tau - \Delta)\,[1 + g(\tau - \Delta)F_i(\tau - \Delta)]^{\Delta}$$
$$(i = 1, ..., N;\ k \epsilon \{K\} \text{ and } k = 0).$$

Multiplying each $\overline{K}_{ki}$ by the appropriate *physical* depreciation rate $\delta_{ki}{}^K$ and summing over sectors gives a vector of replacement demands by capital goods–producing sectors (sectors of origin):

$$I_k(\tau) = \sum_{i=1}^{N} \delta_{ki}{}^K K_{ki}(\tau - \Delta)\,[1 + g(\tau - \Delta)F_i(\tau - \Delta)]^{\Delta}$$
$$(k \epsilon \{K\} \text{ and } k = 0) \tag{7.33}$$

Commodity Balances

The demand-supply balance equations for the N domestically produced goods take the form

$$X_i = \sum_{j=1}^{N} a_{ij}X_j + D_i + I_i + Q_i + G_i + E_i.$$

On the right side of this equation, the first term gives intermediate demands for commodity i, and the next two terms (which will be zero for noncapital goods–producing sectors) respectively give demands for capital formation and replacement investment. The term Q_i gives consumption demand, G_i is government demand, and E_i is exports from sector i. Competitive imports are not included, since we have no reasonable theory about how to determine their levels. For similar reasons, we do not carry inventory changes in the accounting. Merely making them proportional to output changes or something similar would not be very illuminating.

Define a matrix with typical element $\gamma_{ij} - a_{ij}$ (where $\gamma_{ij} = 1$ when $i = j$, and $\gamma_{ij} = 0$ otherwise) and invert it. Calling the elements of the inverse h_{ij}, we can rewrite the above balance equations as

$$X_i = \sum_{j=1}^{N} h_{ij} [D_j + I_j + Q_j + G_j + E_j - M_j] \quad (i = 1, ..., N). \tag{7.34}$$

All terms on the right-hand side of this equation are given within each period except the consumption term Q_j, which depends on the X_i (or the value added levels V_i) through the income generation mechanisms discussed in previous sections. As discussed in more detail in the appendix, this type of functional dependence suggests the following algorithm for solving (7.34):

1. Guess an initial output vector with elements X_i (perhaps last period's output vector, scaled up).
2. Set $V_i = v_i X_i$ and use the V_i to calculate an equilibrium set of prices and input-output coefficients from equations (7.1) to (7.14).
3. Use equations (7.15) to (7.31) to calculate factor payments and then a new vector of consumption levels Q_i.
4. Use the Q_i along with the exogenous terms on the right side of (7.34) to get a new output guess, and iterate back through step 2 until the old and new values of X_i agree to a given tolerance.

Unless a negative denominator shows up in equation (7.7), because of an insufficient capital stock in some sector, this procedure converges rapidly. Its stability stems largely from the simplicity of the direct addilog demand functions and the leakages in the system because of saving and taxes taken from capital and labor incomes.

National Accounting

To check the performance of the model, it is useful to have the standard national accounting summaries of its output. The most convenient ones follow.

Balance of Payments

In terms of domestic prices, the current account deficit BD is

$$BD = r^F \left[\pi_0{}^X \sum_{i=1}^{N} a_{0i} X_i + \pi_0{}^K (I_0 + D_0) + \pi_0{}^Q (Q_0 + G_0) - \sum_{i \in \{E\}} \pi_i^E E_i \right]. \tag{7.35}$$

We assume here that all world prices (the π's) are specified exogenously, along with the exchange rate. All other variables in the equation are either exogenous or depend on the X_i, so that the payments deficit (and therefore foreign saving) is treated as endogenous. Of course, one can simulate the impacts of different levels of capital inflow by varying the exchange rate r^F and other variables to see how BD responds.

Government

Total government expenditures GE are given by the equation

$$GE = \sum_{m=1}^{L} w_{mg}(1 + t_{mg}{}^L) L_{mg} + \sum_{i=1}^{N} P_i G_i + P_0^Q G_0 + \sum_{i \in \{E\}} (P_i - r^F \pi_i^E) E_i, \tag{7.36}$$

that is, the sum of expenditures on employment of persons (including social security taxes, which will also be entered on the other side of the ledger as government revenue), purchases of goods for consumption and investment (with imports valued at post-tariff prices), and subsidies paid to make up the difference between the foreign and domestic price of exports. Note that GE is a value sum, since wages, the exchange rate, and prices enter into its determination.

Government revenue GR is given by an even more complicated expression,

$$GR = \sum_{i=1}^{N} X_i \left[v_i c_i \sum_{m=1}^{L} t_{mi}{}^L w_{mi} c_{mi} + t_i^K \frac{r_i^K}{1 - t_i^K} v_i b_i \left(b_{0i} P_0^K + \sum_{k \in \{K\}} b_{ki} P_k \right) + P_i t_i^V v_i \right] + \sum_{m=1}^{L} t_{mg} w_{mg} L_{mg}$$

$$+ \sum_{u=1}^{U} \left(\sum_{s \in \{S_u\}} L_s \right) (A_u + B_u y_u) + r^F \left[\pi_0{}^X t_0{}^X \sum_{i=1}^{N} a_{0i} X_i \right.$$

$$\left. + \pi_0{}^K t_0{}^K (I_0 + D_0) + \pi_0{}^Q t_0{}^Q (Q_0 + G_0) \right], \qquad (7.37)$$

that is, the sum of social security taxes on business employment, profit taxes, value added taxes, social security taxes on government employees, income taxes from persons, and tariffs on noncompetitive intermediate imports and on imports of capital goods and consumption goods.

Government saving GS is defined as government revenue less government expenditure,

$$GS = GR - GE. \qquad (7.38)$$

Since it is essentially defined as a residual, GS is an endogenous variable. Once again, we can simulate various values for it by varying exogenous items in the government expenditure basket.

Private Saving

Equating the value of factor payments to the value of expenditures and applying the cost and revenue functions developed above, we find that the savings-investment balance (or, equivalently, Walras's law) in the present model reduces to the form

$$\sum_{i=1}^{N} \left(P_0{}^K D_{0i} + \sum_{k \in \{K\}} P_k D_{ki} \right) + P_0{}^K I_0 + \sum_{k \in \{K\}} P_k I_k$$

$$- GS - BD = PS, \qquad (7.39)$$

in which the new symbol PS denotes private saving. Expressed directly, private saving is given by the following equation:

$$PS = \sum_{i=1}^{N} \sum_{s=1}^{S+N+Z} (1 - R_{is}) X_i v_i b_i r_i{}^K \left[\sum_{k \in \{K\}} b_{ki} P_k + b_{0i} P_0{}^K \right]$$

$$+ \sum_{i=1}^{N} X_i v_i b_i \left[\sum_{k \in \{K\}} d_{ki} b_{ki} P_k + d_{0i} b_{0i} P_0{}^K \right]$$

$$+ \sum_{u=1}^{U} \left(\sum_{s \in \{S_u\}} L_s \right) [y_u - (A_u - B_u y_u) - z_u], \qquad (7.40)$$

that is, the sum of retained after-tax profits, depreciation allowances, and personal saving.

Gross National Product

The foregoing equations in effect lay out accounting identities for the foreign sector, government, and private saving and investment. Most presentations also contain product and income accounts for GNP. Since the equations for these are well known, we refrain from stating them in detail here.

Closing the Model

As shown in detail in the appendix, the model can be solved in two major iterations, one nested inside the other. The outer one begins with specification of the wages of the different types of labor and uses equation (7.1) to determine each sector's labor cost P_i^L. The inner iteration begins with a guess at sector output levels X_i and uses these to determine levels of value added V_i. Together with the P_i^L, the V_i provides sufficient information to work through equations (7.2) through (7.34) to get a new set of demands for commodities from (7.34). Supplies are then confronted with demands, and output levels are modified until the demand-supply balances for all commodities are satisfied, concluding the inner iteration.

In most solutions reported in this book, we closed the outer iteration in one of two ways. The simpler was to retain the nominal wage levels generated by a base solution of the model and not iterate on wages at all, as we undertook variations in parameters or exogenous variables. In the fixed capital stock solutions of each period, fixed nominal wages make the model behave in traditional short-run Keynesian fashion—employment levels can increase in response to increases in aggregate demand via reduction in the real wage. Such demand-determined solutions are analyzed in chapters 9 and 10 in connection with recent discussion among Brazilian and Brazilianist scholars about the impact of government expansionary policy on the income distribution.

For given wages, labor demands for the L skill types are given by the equations

$$L_m = \sum_{i=1}^{N} X_i v_i c_i c_{mi} + L_{mg} \quad (m = 1, ..., L). \qquad (7.41)$$

Our alternative method for completing the outer iteration was to confront these demand levels with exogenously fixed labor supplies $\overline{L}_m$ to generate excess labor demand functions of the form

$$L_m^{ED}(w_1, ..., w_L) = L_m - \overline{L}_m \quad (m = 1, ..., L). \qquad (7.42)$$

With six labor types, equations (7.42) define a system of six highly nonlinear equations which can be solved to determine fixed-employment equilibria for the general equilibrium model.[3]

Appendix: Solving the General Equilibrium Model

As should be obvious from its description in the preceding text, our general equilibrium model can be viewed as a system of simultaneous equations to which we want a numerical solution. Which numerical method is used to find the solution, however, is really not of the highest importance. If a method works, it is just as good as some other that costs about the same. The answers produced by either method are (one hopes) the same.

It turned out that with present computers and at a cost of \$15 to \$35, it was possible to obtain a four-period solution to the general equilibrium model with six labor classes, twenty-five sectors, and four household classes. There was therefore no real need to simplify the model. Since it would be easy with this type of model to come up with a solution method that would cost considerably more, the procedure we ended up using should be of some interest. This appendix describes the solution method, as well as some points raised in solving the model that may shed light on the actual adjustment processes of the Brazilian economy.

The method we used follows directly from the logical structure of the model. The almost recursive form into which its equations can be thrown leads naturally to iterative procedures for solving it block by block. Our algorithm follows the standard (at least since Keynes) textbook approach to macro models by using the

3. As discussed in more detail in chapter 6, we do not specify excess demand functions for proprietors, whose economywide remuneration level P^E serves as the numeraire in equation (7.14). In effect, total employment of proprietors is determined by aggregate demand, that is, by government expenditures, net exports, and investment. In practice, we find that model solutions in which aggregate demand is "too" high generate unreasonably high wage levels as well as high employment levels for proprietors. Hence, the latter are kept near historical levels by modification of aggregate demand to keep wages stable.

notions that wages are in some sense "prior to" prices and output levels, and that prices and output levels are jointly determined in a nonconstant returns system by a savings-investment balance. By some stretch of the imagination, one might suppose that the algorithm reflects the operation of two markets: that for products, which is cleared within each wage iteration, and that for labor types. One could then see how difficult it is to solve the equations for these markets. If it does prove difficult, then one may look with doubt (or with wondrous awe) on their operation in the real world. But one must be extremely careful in such interpretations, since it was never our purpose to try to model the actual working of any existing market. Nevertheless, it is significant, as we discuss in detail below, that for several types of labor skills the cross-wage elasticities of demand were so strong that lowering the wage of one labor type to lower its unemployment would *increase* the level of unemployment in the economy as a whole. Such responses, of course, make it very difficult to clear labor markets by a simple Walrasian *tâtonnement*.

Numerically, solving the general equilibrium system in almost block recursive fashion takes advantage of all the "zeros" that economic theory leads us to believe should be in such a system of simultaneous equations. In a general equilibrium system, all variables matter, but only a very few matter *directly* to any given variable. The rest operate indirectly by affecting some intermediate variable, which then affects directly the variable of interest. Of course there may be, and probably are, several intermediate stages. An efficient numerical procedure will take advantage of these zeros.

Our overall strategy was to set up layers of iterations, where the solution to an inside layer is necessary to get the solution to a layer further out. One can use any method, of course, to solve any of these layers; there is no reason why the same procedure has to be used for every layer. We always tried first some simple procedure in solving a particular layer. If it worked, we kept it. If not, only then would we go on to some fancier procedure which might use, for example, derivatives.

The Solution Procedure

The primary breakdown of the model is through time. It is recursive in time, so that the solution in any particular period depends on solutions from previous periods. This means that we can get a solution for any one period, update the exogenous variables and parameters that change in time, and then solve for the next period.

Within each time period, we have two main layers of iterations: an outer one where wages are adjusted and an inner one where outputs are adjusted. In the description below, we follow the equations set out in this chapter and will ignore any side equations used only to aggregate variables or to calculate various statistics.

Step 1. Guess the base wages w_m of each of the six labor types. By equation (7.12), this gives the wage of each labor type in every sector.

Step 2. Guess sectoral output levels X_i. Since value added is related to outputs by a fixed proportion, $V_i = v_i X_i$, this gives value added. Since the aggregate capital stock is fixed in each sector in each time period, we also get the ratio of value added to aggregate capital stock V_i/K_i^*.

A. Obtain the price structure:

1. P_i^L from equation (7.1). Since this depends only on the wages and not on output, this could actually be taken out of the output loop.
2. P_i^V from equation (7.7) and V_i/K_i^*
3. P_i^K from equation (7.6), P_i^V, and V_i/K_i^*
4. P_i from equation (7.8) and P_i^V. Remember that P^E is numeraire, and P_i^E comes from P^E through equation (7.13).
5. r_i^K from equation (7.21), P_i, and P_i^K
6. P_i^u from equations (7.26), (7.27), and P_i.

B. Use equations (7.2) and (7.4) (Shephard's lemma) to obtain L_{mi}/L_i^* and L_i^*/V_i from the price structure. Given the current guesses of the V_i's, these give employment levels from equations (7.15) and (7.16); and given the current price structure, wages, and profit rates, they give all household incomes from equations (7.17), (7.18), (7.22), (7.23), and (7.24).

C. To get household consumption demands:

1. Obtain per household total consumption expenditure z_u from the consumption and household income tax function, equation (7.25).

2. Use the demand functions, equations (7.29) and 7.30), to get per household consumption demands of each sector, using a simple search procedure to eliminate the scaling factor χ_u from (7.29).
3. Use equation (7.31) to aggregate to total consumption demands of each sector.

D. Given the exogenous final demand items (government spending and exports), investment and capital replacement demands—computed from equations (7.32) and (7.33), but exogenous within any time period—and the computed household consumption demands, use the material balance equations (7.34) to get a new guess at output levels.

E. Go back to the beginning of Step 2 with this new guess at outputs and iterate until convergence.

Step 3. With the equilibrium output levels, compute labor demands by using equation (7.41). Compare with the exogenous labor supplies. Use the excess demands for each labor type to compute a new guess of the wage levels. Go back to Step 1 with this new set of guesses and iterate until the excess demands for labor go to zero.

To arrive at the new guesses of outputs in the inner iteration, we used a simple Gauss-Seidel procedure where the new guess of outputs is basically that obtained from the material balance equations. In matrix notation, the material balances can be written as

$$X = AX + Q(X) + \overline{F},$$

where X is the vector of outputs, A is the matrix of input-output coefficients, Q is the vector of consumption demands (which are nonlinear functions of output levels X), and $\overline{F}$ is the vector of other, exogenous, final demands. To cut down on the number of Gauss-Seidel iterations, we partially solved this system for the X's:

$$X^{t+1} = (I - A)^{-1}[Q(X^t) + \overline{F}].$$

The guess of the X's in iteration $t + 1$ would be set equal to the result of the computation of the right-hand side of the equation, where consumption final demand is a function of the guess of the X's in iteration t.

To solve the outer wage iteration, we first tried a simple procedure where we used only the excess labor supplies computed in each wage iteration. If we found some labor type to be in 10 percent excess supply, we would lower its wage by 10 percent (or less, in a crude attempt to avoid instability) to try to drive the excess supply toward zero. For reasons that will become clear shortly, this procedure always strongly perturbed the excess supplies of other labor types and diverged rapidly, driving wages toward zero or infinity. In line with the basic approach sketched above, we then turned to a fancier numerical procedure.

This better method turned out to be an algorithm working with the full Jacobian matrix of all own- and cross-wage derivatives. The one we used was designed and programmed in FORTRAN IV by Powell (1970*a*, 1970*b*), and a copy of the deck was kindly provided us by Sherman Robinson. The Powell method basically treats the excess labor demand equations (7.42) as an implicit six-equation system, and varies wages to solve it on the basis of a continuously updated numerical estimate of the Jacobian.[4] On computers such as an IBM 360/65, the cost of a one-period solution using the Powell algorithm usually varied between $5 and $10 (half of which was printing cost). With costs in this range, even the highly complex general equilibrium model turns out to be a tool of economic analysis cheap enough to use in practice.

Experience with Solving the Model

As just mentioned, the algorithm we used in the wage iteration computed the full Jacobian of excess labor supplies with respect

4. The Powell algorithm uses its first $N + 1$ iterations to set up an initial estimate of the Jacobian (in our case $N = 6$, for the six labor types). Since the cost in solving our model is roughly proportional to the number of wage iterations, one wants to minimize their number. We therefore did not go to an algorithm requiring second derivatives, since it would normally require at least $0.5\ N^2 + 1.5\ N$ iterations just to set up the Hessian. With $N = 6$ this would mean a minimum of twenty-seven iterations before the algorithm even began to search for the solution. Of course, given the Hessian, it should take fewer iterations to arrive at the final solution, but since most of our problems (say, after some parametric change or a tax rate change) took only twenty to thirty iterations (and often only ten to fifteen) to solve, it was clearly not worthwhile to compute a Hessian. These results are consistent with a study by Fair (1974), who found that in determining optimal controls for an econometric model (a problem mathematically very similar to our own), an algorithm using first derivatives clearly worked faster than one requiring second derivatives.

to wage changes. This Jacobian is of some interest in itself, since it gives the general equilibrium effects of a wage change on the demand for labor. The computed Jacobian for the 1971 base solution is given in table 7-2, and table 7-3 shows the matrix of elasticities of excess labor demands with respect to wage changes, given the computed 1971 wage levels and labor demands.

First of all, notice that the Jacobian is not symmetrical, as theorists often assume. Asymmetry results from general equilibrium demand effects, where different households consume, save, and are taxed differently. Next, note that at least as it is estimated numerically by the computer, the Jacobian has a diagonal which is *not* dominant in four of its six columns. Lack of diagonal dominance is important in considerations of Walrasian stability and will be discussed below. Finally, and most obviously, note the positive entries in four off-diagonal positions in the Jacobian, or, equivalently, the negative corresponding entries in the elasticity matrix. Two of these entries, viewed in elasticity form, are almost zero and could be due to computing errors, but the other two probably are not. The various labor types are clearly not gross substitutes, as must often be assumed by theorists in their proofs of uniqueness, stability, and optimality of competitive equilibrium (see Arrow and Hahn 1971).

Why don't the excess labor supply functions demonstrate the nice properties that theorists like to assume in their stability proofs? We have already noted that differential income effects across consumer households may spoil symmetry in the Jacobian, but some additional difficulties can be added to this.

To begin, note that the diagonal elements in the elasticity matrix look quite reasonable. All are quite a bit above one, the natural result when elasticities of substitution among labor types are high. The own-wage elasticities also decline, as one would expect, from values of around minus five or six for unskilled labor, down to minus two or three for educated labor. (Details on labor skill definitions appear in chapter 8.)

The problems arise when one looks at the off-diagonal elements of the Jacobian. These indirect effects on employment, which are often assumed to be zero, turn out to dominate in four of the six cases. As indicated by the negative column sums in the Jacobian of table 7-2, if one tries to lower the wage of labor types 2, 4, 5, or 6 to reduce their unemployment, one will end up increasing total unemployment. Clearly, quite an intelligent algorithm will be necessary to reduce all excess labor supplies to

Table 7-2. Jacobian of Excess Labor Supplies, 1971, Base Run

$$J_{kj} = \frac{\partial f_k(w_1, \ldots, w_6)}{\partial w_j}$$

(change in number of workers)

Equations (7.42)	*Labor skill types*[a] 1	2	3	4	5	6
1.	4,048,000	−158,300	−559,600	−1,278,000	−5,650	3,218
2.	−135,700	608,500	−164,600	−383,500	−1,783	945
3.	−467,900	−161,900	2,538,000	−1,594,000	−47,850	−5,668
4.	−997,900	−344,400	−1,511,000	3,458,000	−289,800	−46,000
5.	−4,245	1,005	−79,170	−501,900	250,800	−40,750
6.	−983	103	−16,020	−101,800	−37,170	39,660
Total	2,441,272	−54,992	207,610	−401,200	−131,453	−48,495

Note: In this table f_k is the excess demand function for labor type k, and in Table 7-3 L_k^D is the corresponding level of labor demand. The cost of labor type j is w_j.

a. Labor skill types are defined as: 1, family farm workers; 2, sharecroppers; 3, uneducated; 4, primary-educated; 5, secondary-educated; 6, highly educated.

Table 7-3. Matrix of Elasticities of Excess Labor Demands with Respect to Wage Changes

$$E_{kj} = -J_{kj}\,(w_j/L_k^D)$$

(percentage change)

Equations (7.42)	Labor skill types[a] *1*	2	3	4	5	6
1.	−5.7906	0.5189	1.6674	4.7721	0.0728	−0.0765
2.	0.6440	−6.6176	1.6272	4.7510	0.0762	−0.0746
3.	0.4577	0.3629	−5.1707	4.0698	0.4214	0.0922
4.	0.2865	0.2266	0.9035	−2.5914	0.7491	0.2196
5.	0.0048	−0.0026	0.1847	1.4670	−2.5285	0.7587
6.	0.0043	−0.0010	0.1451	1.1556	1.4554	−2.8677
Wage (per ten workers)	0.4306	0.9867	0.8969	1.1240	3.8769	7.1595
Employment (in tens)	301,016	90,729	440,236	1,499,901	384,548	99,015

Note: Same as table 7-2.

a. Labor skill types same as table 7-2.

zero. A Gauss-Seidel procedure, which looks only at the excess demand–excess supply status of each single labor type to decide whether to raise or lower its wage, would not work. Nor would it help to take the first derivatives of the changes, that is, to use the diagonal but only the diagonal of the Jacobian. Decentralized labor markets would work only with great difficulty here, a result that should be disconcerting to economists.

Although the Jacobian includes all the general equilibrium interactions in the model, the problem of the nondominant diagonal results primarily from our neoclassical treatment of the labor market. The different types of labor substitute for each other with a high elasticity of substitution, but the wage of college-educated labor, for example, is eight times that of illiterate labor. For illustrative purposes, take the extreme case of infinite substitutability between labor types. A wage eight times that of another then implies that the first type of labor is eight times as efficient as the second. One person of the first type will replace eight of the second. Say the primary choice in production is the use of some combination of these two types of labor. If there is unemployment of the first (efficient) type of labor, an attempt to remedy it by lowering its wage may remove some of its unemployment. But eight of the second type of laborers will be thrown out of work for each of the first type brought back into employment. Total unemployment in the economy (in people, not in "labor efficiency units") will rise.

The results will be mitigated somewhat by the facts that there is not infinite substitutability between labor types, and that aggregate demand effects will arise to a small extent when the wage of one labor type is lowered. As long as the elasticity of substitution is greater than unity, the immediate effect of lowering the wage of the higher skilled worker will still be to create a net increase in unemployment. The increase will not be as much as if the elasticity were infinite, but it will still be there.

The aggregate demand effect, though small, does operate to reduce net unemployment eventually. When the wage of the higher skilled workers is reduced, the entire price level will fall a little. In our model, this has the primary effect of increasing the real value of payments to proprietors and transfers, which increase aggregate demand. This mechanism was outlined in the description of the one-sector model of chapter 6. The important point to keep in mind is that when several labor types substitute for each other with a high elasticity, this effect is weak compared with the substitution effect described above whereby net unemployment increased. The wages of all the labor types will have to fall, even if only one type had some unemployment, to cancel out the substitution effect. Eventually the price level will have fallen enough to increase the total demand for labor.

A falling price level is the mechanism giving the model a way out of the dilemma noted above. Reducing the wage of the efficient workers increases net unemployment because they substitute for a greater number of less efficient workers. But in the second round, the wage of the less efficient workers would fall, and they would get back their jobs, but at the expense of the higher skilled workers. If there were no aggregate demand effects, we would be back where we started, but with a lower price level. The spiral downward into the abyss would simply continue, without a decrease in unemployment.

The misbehavior of the Jacobian raises several theoretical issues. Obviously, any proofs that require the Jacobian to exhibit gross substitution, a dominant diagonal, or symmetry will fall apart. These assumptions are often used in proofs of the uniqueness, stability, and optimality of competitive equilibrium, and theorists have found great difficulty in weakening them (see Arrow and Hahn 1971). Another issue is whether, with a Jacobian such as we found, it is possible for the economy to get stuck in a local minimum where unemployment exists for all labor classes and where a decrease in any wage would result in higher unemployment. In fact, this may have occurred in several of the experiments we conducted. But it was always possible to get around the problem by some ad hoc means, such as tightening the output iteration (which would mean the problem arose because product markets did not clear fully before the algorithm got back information on excess labor demands owing to the current wage guess—a situation that might well occur in the real world), or shocking the wage structure by, say, increasing or decreasing all wages by 10 or 20 percent and letting the algorithm proceed from there. (It would mean a local minimum really had been found, if the algorithm did not return to the same spot).

References

Arrow, Kenneth J., and Frank H. Hahn. 1971. *General competitive analysis*. San Francisco: Holden-Day.

Fair, Ray C. 1974. On the solution of optimal control problems as maximization problems. *Annals of economic and social measurement* 3:135–54.

Fishlow, Albert. 1973. Brazilian income size distribution: Another look. Berkeley: University of California, Department of Economics; processed. Published in Portuguese as: Distribuição da renda no Brasil: Um novo exame. *Dados* 11 (1973):10–80. (Published by Instituto Universitario de Pesquisas, Rio de Janeiro.)

Frisch, Ragnar. 1959. A complete scheme for computing all direct and cross demand elasticities in a model with many sectors. *Econometrica* 27:177–96.

Johansen, Leif. 1974. *A multi-sectoral study of economic growth.* 2nd ed. Amsterdam: North-Holland.

Mata, Milton da, and Edmar L. Bacha. 1973. Emprêgo e salarios na indústria de transformação, 1949–69. *Pesquisa e planajamento economico* 3(2):303–40.

Powell, M. J. D. 1970*a*. A hybrid method for nonlinear equations. In Philip Rabinowitz, ed. *Numerical methods for nonlinear algebraic equations*. London: Gordon and Breach.

———. 1970*b*. A FORTRAN subroutine for solving systems of nonlinear algebraic equations. In Philip Rabinowitz, ed. *Numerical methods for nonlinear algebraic equations*. London: Gordon and Breach.

Sato, Kazuo. 1972. Additive utility functions for double-log consumer demand functions. *Journal of political economy* 80: 102–24.

8

Data for the General Equilibrium Model and a Base Solution

Frank J. Lysy and Lance Taylor

SINCE MULTISECTORAL MODELS USE NUMBERS referring to all parts of the economy, they are very data intensive. Their designers typically draw on disparate, not mutually consistent sources to get a complete data set, and in the best of cases many of the parameters or even basic flows are guesstimated. This data problem is only made worse when the model is extended to deal with income distribution, as in the present study. An honest modelbuilder can never assert that he has numbers truly descriptive of the economy of a country such as Brazil; he has an approximation, and in many cases it may be a bad one. In getting together a data set, one can only hope to design an approximation as free of error as possible, at least with respect to the more important bits of data. Our techniques for doing this are described here.

The basic approach adopted for data generation was to find a complete, consistent data set for a base year. Such an approach is not strictly necessary; for example, one could find some baseyear numbers for variables exogenous to a general equilibrium model, and then solve it for the endogenous items. We chose not to do this, on the ground that forcing the model to reproduce a completely specified base year would be a good test of whether it were well formulated in terms of both theory and computer programming. This turned out to be a sensible choice, for by the time the model did duplicate the base-year data set (to a precision of around 0.1 percent), small but potentially serious logical errors in both its algebraic equations and FORTRAN coding had to be discovered and remedied. At least we now have this minor assurance that the logical structure of the model is error-free.

One major purpose of the present study is to explain trends in Brazilian income distribution over the 1960s. For this reason, a base year near the beginning of that decade is convenient. Because there were industrial and demographic censuses in 1960 (and an input-output table for 1959 based on the former), we selected 1959 as the starting point. In succeeding sections, we describe how a complete data set was constructed from a variety of sources.

Interindustry Flow Data

The accounting conventions underlying the model are built around interindustry flows. The basic source is the 1959 input-output table constructed by van Rijckeghem (1969). The documentation on this table is far from complete, but it appears to be set up in producers' prices. The original table has thirty-two sectors (including three fictional accounting sectors), but we aggregated these to twenty-four for use in the model. In addition, we added a twenty-fifth sector without intermediate flows to represent employment of domestic servants in households, an activity treated as part of value added in the original table. The sector names appear in table 8-1, along with intermediate and final demand flows for 1959.

Table 8-1 shows that the first two sectors are agricultural (plant and animal products, respectively), and sectors 3 through 5 represent tertiary activities in the economy. Sector 3, commerce, is an aggregate of van Rijckeghem's commerce and transport sectors. As discussed below, demands for its output are determined by markups on final demands for consumption and investment goods. Sectors 6 through 23 are mining and manufacturing activities, 24 is construction, and 25 represents domestic servants. As usual in input-output tables, this aggregation scheme lumps together a number of large subsectors in agricultural and tertiary activities and is excessively detailed for manufacturing. We chose to maintain the manufacturing disaggregation because of the possible importance of differing income elasticities of demand for products of different sectors, and we would have preferred a parallel treatment of the other parts of the economy as well. In any case, intermediate flows appear in the first twenty-five rows and columns of table 8-1.

Besides aggregation and addition of the twenty-fifth sector, we modified the accounting of imports and consumption expenditures in the 1959 table. All imports in the original table were treated as competitive, but we thought it more realistic to assume they are noncompetitive for intermediate, investment, and consumption use. Control totals for imports by these three classes are available for Brazil (for example, Baer and Kerstenetzky 1972, tables 8 and 9). The consumption and capital goods import totals appear in row 26 of table 8-1, in columns 31 and 35 respectively. These were broken down by sector according to rough correspondences between the input-output classification and the import classification of Baer and Kerstenetzky (1972), and the resulting imports were subtracted from both the original table's final demands and competitive imports to maintain double-entry accounting totals. The remaining imports were then treated as noncompetitive intermediates, calculated for each sector in proportion to import coefficients from a 1971 Brazilian input-output table (see Carneiro Leão and others 1973). To compensate for the increased intermediate import costs, domestic input-output coefficients from the van Rijckeghem table were reduced to maintain total sectoral costs constant. In most sectors all coefficients were cut back proportionately, but in sectors 1, 8, and 16 larger reductions in the original coefficients for fuel and fertilizer inputs were made. More elaborate coefficient-scaling procedures such as the well-known RAS method might have been used for these calculations, but given the imprecision of the basic data, our more rough and ready procedures seemed adequate. The noncompetitive intermediate import levels by sector that these calculations generated appear in columns 1 through 25 of row 26 of table 8-1.

Since consumption patterns differ according to income level and social station, in a model focusing on income distribution it is useful to group consumers into various classes. We used four—one class made up of rural consumers at fairly low income levels, and three classes of urban consumers grouped by increasing income. Details on the makeup of these groupings are given in table 8-8, but their base-year consumption levels appear in columns 27 through 30 of table 8-1.

Table 8-1. Interindustry Accounting for 1959
(thousands of cruzeiros)

	1	2	3	4	5
Sector	Crop agriculture	Animal agriculture	Commerce	Electricity	Services
1. Crop agriculture	11,118	19,382	7,374	297	591
2. Animal agriculture	18	0	0	0	338
3. Commerce	2,716	235	25,474	408	2,882
4. Electricity	150	95	1,911	3,639	895
5. Services	4,780	1,754	50,855	1,819	16,383
6. Mining	578	0	3,081	124	124
7. Nonmetallic minerals	203	0	295	0	343
8. Metallurgy	2,685	1,713	635	0	178
9. Machine tools	0	0	0	0	196
10. Electrical goods	0	0	0	0	196
11. Transport goods	150	0	10,359	0	978
12. Wood and furniture	237	0	345	0	147
13. Paper	669	0	974	0	49
14. Rubber	43	0	9,535	0	0
15. Leather	0	0	0	0	820
16. Chemicals	4,822	3,165	30,747	1,136	7,379
17. Textiles	506	0	736	0	1,306
18. Clothing	0	0	72	0	981
19. Food	0	1,218	0	0	981
20. Beverages	0	0	0	0	1,989
21. Tobacco	0	0	0	0	0
22. Publishing	0	0	2,933	0	4,675
23. Miscellaneous	0	0	0	0	2,378
24. Construction	1,817	0	1,955	0	24,513
25. Domestic servants	0	0	0	0	0
26. Noncompetitive imports	19,514	1,904	3,382	272	1,357
27. Total intermediate purchases	50,007	29,466	150,664	7,695	69,680
28. Value added	129,857	43,845	180,199	10,051	222,460
29. Payments to entrepreneurs	130,628	44,103	82,410	0	44,820
30. Value added taxes	35,521	11,993	46,343	1,117	47,167
31. Total output	346,014	129,406	459,616	18,863	384,127

6 Mining	7 *Non-metallic minerals*	8 *Metal-lurgy*	9 *Machine tools*	10 *Elec-trical goods*	11 *Trans-port goods*	12 *Wood and furni-ture*	13 *Paper*	14 *Rub-ber*
742	716	1,135	53	93	135	7,654	646	4,371
0	1	4	0	3	0	14	0	0
1,636	4,774	4,505	826	1,527	1,248	3,147	2,035	635
67	625	1,400	139	156	214	287	406	119
940	3,282	6,409	2,173	2,995	6,358	2,853	1,864	1,421
1,641	2,612	3,664	47	46	90	44	81	18
5	4,040	813	90	643	363	589	1,042	110
56	1,418	35,594	10,628	13,517	18,226	2,493	3,932	1,435
0	2	16	349	1,385	229	4	0	0
3	57	94	928	3,580	1,439	12	0	0
0	0	1	6	10	11,893	0	0	0
7	537	946	383	616	639	9,627	1,266	88
15	1,484	3,706	57	212	181	1,196	16,074	536
1	99	243	57	63	1,734	108	247	3,538
0	4	1	19	1	23	61	1	12
2,908	4,113	4,794	396	1,782	1,131	1,322	2,395	1,404
12	1,119	2,340	69	271	223	2,104	3,012	2,254
0	0	0	0	0	2	0	0	0
0	4	41	0	6	8	21	30	0
0	1	3	0	1	1	23	3	0
0	0	0	0	0	0	0	0	0
86	281	225	117	170	206	296	59	48
0	0	12	0	0	0	0	0	0
0	0	0	0	0	0	0	0	0
0	0	0	0	0	0	0	0	0
316	430	14368	901	1,354	1,014	150	529	342
8,436	25,597	80,314	17,238	28,440	45,358	32,005	33,622	16,332
9,578	21,280	44,268	14,189	16,418	31,007	17,447	12,371	12,515
866	3,780	1,687	730	404	607	5,481	464	197
1,033	5,500	10,088	1,476	1,664	3,127	1,725	819	1,571
19,912	56,158	136,357	33,631	46,925	80,098	56,660	47,276	30,615

(Table continues on the following page.)

Table 8-1 (continued)

	15	16	17	18	19
Sector	*Leather*	*Chemicals*	*Textiles*	*Cloth-ing*	*Food*
1. Crop agriculture	325	14,366	19,367	21	82,265
2. Animal agriculture	2,070	1,069	669	100	53,595
3. Commerce	866	12,896	5,458	1,777	10,149
4. Electricity	66	762	1,122	107	1,294
5. Services	674	8,059	7,377	2,715	10,208
6. Mining	26	2,614	136	6	1,213
7. Nonmetallic minerals	65	905	842	207	1,389
8. Metallurgy	115	2,307	2,510	401	2,581
9. Machine tools	0	100	24	0	0
10. Electrical goods	0	29	0	0	0
11. Transport goods	4	0	11	0	0
12. Wood and furniture	41	813	945	335	1,405
13. Paper	69	2,814	2,902	461	3,959
14. Rubber	1	175	209	1,599	256
15. Leather	2,068	73	34	6,056	0
16. Chemicals	1,101	55,503	13,029	471	7,040
17. Textiles	134	2,270	38,258	9,120	2,996
18. Clothing	0	4	0	75	1
19. Food	3	346	82	2	31,400
20. Beverages	1	448	6	3	53
21. Tobacco	0	0	0	0	0
22. Publishing	44	421	273	137	654
23. Miscellaneous	10	0	0	54	0
24. Construction	0	0	0	0	0
25. Domestic servants	0	0	0	0	0
26. Noncompetitive imports	56	31,122	1,568	107	1,594
27. Total intermediate purchases	7,738	137,097	94,823	23,755	212,053
28. Value added	3,891	48,478	47,776	10,308	53,899
29. Payments to entrepreneurs	835	1,889	4,799	3,736	12,475
30. Value added taxes	302	11,056	9,278	2,478	6,565
31. Total output	12,766	198,521	156,676	40,277	284,992

20 Beverages	21 Tobacco	22 Publishing	23 Miscellaneous	24 Construction	25 Domestic servants	26 Total intermediate sales	27 Consumer class 1
2,770	1,872	11	101	318	0	175,723	89,497
27	1	0	73	0	0	57,982	8,619
1,514	360	928	401	31,058	0	117,456	45,019
129	20	128	68	0	0	13,799	673
2,144	492	2,005	1,243	7,681	0	146,484	66,265
29	2	6	112	133	0	16,426	46
269	129	11	208	35,347	0	47,928	560
618	276	264	1,298	24,136	0	127,016	190
0	0	0	0	0	0	2,305	192
0	0	0	51	3,653	0	10,042	1,110
0	0	0	14	1,033	0	24,459	74
336	150	25	461	14,393	0	33,742	2,814
948	703	8,138	449	0	0	45,596	185
62	27	2	72	0	0	18,071	54
0	0	7	88	0	0	9,267	176
1,091	50	1,109	934	2,825	0	150,646	10,540
717	321	118	515	0	0	68,401	14,339
0	0	0	0	0	0	1,135	6,163
3,071	9	1	2	0	0	37,226	41,403
1,079	1	1	4	0	0	3,617	4,457
0	2,280	0	0	0	0	2,280	3,547
133	22	452	65	0	0	11,297	930
0	0	24	163	0	0	2,651	2,057
0	0	0	0	0	0	28,285	6,167
0	0	0	0	0	0	0	3,079
247	0	254	468	3,486	0	84,734	696
15,204	6,713	13,484	6,789	124,063	0	1,236,565	308,853
7,393	2,045	11,172	7,037	36,749	45,925	1,040,156	0
894	147	1,490	364	17,500	0	360,793	0
4,462	4,256	808	594	1,108	0	210,049	0
27,952	13,158	26,954	15,274	179,419	45,925	2,847,561	308,853

(Table continues on the following page.)

Table 8-1 (continued)

Sector	28 Con- sumer class 2	29 Con- sumer class 3	30 Con- sumer class 4	31 Total house- hold con- sumption	32 Govern- ment demand
1. Crop agriculture	39,205	11,918	10,570	151,190	651
2. Animal agriculture	16,903	10,428	24,140	60,090	500
3. Commerce	98,733	42,265	72,471	258,488	27,096
4. Electricity	1,088	667	1,428	3,857	1,207
5. Services	76,914	32,906	61,560	237,645	0
6. Mining	68	43	57	215	662
7. Nonmetallic minerals	1,519	1,090	2,655	5,824	2,203
8. Metallurgy	301	143	361	994	5,175
9. Machine tools	669	682	2,226	3,770	3,251
10. Electrical goods	5,450	4,904	12,309	23,772	1,940
11. Transport goods	2,381	2,040	12,201	16,696	3,545
12. Wood and furniture	5,971	3,625	6,126	18,535	432
13. Paper	227	137	280	829	850
14. Rubber	2,048	2,957	7,146	12,206	303
15. Leather	512	228	490	1,406	30
16. Chemicals	15,114	5,154	4,150	34,958	6,222
17. Textiles	31,753	14,165	26,201	86,459	892
18. Clothing	13,726	6,261	12,451	38,601	512
19. Food	100,829	27,582	12,899	182,713	2,012
20. Beverages	7,521	4,401	7,940	24,319	1
21. Tobacco	4,486	1,251	1,460	10,744	0
22. Publishing	5,053	2,280	6,011	14,274	1,307
23. Miscellaneous	3,972	1,798	3,299	11,126	140
24. Construction	9,935	4,834	10,199	31,135	10,000
25. Domestic servants	4,521	5,044	33,280	45,925	0
26. Noncompetitive imports	2,767	1,635	4,969	10,068	0
27. Total intermediate purchases	451,667	188,437	336,879	1,285,834	68,931
28. Value added	0	0	0	0	89,481
29. Payments to entrepreneurs	0	0	0	0	0
30. Value added taxes	0	0	0	0	0
31. Total output	451,667	188,437	336,879	1,285,834	158,412

Note: See table 8-8 for definitions of consumer classes.

33	34	35	36	37	38
New capital demand	*Replacement capital demand*	*Total capital demand*	*Export demand*	*Competitive import supply*	*Total output*
0	0	6,555	11,897	0	346,014
0	0	10,445	391	0	129,406
0	0	22,730	33,838	0	459,616
0	0	0	0	0	18,863
0	0	0	0	0	384,127
0	0	0	2,609	0	19,912
0	0	0	203	0	56,158
0	0	3,152	19	0	136,357
0	0	24,155	151	0	33,631
0	0	11,161	11	0	46,925
0	0	35,308	91	0	80,098
0	0	3,873	78	0	56,660
0	0	0	1	0	47,276
0	0	0	35	0	30,615
0	0	0	2,062	0	12,766
0	0	0	6,694	0	198,521
0	0	0	924	0	156,676
0	0	0	29	0	40,277
0	0	0	63,043	0	284,992
0	0	0	15	0	27,952
0	0	0	133	0	13,158
0	0	0	76	0	26,954
0	0	1,301	56	0	15,274
0	0	110,000	0	0	179,419
0	0	0	0	0	45,925
0	0	55,099	0	149,901	149,901
0	0	283,779	122,366	149,901	2,847,561
0	0	0	0	0	1,129,637
0	0	0	0	0	360,793
0	0	0	0	0	210,049
0	0	283,779	122,366	149,901	4,548,051

Total consumption levels from the input-output table were used as controls for disaggregation of demands across the consumer classes, as were total expenditures by the four groups. Budget shares for the goods entering the consumers' demand functions (equation 7.29) were then assumed to vary more or less in line with cross-section consumption regressions based on 1962 data from Lopes (1972), as were the Engel elasticities across groups. Total consumer demand for the output of commerce (sector 3) is given by the product of commercialization margins and consumer demands for the other sectors' outputs (see equation 7.30). As equation (7.26) shows, the consumers' price for any product is the sum of its producers' price and its trade markup. Since producers' prices in the base period were set at unity, the consumers' price is one plus the markup. [1] Given these prices and income by consumer groups, the base-year budget shares were converted to the demand levels appearing in table 8-1. Table 8-2 gives the trade margins for consumer goods, budget shares, and income elasticities used in the model. Price elasticities of demand were calculated as described in chapter 7, with the scaling parameter σ^u set to a value of 0.5 for all four consumer classes.

The remaining columns of table 8-1 give final demands for government purchases, capital investment, exports, and competitive imports. Since the van Rijckeghem input-output table does not give a breakdown of investment into replacement and net capital formation, these categories are left blank, although his total investment figures (modified for import content, as discussed above) appear in column 35. Column 37 is largely blank because of our treatment of all imports as noncompetitive.

The last rows of table 8-1 give a breakdown of nonintermediate purchases of sectors into our concept of value added (that is, payments to employed workers and to capital) in row 28, payments to proprietors in row 29, and value added taxes in row 30. How these totals were broken down into a detailed functional distribution of income is discussed next.

1. Consumer goods trade margins were derived from the 1960 Brazilian Census of Commerce, and then rescaled to correspond to total demands for output of sector 3 from the input-output table. Rural margins for agricultural products were set lower than the corresponding urban margins to account for less processing in the countryside. Margins on capital goods appear in row 3 of table 8-5.

Employment and Labor Payments

To break down the input-output table's concept of value added into our own accounting categories, we began by subtracting indirect taxes, which appear in row 30 of table 8-1 and also in table 8-3. These levels were calculated according to a set of indirect tax rates, which were in turn derived from the known total of indirect tax receipts in 1959 (see the GNP accounts in Vargas Foundation 1971) and from a breakdown of tax payments by sector in table 44 of Langoni (1974). These tax rates appear in table 8-3.

The next component of value added in the input-output table to be split out is payments to proprietors. For manufacturing sectors, both the number of and total payments to proprietors were taken directly from the industrial census. Division of the one by the other gave the average remuneration of these people by sector. For the other sectors, we relied on a computer printout summarizing the data used by Fishlow in his studies of the Brazilian income distribution (Fishlow 1972 and 1973, and Fishlow and Meesook 1972), which he kindly made available. This printout is based on a subsample of the 1960 demographic census and gives income distribution by five classes in the economically active population (family workers and sharecroppers in agriculture, and employees, self-employed, and employers in agriculture, manufacturing, services, commerce, and government). We treated Fishlow's self-employed category as being equivalent to our proprietors, and used his data to determine their numbers and remuneration levels in nonmanufacturing sectors. The results of these calculations appear in the first two columns of table 8-4.[2] For some of our sectors that are aggregated in Fishlow's data (such as the two types of agriculture and construction), estimates of numbers of both proprietors and employees were made in proportion to either gross output from the van Rijckeghem table or total economically active population from the censuses, whichever seemed more appropriate.

2. Note that all employment levels in table 8-4 are measured in *tens* of persons. We followed this convention in all work with the model, to scale labor payments per ten persons per year around unity, the same as in the price system. Unless otherwise indicated, all model results should be interpreted as per ten people instead of per capita.

Table 8-2. Consumption Parameters for the Four Consumer Classes

	Commercialization markups		Rural households (class 1)	
Sector	Rural (class 1)	Urban (classes 2–4)	Budget shares	Engel elasticities
1. Crop agriculture	0.075	0.221	0.31150	0.64
2. Animal agriculture	0.075	0.221	0.03000	1.92
3. Commerce	n.c.	n.c.	n.c.	n.c.
4. Electricity	—	—	0.00218	1.38
5. Services	—	—	0.21455	1.19
6. Mining	—	—	0.00015	1.00
7. Nonmetallic minerals	0.665	0.665	0.00302	1.80
8. Metallurgy	0.560	0.560	0.00096	1.15
9. Machine tools	0.560	0.560	0.00097	1.80
10. Electrical goods	0.670	0.670	0.00600	1.80
11. Transport goods	0.470	0.470	0.00035	2.31
12. Wood and furniture	0.650	0.650	0.01503	1.40
13. Paper	0.650	0.650	0.00099	1.21
14. Rubber	0.650	0.650	0.00029	2.10
15. Leather	0.650	0.650	0.00094	0.90
16. Chemicals	0.600	0.600	0.05460	0.99
17. Textiles	0.505	0.505	0.06987	1.04
18. Clothing	0.505	0.505	0.03003	1.04
19. Food	0.305	0.305	0.17494	1.08
20. Beverages	0.305	0.305	0.01883	0.84
21. Tobacco	0.305	0.305	0.01500	0.56
22. Publishing	0.650	0.650	0.00497	1.44
23. Miscellaneous	0.650	0.650	0.01099	1.10
24. Construction	—	—	0.01997	1.30
25. Domestic servants	—	—	0.00997	1.68
26. Noncompetitive imports	0.730	0.730	0.00390	2.10

— Not applicable; that is, there were no markups.
n.c. Not calculated the same way as the other sectors.
Note: See table 8-8 for definitions of consumer classes.

Poor urban households (class 2)		*Mid-income urban households (class 3)*		*Rich urban households (class 4)*	
Budget shares	*Engel elasticities*	*Budget shares*	*Engel elasticities*	*Budget shares*	*Engel elasticities*
0.10595	0.48	0.07720	0.32	0.03830	0.24
0.04568	1.80	0.06755	1.44	0.08747	1.20
n.c.	n.c.	n.c.	n.c.	n.c.	n.c.
0.00241	1.38	0.00354	1.44	0.00424	1.44
0.17029	1.00	0.17463	1.07	0.18274	1.14
0.00015	1.00	0.00023	0.90	0.00017	0.80
0.00560	1.70	0.00963	1.30	0.01312	1.10
0.00104	1.10	0.00118	1.20	0.00167	1.10
0.00231	1.80	0.00565	1.90	0.01031	1.30
0.02015	1.80	0.04346	1.90	0.06102	1.30
0.00775	2.42	0.01591	2.75	0.05324	1.87
0.02181	1.40	0.03174	0.90	0.03000	0.80
0.00083	1.43	0.00120	1.21	0.00137	1.10
0.00748	2.20	0.02588	1.80	0.03499	1.30
0.00187	1.10	0.00200	1.00	0.00240	0.90
0.05354	0.83	0.04376	0.66	0.01971	0.55
0.10580	0.96	0.11313	0.84	0.11705	0.64
0.04573	0.96	0.05000	0.84	0.05562	0.64
0.29133	0.84	0.19102	0.54	0.04997	0.42
0.02173	0.91	0.03048	0.77	0.03076	0.63
0.01297	0.49	0.00867	0.42	0.00566	0.35
0.01846	1.44	0.01996	1.68	0.02944	1.20
0.01451	1.10	0.01574	1.10	0.01616	1.00
0.02200	1.30	0.02566	1.30	0.03028	1.10
0.01001	1.76	0.02677	1.76	0.09879	1.04
0.01060	2.20	0.01501	1.90	0.02552	1.50

Table 8-3. Tax Rates and Receipts, 1959
(receipts in thousands of cruzeiros)

	Value added taxes		*Labor taxes*		*Profit taxes*	
Sector	*Rate*	*Receipts*	*Rate*	*Receipts*	*Rate*	*Receipts*
1. Crop agriculture	0.12	35,521	—	—	—	—
2. Animal agriculture	0.12	11,993	—	—	—	—
3. Commerce	0.15	46,343	—	—	0.20	11,299
4. Electricity	0.10	1,117	—	—	0.20	904
5. Services	0.15	47,167	—	—	0.20	31,791
6. Mining	0.09	1,033	0.18	637	0.20	929
7. Nometallic minerals	0.18	5,500	0.18	1,815	0.20	1,539
8. Metallurgy	0.18	10,088	0.18	3,138	0.20	3,995
9. Machine tools	0.09	1,476	0.18	1,246	0.20	981
10. Electrical goods	0.09	1,664	0.18	1,123	0.20	1,532
11. Transport goods	0.09	3,127	0.18	1,755	0.20	3,241
12. Wood and furniture	0.07	1,725	0.18	1,702	0.20	1,004
13. Paper	0.06	819	0.18	648	0.20	1,281
14. Rubber	0.11	1,571	0.18	427	0.20	1,641
15. Leather	0.06	302	0.18	303	0.20	311
16. Chemicals	0.18	11,056	0.18	2,431	0.20	5,321
17. Textiles	0.15	9,278	0.18	4,073	0.20	3,234
18. Clothing	0.15	2,478	0.18	1,141	0.20	398
19. Food	0.09	6,565	0.18	3,023	0.20	5,601
20. Beverages	0.35	4,462	0.18	675	0.20	433
21. Tobacco	0.66	4,256	0.18	197	0.20	119
22. Publishing	0.06	808	0.18	1,052	0.20	691
23. Miscellaneous	0.07	594	0.18	576	0.20	394
24. Construction	0.02	1,108	—	—	—	—
25. Domestic servants	—	—	—	—	—	—
26. Government	—	—	0.18	16,107	—	—

— Not applicable.

Since there has been a good deal of discussion in Brazil about the role of education in determining the income distribution (see the Fishlow papers cited above and Langoni 1973), we thought it useful to disaggregate the employed labor force by educational categories. To arrive at an approximate disaggregation, we went through several steps. First the total payments to labor and employment were calculated for each sector, most from the industrial census for manufacturing sectors, and the rest from Fishlow's data and the demographic census. Next, labor taxes were subtracted from total labor payments, after assuming with Bacha and others (1972) a labor tax rate of 18 percent for all types of labor in manufacturing and government employment. The corresponding sectoral tax receipts appear in table 8-3.

The employment totals themselves were broken down by educational classes (those who had completed less than four years of school, four to eight years, eight to twelve years, and more than twelve years) according to the average proportions from the five published state volumes of the 1960 demographic census (which refer in principle to economically active population, not employment). Employment levels by labor type and sector appear in table 8-4. Employees are classified by education under the headings "uneducated," "primary-educated," "secondary-educated," and "highly educated." In line with Fishlow, two specifically agricultural labor types—family workers and sharecroppers—are also separated in the data.[3]

Given employment and total labor payments net of taxes, one can easily derive an average wage in each sector. In the manufacturing sectors, this was broken down into wages by each of the educational types in two steps. First, the wage level for highly educated workers was set equal to the wage of "technical" employees in each sector from the industrial census. Wages for uneducated, primary-educated, and secondary-educated workers were then set in the proportions 1:1.9009:5.0450 so as just to exhaust the labor payments remaining after subtracting payments to highly educated workers. These proportions are roughly in line with observed income differentials by educational level in 1960 (see Langoni 1973, chap. 4). In nonmanufacturing sectors, wages by education type were set in line with the 1960 size distribution of income by sector and the breakdown of the labor force by education level. The wage relatives for the two types of agricultural workers are from Fishlow's computer printout. All wage levels appear in table 8-4.

3. Fishlow actually constructed two sets of income distribution estimates for 1960, one without and one with imputation of incomes to groups of workers receiving a substantial share of their income in kind. (For details on the differences between the two sets of estimates, see Fishlow and Meesook 1972.) Our data are based on his income-imputed estimates, that is, the "wages" of agricultural family workers and domestic servants in table 8-4 include substantial nonmonetary components. The demographic census puts the incomes of many of these people at zero.

Table 8-4. Employment and Labor Payments in the Base Year
(employment in tens; payment in thousands of 1959 cruzeiros)

	Proprietors		*Family farm workers*		*Sharecroppers*	
Sector	*Number*	*Payment*	*Number*	*Wage*	*Number*	*Wage*
1. Crop agriculture	419,220	0.31159	311,020	0.0979	61,600	0.2349
2. Animal agriculture	141,540	0.31159	60,000	0.0979	20,000	0.2349
3. Commerce	116,000	0.71043	—	—	—	—
4. Electricity	—	—	—	—	—	—
5. Services	112,500	0.39840	—	—	—	—
6. Mining	117	5.00007	—	—	—	—
7. Nonmetallic minerals	1,550	2.43911	—	—	—	—
8. Metallurgy	286	5.89738	—	—	—	—
9. Machine tools	83	8.80133	—	—	—	—
10. Electrical goods	32	12.81968	—	—	—	—
11. Transport goods	141	4.30795	—	—	—	—
12. Wood and furniture	1,610	3.40534	—	—	—	—
13. Paper	26	18.11914	—	—	—	—
14. Rubber	10	20.48333	—	—	—	—
15. Leather	208	4.01785	—	—	—	—
16. Chemicals	186	10.14329	—	—	—	—
17. Textiles	244	19.65780	—	—	—	—
18. Clothing	611	6.11452	—	—	—	—
19. Food	2,524	4.94336	—	—	—	—
20. Beverages	239	3.74504	—	—	—	—
21. Tobacco	17	8.85783	—	—	—	—
22. Publishing	193	7.70802	—	—	—	—
23. Miscellaneous	140	6.08576	—	—	—	—
24. Construction	3,500	5.00000	—	—	—	—
25. Domestic servants	—	—	—	—	—	—
26. Government	—	—	—	—	—	—

— Not applicable.

Payments to Capital

After accounting for indirect taxes and payments to proprietors and employed workers, we assumed that the rest of sectoral costs could be assigned as quasi rents to fixed capital stocks. Per unit of capital, these quasi rents (or capital costs) are directly related to the share of profits in total value added and inversely related to the capital–value added ratio, since by simple accounting the following identity must hold:

Capital share in value added = (Quasi rent) × (Capital/value added).

Further, the derivation leading to equation (7.21) shows that the

Workers by educational level							
Uneducated		*Primary-educated*		*Secondary-educated*		*Highly educated*	
Number	*Wage*	*Number*	*Wage*	*Number*	*Wage*	*Number*	*Wage*
314,111	0.2055	15,090	0.4110	—	—	—	—
35,889	0.2055	5,000	0.4110	—	—	—	—
68,800	0.2955	82,560	0.5910	19,780	1.4774	860	5.0000
3,017	0.3294	2,953	0.6588	424	1.6470	26	5.5000
131,350	0.1859	49,950	0.3718	3,515	0.9294	185	6.0800
3,781	0.6974	625	1.3257	18	3.5184	1	7.9195
12,551	0.5823	2,125	1.1068	139	2.9375	3	5.2836
8,619	0.6342	7,882	1.2055	506	3.1994	135	6.2645
2,387	0.6489	3,377	1.2334	360	3.2735	8	3.8846
1,730	0.5437	3,399	1.0336	608	2.7431	23	5.2701
3,133	0.6953	4,431	1.3217	472	3.5078	11	5.5846
8,700	0.5126	4,636	0.9740	181	2.5861	3	4.4050
2,617	0.6485	1,394	1.2327	55	3.2716	1	5.4234
748	0.6186	1,164	1.1758	156	3.1206	10	5.0843
1,583	0.5574	635	1.0595	45	2.8119	1	4.0694
4,547	0.5795	7,074	1.1030	947	2.9365	63	4.5120
20,914	0.5140	11,385	0.9770	280	2.5929	7	4.1408
4,972	0.4581	3,949	0.8708	266	2.3111	2	4.2200
16,071	0.5205	7,556	0.9895	355	2.6262	5	4.0989
2,780	0.6719	1,307	1.2772	61	3.3898	1	3.8106
871	0.6252	410	1.1884	19	3.1541	1	3.9000
1,388	0.4859	3,868	0.9236	591	2.4513	22	6.7411
1,496	0.5025	1,915	0.9555	232	2.5359	8	3.5771
54,166	0.2519	22,765	0.5039	1,335	1.5115	236	4.0000
111,000	0.2688	38,100	0.4032	900	0.8047	—	—
30,325	0.2195	54,585	0.4390	31,538	1.0970	4,852	5.0010

quasi rent is in turn broken down according to the following formula:

$$\text{Quasi rent} = \frac{\text{Profit rate}}{1 - \text{Profit tax rate}} + \text{Depreciation charge.}$$

These two relationships in effect mean that once a sector's capital–value added ratio is determined, its profit rate follows as a residual, and the reverse is also true. According to our scheme of calculation, the capital share is given after subtraction of all other payments from value added in the van Rijckeghem table, and the depreciation charge is fixed once the makeup of each sector's capital aggregate (the b_{ki} of equation 7.3) and depreciation rates are known. Values for the b_{ki} were calculated by Lopes

Table 8-5. Makeup of the Aggregate Capital Stock by Sector and Depreciation Rates

	Sector of origin										
Sector of destination	Crop agriculture	Animal agriculture	Commerce	Metallurgy	Machine tools	Electrical goods	Transport goods	Wood and furniture	Miscellaneous	Construction	Noncompetitive imports
1. Crop agriculture	0.3905	—	0.0483	—	0.0835	0.0429	0.0777	—	—	0.2365	0.1200
2. Animal agriculture	—	0.6209	0.0225	—	—	—	—	—	—	0.2360	0.1200
3. Commerce	—	—	0.1020	—	0.1540	0.0780	0.3985	—	—	0.1985	0.0690
4. Electricity	—	—	0.0887	—	0.3120	0.1605	—	—	—	0.3550	0.0838
5. Services	—	—	0.0223	—	0.0532	0.0274	0.0538	—	—	0.8244	0.0189
6. Mining	—	—	0.0241	—	0.0854	0.0441	—	—	—	0.7450	0.1014
7. Nonmetallic minerals	—	—	0.0762	—	0.2327	0.1198	0.0766	—	—	0.3389	0.1558
8. Metallurgy	—	—	0.0882	0.2392	0.1650	0.0849	0.0094	—	—	0.1198	0.2935
9. Machine tools	—	—	0.0775	—	0.2706	0.1402	—	—	—	0.1589	0.3528
10. Electrical goods	—	—	0.0712	—	0.2500	0.1285	—	—	—	0.2569	0.2934
11. Transport goods	—	—	0.0858	—	0.2971	0.1528	0.0094	—	—	0.1615	0.2934
12. Wood and furniture	—	—	0.0870	—	0.1140	0.0440	0.1400	0.3100	—	0.0690	0.2360
13. Paper	—	—	0.0679	—	0.2384	0.1226	—	—	—	0.3347	0.2364
14. Rubber	—	—	0.0781	—	0.2739	0.1410	—	—	—	0.1452	0.3618
15. Leather	—	—	0.0641	—	0.2247	0.1158	—	—	—	0.2602	0.3352
16. Chemicals	—	—	0.0610	—	0.1850	0.1050	—	—	—	0.2890	0.3600
17. Textiles	—	—	0.0789	—	0.2773	0.1427	—	—	—	0.1653	0.3358
18. Clothing	—	—	0.0620	—	0.2174	0.1119	—	—	—	0.2733	0.3354
19. Food	—	—	0.0627	—	0.2038	0.1047	0.0359	—	—	0.3884	0.2045
20. Beverages	—	—	0.0833	—	0.2288	0.1177	0.1354	—	—	0.2304	0.2044
21. Tobacco	—	—	0.0767	—	0.2692	0.1386	—	—	—	0.3115	0.2040
22. Publishing	—	—	0.0826	—	0.2896	0.1456	—	—	—	0.2428	0.2364
23. Miscellaneous	—	—	0.1205	—	0.1066	0.0549	—	—	0.3930	0.0616	0.2634
24. Construction	—	—	0.0919	—	0.2397	0.1233	0.1779	—	—	0.1636	0.2036
Depreciation rate	0.0	0.0	0.0	0.0	0.05	0.05	0.05	0.0	0.05	0.02	0.05

— Not applicable.

(1972) on the basis of 1960 industrial census data, and after some minor modification for import content they were used in this study. They appear in table 8-5, along with depreciation rates by types of capital, which are consistent with those of Langoni (1974). We assume that depreciation rates are the same for each type of capital, regardless of the sector in which it is used, and that the "legal" rates of equation (7.21) and the "physical" rates of equation (7.33) take the same values.

Estimates of capital-output ratios by sector are available in Lopes (1972), while Bacha and others (1971) and Langoni (1974) analyze profit rates, at least for corporate enterprise. We attempted to choose capital–value added ratios and profit rates to be more or less consistent with these sources and with our hypothesized rate of 20 percent for profits taxation in the manufacturing sector (see table 8-3), and arrived at the figures appearing in table 8-6. These have no certain backing, of course, but are perhaps reasonable guesses as to the profit situation of firms in Brazil in the late 1950s and early 1960s.

Distribution of Capital Incomes

The profits just discussed accrue to firms, not to persons. To discuss the role of profits in generating the distribution of income among economically active persons, we have to take into account their distribution from firms to people. In Brazil this is very difficult, for data on wealth holding and even on the amount of earnings that firms retain is virtually nonexistent.

Given this lack of data, we can make only the most general inferences about the distribution of profits. On the one hand, we know that corporate saving is the sum of depreciation allowances and retained net earnings. With some guesses at sectoral corporate savings rates (even the overall rate for the economy does *not* appear in the national accounts) and the table 8-6 specification of depreciation charges, we can infer the proportion of earnings that must have been saved after taxes and depreciation. And on the other hand, Fishlow's worksheet data give numbers and incomes of "employers," whom we can tentatively identify as recipients of capital incomes. Putting these two sets of data together and juggling to get consistency gave rise to the figures appearing in table 8-7 for the number of employers by sector and the shares of net profits which they (along with highly educated

Table 8-6. Capital Cost Data for 1959

Sector	Capital share of value added	Capital–value added ratio	Capital cost	After-tax profit rate	Depreciation charge
1. Crop agriculture	0.1092	1.6	0.0683	0.0473	0.0210
2. Animal agriculture	0.5438	7.5	0.0725	0.0618	0.0108
3. Commerce	0.4304	3.0	0.1435	0.0836	0.0389
4. Electricity	0.6241	5.0	0.1248	0.0719	0.0349
5. Services	0.7870	3.0	0.2623	0.1905	0.0242
6. Mining	0.5643	3.0	0.1881	0.1293	0.0264
7. Nonmetallic minerals	0.4408	2.2	0.2003	0.1315	0.0360
8. Metallurgy	0.5353	2.8	0.1912	0.1289	0.0300
9. Machine tools	0.4242	1.9	0.2233	0.1455	0.0414
10. Electrical goods	0.5516	2.2	0.2507	0.1676	0.0387
11. Transport goods	0.6289	2.6	0.2419	0.1608	0.0409
12. Wood and furniture	0.3606	2.6	0.1386	0.0885	0.0281
13. Paper	0.6567	3.8	0.1728	0.1090	0.0366
14. Rubber	0.7765	2.9	0.2678	0.1808	0.0417
15. Leather	0.4896	2.3	0.2130	0.1391	0.0390
16. Chemicals	0.6713	3.2	0.2098	0.1372	0.0383
17. Textiles	0.4412	2.5	0.1765	0.1083	0.0411
18. Clothing	0.2744	2.1	0.1305	0.0736	0.0387
19. Food	0.6323	3.2	0.1976	0.1299	0.0352
20. Beverages	0.4016	2.8	0.1435	0.0836	0.0389
21. Tobacco	0.3693	2.1	0.1760	0.1112	0.0368
22. Publishing	0.3826	1.9	0.2013	0.1302	0.0386
23. Miscellaneous	0.4639	2.2	0.2107	0.1350	0.0421
24. Construction	0.2361	1.2	0.1972	0.1562	0.0405

workers) receive. These numbers are very crude—far cruder than any others in the model—but perhaps reflect the order of magnitude of the shares to indicate roughly the profit distribution patterns in the Brazilian economy.

Income Levels by Consumer Class

Counting proprietors, employees, and employers in each sector and in government, there are 130 groups of income recipients in the model. These were aggregated into four consumer classes as shown in table 8-8.

All rural income recipients (with the exception of employers, who may be absentee city- or town-dwellers) were grouped into consumer class 1, with a relatively low income per head. Class 2 is urban, made up of workers without education, workers with primary education in tertiary activities, and proprietors in tertiary

Table 8-7. Distribution of Income from Profits

Recipient group	Number (in tens)	Shares of profits received from: Sectors 1 and 2	Sectors 4, 6–24	Sector 3	Sector 5
Employers					
Sectors 1 and 2	29,850	0.7412	—	—	—
Sectors 4, 6–24	7,480	—	0.5789	—	—
Sector 3	12,240	—	—	0.5817	—
Sector 5	1,240	—	—	—	0.7466
Highly educated employees	6,460	—	0.0463	—	0.1120

— Not applicable.
Note: For definition of sectors, see table 8-1.

activities. This group represents the urban economically active poor, with incomes per head a bit less than twice that of the average in rural areas.

The third class is made up of workers with primary education in manufacturing, all workers with secondary schooling, and recipients of capital incomes from agriculture. This is a middle-income group, in number far smaller than the two lower classes. The last high-income class is made up of highly skilled workers (who also are assumed to receive some capital incomes), proprietors in manufacturing, and employers from nonrural production sectors. Their average income level is about thirty-five times that of the poor rural group, and the number of persons in the group is quite small.

As discussed in connection with equation (7.25), incomes received from economic activity in each consumer class are assumed to be modified by government tax and transfer policy. If we let Y and Y^d respectively stand for income before and after taxes and transfers, these variables are related in the base year through the following equations:

Class 1: No taxes or transfers
Class 2: $Y^d = Y - (-0.06 + 0.005Y)$
Class 3: $Y^d = Y - (-0.08 + 0.008Y)$
Class 4: $Y^d = Y - (-0.91 + 0.018Y)$

In each of these relationships, the terms in parentheses are a tax-transfer function—the negative intercept term represents a transfer and the slope term is an income tax more or less in line with the progressivity of Brazilian income taxes. Note that per

Table 8-8. Aggregation of Income Recipients to Consumer Classes
(incomes by function in thousands of 1959 cruzeiros)

Consumer class	Proprietors' income	Labor income
Class 1		
Proprietors, sectors 1 and 2	174,727	—
Family farm workers, sectors 1 and 2	—	36,323
Sharecroppers, sectors 1 and 2	—	19,168
Uneducated workers, sectors 1 and 2	—	71,925
Primary-educated workers, sectors 1 and 2	—	8,257
Subtotal	174,727	135,673
Class 2		
Uneducated workers, sectors 3–25 and government	—	151,327
Primary-educated workers, sectors 3, 4, 5, 24, 25, and government	—	120,106
Proprietors, sectors 3 and 5	127,230	—
Subtotal	127,230	271,433
Class 3		
Primary-educated workers, sectors 6–23	—	71,892
Secondary-educated workers, all sectors and government	—	85,737
Employers, sectors 1 and 2	—	—
Subtotal	—	157,630
Class 4		
Highly educated workers, all sectors and government	—	32,445
Proprietors, sectors 6–24	58,833	—
Employers, sector 3	—	—
Employers, sectors 4, 6–24	—	—
Employers, sector 5	—	—
Subtotal	58,833	32,445
Total	360,790	597,180

— Not applicable.
Note: For definition of sectors, see table 8-1.

Capital income	*Total income*	*Number of persons (tens)*	*Income per ten persons*	*Disposable income per ten persons*	*Consumption per ten persons*
—	174,727	560,760	0.31159		
—	36,323	371,020	0.09790		
—	19,168	81,600	0.23490		
—	71,925	350,000	0.20550		
—	8,257	20,090	0.41100		
—	310,400	1,383,470	0.22436	0.22436	0.22324
—	151,327	497,546	0.30415		
—	120,106	250,913	0.47867		
—	127,230	228,500	0.55681		
—	398,663	976,959	0.40807	0.46603	0.46230
—	71,892	67,132	1.07091		
—	85,737	62,782	1.36564		
22,332	22,332	29,850	0.74815		
22,332	179,962	159,764	1.12643	1.19741	1.17945
20,798	53,243	6,460	8.24156		
—	58,833	11,744	5.00955		
26,290	26,290	12,240	2.14791		
81,968	81,968	7,480	10.95853		
94,938	94,938	1,240	76.56260		
223,994	315,271	39,164	8.04994	8.81504	8.60157
246,326	1,204,296	2,559,357	0.47054	—	—

person transfers—including social security payments, disaster relief and similar items, and interest on the public debt—also rise with income level. In 1959 transfers exceeded income tax revenues, and as table 8-8 shows, disposable income for all consumer classes is assumed to exceed income from economic activity. In addition, since transfers are described by a constant term they will vary countercyclically as long as prices and real output increase together (as in the model they do). This affects government saving, as shown below.

Finally, to get from disposable income to consumption expenditures, we have to make assumptions about personal savings parameters, consistent with the overall savings-investment balance in the model. Studies based on consumer budget data such as Cline (1972) suggest that savings shares in Brazil rise with personal income. The following shares are broadly consistent with these results and with our own implicit estimates of total personal saving in 1959 as a residual after other sources are accounted for:

Class 1: 0.0050
Class 2: 0.0080
Class 3: 0.0150
Class 4: 0.0242

The resulting levels of consumption per ten persons per year are given in the last column of table 8-8. It is easy to verify from the numbers in the table that the richest class accounts for a bit more than half of all personal saving.

Cost Function Parameters and Rates of Technical Change

The preceding section concludes the description of most economic flow data for the base year. To find variations around these flows, it is necessary to look at substitution possibilities in production.

Substitution possibilities in the model are essentially determined by the cost functions for the labor aggregate and value added discussed in chapter 7. To find all parameters of the cost functions (7.1) and (7.3), it is only necessary to specify elasticities of substitution and shares of capital and the various labor types in value added and total labor cost. Since the data on shares can be easily derived from numbers in tables 8-1 through 8-8, we take up the elasticities of substitution. For substitution between capital and labor, these elasticities have been estimated in several studies of manufacturing sectors in Brazil; the results are summarized by Macedo (1974). We initially chose values for the capital-labor elasticity in each manufacturing sector in line with Macedo's summary, and in agriculture and tertiary sectors we followed the general presumption in the literature that the elasticity of substitution exceeds one. During the calibration of the model, some elasticities (and rates of technical change) were modified in order to bring sectoral rates of growth of employment and output more in line with observed values. The final choices appear in table 8-9.

Table 8-9. Elasticities of Substitution and Rates of Technical Change

	Elasticity of substitution		*Rate of technical change*	
Sector	*Between labor types*	*Between capital and labor*	*Employed labor*	*Proprietors*
1. Crop agriculture	7.0	2.2	−0.023	0.04
2. Animal agriculture	7.0	0.7	0.067	0.06
3. Commerce	5.0	1.4	−0.043	0.04
4. Electricity	5.0	0.8	0.000	0.00
5. Services	5.5	1.3	−0.057	0.02
6. Mining	5.5	0.7	0.060	0.04
7. Nonmetallic minerals	5.0	0.4	0.067	0.04
8. Metallurgy	5.0	0.6	0.063	0.04
9. Machine tools	5.0	0.6	0.068	0.04
10. Electrical goods	4.5	0.5	0.024	0.04
11. Transport goods	4.5	0.8	0.020	0.04
12. Wood and furniture	5.5	0.7	0.050	0.05
13. Paper	5.0	0.6	0.063	0.04
14. Rubber	5.5	0.6	0.010	0.04
15. Leather	5.5	0.7	0.057	0.05
16. Chemicals	4.0	0.8	0.030	0.04
17. Textiles	5.5	0.8	0.080	0.04
18. Clothing	5.5	0.5	0.034	0.05
19. Food	5.5	0.5	0.026	0.05
20. Beverages	5.5	0.8	0.020	0.04
21. Tobacco	5.5	0.4	0.000	0.04
22. Publishing	4.0	0.4	0.042	0.04
23. Miscellaneous	5.0	0.6	0.063	0.04
24. Construction	5.0	1.2	−0.065	0.05
25. Domestic servants	6.0	—	—	—

—Not applicable.

The other important substitution elasticity is between labor types. This has been much less studied in Brazil, although Fishlow (1973) does present cross-section estimates based on the 1960 demographic census. His general finding is that the elasticity is high, although substitution possibilities between skill groups seem to decline as skill increases. The elasticities in table 8-9 have values near those of Fishlow and are lower in sectors having a labor force with high skill content.

Rates of technical progress for employed labor (see equation 7.10) were originally calculated as the difference between estimates of output and employment growth by sector over the decade of the 1960s. (The basic data came from worksheets used for Bacha and others 1972, which were kindly provided by Edmar Bacha.) These were modified during calibration of the model. The final values also appear in table 8-9. The type of labor-saving technical progress assumed here will lead to a *decrease* in the labor-capital ratio (for constant labor and capital input costs) when the elasticity of substitution σ^V is less than one, and to an *increase* in the ratio when σ^V exceeds one. The fact that some sectoral rates of technical change were set to negative values in table 8-9 follows from this observation. It is precisely in these sectors that the elasticity of substitution exceeds unity, so negative technical progress means that they can release labor over time without perturbing factor price changes. In effect, agriculture and the tertiary sectors act as reservoirs of surplus labor that are gradually tapped by the manufacturing sectors.

Finally, rates of technical change for proprietors essentially reflect the speed with which these economic actors are absorbed into corporate and other business forms. As shown below, the rates given in table 8-9 generate a steady decline in the shares of proprietors in value added and in the economically active population, and this is probably realistic.

Summary Description of the Base-Year Data

Table 8-10 contains a set of national accounts calculated from the base-year data just described. The accounts can be compared, section by section, with the official accounts published by the Vargas Foundation (1971).

Total GNP in 1959 was Cr$1,987.6 million according to the official estimate, rather higher than our value of Cr$1,728.9 million. Here, we are probably in error (particularly since a recent, as yet unpublished revision of the official accounts increased the 1959 estimate still more), but consciously so. Since it provides the only disaggregated system of accounts, we had to use the input-output table and, perforce, its implicit level of GNP.

Our consumption share of 0.74 in GNP is above the official estimate, which runs a bit less than 0.7 for most years in the late 1950s and early 1960s. Part of the discrepancy is probably due to inventory investment, which is apparently included in consumption in the van Rijckeghem table. (Changes in stocks are explicit in the national accounts but are estimated by very crude methods; see Vargas Foundation 1972.)

The official accounts do not give a breakdown of factor payments such as appears in the second section of table 8-10 under "income accounts." A concept equivalent to our "total factor payments" can be calculated, however, and is about 79 percent of GNP in 1959. This is quite close to our value of 82 percent. Similarly, our estimates of 45 percent and 25 percent for shares of wage-earners and proprietors in factor payments are close to figures usually cited for Brazil.

Our figure of 10 percent as the share of government consumption (purchases of goods plus labor payments) in GNP is close to the official one. Under "government accounts," however, we show transfers as amounting to 43 percent of government revenue net of transfers. The corresponding figure in the national accounts is 25 percent. Our higher transfers are offset by higher taxes, particularly direct ones. Since we relied partly on legal sources in parameterizing tax and transfer policy, it is quite possible that we overestimated their true impact. We shall have to bear this possibility in mind when discussing the influence of tax and transfer instruments on the income distribution.

We show a small balance of payments deficit in world prices, as do the accounts. Our tariff receipts are also close to estimates for the early 1960s. These were calculated by assuming tariffs of 10, 15, and 25 percent on imports of investment, intermediate goods, and consumption goods respectively, and by scaling world prices so that domestic prices of imported goods are unity in the base year. For example, the exchange rate of r^F and the domestic price are both one, so that by equation (7.9) the foreign price of consumption imports becomes 1/1.15 = 0.8696. In 1959 producers' prices of all exports are also one, and we assumed a 5 percent subsidy for all, so that their world prices are 0.9524.

Table 8-10. National Accounts for 1959

Item	Level (thousands of cruzeiros)	Share	
Product accounts (current prices)		*In GNP*	
1. Personal consumption	1,285,842.000	0.7437	
2. Government			
Purchases of goods	68,932.375	0.0399	
Labor payments	105,587.687	0.0611	
3. Capital formation	198,166.937	0.1146	
4. Capital replacement	85,630.375	0.0495	
5. Less balance of payments deficit	−15,287.500	−0.0088	
GNP (current prices)	1,728,869.000[a]	—	
Income accounts		*In GNP*	*In factor payments*
1. Depreciation	85,630.375	0.0495	
2. Indirect business taxes	210,048.562	0.1215	
3. Net tariffs	12,245.211	0.0071	
4. Wages and salaries	597,204.437	0.3454	0.4203
5. Labor taxes	42,066.227	0.0243	0.0296
6. Income of entrepreneurs	360,792.562	0.2087	0.2539
7. Capital income distributed to persons	246,337.125	0.1425	0.1734
8. Profit taxes	76,766.250	0.0444	0.0540
9. Retained corporate earnings	97,771.125	0.0566	0.0688
Total factor payments (sum of 4 through 9)	1,420,937.000	0.8219	—
GNP (current prices)	1,728,860.000[a]	—	—

Foreign accounts (world prices)		*In total imports*
1. Noncompetitive intermediate imports	73,681.875	0.5589
2. Noncompetitive capital imports	50,090.004	0.3800
3. Noncompetitive consumption goods imports	8,054.500	0.0611
4. Noncompetitive government goods imports	0.000	0.0000
5. Competitive imports	0.000	0.0000
6. Exports	116,538.875	—
Current balance of payments deficit	15,287.500	—
Government accounts		*In total government expenditure*
Expenditures		
1. Wages of government workers	89,481.125	0.4962
2. Wage taxes of government workers	16,106.598	0.0893
3. Goods purchased	68,932.375	0.3822
4. Export subsidies	5,829.695	0.0323
Total government expenditures	180,349.750	—
Receipts		*In total government receipts*
1. Labor taxes	42,066.227	0.1689
2. Profit taxes	76,766.250	0.3083
3. Value added taxes	210,048.562	0.8435
4. Tariffs	18,074.906	0.0726
5. Income taxes	9,108.156	0.0366
6. Less personal transfers	−107,042.125	−0.4299
Total government revenue	249,021.875	—
Net government saving	68,672.125	—

(Table continues on the following page.)

Table 8-10 (continued)

Item	Level (thousands of cruzeiros)	Share
Investment and savings accounts		
Investment		*In total investment*
1. Capital formation	198,166.937	0.6983
2. Capital replacement	85,630.375	0.3017
Total investment	283,797.312	—
Saving		*In total saving*
1. Depreciation	85,630.375	0.3017
2. Retained corporate earnings	97,771.125	0.3445
3. Personal saving	16,425.020	0.0579
4. Balance of payments deficit	15,287.500	0.0539
5. Government saving	68,672.125	0.2420
Total saving	283,786.125	—

— Not applicable.

a. Discrepancy between levels of GNP is caused by rounding.

The official accounts show the following breakdown of saving:

Depreciation	0.2310
Private	0.5132
Trade deficit	0.0436
Government	0.2122

We show higher saving from depreciation, although this means little since depreciation is simply estimated as a constant share of GNP in the official data. Our total for other private saving (retained earnings and personal saving) is correspondingly less. We show about 86 percent of this saving as coming from retained earnings. This is reasonable, although the Vargas Foundation accounts do not give a similar breakdown of corporate and private savings which we can use to check ours.

As another check on the data, we can consider the comparison in table 8-11 between the after-tax and after-transfers size distribution of income generated by the base-year data (using each of the 130 classes of income as a data point) and the size distribution for the economically active population (including imputations for income in kind) estimated by Fishlow (1972). In comparison with Fishlow's data, it can be seen that ours somewhat overestimate income shares at both extremes, and underestimate shares in the middle. Thus, Fishlow calculates that the bottom 54.6 percent of the population receives 18.7 percent of the income, while we get

Table 8-11. Size Distribution of Income for the Economically Active Population: A Comparison of Base-Year Data and Fishlow's Estimates
(percent)

Percentage of economically active population by income group[a]	*Income share*	
	Fishlow	*Model*
0.0–26.6	5.2	7.0
26.7–42.8	6.1	8.5
42.9–54.6	7.1	8.5
54.7–68.6	11.3	8.0
68.7–85.9	21.0	17.0
86.0–96.4	23.6	18.0
96.5–99.5	16.8	17.5
99.6–100.0	8.6	15.5

a. The population share is given in ascending order of amount of income received; thus 0.0–26.6 percent are in the lowest income group.

Source: Fishlow (1972) and the general equilibrium model.

24 percent. Similarly, he has the top 14 percent receiving 49 percent, while we estimate 51 percent, with an extremely high share for the top 0.5 percent. These biases may well result from excessive aggregation in our data set at the bottom of the income distribution (that is, there are substantial differences in income among the rural self-employed, whom we treat as one group) and excessive disaggregation (such as for skilled workers and proprietors in each sector of manufacturing) at the top. In any case, our overall distribution measures such as the Gini coefficient resemble those of other investigators. For example, our Gini for after tax income in 1959 is 0.500, while Fishlow got 0.52 and Langoni (1973) got 0.4999.

Data for Simulations over Time

To run the model over time, we have to specify its exogenous variables for all years in which it is to be solved. Our main interest is not in simulating the 1960s, but rather in seeing how the model economy responds to policy and institutional changes. Nonetheless, we need a fairly plausible reproduction of the 1960s to serve as a background for policy variations, and to build this up we solved the model for the years 1962, 1965, 1968, and 1971. In a crude way, we tried to incorporate changes in exogenous variables over this turbulent period into the specification.

The national accounts provide somewhat incomplete data on government expenditures, especially the breakdown between purchases of goods and remuneration of employees. There is, however, a distinction made between government current consumption and investment, though no attempt at cumulation of capital stocks in the control of the government. For our model, the major expenditure categories are purchases of goods by the government, its wage payments, and transfers to persons. Both the volume of purchases and the level of employment are fixed in real terms, hence their value is determined by the model's endogenous prices (in terms of payments to proprietors, the numeraire). Transfers, however, are specified in nominal terms.

In tuning the model, we varied these three expenditure categories so as to keep the shares of total government expenditure and transfers more or less in line with published figures in the national accounts. Because of the lack of theory about the different ways in which public sector capital stocks may affect overall economic performance, we combined government and private investment in our accounting. The levels of the public sector's purchases of goods and employment (in real terms) appear in tables 8-12 and 8-13 respectively. Tax and transfer functions are given above (the section on "Income Levels by Consumer Class") for the base year; thereafter we assumed that the intercept terms giving transfers per head in the different consumption groups grew in absolute magnitude at 4.4 percent a year during 1959–62, 4.7 percent during 1962–65, 0.67 percent during 1965–68, and 20.0 percent during 1968–71. As mentioned earlier, we somewhat overestimated the share of transfers in GNP during 1959. These growth rates serve to bring the shares resulting from the model somewhat closer to official estimates for succeeding years.

Data on growth in demand for exports by input-output sectors are difficult to obtain in most countries because foreign trade and industrial classifications differ. Brazil is a partial exception, since some of the necessary reclassification has been done by Von Doellinger and others (1973). Subject to some additional reclassification (for example, van Rijckeghem appears to treat coffee exports as coming from the food sector, and others do not), we used the Von Doellinger estimates for 1965 and 1968. We interpolated between 1959 and 1965 to get estimates for 1962 and extrapolated crudely from 1970 (taking into account overall growth of exports) to get our numbers for 1971. The results appear in table 8-12. In most sectors exports increase throughout the decade, especially after 1968.

Labor supply growth over the decade can be calculated by comparing demographic census data for 1959 and 1969, although the 1969 census does not split out sharecroppers in agriculture. Applying decadal growth rates (with a guess at sharecroppers) gives supply estimates for 1971. Because very few data are available on intervening years, we made supply guesstimates by interpolating between the end years in a crude way (taking into account GNP growth between the years of the model and the rapid expansion of higher education toward the end of the decade). The resulting figures appear in table 8-13. Volume of government labor demand was estimated in connection with government purchases, and the makeup of the labor force was assumed to change more or less in line with the overall labor supply. These demand estimates are also given in table 8-13. Finally, we assumed that the number of employers (or recipients of capital income) grew

Table 8-12. Government Purchases and Exports
(thousands of 1959 cruzeiros)

	Government purchases					*Exports*				
Sector	*1959*	*1962*	*1965*	*1968*	*1971*	*1959*	*1962*	*1965*	*1968*	*1971*
1. Crop agriculture	651	1,212	2,052	3,654	3,670	11,897	12,775	12,409	13,098	18,500
2. Animal agriculture	500	931	1,575	2,807	2,818	391	420	132	116	174
3. Commerce	27,096	50,480	85,445	152,100	152,797	33,848	36,347	44,900	52,000	60,000
4. Electricity	1,207	2,248	3,806	6,774	6,807	0	0	0	0	0
5. Services	0	0	0	0	0	0	0	0	0	0
6. Mining	662	1,233	2,086	3,714	3,731	2,609	2,802	13,151	13,089	28,240
7. Nonmetallic minerals	2,203	4,104	6,946	12,366	12,423	203	218	79	468	1,904
8. Metallurgy	5,175	9,641	16,321	29,050	29,185	19	20	3,222	2,257	22,571
9. Machine tools	3,251	6,057	10,251	18,246	18,335	151	162	1,055	1,814	11,349
10. Electrical goods	1,940	3,613	6,116	10,889	10,938	11	12	309	388	3,522
11. Transport goods	3,545	6,604	11,180	19,899	19,991	91	98	640	405	4,675
12. Wood and furniture	432	805	1,364	2,427	2,438	78	84	362	892	5,468
13. Paper	850	1,583	2,679	4,773	4,792	1	1	338	107	1,259
14. Rubber	303	565	257	1,702	1,712	35	38	241	35	814
15. Leather	30	56	97	169	172	2,062	2,214	358	392	3,120
16. Chemicals	6,222	11,591	19,619	34,924	35,083	6,694	7,188	4,210	5,016	24,179
17. Textiles	892	1,662	2,813	5,008	5,029	924	992	1,099	907	5,870
18. Clothing	512	954	1,615	2,873	2,889	29	31	31	59	2,274
19. Food	2,012	3,749	6,346	11,293	11,348	63,043	67,697	89,933	108,000	83,553
20. Beverages	1	1	2	4	4	15	16	13	47	296
21. Tobacco	0	0	0	0	0	133	143	21	50	275
22. Publishing	1,307	2,434	4,122	7,336	7,370	76	62	17	5	476
23. Miscellaneous	140	261	442	784	788	56	60	138	20	1,481
24. Construction	10,000	18,631	31,535	56,138	56,395	0	0	0	0	0
Total	68,931	128,416	217,368	386,929	388,711	122,366	131,380	172,658	199,165	280,000

somewhat more slowly than the Brazilian population as a whole, at 2 percent a year.

A number of changes in the tax system occurred during the decade, two of which we incorporated. First, according to Bacha and others (1972), labor taxes in manufacturing increased fairly steadily over the decade. The tax rates we used were 1959, 18 percent; 1962, 27 percent; 1965, 39 percent; 1968, 44 percent; 1971, 44 percent. Second, in 1965 all value added tax rates were increased by 21 percent and in 1968 by an additional 10 percent to represent the tax law changes of that period.

The main source of exogenous demand in the model is capital formation, determined by the parameters g and F_i discussed in connection with equation (7.32). The growth rate of capital stock g was set at 6.5 percent a year in 1962, 5.2 percent in 1965, 4.0 percent in 1968, and 6.7 percent in 1971. The low growth in 1968 is supposed to reflect general economic inactivity around that time. Thereafter, a boom period began, and we assumed *actual* capital growth between 1968 and 1971 to be 6.0 percent annually.

Values for the animal spirits parameters F_i appear in table 8-14. These were varied informally during the calibration of the model to take into account a number of its peculiarities. First, very rapid growth was assumed in the capital stocks of sectors 9 and 10 in the base year to take into account the fact that these sectors' share of investment demand as generated by the b_{kj} coefficients of table 8-5 is far higher than their share in the van Rijckeghem data.

Table 8-13. Labor Supplies and Government Employment
(tens of workers)

Workers	*1959*	*1962*	*1965*	*1968*	*1971*
Labor supplies					
1. Family farm workers	371,020	370,000	319,000	320,000	301,000
2. Sharecroppers	81,600	85,000	80,100	88,400	90,800
3. Uneducated	847,546	830,000	720,000	660,000	440,200
4. Primary-educated	338,135	630,000	783,000	1,100,000	1,500,000
5. Secondary-educated	62,782	110,000	171,000	275,000	384,000
6. Highly educated	6,460	12,500	27,000	55,000	99,100
Government employment					
3. Uneducated	30,325	29,000	28,090	22,880	18,750
4. Primary-educated	54,585	68,500	94,340	120,120	187,500
5. Secondary-educated	31,538	39,000	51,940	71,760	70,000
6. Highly educated	4,852	7,500	12,720	19,760	20,000

Table 8-14. Animal Spirits Parameters by Sector

Sector	*1959*	*1962*	*1965*	*1968*	*1971*
1. Crop agriculture	0.8	1.2	1.0	1.0	1.0
2. Animal agriculture	1.0	1.0	1.0	1.0	1.0
3. Commerce	1.25	1.7	1.3	1.5	1.0
4. Electricity	1.1	1.0	1.0	1.0	1.0
5. Services	1.5	1.6	1.5	1.3	1.2
6. Mining	1.0	1.8	1.0	1.85	1.0
7. Nonmetallic minerals	1.0	1.0	1.0	1.0	1.0
8. Metallurgy	1.0	1.0	1.0	1.0	1.0
9. Machine tools	2.5	1.2	1.2	1.2	1.3
10. Electrical goods	2.7	1.2	1.2	1.7	1.4
11. Transport goods	1.5	1.2	1.2	1.2	1.3
12. Wood and furniture	1.0	1.0	1.0	1.0	1.2
13. Paper	1.0	1.0	1.0	1.0	1.0
14. Rubber	2.0	1.25	1.75	2.2	1.2
15. Leather	1.0	1.0	1.0	1.0	1.0
16. Chemicals	1.0	1.0	1.0	1.0	1.0
17. Textiles	0.9	0.75	0.65	0.8	1.0
18. Clothing	0.9	1.4	1.0	1.0	1.0
19. Food	1.0	1.0	1.0	1.0	1.0
20. Beverages	1.0	1.4	1.0	1.0	1.0
21. Tobacco	1.0	1.5	1.0	1.4	1.0
22. Publishing	1.0	1.0	1.5	1.5	1.0
23. Miscellaneous	1.0	1.0	1.0	1.0	1.0
24. Construction	1.0	1.0	1.0	1.0	1.1

The additional base-year capital formation creates capacity to meet this demand in later years.

Second, table 8-5 shows that sectors 5 and 14 had high capital shares in the base year, which can be shown to lead to high α_{Ki} coefficients in sectoral cost functions. From equation (7.7) high α_{Ki}'s can lead to computational problems when the value added–capital ratio (V_i/K_i^*) in the denominator for sector i gets too large. The high values for F_i for sectors 5 and 14 are to rule out this contingency.

Finally, other animal spirits parameters were set at values exceeding (falling short of) one to offset very high (very low) profit rates in the following period. In general, this has the effect of giving high (low) growth rates of capital to sectors with high (low) income elasticities of demand.

A final exogenous variable to be specified is the exchange rate r^F, which determines domestic prices of imported goods in equations (7.9), (7.20), and (7.27), and also influences the amount of export subsidies in (7.36) and tariff receipts in (7.37). As discussed in the next section, the implicit GNP deflator in the model varies over time as prices shift in relation to the numeraire. We set r^F approximately equal to the deflator in each year to keep constant the real cost of foreign resources and the volume of export subsidies and import tariff receipts. The values of r^F are: 1959, 1.0; 1962, 1.22; 1965, 1.05; 1968, 0.80; 1971, 1.90. The GNP deflator in the base solution has values of 1959, 1.0; 1962, 1.41; 1965, 1.63; 1968, 1.09; and 1971, 2.37, so that we are in effect permitting a small revaluation of the cruzeiro, compensated by increased tariffs and subsidies.

Results from the Base Solution of the Model

All the foregoing data were put together to generate a base solution of the model, which we now describe in some detail since it will serve as a point of reference for future variations.

Beginning with macroeconomic data, growth of GNP in base-year prices over the 1959–71 period turned out to be 7.1 percent a year in the base solution, comparable to about 7.0 percent in the official data. Since the model, by permitting no excess capacity, generates data on *potential* GNP, and both 1959 and 1971 were years of relatively full employment, the agreement is reassuring. Our crude attempts to capture cyclical fluctuations during the period were less successful, as the three-year growth rates for GNP in table 8-15 demonstrate.[4] A model like ours is obviously better used for full-employment comparisons than for reflections of business cycles.

As discussed in chapters 6 and 7, when aggregate demand increases, the model's macro-distribution responses are mediated by inflation of wages and prices in relation to payments, such as transfers and remuneration of proprietors, with values fixed in nominal terms. Table 8-15 gives values for the implicit deflator of GNP; the correlation of this price index with the shares in GNP of exogenous demand categories such as exports and investment is clear. In table 8-16 it can be seen that the share of wages and retained profits in total factor payments increase in years with high aggregate demand, especially 1971. The counter-

4. Growth rates of GNP from the national accounts are: 1959–62, 0.0806; 1962–65, 0.0237; 1965–68, 0.0614; 1968–71, 0.0950; and 1959–71, 0.0699. In effect, the model solution smooths the severe decline during mid-decade toward succeeding years.

Table 8-15. Output, Price, Expenditure, and Wage Variations: Base Solution

Item	*1959*	*1962*	*1965*	*1968*	*1971*
Output and prices					
GNP (millions of 1959 cruzeiros)	1,729	2,295	2,755	3,449	4,185
GNP deflator	1.0000	1.3837	1.0721	1.0333	2.7106
GNP growth rate (percentage over previous period)	—	9.44	6.09	7.49	6.45
Final demands					
Personal consumption/GNP	0.7438	0.6989	0.6902	0.6874	0.6466
Government					
Purchases of goods/GNP	0.0399	0.0591	0.0836	0.1212	0.1045
Labor payments/GNP	0.0611	0.0586	0.0684	0.0694	0.0679
Investment					
New capital formation/GNP	0.1146	0.1473	0.1134	0.0826	0.1335
Capital replacement/GNP	0.0495	0.0535	0.0548	0.0490	0.0548
Foreign trade					
Exports/GNP	0.0674	0.0481	0.0585	0.0426	0.0447
Less imports/GNP	0.0763	0.0655	0.0689	0.0521	0.0521
Transfers/GNP	0.0619	0.0469	0.0657	0.0720	0.0531
Wage levels[a]					
Family farm workers	0.0979	0.1561	0.1354	0.1361	0.4306
Sharecroppers	0.2349	0.3723	0.3186	0.3156	0.9867
Uneducated	0.2055	0.3193	0.2714	0.2730	0.8969
Primary-educated	0.4110	0.5422	0.4190	0.3867	1.1240
Secondary-educated	2.0000	2.4662	1.7124	1.4703	3.8769
Highly educated	5.0000	5.8457	3.6560	2.8999	7.1595

a. Thousands of cruzeiros per ten workers.

point is the negative response to aggregate demand of the shares of proprietors ("entrepreneurial income" in table 8-16), and transfers (table 8-15).

Additional insight into savings-investment interactions comes from the decomposition of sources of saving at the top of table 8-17. The major observation is that savings supplies which tend to have small fluctuations in value in relation to the overall price level and level of economic activity (such as depreciation and retained earnings) are more important in slack years such as 1968. Government saving, on the other hand, is large in high demand years such as 1971. (Foreign saving is important in the earlier

Table 8-16. *Functional Income Distribution Measures: Base Solution, Shares of GNP*

Item	*1959*	*1962*	*1965*	*1968*	*1971*	*1971 level*[a]
Wages and salaries	0.3454	0.3656	0.3520	0.3532	0.3931	4,458,694
Family farm workers	0.0210	0.0182	0.0147	0.0122	0.0114	129,616
Sharecroppers	0.0111	0.0100	0.0086	0.0078	0.0079	89,518
Uneducated	0.1291	0.1023	0.0780	0.0581	0.0395	447,741
Primary-educated	0.1158	0.1504	0.1458	0.1491	0.1766	2,003,687
Secondary-educated	0.0496	0.0616	0.0715	0.0814	0.0962	1,091,394
Highly educated	0.0188	0.0231	0.0334	0.0446	0.0614	696,739
Entrepreneurial income	0.2087	0.1249	0.1354	0.1193	0.0390	442,541
Profits and depreciation allowance	0.2486	0.3044	0.2719	0.2763	0.3115	3,532,975
Distributed profits	0.1425	0.1770	0.1522	0.1585	0.1774	2,012,077
Agricultural capitalists	0.0129	0.0154	0.0141	0.0141	0.0165	187,036
Manufacturing capitalists	0.0474	0.0697	0.0592	0.0625	0.0760	862,356
Commerce capitalists	0.0152	0.0165	0.0169	0.0193	0.0204	231,302
Services capitalists	0.0549	0.0606	0.0498	0.0501	0.0508	576,084
College-educated labor	0.0120	0.0147	0.0122	0.0125	0.0137	155,401
Other workers	0.0000	0.0000	0.0000	0.0000	0.0000	0
Retained profits	0.0565	0.0739	0.0648	0.0687	0.0793	899,056
Depreciation allowance	0.0495	0.0535	0.0548	0.0490	0.0548	621,842
Taxes	0.1973	0.2051	0.2407	0.2512	0.2564	2,908,891
Value added tax	0.1215	0.1220	0.1462	0.1657	0.1677	1,901,678
Labor wage tax	0.0243	0.0367	0.0472	0.0494	0.0510	578,725
Profit tax	0.0444	0.0428	0.0421	0.0443	0.0561	636,241
Net tariffs	0.0071	0.0036	0.0052	−0.0082	−0.0183	−207,751
Gross national product						11,343,101

a. In thousands of cruzeiros.

Table 8-17. Saving, Taxes, and Size Distribution Measures: Base Solution

Item	*1959*	*1962*	*1965*	*1968*	*1971*
Savings ratios					
Total saving/GNP	0.1641	0.2008	0.1682	0.1316	0.1884
Depreciation allowance/saving	0.3017	0.2666	0.3260	0.3725	0.2910
Retained corporate earnings/saving	0.3445	0.3679	0.3854	0.5223	0.4208
Personal saving/saving	0.0579	0.0485	0.0574	0.0761	0.0534
Balance of payments deficit/saving	0.0539	0.0867	0.0622	0.0724	0.0394
Government saving/saving	0.2420	0.2304	0.1691	−0.0434	0.1954
Tax ratios					
Total government taxes/GNP	0.2060	0.2164	0.2506	0.2725	0.2880
Labor tax/total taxes	0.1181	0.1696	0.1883	0.1814	0.1772
Profit tax/total taxes	0.2156	0.1977	0.1680	0.1624	0.1948
Value added tax/total taxes	0.5899	0.5640	0.5834	0.6082	0.5822
Tariffs/total taxes	0.0508	0.0425	0.0388	0.0275	0.0255
Income tax/total taxes	0.0256	0.0263	0.0215	0.0205	0.0203
Size distribution before taxes and transfers					
Gini coefficient	0.5032	0.5362	0.5059	0.5076	0.5724
Theil measure	0.8470	1.0402	0.8930	0.9279	1.0921
Variance log income	0.5349	0.5167	0.4858	0.4779	0.7111
Atkinson measure	0.4933	0.5090	0.4774	0.4781	0.5885
Size distribution after taxes and transfers					
Gini coefficient	0.5086	0.5413	0.5193	0.5245	0.5776
Theil measure	0.8383	1.0187	0.8870	0.9200	1.0692
Variance log income	0.5707	0.5499	0.5354	0.5338	0.7367
Atkinson measure	0.5090	0.5207	0.4997	0.5033	0.5965

years, but much less so in 1971 because of the great expansion of exports that year.)

The evolution of government saving is conditioned by two things. One is the countercyclical fluctuation of transfers (already mentioned several times), and the other is the pro-cyclical response of tax revenues as the price times the quantity base of the value added tax increases with output and inflation. Superimposed on this short-term behavior is a steadily increasing trend in both nominal transfer payments and tax rates. The very high level of government saving in 1971 is the culmination of both tendencies—transfers are low in real terms and tax revenues are high because of high aggregate demand, and at the same time the steady increases in government taxing power comes to the fore.[5]

Another aspect of the income distribution is presented in table 8-18, which shows changes in relative wages of the six types of labor skill over time. As might be expected from a model with an essentially neoclassical labor market specification, the wage structure narrows as supplies of initially scarce skilled laborers go up. For example, as highly educated workers increase from one-fiftieth to one-third the number of family farm workers, their wage in relation to that of the family workers drops off from 51 to 17. Similar shifts are observed for other labor types.

Scattered evidence (for example, Bacha 1976), mostly for urban industrial workers, suggests that the wage structure widened during the 1960s. Moreover, the shares of high-skill groups in income surely increased, as their employment went up as well. As discussed in chapter 10, the "correct" decomposition of these share increases into increasing wage spread and employment is a subject of acrimonious and unresolved debate in Brazil. Within the model, the decomposition is unambiguous: wages of skilled workers fall as their supplies increase, but because of high substitution elasticities among labor types, skilled shares increase (for example, from 3.1 percent of personal income for highly educated workers in 1959, to 7.9 percent in 1971). Whether this

5. Officially, percentage shares of taxes and transfers in GNP were:

	1962	*1965*	*1968*	*1971*
Transfers	5.3	6.0	8.1	7.5
Taxes	17.8	21.8	26.5	24.2

The estimates for 1971 are based on a new accounting methodology and are not strictly comparable with those of the other years. For more detail on public sector accounting, see Maneschi (1972).

Table 8-18. *Wage and Employment Structure: Base Solution*

Type of labor skill	*1959*		*1962*		*1965*		*1968*		*1971*	
	Wage ratio	*Employment ratio*	*Wage ratio*	*Employment ratio*	*Wage ratio*	*Employment ratio*	*Wage ratio*	*Employment ratio*	*Wage ratio*	*Employment ratio*
Sharecroppers/ Family farm workers	2.40	0.22	2.38	0.23	2.35	0.25	2.32	0.28	2.29	0.30
Uneducated/ Family farm workers	2.10	2.28	2.05	2.24	2.00	2.26	2.01	2.06	2.08	1.46
Primary-educated/ Family farm workers	4.20	0.91	3.47	1.70	3.09	2.45	2.84	3.44	2.61	4.98
Secondary-educated/ Family farm workers	20.43	0.17	15.80	0.30	12.64	0.54	10.81	0.86	9.00	1.27
Highly educated/ Family farm workers	51.07	0.02	37.45	0.03	26.99	0.08	21.31	0.17	16.63	0.33
Highly educated/ Primary-educated	12.17	0.02	10.78	0.02	8.73	0.03	7.50	0.05	6.37	0.07

decomposition is in accord with the facts is another question, but even if it is not, we can use the logic of the model to infer some things about labor market behavior.

For example, the equalizing trend of wages in the model is *not* stronger than that in table 8-18 because we assume that elasticities of substitution among labor types are high. Were elasticities lower and the substitution of labor skills more difficult, the fall in wages for skilled workers would have to have been much sharper for all of them to be hired in the last years of the simulation. As discussed in chapter 10, some explanations of Brazilian inequality trends essentially postulate low wage elasticities of demand for the skilled. Taken literally, this implies that shares of the skilled should have *fallen* during the 1960s with the large increase in the number of such workers. Both the model simulation and what is known of the facts contradict this assertion.

Other explanations of inequality push this argument further and assume no substitutability among labor types, that is, employment of each skill group is determined by output levels alone. Zero elasticities of substitution for labor are consistent with any wage structure, so that there can be both a widening wage spread and increases in skilled employment. The question such models beg is how wages are determined. This can be answered in the aggregate by savings-investment widow's cruse theories (as in the KS version of the identity model of chapters 3 to 5), but disaggregated generalizations are difficult. Until they are provided, models simulating independent wage and employment changes lack explanatory power and of course run against the neoclassical presumption that some wage-narrowing is necessary to accommodate large increases in the supply of skilled labor.

In table 8-18 wage equalization seems to be retarded between 1968 and 1971, probably because of increased demands for saving from high-income groups in 1971. Such widow's cruse effects may be a partial explanation for the observed behavior of the Brazilian wage structure. They also illustrate a case in which the short-term macro-distribution theory of the model and medium-term trends in educational redistribution act together in a fairly complicated way.

For another comparison between the model's results and numbers describing the evolution of the Brazilian economy, see tables 8-19 and 8-20, which present data on the evolution of sectoral levels of output and the economically active population

Table 8-19. Changes in Output, 1959–71, by Sector

Sector	1959 output[a]	Historical output growth rate[b] (percent)	1971 output[c]	Model output growth rate[b] (percent)	Model 1971 output
1. Crop agriculture	346,014	3.90	552,514	5.49	668,373
2. Animal agriculture	129,406	4.70	227,456	7.58	321,199
3. Commerce	459,616	6.20	967,187	7.38	1,114,378
4. Electricity	18,863	7.60	46,956	7.99	49,202
5. Services	384,127	4.50	659,164	6.98	887,211
6. Mining	19,912	6.70	44,493	11.32	77,443
7. Nonmetallic minerals	56,158	7.84	143,878	8.05	147,577
8. Metallurgy	136,357	8.93	398,169	9.71	437,437
9. Machine tools	33,631	12.74	155,128	12.88	157,811
10. Electrical goods	46,925	11.49	186,299	10.30	161,420
11. Transport goods	80,098	10.60	285,788	8.42	219,971
12. Wood and furniture	56,660	6.53	124,048	7.57	140,608
13. Paper	47,276	8.58	132,370	7.98	123,177
14. Rubber	30,615	9.20	92,341	8.78	87,826
15. Leather	12,766	2.18	16,583	6.93	29,324
16. Chemicals	198,521	9.58	626,717	7.71	500,611
17. Textiles	156,676	3.81	247,492	7.43	382,120
18. Clothing	40,277	6.74	90,430	7.63	100,610
19. Food	284,992	5.34	540,914	4.86	510,845
20. Beverages	27,952	5.49	54,016	6.98	64,565
21. Tobacco	13,158	4.50	22,579	4.29	22,015
22. Publishing	26,954	6.48	58,658	7.87	69,338
23. Miscellaneous	15,274	8.00	39,891	7.11	35,858
24. Construction	179,419	3.70	279,702	7.55	443,986
25. Domestic servants	45,925	7.99	119,778	7.99	119,778
4, 6–23. Manufacturing	1,303,065	7.76	3,306,750	7.79	3,317,758
Total output	2,847,572	6.37	6,112,551	7.34	6,872,683

a. In thousands of 1959 cruzeiros.
b. Average annual growth rate from 1959 to 1971.
c. Inferred from 1959 output at historical growth rate.
Sources: Historical data from Bonelli (1975), the national accounts, and demographic censuses.

(EAP) between 1959 and 1971. The historical data on output and EAP are taken from a recent compilation for industrial sectors by Bonelli (1975) and the national accounts and demographic censuses.

Figure 8-1 contrasts actual and model-generated 1959–71 growth rates in graphic form. If the model results agreed with historical data perfectly, all points would lie along the 45-degree line. In figure 8-1 most points lie within 1 or 2 percent of this standard, with larger discrepancies for sectors 6 (mining), 15

Table 8-20. Changes in Economically Active Population (EAP), 1959–71, by Sector
(employment in tens of workers)

Sector	1959 EAP	Historical EAP growth rate[a] (percent)	1971 EAP[b]	Model EAP growth rate[a] (percent)	Model 1971 EAP
1. Crop agriculture	1,121,000		1,219,232	2.83	1,574,786
		0.70		2.47	
2. Animal agriculture	262,400		285,394	0.73	286,519
3. Commerce	288,000	3.55	440,963	4.19	476,029
4. Electricity	6,419	8.30	17,379	5.05	11,760
5. Services	297,500	2.90	421,329	1.07	338,451
6. Mining	4,573	5.60	8.955	6.35	9.796
7. Nonmetallic minerals	16,370	2.64	22,472	0.46	17,290
8. Metallurgy	17,426	3.22	25,645	3.81	27,518
9. Machine tools	6,215	9.13	18,589	6.16	13,011
10. Electrical goods	5,790	5.91	11,767	4.11	9,480
11. Transport goods	8,188	5.09	15,082	4.37	13,829
12. Wood and furniture	15,130	3.25	22,347	0.26	15,602
13. Paper	4,093	3,87	6,512	3.53	6,254
14. Rubber	2,089	3.95	3,356	−1.80	1,683
15. Leather	2,472	−0.52	2,322	−1.72	2,011
16. Chemicals	12,816	2.24	16,768	4.98	23,301
17. Textiles	32,834	0.02	32,913	−1.33	27,988
18. Clothing	9,800	3.89	15,630	0.89	10,908
19. Food	26,514	2.12	34,195	−2.88	18,773
20. Beverages	4,389	2.28	5,770	1.55	5,289
21. Tobacco	1,317	0.37	1,377	−0.73	1,207
22. Publishing	6,062	3.58	9,315	0.74	6,624
23. Miscellaneous	3,789	3.70	5,907	−1.93	3,005
24. Construction	82,060	7.90	211,759	7.02	190,554
25. Domestic servants	150,000	6.37	322,334	6.37	322,334
4, 6–23. Manufacturing	186,274	3.29	276,301	1.59	225,315
Total EAP (excluding government)	2,387,360	2.38	3,177,312	2.98	3,413,977

a. Average annual growth rate from 1959 to 1971.
b. Inferred from 1959 EAP at historical growth rate.
Sources: Historical data from Bonelli (1975), the national accounts, and demographic censuses.

(leather), and 24 (construction). The model's overoptimistic assessment of growth in sectors 6 and 24 probably stems from too high projections of their major final demands (exports and investment, respectively). The overly rapid growth of leather goods reflects difficulties of modeling a complex sector made up of both highly traditional and modern export producers in a changing mix.

Figure 8-1. Growth Rates of Sectoral Output: Actual and Calculated by the Model

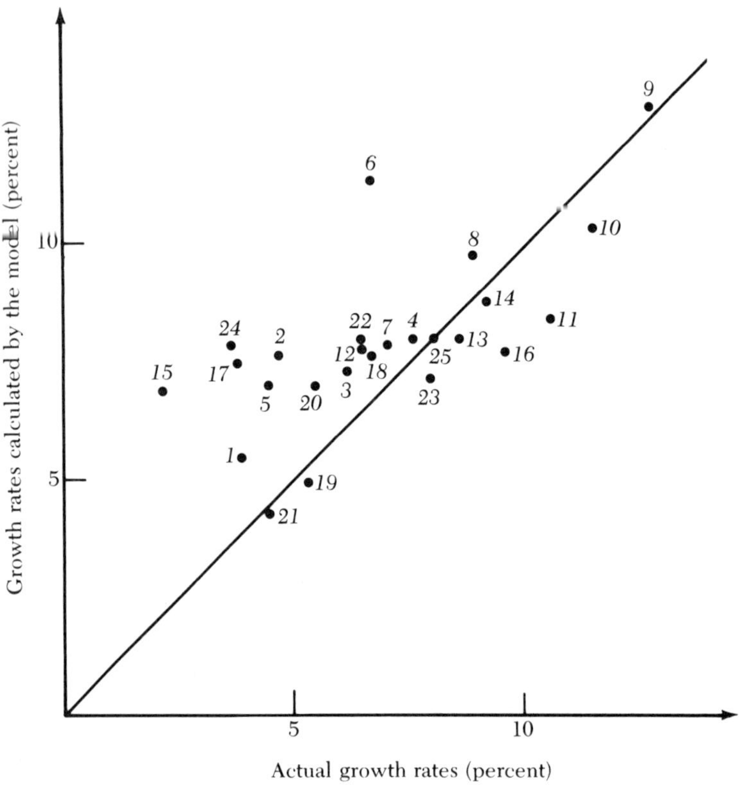

Note: Numbers in the scatter diagram refer to the sectors listed in table 8-19.

Source: Table 8-19.

Our results on shifts in EAP are less auspicious. The model-generated 1971 total EAP in table 8-20 exceeds the later-compiled (and presumably better) historical estimate for 1971 by around 2.4 million workers (employment measured by convention in tens of people). Comparisons of historical and model growth rates have to be made bearing this upward bias in mind.

As it turns out, the model's 1971 EAP in sector 1 (crop agriculture) exceeds the actual by 3.6 million workers; thus the discrepancy is more than made up in this single sector. In other major sources of employment—commerce, services, and electricity and manufacturing—the *absolute* errors in employment estimates are less than a million workers, which is not too far from the errors in the data. The model's EAP estimates in sector 2 (animal agriculture) and sector 24 (construction) are quite close to what was observed.

All in all, the performance is not outstanding. As shown in chapter 9, however, the major play in the model's employment patterns is between employment in manufacturing and "surplus labor" in sectors such as crop agriculture, commerce, services, and construction, and here the base solution appears to capture at least the qualitative aspects of historical change. "Better" results about employment could be obtained by juggling sector-level elasticities of substitution and rates of technical change. But the tedium and expense of such manipulation dissuaded us from attempting it when only small absolute shifts in employment and distribution would result.

Behavior of producers' prices and profit rates over time is set out in table 8-21. Except in a few sectors, particularly in 1971 with its high level of aggregate demand, relative prices and profit rates do not shift markedly. The price behavior is consistent with the scant data available for Brazil (for example, Baer and Kerstenetzky 1972, table 6). Some stability in the structure of rates of profit over time is also apparent in the tabulation in Langoni (1974), table 49. The model results show fairly high profits in certain years for "dynamic" manufacturing sectors (especially sectors 7–11, 13, and 16), but this is probably realistic. In macroeconomic terms, profit rates tend to fluctuate upward in years of high aggregate demand (compare 1968 and 1971). The movements are not large, however, and this stability explains the countercyclical behavior of retained earnings as a share of saving shown in table 8-17.

Certain aggregate distributional trends are summarized in table 8-22. There is a steady gain in real personal income accruing from economic activity per ten participants, at least when nominal totals are deflated by the implicit GNP deflator. As the table indicates, personal income grew from 0.47 in 1959 to 0.68 in 1971, for an annual rate of 3.08 percent.[6] Consumption per ten

6. The units of these ratios are thousands of 1959 cruzeiros per ten persons, or hundreds of cruzeiros per person a year. Dividing by 0.2, the approximate 1959 exchange rate, shows that average payments in the model rise from US$235 in 1959 to US$317 in 1971.

Table 8-21 Producers' Prices and After-tax Profit Rates, by Sector

Sector	1959		1962		1965		1968		1971	
	Price	Profit rate	Price	Profit rate	Price	Profit rate	Price	Profit rate	Price	Profit rate
1. Crop agriculture	1.0	0.047	1.24	0.059	1.09	0.066	1.06	0.078	2.82	0.095
2. Animal agriculture	1.0	0.062	1.20	0.089	0.92	0.069	0.83	0.074	1.80	0.089
3. Commerce	1.0	0.083	1.34	0.081	1.08	0.078	1.09	0.094	2.75	0.085
4. Electricity	1.0	0.072	1.57	0.093	1.25	0.103	1.40	0.159	1.68	0.137
5. Services	1.0	0.191	1.40	0.190	1.01	0.137	1.01	0.136	2.55	0.120
6. Mining	1.0	0.129	1.48	0.175	1.41	0.283	1.29	0.268	3.67	0.314
7. Nonmetallic minerals	1.0	0.131	1.56	0.241	1.16	0.187	1.12	0.222	3.27	0.331
8. Metallurgy	1.0	0.129	1.75	0.308	1.30	0.259	1.23	0.305	4.09	0.518
9. Machine tools	1.0	0.146	1.83	0.454	1.20	0.269	1.03	0.226	3.20	0.366
10. Electrical goods	1.0	0.170	1.61	0.235	1.13	0.156	1.05	0.163	2.97	0.137
11. Transport goods	1.0	0.161	1.70	0.254	1.17	0.176	1.11	0.195	3.24	0.205
12. Wood and furniture	1.0	0.088	1.31	0.093	1.01	0.081	0.94	0.087	2.40	0.103
13. Paper	1.0	0.109	1.59	0.176	1.21	0.170	1.31	0.282	3.68	0.296
14. Rubber	1.0	0.181	1.29	0.142	0.94	0.100	0.86	0.093	1.93	0.024
15. Leather	1.0	0.139	1.29	0.138	0.92	0.069	0.86	0.085	2.19	0.120
16. Chemicals	1.0	0.137	1.41	0.177	1.13	0.159	1.14	0.241	3.10	0.265
17. Textiles	1.0	0.108	1.31	0.108	1.01	0.100	0.95	0.125	2.40	0.118
18. Clothing	1.0	0.073	1.31	0.093	0.99	0.065	0.94	0.090	2.29	0.094
19. Food	1.0	0.130	1.26	0.107	1.01	0.097	0.98	0.119	2.26	0.043
20. Beverages	1.0	0.084	1.39	0.091	1.13	0.072	1.14	0.090	2.97	0.089
21. Tobacco	1.0	0.111	1.40	0.100	1.41	0.035	1.93	0.034	5.06	0.019
22. Publishing	1.0	0.130	1.47	0.182	1.12	0.179	1.08	0.189	2.59	0.102
23. Miscellaneous	1.0	0.135	1.32	0.135	0.97	0.110	0.88	0.120	2.26	0.121
24. Construction	1.0	0.157	1.48	0.206	1.19	0.246	1.18	0.300	3.45	0.432
25. Domestic servants	1.0	0	1.44	0	1.15	0	1.08	0	3.16	0

Table 8-22. Aggregate Distributional Data
(thousands of 1959 cruzeiros per ten workers)

	1959	*1962*	*1965*	*1968*	*1971*
Personal income					
Current prices	0.47	0.72	0.63	0.65	1.83
1959 prices	0.47	0.52	0.59	0.63	0.68
Consumer class[a] (1959 prices)					
Class 1	0.22	0.22	0.26	0.27	0.28
Class 2	0.46	0.46	0.52	0.52	0.45
Class 3	1.18	1.23	1.21	1.13	1.22
Class 4	8.60	10.17	9.19	8.55	7.52
Wage share of highly educated workers' income	0.61	0.61	0.73	0.78	0.82

a. See table 8-8 for definitions of consumer classes.

workers tends also to grow over time, though there are downward fluctuations for classes 2 and 4 in 1971, essentially because of the high aggregate demand built into the model that year. A final observation is that the wage share of skilled workers' income grows over time, largely because of the great increase in their number and the relative stability of their wage (see table 8-18).

References

Bacha, Edmar L. 1976. Hierarquia e remuneração gerencial. In E. L. Bacha. *Os mitos de uma década: Ensaios de economia brasileira*. Rio de Janeiro: Paz e Terra.

Bacha, Edmar L., Aloisio Barboso Araujo, Milton da Mata, and Rui Lyrio Modenesi. 1971. *Analise governmental de projectos de investimento no Brasil*. Rio de Janeiro: Instituto de Planejamento Econômico e Social / Instituto de Pesquisas (IPEA/INPES).

Bacha, Edmar L., Milton da Mata, and Rui Lyrio Modenesi. 1972. *Encargos trabalhistas e absorção de mão-de-obra*. Coleção relatorios de pesquisa no. 12. Rio de Janeiro: Instituto de Planejamento Econômico e Social / Instituto de Pesquisas (IPEA/INPES).

Baer, Werner, and Isaac Kerstenetzky. 1972. The Brazilian economy. In Riordan Roett, ed. *Brazil in the sixties*. Nashville, Tenn.: Vanderbilt University Press.

Bonelli, Regis. 1975. Growth and technological change in Brazilian manufacturing industries during the sixties. Ph.D. dissertation, University of California at Berkeley.

Carneiro Leão, Antonio Sergio, Carlos Alberto Ribeiro da Silva, Elcio Giestes, and Jose Nobrega. 1973. Matriz de insumo-producto do Brasil. *Revista brasileira de economia* 27(3):3–10.

Cline, William R. 1972. *Potential effects of income redistribution on economic growth: Latin American cases*. New York: Praeger.

Fishlow, Albert. 1972. Brazilian size distribution of income. *American economic review (papers and proceedings)* 62(2): 391–402.

———. 1973. Brazilian income size distribution: Another look. Berkeley: University of California, Department of Economics; processed. Published in Portuguese as: Distribuição da renda no Brasil: Um novo exame. *Dados* 11(1973):10–80. (Published by Instituto Universitario de Pesquisas, Rio de Janeiro.)

Fishlow, Albert, and Astra Meesook. 1972. Technical appendix: Brazilian size distribution of income, 1960. Berkeley: University of California, Department of Economics; processed.

Langoni, Carlos Geraldo. 1973. *Distribuição da renda e desenvolvimento econômico do Brasil.* Rio de Janeiro: Editora Expressão e Cultura.

———. 1974. *As causes do crescimento econômico do Brasil*. Rio de Janeiro: Apec Editora.

Lopes, Francisco Lafaite de Padua. 1972. Inequality planning in the developing economy. Ph.D. dissertation, Harvard University.

Macedo, Roberto Bras Matos. 1974. Models of the demand for labor and the problem of labor absorption in the Brazilian manufacturing sector. Ph.D. dissertation, Harvard University.

Maneschi, Andrea. 1972. The Brazilian public sector. In Riordan Roett, ed. *Brazil in the sixties*. Nashville, Tenn.: Vanderbilt University Press.

van Rijckeghem, Willy. 1969. An intersectoral consistency model for economic planning in Brazil. In Howard S. Ellis, ed. *The economy of Brazil*. Berkeley: University of California Press.

Vargas Foundation. 1971. Contas nacionais do Brasil—Actualização. *Conjuntura econômica* 25(9):91–114.

———. 1972. *Contas nacionais do Brasil: Conceitos e metodologia*. Rio de Janeiro.

Von Doellinger, Carlos, Hugo Barros de Castro Faria, Raimundo Nonato Mendonca Ramos, and Leonardo Caserta Cavalcanti. 1973. *Transformação da estrutura das exportacoes brasileiras, 1964–70*. Rio de Janeiro: Instituto de Planejamento Econômico e Social / Instituto de Pesquisas (IPEA/INPES).

9
Income Distribution Simulations, 1959–71

Frank J. Lysy and Lance Taylor

THIS LENGTHY CHAPTER describes almost thirty general equilibrium model simulations for the 1959–71 period. It explores how income distribution in the general equilibrium model responds to a variety of policy or institutional changes. From such information, we hope to infer something about how the real Brazilian income distribution might respond as well. In the next chapter, these model-based inferences are contrasted with hypotheses about Brazilian distribution mechanisms proposed by others. The object there is a preliminary exploration, in light of the model results and other information, of the apparent credibility (or incredibility) of the numerous, sometimes contradictory, "explanations" of deterioration in Brazilian income equality.

Table 9-1 lists the twenty-seven solutions discussed in this chapter. A first group of four variations around the base solution tests model responses to changes in its key parameters: elasticities of substitution in production and income elasticities of demand. Three additional solutions then explore the effects of changes in investment demand functions.

Next, eight solutions in two groups examine the distributional consequences of movements in government policy variables: changes in real expenditure levels, modifications in the pattern

Table 9-1. Catalog of Solutions to the General Equilibrium Model

Designation	*Description*
Base solution	
Base	Complete model simulation, 1959–71, by three-year time steps.
Tests of sensitivity to parameter changes	
SEN 1	Reduce all elasticities of substitution among labor skill groups by 10 percent.
SEN 2	Reduce capital-labor elasticities of substitution by 4 percent in sectors 1, 3, 5, 24 (where the elasticity initially exceeds one).
SEN 3	Change all income elasticities of demand proportionately 25 percent toward one.
Modifications in investment demand functions	
INV 1	Reduce overall growth rate of capital stock by 10 percent (1962–71).
INV 2	Multiply animal spirits parameters by 1.25 in sectors 8, 9, 10, 11, and 16 ("advanced" industrial sectors); multiply by 0.75 in sectors 17, 18, and 19 ("old" industrial sectors); all periods.
INV 3	Modify animal spirits parameters from base run by making them sensitive to previous sectoral growth rates.
Government expenditure variations	
GOV 1	Set real government expenditures on goods and services at 70 percent of base-run values.
GOV 2	Reduce government employment levels by 5 percent.
TRANS 1	Reduce transfers to all recipients by 20 percent.
TRANS 2	Reduce per person transfers to high-income consumer groups by 50 percent; increase transfers to lower two consumer groups by an offsetting amount.
Changes in tax rates and the exchange rate	
TAX 1	Reduce wage tax rates by 50 percent.
TAX 2	Reduce profit tax rates by 50 percent.
TAX 3	Decrease wage tax rates by 50 percent; increase profit tax rates by an offsetting amount.
RATE 1	Devalue the exchange rate by 15 percent.
Changes in labor supplies by education type[a]	
EDUC 1	Increase the supply of highly educated workers by 2.9412 percent of the initial supply of secondary-educated workers; reduce the supply of secondary-educated workers by an equal number of persons.
EDUC 2	Increase the supply of secondary-educated workers by 2.74725 percent of the initial supply of primary-educated workers; reduce the supply of primary-educated workers by an equal number of persons.
EDUC 3	Increase the supply of primary-educated workers by 47.0588 percent of the initial supply of uneducated workers; reduce the supply of uneducated workers by an equal number of persons.

(Table continues on the following page.)

Table 9-1 (continued)

Designation	*Description*
Modifications in profit distributions and wage structures	
DIST 1	Reduce agricultural profits distributed to employers by 50 percent, and transfer the same amount to sharecroppers.
DIST 2	Reduce nonagricultural profits distributed to employers by 50 percent, and transfer an equal amount to uneducated, primary-educated, and secondary-educated workers; distribute the profits to each class of workers in proportion to their total wage payments in the sectors where the profits are produced.
DIST 3	Remove all intersectoral wage differentials for each labor skill group.
DIST 4	Maintain the wages from 1965 in 1968 and 1971.
Changes in export levels	
EXP 1	Reduce exports in all sectors by 10 percent.
EXP 2–5	Increase exports by 50 percent in sectors 1, 9, 16, and 19.

a. In each experiment, enough workers were upgraded from one class to the next higher class so that real GNP would rise by almost Cr$20 million (in 1959 cruzeiros).

of transfer payments to individuals, changes in tax rates, and shifts in the exchange rate. These are followed by solutions which are supposed to reflect more basic institutional changes, such as large shifts in the skill mix of the labor force, redistributions of profits, and movements in the wage structure. A final group of five solutions measures the impact of exports on employment and the income distribution.

As already discussed in chapters 6 and 7, changes in parameters and exogenous variables shift a general equilibrium model solution in two ways. First, the model equilibrium must adjust macroeconomically to bring aggregate supply back in line with aggregate demand (or, what amounts to the same thing, to make saving equal to investment demand). The main adjustment mechanism is movement of the overall price level in relation to payments fixed in nominal terms. When aggregate demand falls, for example, prices fall and the income distribution shifts to favor classes with fixed nominal incomes and low savings propensities. Most of the solutions discussed here are "deflationary" in this sense. They were designed this way since it usually took less time on the computer to solve a deflationary variant than its inflationary mirror image.

The macro adjustment is accompanied by numerous microeconomic changes in the model equilibrium—shifts in employment levels by sector and labor type, consumption levels by sector and consumer class, value added costs and prices of individual goods, profit rates, tax takes, and so on. These changes are considered in a second level of discussion, with particular micro adjustments being more interesting in some solutions than in others.

Each solution is discussed at both levels—first its macroeconomic differences from the base solution, and second its microeconomic adjustments. As discussed in the previous chapters, the macroeconomic adjustment is viewed as taking place in two modes—one in which nominal wages stay at their base solution values and employment varies, and another in which wages shift to bring labor demands by skill type back in line with predetermined supplies. These two types of solution are discussed respectively under the rubrics of "wages fixed" and "wages variable" in what follows.[1] Most of the discussion will be of the "wages variable" simulations.

Tests of Model Sensitivity to Parameter Changes

The first set of variant solutions tests how the model responds to changes in key parameters. Solution SEN 1 explores the consequences of reduced substitutability among labor types, SEN 2 reduces supply responsiveness in the model's "labor surplus" sectors, and SEN 3 makes income effects less important in demand.

Tables 9-2 to 9-4 provide a detailed assessment of the macro differences between the base run and each of the three variant solutions being considered. The first column of table 9-2 gives base solution levels for total output in 1959 prices, the GNP deflator, the components of GNP demand as a share of GNP, and wages. Succeeding columns to the right show the absolute change of each variable and the ratio of its new value to the base solution

1. In the "wages variable" solution, the Powell algorithm discussed in the appendix to chapter 7 was used to drive the sum of squares of excess labor supplies to a value less than 1.0×10^6, corresponding to a root mean square error in each labor excess supply function of about 500—that is, 5,000 workers, since employment is measured in units of ten persons. Because our estimates of labor supplies themselves are much less accurate than this, the precision of the model solutions is exaggerated. The tight tolerances were necessary because the price level (and the resulting income distribution) had to change a great deal in order to change employment demands a little.

Table 9-2. SEN Solutions—Output, Price, Expenditure, and Wage Variations: 1971, Wages Variable

Item	Base level	SEN 1 Absolute change	SEN 1 Ratio to base	SEN 2 Absolute change	SEN 2 Ratio to base	SEN 3 Absolute change	SEN 3 Ratio to base
Output and prices							
GNP (millions of 1959 cruzeiros)	4,185	−43	0.9898	−125	0.9700	−1	0.9997
GNP deflator	2.7106	0.4600	1.1697	14.5414	6.3646	0.0516	1.0190
Final demands							
Personal consumption/GNP	0.6466	−0.0012	0.9982	−0.0160	0.9753	−0.0006	0.9991
Government							
Purchases of goods/GNP	0.1045	0.0005	1.0046	0.0046	1.0440	0.0002	1.0017
Labor payments/GNP	0.0679	0.0007	1.0102	0.0086	1.1267	0.0001	1.0018
Investment							
New capital formation/GNP	0.1335	−0.0003	0.9980	0.0005	1.0039	0.0002	1.0013
Capital replacement/GNP	0.0548	−0.0007	0.9864	−0.0037	0.9318	0.0001	1.0019
Foreign trade							
Exports/GNP	0.0447	−0.0061	0.8631	−0.0375	0.1618	−0.0009	0.9809
Less imports/GNP	0.0521	−0.0072	0.8614	−0.0435	0.1642	−0.0010	0.9813
Transfers/GNP	0.0531	−0.0074	0.8599	−0.0445	0.1619	−0.0010	0.9815
Wage levels[a]							
Family farm workers	0.4306	0.1156	1.2684	2.5256	6.8652	0.0085	1.0198
Sharecroppers	0.9867	0.2573	1.2608	5.7870	6.8650	0.0192	1.0195
Uneducated	0.8969	0.2394	1.2669	5.2713	6.8773	0.0178	1.0199
Primary-educated	1.1240	0.2264	1.2015	6.6143	6.8846	0.0225	1.0200
Secondary-educated	3.8769	0.6050	1.1561	23.1412	6.9690	0.0798	1.0206
Highly educated	7.1595	0.8616	1.1203	43.3848	7.0597	0.1439	1.0201

a. Thousands of cruzeiros per ten workers.

Table 9-3. SEN Solutions—Functional Income Distribution Measures: 1971, Wages Variable

			SEN 1		SEN 2		SEN 3	
Item	*Base level (1959 cruzeiros)*	*Base share in GNP*	*Change in GNP share from base*	*Ratio of GNP share to base*	*Change in GNP share from base*	*Ratio of GNP share to base*	*Change in GNP share from base*	*Ratio of GNP share to base*
Wages and salaries	4,458,694	0.3931	0.0101	1.0257	0.0480	1.1222	0.0007	1.0017
Family farm workers	129,616	0.1140	0.0011	1.0989	0.0013	1.1142	0.0000	1.0031
Sharecroppers	89,518	0.0079	0.0007	1.0939	0.0009	1.1079	0.0000	1.0008
Uneducated	447,741	0.0395	0.0036	1.0914	0.0044	1.1123	0.0000	1.0011
Primary-educated	2,003,687	0.1766	0.0068	1.0384	0.0210	1.1188	0.0004	1.0021
Secondary-educated	1,091,394	0.0962	−0.0000	0.9995	0.0124	1.1290	0.0001	1.0014
Highly educated	696,739	0.0614	−0.0020	0.9670	0.0081	1.1324	0.0002	1.0030
Entrepreneurial income	442,541	0.0390	−0.0056	0.8555	−0.0329	0.1571	−0.0007	0.9811
Profits and depreciation allowance	3,532,975	0.3115	0.0016	1.0053	0.0173	1.0556	0.0007	1.0024
Distributed profits	2,012,077	0.1774	0.0016	1.0090	0.0135	1.0759	0.0004	1.0022
Agricultural capitalists	187,036	0.0165	0.0010	1.0581	0.0018	1.1102	−0.0002	0.9856
Manufacturing capitalists	862,356	0.0760	0.0006	1.0075	0.0048	1.0626	0.0006	1.0077
Commerce capitalists	231,202	0.0204	0.0002	1.0105	0.0051	1.2521	−0.0000	0.9985
Services capitalists	576,084	0.0508	−0.0002	0.9967	0.0012	1.0233	0.0000	1.0006
Highly educated labor	155,401	0.0137	0.0000	1.0015	0.0006	1.0407	0.0001	1.0037
Other workers	0	0.0000	0.0000	1.0000	0.0000	1.0000	0.0000	1.0000
Retained profits	899,056	0.0793	0.0008	1.0100	0.0076	1.0959	0.0002	1.0031
Depreciation allowance	621,842	0.0548	−0.0007	0.9864	−0.0037	0.9318	0.0001	1.0019
Taxes	2,908,891	0.2564	−0.0061	0.9762	−0.0325	0.8734	−0.0007	0.9974
Value added tax	1,901,678	0.1677	0.0010	1.0062	0.0042	1.0250	−0.0002	0.9989
Labor wage tax	578,725	0.0510	0.0007	1.0146	0.0041	1.0807	0.0002	1.0030
Profit tax	636,241	0.0561	0.0002	1.0031	0.0035	1.0620	0.0002	1.0042
Net tariffs	−207,751	−0.0183	−0.0082	1.4456	−0.0444	3.4237	−0.0010	1.0536
Gross national product	11,343,101							

Table 9-4. SEN Solutions—Saving, Taxes, and Size Distribution Measures: 1971, Wages Variable

		SEN 1		SEN 2		SEN 3	
Item	*Base level*	*Change in portion from base*	*Ratio of portion to base*	*Change in portion from base*	*Ratio of portion to base*	*Change in portion from base*	*Ratio of portion to base*
Savings ratios							
Total saving/GNP	0.1884	−0.0011	0.9940	−0.0033	0.9824	0.0002	1.0009
Depreciation allowance/saving	0.2910	−0.0025	0.9915	−0.0151	0.9481	0.0001	1.0002
Retained corporate earnings/saving	0.4208	0.0069	1.0163	0.0487	1.1158	0.0010	1.0024
Personal saving/saving	0.0534	−0.0003	0.9944	−0.0002	0.9956	−0.0000	0.9994
Balance of payments deficit/saving	0.0394	−0.0058	0.8538	−0.0323	0.1808	−0.0008	0.9798
Government saving/saving	0.1954	0.0016	1.0080	−0.0011	0.9943	−0.0004	0.9981
Tax ratios							
Total government taxes/GNP	0.2880	0.0009	1.0032	0.0060	1.0210	0.0001	1.0003
Labor tax/total taxes	0.1772	0.0019	1.0107	0.0102	1.0578	0.0004	1.0020
Profit tax/total taxes	0.1948	−0.0000	0.9999	0.0078	1.0401	0.0008	1.0039
Value added tax/total taxes	0.5822	0.0018	1.0031	0.0024	1.0041	−0.0007	0.9988
Tariffs/total taxes	0.0255	−0.0036	0.8599	−0.0213	0.1642	0.0005	0.9812
Income tax/total taxes	0.0203	−0.0001	0.9941	0.0009	1.0436	0.0001	1.0029
Size distribution before taxes and transfers							
Gini coefficient	0.5724	−0.0013	0.9976	0.0528	1.0922	0.0014	1.0024
Theil measure	1.0921	−0.0127	0.9884	0.1033	1.0946	0.0043	1.0039
Variance log income	0.7111	0.0622	1.0875	1.4848	3.0880	0.0083	1.0117
Atkinson measure	0.5885	0.0211	1.0358	0.2941	1.4998	0.0035	1.0059
Size distribution after taxes and transfers							
Gini coefficient	0.5776	−0.0027	0.9953	0.0455	1.0788	0.0010	1.0017
Theil measure	1.0692	−0.0107	0.9900	0.1187	1.1110	0.0041	1.0038
Variance log income	0.7367	0.0485	1.0658	1.3784	2.8711	0.0067	1.0091
Atkinson measure	0.5965	0.0164	1.0275	0.2798	1.4691	0.0029	1.0048

for each of the variants. Thus, in solution SEN 1, the share of personal consumption in GNP fell by 0.0012 from its base solution level of 0.6466 in 1971 (with wages varying to bring labor demands in line with supplies). The new consumption share of 0.6454 is 99.82 percent of the value in the base. As the reader can easily verify, the absolute changes in the shares of the various final demand components in GNP must sum to zero.

Tables 9-3 and 9-4 provide similar information about other macroeconomic magnitudes. In table 9-3 the absolute changes from the base solution of all components of GNP on the factor payments side must sum to zero; that is, in SEN 1 the wage share rises by 0.0101, the proprietors' share falls by 0.0056, the share of capital payments rises by 0.0016, and the tax share falls by 0.0061. Within the limits of round-off error the sum of these share changes is equal to zero. In table 9-4 a similar shift-share analysis is applied to different sources of saving and taxes. In addition, changes in four summary measures of inequality in the size distribution are given, both before and after taxes and transfers. Usually, the four measures move in the same direction, although there are some exceptions (as in SEN 1 where the Gini and Theil measures improved, while the variance of log income and the Atkinson measure worsened).[2]

Reduced Labor Substitutability: SEN 1

The SEN 1 solution reduces substitution elasticities among labor types by 10 percent, making it more difficult to use workers of one skill level in place of any other. The macroeconomic effect is inflationary, since supply responsiveness in the economy as a whole is reduced by limitation of substitution. It becomes more difficult with fixed labor supplies to meet exogenous demand targets, and the results are an increase in the GNP deflator (table 9-2) and reduction of the shares in GNP of payments fixed in nominal terms—proprietors' income (table 9-3), transfers (table 9-2), and net tariffs (table 9-3). Table 9-4 indicates that the share

2. For a succinct explanation of the inequality measures used here, see Sen (1973). Debate about changes in the Brazilian income distribution invokes all four of the inequality indexes in table 9-4, with different authors emphasizing one or another of them. To ease interpretation, note that the variance of log incomes is measured about the geometric mean income, and that the income elasticity of the marginal utility of additional income in the Atkinson measure is given a value of one-half.

of saving coming from capital income increases with inflation. Total government expenditure (on goods, payments to government workers, transfers, and the implicit subsidies to exports) rises by less than the total rise in the tax take, leading to a small rise in government saving. Other savings sources decline, especially the current account deficit (which is denominated in a fixed exchange rate).

The increase in the overall price level results from substantial wage increases, as shown in the last panel of table 9-2. Wages rise far more in percentage terms for low-skill than for high-skill groups, however, even though a situation in which supply is tight and saving is scarce might be expected to favor the high-skill groups. As already pointed out in chapter 8, the wage structure is narrowed because by 1971 skilled workers are in relatively plentiful supply, and if it becomes more difficult to substitute their services for those of the unskilled, their relative wage in a neoclassical economy must fall. At least in the general equilibrium model, more difficult labor substitution equalizes incomes from wages.

Another way to see this is to look at the changes in the demands for each labor type by sector when the wages are held constant. Table 9-5 shows the labor demand in SEN 1 (with wages not yet allowed to vary to bring about zero excess labor demands) as a proportion of the labor demand in the base. When the elasticity of substitution between labor types falls, the demand for the lower skilled workers rises, while that for the higher skilled

Table 9-5. Labor Demand in SEN 1 as a Proportion of Labor Demand in the Base Solution

	Labor type[a]					
Sector	1	2	3	4	5	6
1. Crop agriculture	1.2642	1.2182	1.2563	0.8642	—	—
2. Animal agriculture	1.2329	1.1942	1.2261	0.8841	—	—
3. Commerce	—	—	1.4981	1.1858	0.9980	0.8580
5. Services	—	—	1.5050	1.1635	0.9627	0.8151
4, 6–23. Manufacturing	—	—	1.3413	1.0753	0.9219	0.8284
24. Construction	—	—	1.4791	1.1704	0.9856	0.8472
25. Domestic servants	—	—	1.2847	0.9708	0.7894	—
Overall	1.2613	1.2150	1.2761	0.9768	0.9601	0.8757

— Not applicable.

a. Labor types are: 1, family farm workers; 2, sharecroppers; 3, uneducated workers; 4, primary-educated workers; 5, secondary-educated workers; and 6, highly educated workers.

workers falls. In a neoclassical model the wage of the lower skilled workers will then have to rise in relation to the wage of the higher skilled workers to bring about zero excess demands (and supplies) for all.

This result, which is expected from a neoclassical labor market of the type specified here, can be seen geometrically in figure 9-1, in which two labor types, L_1 and L_2, are combined to produce a CES aggregate of labor, $\overline{L}$. If the base-year supplies are at point A, with the elasticity of substitution equal to σ_1, the ratio of marginal products at A (and therefore the ratio of wages) will

Figure 9-1. Constant Elasticity of Substitution (CES) Isoquants

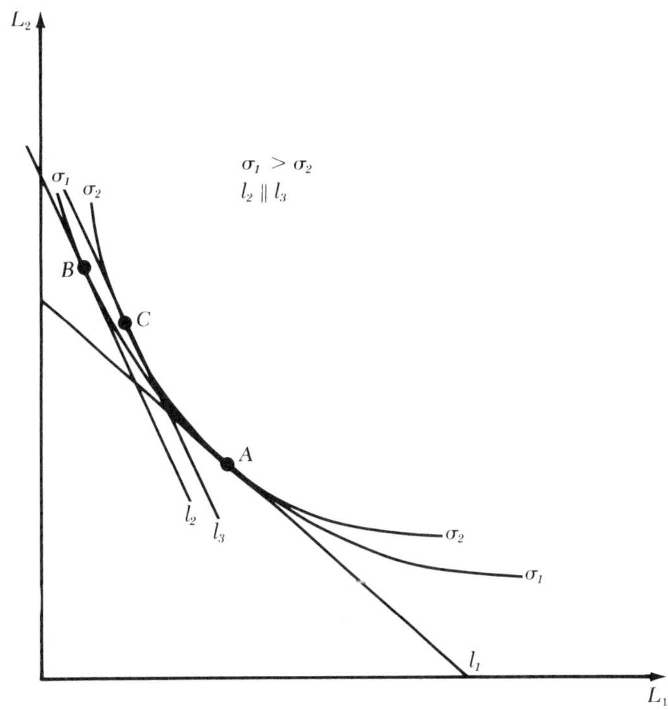

Note: $\left(\frac{MP_1}{MP_2}\right)_A = \left(\frac{w_1}{w_2}\right)_A$, and $\left(\frac{MP_1}{MP_2}\right)_B > \left(\frac{MP_1}{MP_2}\right)_A$, so that $\left(\frac{w_1}{w_2}\right)_B > \left(\frac{w_1}{w_2}\right)_A$

where MP_i = marginal product of labor type i, and
w_i = wage of labor type i.

equal the slope of l_1, the line tangent at A to the isoquant going through A. When the relative supply of L_2 increases and that of L_1 falls, it gives rise to the same aggregate labor "output" $\bar{L}$, but at point B. Because the slope of l_2 is greater than that of l_1, the relative wage of L_2 must fall. In our model of Brazil, the relative supplies of the higher skilled workers increased tremendously by 1971, and their relative wage did fall. If the elasticity of substitution is reduced to σ_2, the isoquant to produce $\bar{L}$ will everywhere have to shift outward (except at A). If relative wages remain as at B, and firms hire as much labor of each type as they wish to produce $\bar{L}$, the CES aggregate of labor will shift to point C. Given the convexity of the isoquants, and the fact that the relative supply of L_2 rose, demand for L_2 will have to fall and that for L_1 rise at C in relation to B. Note also that this argument holds for any σ in the range of zero to infinity. Both the substitution elasticities do not have to be greater than one, as they are in the model.

The shifts in the functional distribution summarized in table 9-3 result in fairly complex shifts in the size distribution. As the data on real consumption in 1959 prices in table 9-6 shows, the poorest consumer group enjoys an increase in real income, while the level of living of the top group drops fairly sharply. Overall, the effect on distribution is ambiguous: two of the aggregate measures given in table 9-4 indicated an improvement and two a deterioration. Although the distribution between labor groups got better, proprietors (generally of low per capita income) lose in inflation, while high-income capitalists gain. Contradictions among the summary inequality measures also show up in other solutions and emphasize the problems inherent in trying to summarize a complex distributional process with a single statistic.

Table 9-6. Real Consumption in 1959 Prices in SEN 1 and the Base Solution
(thousands of 1959 cruzeiros)

	Base		*SEN 1*	
Consumer class[a]	*Total consumption*	*Consumption per ten workers*	*Total consumption*	*Consumption per ten workers*
1	527,163	0.2832	539,906	0.2895
2	556,874	0.4544	543,280	0.4478
3	666,955	1.2209	662,584	1.2148
4	1,065,607	7.5170	1,027,603	7.2517

a. For definitions of consumer classes, see table 8-8.

Less Supply Flexibility in Labor Surplus Sectors: SEN 2

Five sectors—crop agriculture, commerce, services, construction, and domestic servants—have several characteristics in common. They all have capital-labor elasticities of substitution greater than one (except domestic servants, where there is no capital). The average wage is less than that of the industrial sectors (ranging from a half to a tenth of the industrial wage for labor of the same type). Finally, their labor-labor elasticities of substitution are generally higher than those in the industrial sectors. For all these reasons, it is easy to move workers in and out of these sectors—hence we label them "labor-surplus" sectors.

Because of their characteristics, the Harrod-neutral technical progress specified in equation (7.10) is labor-using in the labor-surplus sectors. This means that as the capital-labor elasticity of substitution decreases or the rate of technical change becomes more positive, such a sector's equilibrium labor-capital ratio at any point in time will be higher (for any parametrically specified wage-rental ratio).[3] In effect, the labor-surplus sectors will draw labor from the rest of the economy, but as this occurs overall labor productivity will fall as workers are pulled into industries in which their wages (and marginal productivities) are lower. Less flexible substitution response in labor-surplus sectors can lead to lower real growth for the economy as a whole. One underlying cause is the different productivity of the same type of labor in different sectors built into equations (7.12).

Solution SEN 2 illustrates this effect by incorporating elasticities of substitution in the labor-surplus sectors which are reduced by 4 percent. Aggregate supply fell as a consequence, and with more or less exogenous final demands the economy had to inflate. One reason for this fall in supply should be obvious. The capital-labor elasticity of substitution fell in some sectors, thereby making the economy more rigid. In addition, for the reasons pointed out above, since labor is being drawn into low-productivity employment from industry, aggregate supply will again fall. Employment rose in response to the lower elasticity of

3. That is, when technical change is purely labor-augmenting, as we specify it to be, then for a given capital-labor ratio, the equilibrium wage-rental ratio rises over time in a sector with a capital-labor elasticity of substitution exceeding one. To hold real wages constant, more labor must be absorbed into the sector as technical advance proceeds. For an accessible discussion of biased technical progress, see Kelley, Williamson, and Cheetham (1972), chap. 2.

substitution in the construction and commerce sectors and decreased elsewhere. The increase in construction (from 186,000 in 1971 in the base solution to 238,000 in SEN 2) was quite sharp.

Although its results are not definitive, SEN 2 does support the notion that production possibilities in sectors absorbing large amounts of low-skill labor impose significant constraints on development patterns in the overall economy. As it becomes more difficult to pull labor into industries where its productivity is high, possibilities for growth and equitable distribution are significantly reduced. The general equilibrium model's jargon about "elasticities of substitution" and "technical change" of course does not capture the dialectic of human institutions and micro technology that determine employment patterns in labor-surplus sectors. It does support the long-standing argument of Latin American structuralist economists that without labor and output responsiveness in agriculture and cognate sectors, rapid economic growth is both difficult and inequitable.

Less Diverse Consumer Demand Patterns: SEN 3

SEN 3 tests the impact of diversity of consumer preferences on the income distribution. All income elasticities of demand are moved one-quarter of the way between their initial values and unity (which maintains Engel aggregation), making the distinction between luxuries and necessities less acute.

The macro changes are slight as a result of this rather large change in income elasticities. In addition, the sectoral levels of output and relative prices show very little change. These changes were small because of the small changes in real consumption levels from 1959 to 1971 shown in table 8-22. In a generalized CES type of demand system, as we have here, if real household incomes and relative prices do not change, income elasticities will not matter at all.

The changes that did occur were all in the "right" direction. If household real incomes fall over time, we would expect a relative rise in the base run of consumption of goods which have an income elasticity of less than unity. If all income elasticities less than one are raised, as they are in SEN 3, the consumption levels of these income inelastic goods should fall in SEN 3 compared with the base. This occurs in every case, even when relative price changes are not taken into account (they were small in SEN 3 compared with the base run for 1971). In other words, the household consumption levels in 1971 of SEN 3 compared with 1971 of the base will fall for income inelastic goods (whose elasticities were raised) and rise for income elastic goods (whose elasticities were lowered) when household incomes fall between 1959 and 1971.

The actual movement of the average real consumption level is a little ambiguous since, as seen in table 8-22, the real consumption levels in consumer classes 2 and 4 fell, but those in classes 1 and 3 rose between 1959 and 1971. If the measure of the "average" is the absolute differences in real consumption levels, weighted by either the number of households of each type or by their importance in total household consumption in the economy, average household consumption will fall. If all relative prices do not shift by a significant amount, in SEN 3 the demand for income inelastic goods should fall in 1971 and the demand for income elastic goods should rise. This is, in fact, what did occur in eighteen sectors. In six it did not, and in one we cannot tell since it was income elastic for two consumer classes but inelastic for the other two.

Since income inelastic goods (food, clothing, and so on) are also more labor intensive (especially unskilled labor intensive), the relative wage of the lower skilled and agricultural labor groups should fall in SEN 3. This does occur, to a very small degree, as is seen in tables 9-2 and 9-3. As a result, we should also see that aggregate distribution measures indicate a deterioration in the income distribution, and this prediction also holds, as seen in table 9-4.

There is still some ambiguity in these conclusions. Since the experiment was slightly inflationary, and since the generally low-income proprietors are hurt in an inflation, the distribution measures may have indicated a deterioration solely for this reason. This is doubtful, since the inflation was slight. But clearer results can be found by examining the SEN 3 results for 1965. In that year the household incomes of *each* consumer class had risen in relation to the base period. By the reasoning given above, the demand for income inelastic goods should therefore rise (since their elasticities were raised toward unity) and the demand for income elastic goods fall. Demand did respond like this in twenty cases, in two it did not, in two there was no change, and in one we could not predict. The demand for unskilled labor-intensive goods rose, and the wage changes of the six labor types were, as a ratio to their base run values, 1.0081, 1.0073, 1.0071, 1.0066, 1.0064, and 1.0064 (for types 1–6 respectively). The wage spread narrowed, and all the aggregate distribution measures indicated an improvement in the income distribution. Yet the experiment for 1965 was slightly inflationary and therefore hurt proprietors.

All of this gives modest quantitative support for the structuralist argument that diversity in demand patterns leads to unequalizing growth. As per capita incomes rise, if income elasticities lie farther from unity, distribution becomes worse.[4]

Shifts in Investment Demand Levels

Aside from technical progress and growth in the labor force, the major dynamic element in the model is investment. Tables 9-7 to 9-9 give details on three simulations in which overall levels of investment demand are modified and there are shifts in demand across sectors.

Reduced Overall Investment Demand: INV 1

As discussed in chapter 7, investment in each period τ is determined by the expected growth of the economy $g(\tau)$ and the "animal spirits" parameters $F_i(\tau)$ which move the expected growth rates of sectors up or down from the economywide average. Solution INV 1 incorporates a less ambitious growth program than that in the base solution, multiplying $g(\tau)$ in each period by the factor 0.9.

At the macroeconomic level, two effects that result from less investment over time must be separated. The immediate effect is a sharp fall in exogenous demand, leading to a strong deflation. Over time, however, less investment results in a smaller stock of physical capital.[5] If aggregate demand were the same, this would be inflationary since there would be less aggregate supply. At first, the deflationary effect of lower investment demand dominates, but as the capital stock becomes smaller and smaller, the second effect will become more important.

4. See Taylor and Bacha (1976) for a different version of this line of reasoning, expressed in terms of widow's cruse savings effects like those built into the general equilibrium model. Demand composition effects are further discussed in this and the next chapter as well.

5. In 1971 total capital in the base solution is 6,934,093 (thousands of 1959 cruzeiros) and 6,511,400 in INV 1, a decline of 6.1 percent. Investment declines from 713,044 to 622,048 or 12.8 percent.

Table 9-7. INV Solutions—Output, Price, Expenditure, and Wage Variations: 1971, Wages Variable

Item	Base level	INV 1		INV 2		INV 3	
		Absolute change	*Ratio to base*	*Absolute change*	*Ratio to base*	*Absolute change*	*Ratio to base*
Output and prices							
GNP (millions of 1959 cruzeiros)	4,185	−119	0.9717	36	1.0087	−14	0.9966
GNP deflator	2.7106	−0.8224	0.6966	−0.5271	0.8055	−0.4939	0.8178
Final demands							
Personal consumption/GNP	0.6466	0.0159	1.0246	0.0184	1.0284	0.0079	1.0123
Government							
Purchases of goods/GNP	0.1045	0.0025	1.0244	−0.0068	0.9354	−0.0015	0.9853
Labor payments/GNP	0.0679	−0.0033	0.9514	0.0011	1.0159	−0.0008	0.9883
Investment							
New capital formation/GNP	0.1335	−0.0165	0.8767	−0.0036	0.9729	−0.0037	0.9725
Capital replacement/GNP	0.0548	−0.0003	0.9938	−0.0048	0.9124	−0.0006	0.9893
Foreign trade							
Exports/GNP	0.0447	0.0213	1.4763	0.0103	1.2298	0.0101	1.2260
Less imports/GNP	0.0521	0.0196	1.3754	0.0144	1.2773	0.0113	1.2177
Transfers/GNP	0.0531	0.0251	1.4722	0.0123	1.2312	0.0119	1.2234
Wage levels[a]							
Family farm workers	0.4306	−0.1539	0.6426	−0.0752	0.8253	−0.0832	0.8067
Sharecroppers	0.9867	−0.3529	0.6423	−0.1724	0.8253	−0.1911	0.8063
Uneducated	0.8969	−0.3202	0.6429	−0.1564	0.8257	−0.1739	0.8061
Primary-educated	1.1240	−0.4004	0.6437	−0.1962	0.8255	−0.2180	0.8060
Secondary-educated	3.8769	−1.3721	0.6461	−0.6740	0.8262	−0.7533	0.8057
Highly educated	7.1595	−2.5654	0.6417	−1.2612	0.8238	−1.4060	0.8036

a. Thousands of cruzeiros per ten workers.

Table 9-8. *INV Solutions—Functional Income Distribution Measures: 1971, Wages Variable*

Item	Base level (1959 cruzeiros)	Base share in GNP	INV 1 Change in GNP share from base	INV 1 Ratio of GNP share to base	INV 2 Change in GNP share from base	INV 2 Ratio of GNP share to base	INV 3 Change in GNP share from base	INV 3 Ratio of GNP share to base
Wages and salaries	4,458,694	0.3931	−0.0201	0.9490	0.0038	1.0096	−0.0059	0.9851
Family farm workers	129,616	0.0114	−0.0006	0.9494	0.0002	1.0195	−0.0001	0.9897
Sharecroppers	89,518	0.0079	−0.0004	0.9488	0.0001	1.0153	−0.0001	0.9892
Uneducated	447,741	0.0395	−0.0020	0.9498	0.0006	1.0151	−0.0006	0.9839
Primary-educated	2,003,687	0.1766	−0.0090	0.9493	0.0020	1.0112	−0.0025	0.9857
Secondary-educated	1,091,394	0.0962	−0.0053	0.9447	0.0003	1.0031	−0.0016	0.9835
Highly educated	696,739	0.0614	−0.0027	0.9558	0.0007	1.0111	−0.0008	0.9868
Entrepreneurial income	442,541	0.0390	0.0169	1.4342	0.0093	1.2376	0.0086	1.2209
Profits and depreciation allowance	3,532,975	0.3115	−0.0107	0.9656	−0.0170	0.9455	−0.0116	0.9627
Distributed profits	2,012,077	0.1774	−0.0060	0.9662	−0.0069	0.9610	−0.0068	0.9616
Agricultural capitalists	187,036	0.0165	−0.0014	0.9160	0.0002	1.0111	−0.0006	0.9652
Manufacturing capitalists	862,356	0.0760	−0.0052	0.9318	−0.0114	0.8495	−0.0061	0.9201
Commerce capitalists	231,202	0.0204	−0.0012	0.9416	0.0023	1.1108	−0.0002	0.9912
Services capitalists	576,084	0.0508	0.0019	1.0374	0.0026	1.0510	0.0004	1.0087
Highly educated labor	155,401	0.0137	−0.0001	0.9905	−0.0005	0.9616	−0.0004	0.9694
Other workers	0	0.0000	0.0000	1.0000	0.0000	1.0000	0.0000	1.0000
Retained profits	899,056	0.0793	−0.0044	0.9448	−0.0053	0.9336	−0.0042	0.9468
Depreciation allowance	621,842	0.0548	−0.0003	0.9938	−0.0048	0.9124	−0.0006	0.9893
Taxes	2,908,891	0.2564	0.0138	1.0539	0.0039	1.0153	0.0089	1.0346
Value added tax	1,901,678	0.1677	−0.0026	0.9845	−0.0053	0.9683	−0.0018	0.9891
Labor wage tax	578,725	0.0510	−0.0029	0.9424	−0.0013	0.9737	−0.0014	0.9730
Profit tax	636,241	0.0561	−0.0018	0.9687	−0.0032	0.9426	−0.0025	0.9558
Net tariffs	−207,751	−0.0183	0.0210	−0.1483	0.0137	0.2510	0.0144	0.2105
Gross national product	11,343,101							

Table 9-9. INV Solutions—Saving, Taxes, and Size Distribution Measures: 1971, Wages Variable

Item	Base level	INV 1 Change in portion from base	INV 1 Ratio of portion to base	INV 2 Change in portion from base	INV 2 Ratio of portion to base	INV 3 Change in portion from base	INV 3 Ratio of portion to base
Savings ratios							
Total saving/GNP	0.1884	−0.0169	0.9103	−0.0085	0.9548	−0.0044	0.9769
Depreciation allowance/saving	0.2910	0.0265	1.0909	−0.0131	0.9549	0.0035	1.0119
Retained corporate earnings/saving	0.4208	0.0161	1.0383	−0.0092	0.9781	−0.0128	0.9695
Personal saving/saving	0.0534	0.0067	1.1259	0.0035	1.0662	0.0016	1.0306
Balance of payments deficit/saving	0.0394	−0.0064	0.8385	0.0249	1.6331	0.0075	1.1912
Government saving/saving	0.1954	−0.0430	0.7797	−0.0062	0.9681	0.0001	1.0004
Tax ratios							
Total government taxes/GNP	0.2880	−0.0047	0.9838	−0.0080	0.9722	−0.0042	0.9853
Labor tax/total taxes	0.1772	−0.0076	0.9573	0.0002	1.0009	−0.0023	0.9869
Profit tax/total taxes	0.1948	−0.0030	0.9846	−0.0059	0.9695	−0.0058	0.9700
Value added tax/total taxes	0.5822	0.0005	1.0009	−0.0022	0.9962	0.0024	1.0041
Tariffs/total taxes	0.0255	0.0102	1.3981	0.0076	1.2970	0.0059	1.2296
Income tax/total taxes	0.0203	−0.0001	0.9957	0.0004	1.0199	−0.0001	0.9965
Size distribution before taxes and transfers							
Gini coefficient	0.5724	−0.0274	0.9522	−0.0205	0.9642	−0.0181	0.9685
Theil measure	1.0921	−0.0360	0.9670	−0.0666	0.9391	−0.0454	0.9585
Variance log income	0.7111	−0.1560	0.7806	−0.0837	0.8823	−0.0901	0.8733
Atkinson measure	0.5885	−0.0641	0.8912	−0.0396	0.9327	−0.0391	0.9336
Size distribution after taxes and transfers							
Gini coefficient	0.5776	−0.0177	0.9694	−0.0160	0.9723	−0.0135	0.9766
Theil measure	1.0692	−0.0370	0.9654	−0.0619	0.9421	−0.0430	0.9598
Variance log income	0.7367	−0.1193	0.8381	−0.0676	0.9082	−0.0722	0.9019
Atkinson measure	0.5965	−0.0481	0.9194	−0.0320	0.9463	−0.0312	0.9477

To separate these two effects, we ran an additional experiment where the capital stock in 1971 was kept at its base-run levels, but where total investment demand was reduced to be the same as in INV 1 for that year. As should be expected, real GNP stayed about the same as in the base, in contrast to the Cr$119 million drop for INV 1.[6] The deflation was therefore stronger than in INV 1, with the GNP deflator dropping 43 percent as compared with 30 percent in INV 1.

The most interesting result is the way the GNP shares of labor and capital fall. Both fall relative to proprietors in the deflations. But in INV 1 the share of profits falls by less than that of wages (4 percent for distributed plus retained profits as against 5.1 percent for wages), while in the experiment where only demand was reduced the share of profits falls by much more than that of wages (11.3 percent as against 6.4 percent).

The reason for this macro result can be easily seen as resulting from the neoclassical specification of the production functions, by using equation (6.22) for the real wage rate in the one-sector model of chapter 6, and the corresponding equation for the real cost of capital. These are:

$$\frac{P^L}{P} = \frac{\alpha_L}{v}\left(\frac{V}{L}\right)^{1/\sigma}\left(1 - \frac{eP^E}{P}\right) \tag{9.1}$$

and

$$\frac{P^K}{P} = \frac{\alpha_K}{v}\left(\frac{V}{K}\right)^{1/\sigma}\left(1 - \frac{eP^E}{P}\right). \tag{9.2}$$

With no taxes or depreciation, $P^L = w$ and $P^K = rP$. The ratio of profits to the wage, that is, the ratio of (9.2) to (9.1), gives

$$\frac{rP}{w} = \frac{\alpha_K}{\alpha_L}\left(\frac{K}{L}\right)^{-1/\sigma} \tag{9.3}$$

The elasticity of the profit-wage ratio with respect to changes in the capital-labor ratio is therefore just $-(1/\sigma)$. The general equilibrium nature of our model does not change this neoclassical result because of the way labor and capital are tied to each other.

Since the capital-labor elasticity of substitution is less than one in the sectors where the majority of the profits are generated, the share of profits should rise (compared with the share of labor) when there is a smaller capital stock and when aggregate demand

6. All money amounts in this chapter are in constant 1959 cruzeiros.

is controlled for. This is the result noted above. Furthermore, a check by each sector in the full model shows that our prediction holds in every case. The profit share as a ratio to the wage share rises in every sector where the elasticity of substitution is less than one, and falls where it is greater than one.

The moral of this story is that if investment is lowered, the immediate effect is equalizing, as the economy is under less pressure to produce saving. But after a while the share of profits rises, in a neoclassical way, resulting in a less equal distribution. In addition, with less aggregate supply, the economy eventually comes under inflationary pressures to meet the given final demands, which further worsens distribution.

The principal microeconomic results center around the unequal changes in exogenous demands when investment falls. The investment-goods-producing industrial sectors are of course most affected. The demand for their products drops substantially, but their capital stock is immobile. The profit rates on the capital stocks of these sectors, which are really rentals when compared across sectors, therefore fall a great deal—75 to 85 percent of their base values—while in the other sectors profit rate changes range from −5 to +23 percent. Workers, however, are mobile and are therefore pushed out of the investment-goods sectors to ones where their marginal product (and therefore their wage, in a neoclassical model) is lower. Real GNP falls a little solely because of this shifting of the labor force, even when the capital stock is constant, as in 1962 or in our special experiment with 1971.

The other results of tables 9-7 to 9-9 should be clear, except possibly the fact that depreciation allowances as a share of GNP stayed about constant, even though the real capital stock had declined by 6.1 percent by 1971. This was the result of relative price changes, mainly the price of imported capital, which was tied to a constant world price. With the deflation, its relative price rose, thus increasing the level of depreciation allowances when domestic prices fell. In the experiment where the capital stock was kept constant, the share of depreciation allowances rose by 4.5 percent.

Shifts in Investment by Sector: INV 2 and INV 3

Both these solutions test the effect of shifting investment demand toward rapidly growing sectors. In INV 2 the animal spirits parameters F_i (defined in chapter 7 under "Investment Functions") for sectors 8 through 11 (basic metals and producers' goods) and sector 16 (chemicals) are increased by 25 percent, while those in sectors 17 through 19 (textiles, clothing, and food products—the old industrial sectors) are reduced by the same proportion. In INV 3 the base solution value of F_i in any period τ is multiplied by $(\hat{g}_i/\bar{g})^{0.5}$, where $\hat{g}_i$ is the growth rate of sector i between periods $\tau - 2$ and $\tau - 1$, and $\bar{g}$ is the economywide growth rate over the same time span.

The microeconomic results are the most interesting. The sectoral shifts in relative sizes of capital stocks were major, especially in INV 2. There, the dynamic industrial sectors ended up in 1971 with capital stocks at 119 to 133 percent of their base values, and the old industrial sectors had 83 to 87 percent of their base capital stocks. In INV 3 there were a few outliers (mining had 126 percent of its base capital stock, machinery had 111 percent, leather had 87 percent, and tobacco had 86 percent), but all the rest were in the range of 93 to 106 percent of base values.

When capital stocks changed, profit rates (rents) on the immobile capital moved in the opposite direction, often quite sharply. In INV 2 sectors with more capital ended up with profit rates on that capital of 38 to 59 percent of their base profit rates, while sectors with less capital had their profit rates increase to 173 to 333 percent of their base values. These large changes were caused by the relative inelasticity of most demands. Relative prices changed a great deal, but only consumption responds to relative prices, and household consumption forms only a very small part of total demand for most of the sectors in which capital stocks changed significantly. The relative producer prices of sectors 8 to 11 fell to about 73 percent of their base values in INV 2 (expressed as a proportion of sector 1 prices, to remove the effects of general deflation).

With the prices of goods falling in sectors with an increased capital stock (and rising if the capital stock fell), mobile labor was pushed out of the dynamic industrial sectors and pulled into the old industrial sectors. To produce the amount of output demanded (which stayed about constant), if there were more immobile capital then there was less need for labor. Even though capital and labor do not substitute easily in production in these sectors (with elasticities of substitution in the range 0.5 to 0.8), if there is more capital, there is less need for labor. Directing investment toward the modern, dynamic sectors lowers employment opportunities in them.

In INV 2 the final total capital stock is 1.85 percent higher than in the base run, and in INV 3 it is 0.8 percent lower. Real GNP moves in the same way because of full employment of all factors. Both solutions are deflationary even though physical investment demand in 1971 was higher in each (in INV 2 it rose by over 10 percent). Real consumption demand rose a little in INV 2 and stayed about the same in INV 3. All other final demands were constant. Why then did they deflate? In INV 2 things were helped a little by the small rise in real GNP supply, but the main explanation lies in the relative price changes. As noted above, it was in the dynamic industrial sectors that relative prices declined. These are also the sectors that produce much of the investment goods in the economy. When their relative prices fell, the cost of accomplishing a given amount of real investment declined. Nominal investment demand therefore actually fell as a share of GNP, even though real investment rose, and the economy deflated.

The labor share of GNP rose in INV 2 and fell only slightly in INV 3. Normally, a deflation would lead to a sharp decrease. Our wage index did fall—by about 20 percent, in fact. This is the only way a general equilibrium model in which price is made equal to cost can bring about a change in the price level. The GNP shares of labor nevertheless held firm because of the offsetting movements of labor between sectors that paid different wage rates in relation to the index. The share in GNP of the manufacturing capitalists' profits fell by 15 percent in INV 2, while the GNP shares of the other capitalists held steady or rose. Similar movements, but not nearly so strong, occurred in INV 3. With the deflation and favorable movements in GNP shares, the income distribution gets significantly better.

In contrast to simple forced savings stories, the general equilibrium model permits the income distribution to improve, even when aggregate real demand increases, via intersectoral price shifts. These can lower nominal demands and lead to a general deflation, helping the low-income entrepreneurs. Of course, profit rates in the investment-goods-producing sectors must fall when additional capital is directed toward them. If this assumption of perfect competition does not hold and profits stay high, the beneficial effects on the income distribution will not follow.

Table 9-10. GOV and TRANS Solutions—Output, Price, Expenditure, and Wage Variations: 1971, Wages Variable

Item	Base level	GOV 1		GOV 2		TRANS 1		TRANS 2	
		Absolute change	*Ratio to base*	*Absolute change*	*Ratio to base*	*Absolute change*	*Ratio to base*	*Absolute change*	*Ratio to base*
Output and prices									
GNP (millions of 1959 cruzeiros)	4185	−17	0.9959	−2	0.9995	−5	0.9987	0	1.0001
GNP deflator	2.7106	−1.3221	0.5122	−0.3472	0.8719	−0.9128	0.6632	−0.0292	0.9892
Final demands									
Personal consumption/GNP	0.6466	0.0322	1.0497	0.0035	1.0055	−0.0012	0.9981	0.0010	1.0016
Government									
Purchases of goods/GNP	0.1045	−0.0334	0.6805	−0.0001	0.9993	−0.0004	0.9963	−0.0002	0.9979
Labor payments/GNP	0.0679	−0.0050	0.9260	−0.0047	0.9306	−0.0033	0.9508	0.0001	1.0012
Investment									
New capital formation/GNP	0.1335	0.0057	1.0429	0.0013	1.0099	0.0044	1.0333	−0.0004	0.9967
Capital replacement/GNP	0.0548	0.0047	1.0863	0.0010	1.0183	0.0033	1.0593	−0.0003	0.9949
Foreign trade									
Exports / GNP	0.0447	0.0429	1.9587	0.0066	1.1466	0.0227	1.5085	0.0004	1.0100
Less imports / GNP	0.0521	0.0470	1.9013	0.0075	1.1448	0.0254	1.4875	0.0005	1.0095
Transfers / GNP	0.0531	0.0504	1.9487	0.0078	1.1462	0.0110	1.2068	0.0003	1.0053
Wage levels[a]									
Family farm workers	0.4306	−0.2252	0.4769	−0.0623	0.8552	−0.1594	0.6298	−0.0025	0.9942
Sharecroppers	0.9867	−0.5162	0.4768	−0.1433	0.8548	−0.3652	0.6298	−0.0060	0.9939
Uneducated	0.8969	−0.4695	0.4765	−0.1302	0.8548	−0.3317	0.6301	−0.0064	0.9929
Primary-educated	1.1240	−0.5891	0.4759	−0.1637	0.8543	−0.4158	0.6301	−0.0096	0.9915
Secondary-educated	3.8769	−2.0523	0.4706	−0.5685	0.8534	−1.4360	0.6296	−0.0430	0.9889
Highly educated	7.1595	−3.8100	0.4678	−1.0592	0.8521	−2.6559	0.6290	−0.0773	0.9892

a. Thousands of cruzeiros per ten workers.

Changes in Government Expenditure Policies

The previous two sections dealt with experiments that were conducted to get a better feel for the process of growth and distribution in Brazil. There was no supposition of any direct policy intervention affecting this process. This section begins the discussion of experiments in which policymakers have a direct hand, and four experiments are reviewed in which government expenditure patterns are altered (see tables 9-10 to 9-12).

Reduced Government Spending on Goods and Services: GOV 1

To assess the impact of the level of government spending on the economy, in GOV 1 we reduced all government purchases of goods and services by 30 percent. Direct government employment and government expenditures on transfers and export subsidies were kept at their base rates.

Once again, the results can be separated into macro effects and micro effects. We go into detail in this section on the macro effects of this deflationary policy, so that the descriptions of the macro results of later experiments can be brief. The main process is always the same.

The macro results can best be described through the analysis of changes in saving (see table 9-12). Since saving must equal investment, if total investment is constant then total saving must be constant too, although this identity holds only in nominal terms. Because of relative price changes, nominal investment as a share of GNP may change even though real investment is constant, as it is in GOV 1. Normally these relative price changes are not very important, and nominal saving as a share of GNP will be about constant.

With the 30 percent fall in government expenditures on goods and services, government saving rises dramatically. Aggregate demand falls and, with the *initial* level of wages, there is unemployment. With the lower employment level, real GNP falls. Since we assume that the fixed capital stock is still fully employed, profit rates have to fall a great deal. The GNP share of profits falls, and that of labor rises, even though there is still unemployed labor. This is the other side of the coin that we noted with regard to the INV 1 experiment, where the capital stock was reduced. Here, the level of employed labor falls, and with an average

Table 9-11. GOV and TRANS Solutions—Functional Income Distribution Measures: 1971, Wages Variable

Item	Base level (1959 cruzeiros)	Base share in GNP	GOV 1: Change in GNP share from base	GOV 1: Ratio of GNP share to base
Wages and salaries	4,458,694	0.3931	−0.0316	0.9196
Family farm workers	129,616	0.0114	−0.0007	0.9369
Sharecroppers	89,518	0.0079	−0.0005	0.9353
Uneducated	447,741	0.0395	−0.0029	0.9271
Primary-educated	2,003,087	0.1766	−0.0137	0.9222
Secondary-educated	1,091,394	0.0962	−0.0087	0.9097
Highly educated	696,739	0.0614	−0.0050	0.9187
Entrepreneurial income	442,541	0.0390	0.0371	1.9521
Profits and depreciation allowance	3,532,975	0.3115	−0.0330	0.8941
Distributed profits	2,012,077	0.1774	−0.0240	0.8650
Agricultural capitalists	187,036	0.0165	−0.0017	0.8946
Manufacturing capitalists	862,356	0.0760	−0.0165	0.7829
Commerce capitalists	231,202	0.0204	−0.0031	0.8484
Services capitalists	576,084	0.0508	−0.0011	0.9777
Highly educated labor	155,401	0.0137	−0.0015	0.8912
Other workers	0	0.0000	0.0000	1.0000
Retained profits	899,056	0.0793	−0.0138	0.8264
Depreciation allowance	621,842	0.0548	0.0047	1.0863
Taxes	2,908,891	0.2564	0.0275	1.1071
Value added tax	1,901,678	0.1677	−0.0090	0.9463
Labor wage tax	578,725	0.0510	−0.0050	0.9021
Profit tax	636,241	0.0561	−0.0085	0.8478
Net tariffs	−207,751	−0.0183	0.0499	−1.7273
Gross national product	11,343,101			

capital-labor elasticity of substitution of less than one, the share of labor must rise.

With profit rates down on a fixed capital stock, profits and therefore retained corporate earnings are also down. The fall in this source of saving largely makes up for the rise in government saving. This, then, is the mechanism by which aggregate supply is made equal to aggregate demand (that is, saving made equal to investment), even though wages are still constant. We have an equilibrium, although it is an unemployment equilibrium.

To attain full employment, the model is then allowed to adjust wages. For the reasons given in the appendix to chapter 7, the general level of wages will have to fall a great deal. There is no direct capital-labor substitution, since the price of capital

GOV 2		*TRANS 1*		*TRANS 2*	
Change in GNP share from base	*Ratio of GNP share to base*	*Change in GNP share from base*	*Ratio of GNP share to base*	*Change in GNP share from base*	*Ratio of GNP share to base*
−0.0078	0.9801	−0.0197	0.9498	0.0002	1.0005
−0.0002	0.9812	−0.0005	0.9552	0.0001	1.0059
−0.0001	0.9815	−0.0004	0.9503	0.0000	1.0040
−0.0008	0.9806	−0.0020	0.9502	0.0000	1.0001
−0.0034	0.9807	−0.0087	0.9506	0.0002	1.0011
−0.0020	0.9797	−0.0050	0.9480	−0.0001	0.9995
−0.0013	0.9795	−0.0030	0.9507	0.0000	1.0008
0.0059	1.1514	0.0198	1.5073	0.0006	1.0144
−0.0027	0.9914	−0.0155	0.9501	−0.0010	0.9967
−0.0024	0.9867	−0.0127	0.9284	−0.0004	0.9978
−0.0004	0.9754	−0.0017	0.8978	0.0002	1.0098
−0.0011	0.9859	−0.0058	0.9231	−0.0007	0.9912
−0.0005	0.9733	−0.0016	0.9201	0.0000	1.0010
−0.0002	0.9955	−0.0027	0.9474	0.0001	1.0026
−0.0001	0.9913	−0.0009	0.9366	−0.0000	0.9976
0.0000	1.0000	0.0000	1.0000	0.0000	1.0000
0.0013	0.9835	−0.0061	0.9232	−0.0004	0.9953
0.0010	1.0183	0.0033	1.0593	−0.0003	0.9949
0.0046	1.0180	0.0155	1.0604	0.0003	1.0011
−0.0006	0.9967	−0.0041	0.9754	0.0001	1.0006
−0.0018	0.9645	−0.0026	0.9494	−0.0001	0.9983
−0.0007	0.9871	−0.0040	0.9291	−0.0002	0.9956
0.0076	0.5851	0.0261	−0.4248	0.0004	0.9785

changes at the same time the price of labor does. But after a long fall in wages in relation to the remuneration rate of proprietors (the numeraire), the unit cost of labor eventually falls enough in relation to the price of the product to lead to the full employment of all labor.

Profit rates remain low and, at full employment, are again the principal source of reduced saving to make up for the rise in government saving. During the deflation, however, other changes in the various savings components occur which sometimes increase saving and sometimes decrease it. The balance of payments deficit is almost fixed in real terms, since exports are exogenous and since most imports are tied rigidly to real output levels. With the deflation and a fixed cruzeiro-dollar exchange

Table 9-12. GOV and TRANS Solutions—Saving, Taxes, and Size Distribution Measures: 1971, Wages Variable

		GOV 1		GOV 2		TRANS 1		TRANS 2	
Item	Base level	Change in portion from base	Ratio of portion to base	Change in portion from base	Ratio of portion to base	Change in portion from base	Ratio of portion to base	Change in portion from base	Ratio of portion to base
Savings ratios									
Total saving/GNP	0.1884	0.0104	1.0550	0.0022	1.0118	0.0076	1.0404	−0.0008	0.9956
Depreciation allowance/saving	0.2910	0.0084	1.0289	0.0016	1.0056	0.0051	1.0174	−0.0004	0.9985
Retained corporate earnings/saving	0.4208	−0.0911	0.7835	−0.0116	0.9723	−0.0473	0.8876	−0.0000	1.0000
Personal saving/saving	0.0534	−0.0012	0.9771	−0.0003	0.9938	−0.0027	0.9491	−0.0011	0.9798
Balance of payments deficit/saving	0.0394	0.0185	1.4690	0.0046	1.1169	0.0120	1.3034	0.0003	1.0076
Government saving/saving	0.1954	0.0653	1.3344	0.0056	1.0288	0.0329	1.1683	0.0011	1.0058
Tax ratios									
Total government taxes/GNP	0.2880	−0.0166	0.9425	−0.0021	0.9927	−0.0075	0.9741	−0.0002	0.9994
Labor tax/total taxes	0.1772	−0.0077	0.9565	−0.0051	0.9710	−0.0046	0.9740	−0.0003	0.9983
Profit tax/total taxes	0.1948	−0.0196	0.8995	−0.0011	0.9943	−0.0090	0.9538	−0.0007	0.9962
Value added tax/total taxes	0.5822	0.0024	1.0042	0.0025	1.0042	0.0009	1.0015	0.0008	1.0014
Tariffs/total taxes	0.0255	0.0252	1.9880	0.0038	1.1502	0.0130	1.5108	0.0002	1.0086
Income tax/total taxes	0.0203	−0.0004	0.9827	−0.0000	0.9982	−0.0003	0.9871	−0.0000	0.9992
Size distribution before taxes and transfers									
Gini coefficient	0.5724	−0.0600	0.8951	−0.0093	0.9838	−0.0340	0.9405	−0.0011	0.9981
Theil measure	1.0921	−0.1443	0.8678	−0.0141	0.9871	−0.0779	0.9287	−0.0041	0.9963
Variance log income	0.7111	−0.2358	0.6684	−0.0634	0.9109	−0.1645	0.7687	−0.0043	0.9939
Atkinson measure	0.5885	−0.1123	0.8091	−0.0249	0.9577	−0.0724	0.8770	−0.0021	0.9965
Size distribution after taxes and transfers									
Gini coefficient	0.5776	−0.0379	0.9343	−0.0065	0.9888	−0.0264	0.9543	−0.0238	0.9587
Theil measure	1.0692	−0.1296	0.8788	−0.0144	0.9866	−0.0716	0.9330	−0.0590	0.9448
Variance log income	0.7367	−0.1702	0.7689	−0.0508	0.9311	−0.1402	0.8097	−0.0812	0.8898
Atkinson measure	0.5965	−0.0792	0.8672	−0.0197	0.9669	−0.0605	0.8986	−0.0367	0.9385

rate, the value of this deficit in total saving rises. In addition, since the final full-employment equilibrium will have a higher real output level than the initial unemployment equilibrium, real imports will rise (since they are tied to real outputs), and the balance of payments deficit will rise in constant dollar terms. This further increases the contribution of the deficit to saving. Although the increase is large in relative terms (the contribution of the deficit to total saving rises by 47 percent in GOV 1), the deficit starts out as such a small contribution to total saving (3.9 percent in the base run), that its absolute contribution to saving changes little.

With the deflation, government saving also rises beyond the initial change caused by the reduction in purchases. There are two forces which partly offset each other. First, expenditure on transfers, which are fixed in nominal terms, rises with the deflation. This would reduce government saving. Offsetting this is a fall in government expenditures on export subsidies. In order for Brazil to be able to sell its exports on the world market through a generally overvalued exchange rate, we assume that the government subsidizes exports to the extent necessary to make Brazilian prices and world prices equal. In practice, these operate through various tax breaks given exporters, but it is easier to think of them as direct expenditures. With the deflation, there is less need for such subsidies, as Brazilian prices come more in line with the world's, and these expenditures therefore fall, increasing government saving.

The other sources of saving are depreciation allowances and personal saving. Personal saving is tied to household income levels, with the richer households saving a higher proportion of their income. With a more equal distribution of income personal saving will fall somewhat. Since it is such a small absolute source of saving, and since the household distribution of income generally changes little, it is never a large source of change in total saving. Depreciation allowances are a large absolute source, but they are tied to a capital stock that does not change. Depreciation allowances can change as a source of saving only through relative price changes. With a deflation, they generally rise a little, since imported capital makes up a significant portion of the total capital stock, and the relative price of this imported good rises in inverse proportion to the deflation (since it is fixed in world prices).

To summarize, if some source of saving rises, leading to a shortfall of aggregate demand, retained corporate earnings must fall to bring total saving back in line with total investment (or, equivalently, make aggregate supply equal aggregate demand).

The deflation is strongly equalizing. Both capital incomes and labor incomes fall, while the real incomes of proprietors rise. Since most of the proprietors in the model (small farmers, shopkeepers, and the like) are fairly poor, deflation leads to a more equal distribution of income. Relative incomes of different labor groups do not normally change; since different types of labor can substitute for each other with a high elasticity, the wage structure is rigid. And the relative incomes of capital and labor do not change very much since total profits fall just about as fast as the wage bill in the general deflation.

The aggregate distribution measures given in table 9-12 reflect this equalizing result of deflation. All the measures show a significant improvement in distribution, especially the variance of log incomes. The log variance gives a higher weight to low-income recipients,[7] and the improvement in the situation of the low-income proprietors therefore shows up as an especially sharp fall in this measure of inequality.

The micro results of GOV 1 are similar to the ones noted for INV 1. Sectors with a relatively large part of their demand from government are especially hurt by the fall in expenditures. These are mainly the manufacturing sectors, with sectors 4, 7, 8, 9, 10, 11, 16, and 22 all receiving a higher than average share of government purchases. With a fixed capital stock and decreased demand, their profit rates fall more than the average, their prices fall, and labor is pushed out of them and into the lower productivity labor-surplus sectors. As table 9-11 shows, manufacturing capitalists experience the largest fall in GNP share because of the sectoral impact of government spending.

A rise in government spending would result in the mirror image of the above. Government spending on goods as a proportion of GNP did rise in the 1960s in the model's base solution, from 4 percent of GNP in 1959 to 10.5 percent in 1971. Without a concomitant rise in taxes, the reduced government saving would be inflationary and would have to be financed, in the model, by a rise in corporate profits. Both of these results lead to a worse distribution of income.

7. See Sen (1973), p. 29, for example, or merely note that the log function becomes less concave at higher income levels.

Reduced Government Employment: GOV 2

In this experiment, government demands for each type of labor it hires is reduced by 5 percent. This should have two main effects. First, government saving will rise, leading to a deflation. Second, with less of the fully employed labor supply being used by government, private production should be able to expand. We should also see a narrowing of the wage structure, since government employs a relatively higher share of the higher skilled labor types. Indeed, it employs none of the lowest two labor groups.

In fact, this second effect is of minor importance, since the amount of extra labor released is very small. The total labor supply available for private employment rises by only about 0.25 percent for uneducated workers, 0.75 percent for the primary-educated, 1 percent for the secondary-educated, 1.5 percent for the highly educated, and, of course, none at all for family farm workers and sharecroppers. One may be able to note a very slight narrowing of the wage structure in table 9.10, but the high elasticity of substitution between labor types mitigates any further narrowing that might have resulted.

The main effect of more government saving is therefore deflationary. The GNP deflator falls by 13 percent, and all of the standard deflationary results described for GOV 1 follow. Retained corporate earnings fall, the GNP shares of labor and capital fall while that of properties rises, and the distribution of income becomes more equal.

Changes in Government Transfer Policies: TRANS 1 and TRANS 2

In these two experiments we had the government change its policies on transfers to households. As explained in chapter 8, the model allows for government transfers to households as payments fixed in nominal terms to the upper three classes of consumers (see table 8-8). For Brazil, these include social security payments, interest on the public debt, and the like. In TRANS 1 they were reduced by 20 percent in nominal terms for each household. In TRANS 2, the total amount of nominal transfers to the richest class of households was cut in half, and this was distributed in equal amounts to the two poorest classes of household. Since the very poorest type of household was about 50 percent more numerous than the second poorest, the poorest received only two-thirds the per household transfer of the second poorest. This is a reasonable assumption in view of what is politically possible.

Since government expenditure on transfers falls in TRANS 1, there is a deflation, with all the normal results: labor and capital shares of GNP fall while that of proprietors gains, and distribution gets better. Somewhat paradoxically, the share of transfers in GNP actually rises by 21 percent, even though in nominal terms it falls by 20 percent. The immediate cause is the 34 percent fall in the price level, but the question remains, Why does the price level fall by so much? This is another illustration of the difficulty of finding a full-employment equilibrium through changes in nominal wage rates. As discussed in the appendix to chapter 7, a very large fall in nominal wages, and therefore in the general price level, is necessary to increase the general demand for labor by a small amount. Transfers constitute only 5.3 percent of GNP in the base run, and yet a fall of only 20 percent in their nominal value (1.06 percent of GNP in base prices) necessitated a fall of 37 percent in the general wage level to achieve full employment again.

The real value of transfers to the top three classes of household therefore rose (the poorest household class got no transfers) in TRANS 1. As noted before, the tax and transfer system in Brazil is generally regressive (for example, the aggregate distribution measures in the base run are worse in three cases out of four after taxes and transfers). The real value of transfers, to those that received any, rose in TRANS 1. We therefore see in table 9-12 that by all four distribution measures the improvement in distribution was substantially greater before taxes and transfers were added.

In TRANS 2 the reduction in transfers to the richest class of household is balanced by increases to the two poorest classes of household, so that there is no deflation. Most macro items stay the same. Aggregate income distribution *does* become significantly better. The transfer system becomes, at least in relation to the old one, much more progressive. Before taxes and transfers, the aggregate distribution measures remain about the same, but after taxes and transfers are added, they improve by about 4 to 11 percent. These are substantial jumps for such stable measures.

The shift in distribution to the poorer classes results in significant shifts in consumer demand from luxury goods to necessities. As a result, in the sectors that have a substantial amount of their demand coming from the sale of luxury goods, profit rates (on fixed capital stock) fall. They fell by almost 20 percent for rubber goods and about 5 percent for electrical goods, transport goods, and publishing. The output of the domestic servants sector falls more than 4 percent. In sectors that produce necessities profits rise (by as much as 13.5 percent in the food sector).

The mobile labor force follows these shifts in sectoral demand. Since luxury goods sectors employ more highly skilled labor than do sectors producing necessities, the wage spread narrows a little (table 9-10).

TRANS 2 supports the idea that government policy, through direct redistribution of incomes, can have a significant effect in reducing inequality. Like the SEN 3 experiment, it supports the structuralist argument that less diverse consumer demand patterns would require a production mix less oriented toward luxury goods. It also indicates that beyond those directly affected by the change in transfer policies, there may be those with important vested interests in the luxury goods sectors who would oppose any change that deprived them of profit.

Modifying Tax Rates and the Foreign Exchange Rate

In this series of experiments, we changed the rates for various government policy instruments that affect the levels of various economic activities only indirectly (see tables 9-13 to 9-15).

Reducing Wage Tax Rates by 50 Percent: TAX 1

Wage taxes increased enormously in Brazil in the 1960s, and there has been a good deal of debate on the effect these taxes would have on employment demand. In the model, wage taxes are paid in the industrial sectors (6 through 23). In the base year (1959) they were set at 18 percent of wages and by 1971 they had risen to 44 percent of wages. This is in line with the figures found by Bacha, Mata, and Modenesi (1972). In TAX 1 they are lowered to 22 percent.

With a fixed level of government spending, but lower taxes, government saving falls. With fixed investment demand, the model inflates. The results are therefore the mirror image of those coming from the normal deflation. The GNP share of proprietors falls, that of capital and labor rises, retained corporate earnings rise as a share of saving, and the income distribution gets worse.

Table 9-13. *TAX and RATE Solutions—Output, Price, Expenditure, and Wage Variations: 1971, Wages Variable*

Item	Base level	TAX 1 Absolute change	TAX 1 Ratio to base	TAX 2 Absolute change	TAX 2 Ratio to base	TAX 3 Absolute change	TAX 3 Ratio to base	RATE 1 Absolute change	RATE 1 Ratio to base
Output and prices									
GNP (millions of 1959 cruzeiros)	4,185	14	1.0033	6	1.0014	10	1.0023	−9	0.9979
GNP deflator	2.7106	2.4719	1.9120	6.9864	3.5775	−0.2857	0.8946	−0.3447	0.8728
Final demands									
Personal consumption/GNP	0.6466	0.0128	1.0197	−0.0001	0.9999	0.0113	1.0184	−0.0017	0.9973
Government									
Purchases of goods/GNP	0.1045	−0.0003	0.9970	0.0008	1.0073	−0.0009	0.9917	−0.0002	0.9985
Labor payments/GNP	0.0679	−0.0041	0.9400	0.0048	1.0707	−0.0076	0.8875	−0.0016	0.9768
Investment									
New capital formation/GNP	0.1335	−0.0062	0.9533	−0.0058	0.9562	−0.0012	0.9908	0.0031	1.0229
Capital replacement/GNP	0.0548	−0.0050	0.9091	−0.0043	0.9209	−0.0013	0.9772	0.0023	1.0412
Foreign trade									
Exports/GNP	0.0447	−0.0214	0.5209	−0.0322	0.2789	0.0051	1.1144	0.0143	1.3193
Less imports/GNP	0.0521	−0.0244	0.5326	−0.0371	0.2888	0.0059	1.1138	0.0160	1.3074
Transfers/GNP	0.0531	−0.0254	0.5209	−0.0382	0.2797	0.0060	1.1125	0.0078	1.1476
Wage levels[a]									
Family farm workers	0.4306	0.4843	2.1247	1.2160	3.8239	−0.0262	0.9393	−0.0642	0.8510
Sharecroppers	0.9867	1.1093	2.1242	2.7838	3.8214	−0.0598	0.9394	−0.1476	0.8504
Uneducated	0.8969	1.0078	2.1237	2.5337	3.8250	−0.0548	0.9389	−0.1339	0.8507
Primary-educated	1.1240	1.2629	2.1235	3.1796	3.8288	−0.0694	0.9382	−0.1677	0.8508
Secondary-educated	3.8769	4.3820	2.1303	11.0170	3.8417	−0.2360	0.9391	−0.5789	0.8507
Highly educated	7.1595	8.1024	2.1317	20.3271	3.8392	−0.4311	0.9398	−1.0736	0.8500

a. Thousands of cruzeiros per ten workers.

In the microeconomics, the lower wage tax rate for sectors 6 to 23 does lower the cost of labor, P_i^L from equation (7.1), by a great deal. In the fixed wage solution, the cost of labor to the industrial sectors falls to 85 percent of its base-run cost. After the wages are allowed to vary to achieve full employment, the wage structure remains the same because of the high elasticities of substitution between labor types. All wages inflate by about 13 percent as seen in table 9-13. Therefore, even after wages are allowed to vary, the cost of labor to the industrial sectors remains at 85 percent of the cost to the other sectors, all in relation to the base run.

In spite of this enormous shift in relative labor costs between the industrial and nonindustrial sectors, employment shifts were fairly small. The industrial sectors as a whole had only a 2 percent increase in employment. Commerce had a 2.5 percent rise, services a 1.5 percent fall, domestic servants a 4.8 percent fall, and agriculture stayed the same.[8]

Such a small shift of labor into industry in spite of the 15 percent fall in its relative cost would seem surprising. The model does allow for capital-labor substitution with elasticities around one. Such shifts did not, in fact, occur because the cost of capital, P_i^K, moved in the same way as the cost of labor. The cost of capital also fell about 15 percent in the industrial sectors in relation to the nonindustrial, which left the relative cost of labor to capital almost the same. The various sectors therefore had no reason to try to substitute labor for capital, even though they could have.

Why did the cost of capital fall for the industrial sectors? There are two reasons. First, since the capital stock for the industrial sectors is mainly produced by the industrial sectors, if the cost of industrial goods falls (as it does when the wage costs are lowered), the cost of capital to the industrial sectors will fall also. Since the capital stock of the nonindustrial sectors is mainly produced by the nonindustrial sectors, its cost does not fall.

To the extent that the B matrix (table 8.5) "crosses" between the industrial and nonindustrial sectors, these conclusions must be modified. The industrial sectors also purchase capital "goods"

8. Even with wages held fixed, the results are not greatly different. Because of the increase in aggregate demand from the tax reduction, total employment (exclusive of government) rises by 5.29 percent. When this overall growth is netted out, the sectoral changes are: industrial sectors, 2.61 percent; commerce, 1.29 percent; services, 7.70 percent; construction, −3.77 percent; domestic servants, −0.67 percent; and crop agriculture, −1.05 percent.

from commerce, construction, and imports. Because the relative cost of goods from commerce and construction rises when wage taxes are lowered for the industrial sectors, to a certain extent the cost of capital will rise for the industrial sectors. This would lead to substitution of labor for capital if nothing else changed. But this trend will be at least partially offset, and possibly more than fully offset, by the relative decline in the cost of imported capital. The industrial sectors are heavy users of imported machinery, and with the domestic inflation their relative cost falls. This would lead to substitution of capital for labor.

The second reason for the fall in the relative price of capital for the industrial sectors arises from the fixity of the capital stock and the inelasticity of demand to relative price changes. If demand were totally inelastic, then with a fixed capital stock the total amount of labor a sector would hire would also be fixed, no matter what the cost of labor. If a sector hired more labor and combined it with the fixed capital stock, more output would be produced than was demanded. When the cost of labor falls, the cost (rent) of capital will therefore also have to fall by the same proportion. To a large extent this occurred automatically for the first reason discussed above. Any residual change will be achieved by changes in the profit rate earned by the fixed capital stock in that sector.

Demands are not totally inelastic in our model. Consumer demands are quite elastic, but they make up only 29 percent of total demands in the economy. The rest are price inelastic intermediate demands, government demands, and investment, depreciation, and export demands. The fall in the relative price of industrial goods therefore does not lead to a large increase in demand for them, and there is little shift in employment demands. The relevance of this finding of course depends on one's assessment of how credibly the general equilibrium model describes the Brazilian economy, but it casts severe doubt on simple neoclassical prescriptions for increasing employment in manufacturing by cutting labor costs through reductions of social security taxes (or minimum wages).

Reducing Profit Tax Rates by 50 Percent: TAX 2

Profits in sectors 3 to 23 (industry, services, and commerce) are assumed to be taxed at the rate of 20 percent. It is an inside tax, and in TAX 2 we lower the rate to 10 percent.

As in TAX 1, the result is inflation, since taxes are lowered with government spending remaining the same. It is a good deal more inflationary than TAX 1: the GNP deflator shot up to 9.7 in TAX 2 from 2.7 in the base, while in TAX 1 it went only to 5.2. There are two main reasons. In the base the level of profit taxes is higher than that of wage taxes (5.6 percent of GNP as opposed to 5.1 percent). This factor should not be too important, but as pointed out before, small changes in saving lead to wide swings in the level of wages to bring about full employment.

The second reason arises from the fact that government pays wage taxes on the wages of its own workers. Therefore, when wage taxes are lowered, government spending falls. Since government saving is the small difference between two large sums, a small reduction in spending can lead to large proportional shifts in government saving. In both TAX 1 and TAX 2 government revenues fall from about 29 percent of GNP to 27 percent. Government expenditure on wage taxes falls from 2 percent of GNP to 1 percent in TAX 1, but stays at 2 percent in TAX 2. Government saving therefore falls from 3.7 percent of GNP in the base only to 2.8 percent in TAX 1, but to 1.7 percent in TAX 2.

We therefore get more inflation in TAX 2. Again we observe the usual effects of inflation in the model: the share of proprietors in GNP falls, that of labor and capital rises, retained corporate profits rise (both because of the inflation and because capital incomes are now taxed less), and the income distribution gets much worse.

One might expect, as in the case of TAX 1, that the lowering of the profit tax on sectors 3–23 would lead to important shifts in the relative prices of capital and possibly of labor. This does *not* follow, however, because capital is treated as a fixed factor, while labor is mobile. Capital is earning a rent in each sector, and when the tax on it falls, the profit rate on the capital stock of the sector rises in an offsetting way to leave the cost of capital to the sector the same. The profit rates in sectors 3–23 therefore rise an average of 44 percent, while those in the other sectors rise an average of 20 percent. They all rise because of inflation, but rise by different proportions because of the reduced taxes.

Because of the mobility of labor and the rigid wage structure, the relative cost of labor across sectors remains the same. Wages for all labor types rise by a factor of 3.8 in the inflation. The ratio of labor costs to capital costs remains the same in each sector (full-employment situations are compared in each case), and

Table 9-14. TAX and RATE Solutions—Functional Income Distribution Measures: 1971, Wages Variable

Item	Base level (1959 cruzeiros)	Base share in GNP	TAX 1: Change in GNP share from base	TAX 1: Ratio of GNP share to base
Wages and salaries	4,458,694	0.3931	0.0441	1.1122
Family farm workers	129,616	0.0114	0.0013	1.1102
Sharecroppers	89,518	0.0079	0.0009	1.1084
Uneducated	447,741	0.0395	0.0042	1.1073
Primary-educated	2,003,687	0.1766	0.0198	1.1120
Secondary-educated	1,091,394	0.0962	0.0111	1.1158
Highly educated	696,739	0.0614	0.0069	1.1129
Entrepreneurial income	442,541	0.0390	−0.0186	0.5239
Profits and depreciation allowance	3,532,975	0.3115	0.0132	1.0423
Distributed profits	2,012,077	0.1774	0.0132	1.0744
Agricultural capitalists	187,036	0.0165	0.0027	1.1617
Manufacturing capitalists	862,356	0.0760	0.0002	1.0028
Commerce capitalists	231,202	0.0204	0.0040	1.1964
Services capitalists	576,084	0.0508	0.0055	1.1076
Highly educated labor	155,401	0.0137	0.0008	1.0611
Other workers	0	0.0000	0.0000	1.0000
Retained profits	899,056	0.0793	0.0050	1.0624
Depreciation allowance	621,842	0.0548	−0.0050	0.9091
Taxes	2,908,891	0.2564	−0.0387	0.8491
Value added tax	1,901,678	0.1677	0.0039	1.0232
Labor wage tax	578,725	0.0510	−0.0224	0.5609
Profit tax	636,241	0.0561	0.0033	1.0590
Net tariffs	−207,751	−0.0183	−0.0236	2.2893
Gross national product	11,343,101			

there is therefore almost no movement of labor across sectors. What movement there is comes from the income distribution shifts that result from the inflation. Because low-income proprietors are hurt in the inflation, demand falls for income inelastic goods (food, clothing, beverages, tobacco), and employment shifts from these sectors to those that produce goods favored by the rich.

Reducing Wage Taxes by 50 Percent and Raising Profit Taxes by an Offsetting Amount: TAX 3

In this experiment we try to model a tax reform in which wage taxes are lowered by 50 percent and profit taxes are raised by an

TAX 2		*TAX 3*		*RATE 1*	
Change in GNP share from base	*Ratio of GNP share to base*	*Change in GNP share from base*	*Ratio of GNP share to base*	*Change in GNP share from base*	*Ratio of GNP share to base*
0.0281	1.0715	0.0194	1.0493	−0.0094	0.9762
0.0008	1.0693	0.0006	1.0526	−0.0003	0.9766
0.0006	1.0724	0.0004	1.0470	−0.0002	0.9774
0.0027	1.0688	0.0018	1.0459	−0.0009	0.9764
0.0126	1.0711	0.0088	1.0496	−0.0041	0.9769
0.0070	1.0730	0.0049	1.0512	−0.0024	0.9750
0.0046	1.0742	0.0030	1.0491	−0.0014	0.9774
−0.0281	0.2795	0.0047	1.1203	0.0057	1.1474
0.0529	1.1699	−0.0293	0.9060	−0.0070	0.9774
0.0391	1.2203	−0.0185	0.8959	−0.0062	0.9649
0.0023	1.1385	0.0007	1.0441	−0.0008	0.9505
0.0181	1.2381	−0.0134	0.8234	−0.0029	0.9614
0.0052	1.2545	−0.0005	0.9736	−0.0008	0.9584
0.0105	1.2063	−0.0036	0.9287	−0.0012	0.9761
0.0030	1.2204	−0.0016	0.8820	−0.0004	0.9696
0.0000	1.0000	0.0000	1.0000	0.0000	1.0000
0.0182	1.2295	−0.0095	0.8796	−0.0031	0.9614
−0.0043	0.9209	−0.0012	0.9772	0.0023	1.0412
−0.0530	0.7935	0.0052	1.0202	0.0106	1.0415
0.0056	1.0334	−0.0008	0.9953	−0.0027	0.9838
0.0037	1.0723	−0.0240	0.5288	−0.0012	0.9764
−0.0252	0.5501	0.0230	1.4106	−0.0020	0.9649
−0.0371	3.0275	0.0069	0.6245	0.0164	0.1019

amount that would leave total government revenues about the same. This required a rise in profit tax rates of 44.4186 percent.

Macroeconomically, the model deflates a modest amount. The GNP deflator falls 10 percent even though the total take of the wage tax fell by about the same amount as that of the profit tax rose. Indeed, the total take of the two taxes actually fell a very slight bit (0.1 percent of GNP), which would have been inflationary. The model nevertheless deflated because, as explained in the discussion of TAX 2, government spending on the wage taxes of its own workers falls when the wage tax rate is lowered. Government saving therefore rose from 3.7 percent of GNP to 4.5 percent.

Table 9-15. *TAX and RATE Solutions—Saving, Taxes, and Size Distribution Measures: 1971, Wages Variable*

Item	Base level	TAX 1		TAX 2		TAX 3		RATE 1	
		Change in portion from base	*Ratio in portion to base*	*Change in portion from base*	*Ratio of portion to base*	*Change in portion from base*	*Ratio of portion to base*	*Change in portion from base*	*Ratio of portion to base*
Savings ratios									
Total saving/GNP	0.1884	−0.0113	0.9399	−0.0103	0.9454	−0.0026	0.9863	0.0052	1.0277
Depreciation allowance/saving	0.2910	−0.0098	0.9665	−0.0078	0.9733	−0.0029	0.9900	0.0036	1.0124
Retained corporate earnings/saving	0.4208	0.0550	1.1307	0.1266	1.3009	−0.0454	0.8921	−0.0270	0.9358
Personal saving/saving	0.0534	0.0045	1.0845	0.0048	1.0895	0.0005	1.0087	−0.0017	0.9683
Balance of payments deficit/saving	0.0394	−0.0142	0.6401	−0.0249	0.3679	0.0048	1.1222	0.0078	1.1988
Government saving/saving	0.1954	−0.0357	0.8175	−0.0988	0.4943	1.0430	1.2198	0.0172	1.0879
Tax ratios									
Total government taxes/GNP	0.2880	−0.0182	0.9369	−0.0204	0.9292	−0.0012	0.9960	−0.0038	0.9867
Labor tax/total taxes	0.1772	−0.0712	0.5983	0.0272	1.1533	−0.0832	0.5306	−0.0020	0.9889
Profit tax/total taxes	0.1948	0.0254	1.1303	−0.0795	0.5920	0.0811	1.4163	−0.0043	0.9779
Value added tax/total taxes	0.5822	0.0537	1.0923	0.0654	1.1124	−0.0003	0.9995	−0.0016	0.9972
Tariffs/total taxes	0.0255	−0.0108	0.5765	−0.0174	0.3191	0.0029	1.1146	0.0081	1.3160
Income tax/total taxes	0.0203	0.0029	1.1420	0.0043	1.2094	−0.0005	0.9732	−0.0002	0.9916
Size distribution before taxes and transfers									
Gini coefficient	0.5724	0.0310	1.0541	0.0651	1.1137	−0.0220	0.9615	−0.0119	0.9792
Theil measure	1.0921	0.0501	1.0458	0.2324	1.2128	−0.1293	0.8816	−0.0281	0.9743
Variance log income	0.7111	0.4324	1.6081	0.9205	2.2944	−0.0351	0.9506	−0.0672	0.9055
Atkinson measure	0.5885	0.1316	1.2236	0.2344	1.3984	−0.0282	0.9520	−0.0279	0.9525
Size distribution after taxes and transfers									
Gini coefficient	0.5776	0.0253	1.0437	0.0576	1.0997	−0.0188	0.9674	−0.0088	0.9848
Theil measure	1.0692	0.0557	1.0521	0.2408	1.2252	−0.1180	0.8896	−0.0272	0.9745
Variance log income	0.7367	0.3787	1.5141	0.8327	2.1303	−0.0287	0.9611	−0.0540	0.9268
Atkinson measure	0.5965	0.1174	1.1968	0.2184	1.3661	−0.0240	0.9598	−0.0224	0.9625

Relative sectoral costs changed from TAX 1 and TAX 2 as one would expect. The cost of labor to sectors 6–23 fell to 85 percent of the cost to other sectors, since the wage tax rate was lowered again by 50 percent. As noted in TAX 2, the cost of capital would not be changed by changes in the tax on profits (because of offsetting movements in the profit rate); therefore the cost of capital was free to respond in an offsetting way to the change in the cost of labor, as it did in TAX 1. As a result, intersectoral labor movements were again fairly small. A large part of those that did occur can be explained by the shifts in the income distribution, with the resulting changes in demand patterns.

The income distribution improved a great deal as a result of the tax reform, as can be seen by the aggregate distribution measures of table 9-15. The deflation helped, but it cannot explain all the improvement. Other experiments with similar or greater deflations (such as GOV 2, RATE 1, and EXP 1) had less of an improvement in distribution. In TAX 3 the GNP share of labor actually rose, and substantially so, because taxes on labor fell. In addition, the GNP share of profits fell by 9.4 percent. There are two reasons for this in the model. First, as always with a deflation, profits fell to reduce retained corporate earnings so that saving would fall (to offset the increase in government saving). Second, in TAX 3 when profit taxes rose, profit rates (rents) had to fall to keep the cost of capital constant.

If one is willing to believe the model, it would seem to indicate that a significant improvement in the distribution of income can come from changes in the decisions on which factors to tax.

Devalue the Foreign Exchange Rate by 15 Percent: RATE 1

Developing countries are often urged by institutions such as the IMF to devalue their currencies, and they almost invariably resist. Academic economists seem to look only at the effects on the foreign trade balance when coming to their decision to recommend devaluation. In this experiment we consider some of the domestic repercussions—especially on effective demand and on the distribution of income—that might result from a devaluation of the cruzeiro.

Devaluation makes little difference microeconomically. In sectors that must import relatively more of their inputs, their relative costs and therefore prices (in our perfectly competitive world) rise. For the Brazilian economy, however, imports are such a small proportion of total output that relative prices change little.

The interesting results are macroeconomic. A devaluation of the cruzeiro leads to increased saving, which leads to deflation. This is the opposite of the normal assumption that devaluation is inflationary. Economists usually ignore the effects of devaluation on saving and therefore on effective demand. They assume that with a devaluation, foreign goods will become more expensive, which will lead to a curtailment of imports and to a spurt in exports and home-goods production. Many would question the extent to which exports and imports are price responsive in developing countries. In our model, we assume that exports are exogenous and fixed in real terms. Imports are divided into several types. Those required as intermediate inputs are tied by fixed proportions to sectoral output levels. Imports of capital goods are a fixed proportion of the total investment demand by each sector. Both are totally price inelastic, and they constitute 92 percent of all imports in the base run. The rest of the imports, consumer goods, are price elastic, with a price elasticity of around unity, but they are too small to matter.

While output is not stimulated, in the short run at least, by relative price changes, effective demand falls because saving rises. This immediately leads to unemployment and, after wages are allowed to vary to bring back full employment, to deflation. One reason for a rise in saving is that a current account trade deficit is worth more domestically after a devaluation. Then too, government saving rises because of higher tariffs on imports (since the nominal level of imports is higher) and because the export subsidies required to make Brazilian goods competitive on the world market are reduced. With the devaluation there is less of a gap between Brazilian prices and world prices at an overvalued exchange rate.

With the deflation, there are second- and third-round effects on government saving. With a lower domestic price level, export subsidies can be reduced even more, which produces more government saving and more deflation. Eventually, saving falls enough by means of lower corporate retained earnings to bring about a full-employment equilibrium.

Deflation has the usual effects on income distribution. In fact, this is probably the purest case we can study to determine the effects of deflation. Other experiments have some extraneous factor also inciding on the income distribution which is hard to separate out.

As seen in table 9-14, the GNP shares of both labor and capital fall by the same proportion, affected by deflation in the same way. The share of proprietors rises, and the income distribution improves in all the aggregate measures of table 9-15.

Changes in Labor Supplies by Education Type

In this series of experiments, we try to model the results of different education programs. In each case we upgrade enough workers of one skill to the next higher skill to lead to a GNP change of about Cr$20 million. The main macroeconomic results are given in tables 9-16 to 9-18.

Since there is more aggregate supply available to the economy to meet the aggregate demand, the price level falls. This has the normal effects: the GNP share of proprietors rises; shares of labor and capital fall; retained corporate earnings fall; and distribution generally gets better. Even though aggregate supply rises by the same amount in the three experiments, the price level falls by different amounts because the three solutions have different effects on the government wage bill, the total take from wage taxes, and therefore the level of government saving.

As would be expected in a neoclassical modeling of the labor market, when the supply of one labor type rises, its relative wage falls, and if its supply falls its relative wage rises (see table 9-16). Note, however, that relative wages do not change very much. In EDUC 1 the supply of highly educated labor rises by 11.4 percent; in EDUC 2 that of the secondary-educated rises by 10.7 percent; and in EDUC 3 that of the primary-educated rises by 13.8 percent. These are the results of shifts of 11,300 workers from secondary to university level, 41,200 workers from primary to secondary level, and 207,200 uneducated workers to primary level in the respective experiments. Because of the large rise in numbers, but the comparatively small fall in relative wages, the labor type which has an increased supply will have a larger GNP share as shown in table 9-17. The reason for this, of course, is the high elasticity of substitution between different types of labor. This holds the wage structure relatively rigid in the face of large changes in supplies.

The aggregate distribution measures show an improvement in each case, except for the after-tax Gini coefficient of EDUC 1.

Table 9-16. EDUC Solutions—Output, Price, Expenditure, and Wage Variations: 1971, Wages Variable

Item	Base level	EDUC 1 Absolute change	EDUC 1 Ratio to base	EDUC 2 Absolute change	EDUC 2 Ratio to base	EDUC 3 Absolute change	EDUC 3 Ratio to base
Output and prices							
GNP (millions of 1959 cruzeiros)	4,185	20	1.0048	20	1.0049	19	1.0045
GNP deflator	2.7106	−0.1137	0.9581	−0.2623	0.9032	−0.2100	0.9225
Final demands							
Personal consumption/GNP	0.6466	0.0028	1.0044	0.0029	1.0046	0.0024	1.0037
Government							
Purchases of goods/GNP	0.1045	−0.0006	0.9943	−0.0008	0.9920	−0.0005	0.9950
Labor payments/GNP	0.0679	−0.0012	0.9822	−0.0016	0.9759	−0.0015	0.9776
Investment							
New capital formation/GNP	0.1335	−0.0005	0.9962	0.0001	1.0006	0.0001	1.0006
Capital replacement/GNP	0.0548	−0.0001	0.9990	0.0003	1.0062	0.0003	1.0048
Foreign trade							
Exports/GNP	0.0447	0.0017	1.0380	0.0045	1.1010	0.0035	1.0784
Less imports/GNP	0.0521	0.0021	1.0396	0.0053	1.1018	0.0041	1.0793
Transfers/GNP	0.0531	0.0041	1.0763	0.0054	1.1024	0.0045	1.0849
Wage levels[a]							
Family farm workers	0.4306	−0.0196	0.9546	−0.0426	0.9011	−0.0359	0.9165
Sharecroppers	0.9867	−0.0451	0.9543	−0.0978	0.9008	−0.0830	0.9158
Uneducated	0.8969	−0.0414	0.9538	−0.0907	0.8988	0.0039	1.0043
Primary-educated	1.1240	−0.0525	0.9533	−0.1119	0.9004	−0.1195	0.8937
Secondary-educated	3.8769	−0.1701	0.9561	−0.5286	0.8637	−0.3524	0.9091
Highly educated	7.1595	−0.5709	0.9203	−0.8377	0.8830	−0.6551	0.9085

a. Thousands of cruzeiros per ten workers.

Table 9-17. EDUC Solutions—Functional Income Distribution Measures: 1971, Wages Variable

			EDUC 1		EDUC 2		EDUC 3	
Item	*Base level (1959 cruzeiros)*	*Base share in GNP*	*Change in GNP share from base*	*Ratio of GNP share to base*	*Change in GNP share from base*	*Ratio of GNP share to base*	*Change in GNP share from base*	*Ratio of GNP share to base*
Wages and salaries	4,458,694	0.3931	−0.0022	0.9943	−0.0050	0.9873	−0.0043	0.9892
Family farm workers	129,616	0.0114	−0.0001	0.9925	−0.0001	0.9936	−0.0001	0.9885
Sharecroppers	89,518	0.0079	−0.0001	0.9910	−0.0001	0.9923	−0.0001	0.9881
Uneducated	447,741	0.0395	−0.0004	0.9896	−0.0006	0.9836	−0.0165	0.5830
Primary-educated	2,003,687	0.1766	−0.0020	0.9888	−0.0075	0.9576	0.0157	1.0891
Secondary-educated	1,091,394	0.0962	−0.0037	0.9615	0.0050	1.0516	−0.0021	0.9781
Highly educated	696,739	0.0614	0.0041	1.0669	−0.0016	0.9744	−0.0011	0.9821
Entrepreneurial income	442,541	0.0390	0.0017	1.0441	0.0042	1.1078	0.0033	1.0846
Profits and depreciation allowance	3,532,975	0.3115	−0.0011	0.9965	−0.0026	0.9916	−0.0017	0.9944
Distributed profits	2,012,077	0.1774	−0.0006	0.9964	−0.0018	0.9900	−0.0012	0.9932
Agricultural capitalists	187,036	0.0165	−0.0001	0.9947	−0.0001	0.9936	−0.0002	0.9899
Manufacturing capitalists	862,356	0.0760	−0.0002	0.9979	−0.0008	0.9891	−0.0006	0.9915
Commerce capitalists	231,202	0.0204	−0.0003	0.9855	−0.0008	0.9620	−0.0004	0.9784
Services capitalists	576,084	0.0508	−0.0001	0.9987	−0.0000	0.9999	0.0001	1.0019
Highly educated labor	155,401	0.0137	−0.0000	0.9983	−0.0001	0.9951	−0.0000	0.9973
Other workers	0	0.0000	0.0000	1.0000	0.0000	1.0000	0.0000	1.0000
Retained profits	899,056	0.0793	−0.0004	0.9950	−0.0012	0.9853	−0.0008	0.9897
Depreciation allowance	621,842	0.0548	−0.0001	0.9990	0.0003	1.0062	0.0003	1.0048
Taxes	2,908,891	0.2564	0.0016	1.0063	0.0034	1.0132	0.0027	1.0106
Value added tax	1,901,678	0.1677	−0.0002	0.9991	−0.0007	0.9957	−0.0005	0.9971
Labor wage tax	578,725	0.0510	−0.0004	0.9913	−0.0009	0.9825	−0.0008	0.9841
Profit tax	636,241	0.0561	−0.0002	0.9969	−0.0006	0.9887	−0.0004	0.9930
Net tariffs	−207,751	−0.0183	0.0023	0.8753	0.0055	0.6981	0.0043	0.7647
Gross national product	11,343,101							

Table 9-18. EDUC Solutions—Saving, Taxes, and Size Distribution Measures: 1971, Wages Variable

		EDUC 1		EDUC 2		EDUC 3	
Item	*Base level*	*Change in portion from base*	*Ratio of portion to base*	*Change in portion from base*	*Ratio of portion to base*	*Change in portion from base*	*Ratio of portion to base*
Savings ratios							
Total saving/GNP	0.1884	−0.0007	0.9964	0.0003	1.0017	0.0002	1.0013
Depreciation allowance/saving	0.2910	0.0005	1.0018	0.0011	1.0037	0.0008	1.0027
Retained corporate earnings/saving	0.4208	−0.0005	0.9988	−0.0068	0.9839	−0.0047	0.9887
Personal saving/saving	0.0534	0.0008	1.0153	0.0002	1.0043	0.0001	1.0023
Balance of payments deficit/saving	0.0394	0.0019	1.0494	0.0040	1.1014	0.0032	1.0804
Government saving/saving	0.1954	−0.0029	0.9853	0.0014	1.0070	0.0006	1.0028
Tax ratios							
Total government taxes/GNP	0.2880	−0.0005	0.9984	−0.0016	0.9946	−0.0012	0.9960
Labor tax/total taxes	0.1772	−0.0014	0.9922	−0.0023	0.9872	−0.0022	0.9874
Profit tax/total taxes	0.1948	−0.0003	0.9985	−0.0012	0.9940	−0.0006	0.9969
Value added tax/total taxes	0.5822	0.0005	1.0008	0.0008	1.0013	0.0007	1.0013
Tariffs/total taxes	0.0255	0.0010	1.0405	0.0027	1.1060	0.0021	1.0824
Income tax/total taxes	0.0203	0.0002	1.0079	−0.0000	0.9989	−0.0000	0.9990
Size distribution before taxes and transfers							
Gini coefficient	0.5724	−0.0014	0.9975	−0.0079	0.9863	−0.0093	0.9837
Theil measure	1.0921	−0.0029	0.9974	−0.0139	0.9872	−0.0111	0.9898
Variance log income	0.7111	−0.0152	0.9786	−0.0467	0.9343	−0.0413	0.9419
Atkinson measure	0.5885	−0.0061	0.9897	−0.0187	0.9682	−0.0160	0.9728
Size distribution after taxes and transfers							
Gini coefficient	0.5776	0.0003	1.0005	−0.0057	0.9901	−0.0078	0.9865
Theil measure	1.0692	−0.0024	0.9977	−0.0141	0.9868	−0.0122	0.9886
Variance log income	0.7367	−0.0086	0.9884	−0.0376	0.9490	−0.0352	0.9523
Atkinson measure	0.5965	−0.0035	0.9941	−0.0150	0.9748	−0.0134	0.9775

Primarily, this general improvement is because of the deflation. In the after-tax measures, EDUC 2 and 3 showed about the same amount of improvement, and more than EDUC 1. EDUC 3 did not deflate as much as EDUC 2, but its Gini coefficient was the best of the three. Generally, these measures support the conclusion that primary and secondary education will lead to improvements in distribution, while higher education will have less effect.

As cited above, shifts of 11,300, 41,200, and 207,200 workers to the next higher educational level were required in the respective experiments to achieve the same Cr$20 million increase in GNP. These are in the ratio 1:3.65:18.34. The question naturally arises, and has been the subject of much debate in Brazil, of where to spend the limited resources available for education. If growth is the only goal, this turns on the relative costs of educating the three classes of workers. From data in table 37 of Langoni (1974) it can be deduced that in 1969 these annual costs were in the ratio 1:2.8:29, and for 1960, 1:2.6:45. The estimates include all direct current and capital costs. Fishlow (1973) uses these figures as the basis for his estimate of a 1:3:25 cost structure for 1969, and 1:6:50 for 1960. In Brazil five years are generally required to graduate from primary school, eight years from secondary, and four years from university level. Thus the total cost structures of educating a student are, from Langoni's figures, 1:4.5:23.2 for 1969 and 1:4.2:36 for 1960, and from Fishlow's figures, 1:4.8:20 for 1969 and 1:9.6:40 for 1960.

Since the numbers of workers that must be upgraded are in the ratio 1:3.65:18.34 for an equal GNP change, it is obvious that even if growth were the sole consideration, a program to educate illiterates is the one called for. For the cost of educating each person in the higher education category, one could educate 36 or 40 persons in the primary category at 1960 costs, or 23 or 20 at 1969 costs. Our figures indicate that it would be necessary to educate only 18.34 illiterates for each highly educated person to give the same boost to GNP. Comparing secondary with higher programs, the costs are such that for one person in the higher category, Brazil could have educated at the secondary level 8.6 or 4.2 by 1960 estimates, or 5.2 or 4.2 by 1969 estimates. But a ratio of only 1:3.65 would have been necessary for an equal contribution to GNP. None of the cost figures cited include an estimate of the opportunity cost to the student of lost earnings during the period in school. Since these costs are much higher for those who already have some level of education (and could therefore increase the cost ratios more than proportionately for the highly educated), our conclusions are reinforced.

Not only is distribution improved by programs to upgrade the education of illiterate and primary-educated workers, but growth is also aided by education programs for illiterates. Growth and distribution are not at all in conflict, but rather mutually supportive. These conclusions are similar to those of Fishlow and opposed to those of Langoni. Although the GNP share of highly educated workers increased in the 1960s, it does not mean that they were in short supply. In a neoclassical labor market, if the elasticity of substitution between labor types is greater than one (and all empirical studies indicate an elasticity much greater than one), then the GNP share will rise whenever their relative numbers increase. This occurred in all three experiments above. The GNP share of highly educated workers rose because their relative supply increased tremendously in the 1960s.

Other Redistributive Policies

The experiments in this section are more extreme in their redistributive aims. We transfer distributed profits from high- to low-income groups, abolish intersectoral wage differentials, and maintain the wage structure of 1965 in 1968 and 1971 (see tables 9-19, 9-20, and 9-21).

Profit Redistributions: DIST 1 and DIST 2

In DIST 1 half the profits that would have gone to the capitalists in agriculture are distributed to the sharecropper class. In DIST 2 half the profits that would have gone to the nonagricultural capitalists (produced in sectors 3 to 24) are distributed to the workers of type 3, 4, and 5 (the uneducated and those with primary- and secondary-school education). In this experiment the profits generated in commerce (sector 3), services (sector 5), and manufacturing (sectors 4 and 6-24 taken as a whole) were distributed only to the type 3, 4, and 5 workers who were actually employed in those sectors. Furthermore, the profits generated in, say, sector 3 were distributed to the three classes of workers in that sector according to their base-run wage payments. In other words, if type 5 workers received twice the total wage payments of type 4

Table 9-19. DIST 1–3 Solutions—Output, Price, Expenditure, and Wage Variations: 1971, Wages Variable

Item	Base level	DIST 1 Absolute change	DIST 1 Ratio to base	DIST 2 Absolute change	DIST 2 Ratio to base	DIST 3 Base level	DIST 3 Absolute change	DIST 3 Ratio to base
Output and prices								
GNP (millions of 1959 cruzeiros)	4,185	−3	0.9992	18	1.0043		114	1.0273
GNP deflator	2.7106	0.0578	1.0213	−0.2544	0.9062		0.6712	1.2476
Final demands								
Personal consumption/GNP	0.6466	0.0003	1.0004	0.0023	1.0036		0.0338	1.0523
Government								
Purchases of goods/GNP	0.1045	−0.0001	0.9991	−0.0003	0.9975		−0.0150	0.8565
Labor payments/GNP	0.0679	0.0004	1.0056	−0.0014	0.9793		0.0168	1.2478
Investment								
New capital formation/GNP	0.1335	−0.0004	0.9973	0.0001	1.0008		−0.0219	0.8356
Capital replacement/GNP	0.0548	−0.0003	0.9951	0.0003	1.0048		−0.0139	0.7462
Foreign trade								
Exports/GNP	0.0447	−0.0009	0.9791	0.0044	1.0980		−0.0098	0.7796
Less imports/GNP	0.0521	−0.0011	0.9789	0.0053	1.1017		−0.0102	0.8051
Transfers/GNP	0.0531	−0.0012	0.9767	0.0049	1.0924		−0.0117	0.7804
Wage levels[a]								
Family farm workers	0.4306	0.0123	1.0285	−0.0459	0.8934	0.4306	0.3530	1.8198
Sharecroppers	0.9867	0.0280	1.0284	−0.1050	0.8936	0.9867	0.8066	1.8175
Uneducated	0.8969	0.0251	1.0280	−0.0970	0.8918	1.0170	0.6624	1.6513
Primary-educated	1.1240	0.0306	1.0272	−0.1234	0.8902	1.3359	0.6770	1.5068
Secondary-educated	3.8769	0.0974	1.0251	−0.4251	0.8904	2.8381	0.8411	1.2964
Highly educated	7.1595	0.1775	1.0248	−0.7692	0.8926	7.0367	2.4206	1.3440

a. Thousands of cruzeiros per ten workers.

Table 9-20. DIST 1–3 Solutions—Functional Income Distribution Measures: 1971, Wages Variable

			DIST 1		DIST 2		DIST 3	
Item	Base level (1959 cruzeiros)	Base share in GNP	Change in GNP share from base	Ratio of GNP share to base	Change in GNP share from base	Ratio of GNP share to base	Change in GNP share from base	Ratio of GNP share to base
Wages and salaries	4,458,694	0.3931	0.0018	1.0046	−0.0072	0.9817	0.0545	1.1386
Family farm workers	129,616	0.0114	0.0001	1.0116	−0.0002	0.9856	0.0048	1.4246
Sharecroppers	89,518	0.0079	0.0001	1.0084	−0.0001	0.9816	0.0034	1.4248
Uneducated	447,741	0.0395	0.0002	1.0051	−0.0009	0.9767	0.0113	1.2869
Primary-educated	2,003,687	0.1766	0.0009	1.0051	−0.0033	0.9813	0.0310	1.1755
Secondary-educated	1,091,394	0.0962	0.0003	1.0029	−0.0015	0.9846	0.0010	1.0102
Highly educated	696,739	0.0614	0.0003	1.0052	−0.0011	0.9822	0.0031	1.0499
Entrepreneurial income	442,541	0.0390	−0.0007	0.9809	0.0043	1.1105	−0.0076	0.8058
Profits and depreciation allowance	3,532,975	0.3115	−0.0002	0.9994	−0.0013	0.9959	−0.0237	0.9238
Distributed profits	2,012,077	0.1774	0.0002	1.0012	−0.0013	0.9929	−0.0017	0.9902
Agricultural capitalists	187,036	0.0165	−0.0082	0.5046	0.0000	1.0022	0.0079	1.4773
Manufacturing capitalists	862,356	0.0760	−0.0004	0.9945	−0.0379	0.5008	−0.0246	0.6769
Commerce capitalists	231,202	0.0204	0.0000	1.0015	−0.0103	0.4959	0.0042	1.2050
Services capitalists	576,084	0.0508	0.0004	1.0083	−0.0259	0.4893	0.0111	1.2177
Highly educated labor	155,401	0.0137	0.0000	1.0022	−0.0002	0.9887	−0.0003	0.9777
Other workers	0	0.0000	0.0083	1.0000	0.0730	1.0000	0.0000	1.0000
Retained profits	899,056	0.0793	−0.0002	0.9981	−0.0003	0.9965	−0.0081	0.8981
Depreciation allowance	621,842	0.0548	−0.0003	0.9951	0.0003	1.0048	−0.0139	0.7462
Taxes	2,908,891	0.2564	−0.0009	0.9967	0.0042	1.0162	−0.0232	0.9097
Value added tax	1,901,678	0.1677	0.0001	1.0007	0.0001	1.0005	−0.0079	0.9529
Labor wage tax	578,725	0.0510	0.0001	1.0016	−0.0006	0.9880	−0.0071	0.8616
Profit tax	636,241	0.0561	−0.0000	0.9992	−0.0003	0.9940	−0.0056	0.9004
Net tariffs	−207,751	−0.0183	−0.0011	1.0606	0.0049	0.7306	−0.0027	1.1484
Gross national product	11,343,101							

Table 9-21. DIST 1–3 Solutions—Saving, Taxes, and Size Distribution Measures: 1971, Wages Variable

Item	Base level	DIST 1		DIST 2		DIST 3	
		Change in portion from base	Ratio of portion to base	Change in portion from base	Ratio of portion to base	Change in portion from base	Ratio of portion to base
Savings ratios							
Total saving/GNP	0.1884	−0.0007	0.9961	0.0003	1.0014	−0.0360	0.8091
Depreciation allowance/saving	0.2910	−0.0005	0.9982	0.0007	1.0025	−0.0229	0.9214
Retained corporate earnings/saving	0.4208	0.0009	1.0022	−0.0020	0.9953	0.0464	1.1102
Personal saving/saving	0.0534	−0.0002	0.9953	−0.0036	0.9323	0.0118	1.2206
Balance of payments deficit/saving	0.0394	−0.0009	0.9780	0.0047	1.1191	0.0072	1.1817
Government saving/saving	0.1954	0.0006	1.0030	0.0001	1.0003	−0.0425	0.7823
Tax ratios							
Total government taxes/GNP	0.2880	−0.0001	0.9997	−0.0009	0.9967	−0.0221	0.9234
Labor tax/total taxes	0.1772	0.0002	1.0012	−0.0017	0.9906	−0.0120	0.9324
Profit tax/total taxes	0.1948	−0.0001	0.9994	−0.0005	0.9972	−0.0049	0.9751
Value added tax/total taxes	0.5822	0.0007	1.0011	0.0023	1.0039	0.0187	1.0321
Tariffs/total taxes	0.0255	−0.0005	0.9787	0.0026	1.1033	−1.0031	0.8781
Income tax/total taxes	0.0203	−0.0002	0.9904	−0.0027	0.8666	0.0012	1.0610
Size distribution before taxes and transfers							
Gini coefficient	0.5724	−0.0045	0.9922	−0.0690	0.8795	−0.0497	0.9132
Theil measure	1.0921	−0.0115	0.9894	−0.4622	0.5767	−0.1346	0.8767
Variance log income	0.7111	0.0047	1.0066	0.0168	1.0236	0.1247	1.1754
Atkinson measure	0.5885	0.0005	1.0009	−0.0488	0.9171	0.0309	1.0526
Size distribution after taxes and transfers							
Gini coefficient	0.5776	−0.0051	0.9912	−0.0616	0.8933	−0.0497	0.9139
Theil measure	1.0692	−0.0108	0.9899	−0.4219	0.6054	−0.1252	0.8829
Variance log income	0.7367	0.0017	1.0023	0.0199	1.0270	0.0923	1.1252
Atkinson measure	0.5965	−0.0003	0.9996	−0.0423	0.9291	0.0216	1.0362

workers in sector 3, then they were given twice the distributed profits.

Although we do not describe the actual mechanisms that might be used to achieve these profit redistributions, they reflect possible serious proposals for reform. That is, not all the profits generated in each sector are redistributed, but only half of them, and they are redistributed among the labor classes more or less realistically.

While the groups directly affected saw their GNP shares change a great deal, the other groups in the economy were little affected. In DIST 1 the agricultural capitalists lost 0.82 percentage points of their GNP share (half of their initial share of 1.65 percentage points), and the sharecroppers (see "other workers" in table 9-20) gained 0.83 percentage points in profit income. There were no other significant shifts in GNP shares in DIST 1. In DIST 2 there was only a trade of GNP share from the capitalists of sectors 3 to 24 (losing 7.41 percentage points) to the type 3, 4, and 5 workers, who gained profit incomes of 7.30 percentage points of GNP (see "other workers" in table). Other groups in the economy did not lose (or gain) as a result of the redistribution.

The impact on real consumption per household is also clear:

Consumer class	*Base*	*DIST 1*	*DIST 2*
1	0.2832	0.3034	0.2825
2	0.4544	0.4286	0.4801
3	1.2209	1.1581	1.7388
4	7.5169	7.4967	5.4326

Consumer class 1 includes sharecroppers, class 3 includes agricultural capitalists, and the main shifts in real per household consumption levels (which are quite small at such an aggregated level) are seen in these classes in DIST 1. Nonagricultural capitalists are in consumer class 4, types 3, 4, and 5 nonagricultural labor are in classes 2 and 3, and quite significant shifts in real per household consumption levels for those households are evident in DIST 2. The changes are much larger in DIST 2 than in DIST 1 because the share of GNP being shifted in DIST 2 is nine times as big as that in DIST 1 (7.41 percentage points as opposed to 0.82 percentage points).

A third way to look at the results is to analyze the way the various groups moved around in the relative income distribution. In DIST 1 the sharecroppers move from a point where 40 percent of the population (with 11 percent of the income) is poorer than they are, to where 81 percent of the population (with 38 percent of the income) is poorer. The agricultural capitalists move from a point where 94 percent of the population (with 56 percent of the income) is poorer, to where 86 percent of the population (with 43 percent of the income) is poorer. In DIST 2 the richest two capitalist classes (in services and manufacturing) maintain their positions as the richest two classes in the economy (with 99.7 percent of the population poorer than they), even though their incomes have been cut in half. But whereas they formerly got 20 percent of the personal income generated by the economy, now they get "only" 10 percent for their 0.3 percent of the population.

The economy inflates very little in DIST 1 and deflates a significant amount in DIST 2. The deflation is caused by an increase in aggregate supply available to the economy; note that GNP supply rose by CR$18 million in DIST 2, which is almost as much as in the education experiments. The supply increase follows from the shift in demand and employment patterns resulting from the income redistribution. The demand for luxury goods declines and that for necessities increases, leading to significant changes in output levels (see table 9-22). These changes are quite large when one considers that the model forces full employment of all resources and that capital stocks are fixed in each sector. This means that when the demand for some good falls, the rental that the capital of that sector earns will drop sharply, lowering the price of the good and therefore encouraging substitution of it for other goods in household demand.

By far the largest change is the drop in demand for domestic servants, by 11.55 percent, as one would expect with a more egalitarian structure of income distribution. The demand for transport goods (cars) also falls a significant amount. Because of the labor released by these two sectors (and in the machinery and leather sectors to a minor extent), the output of all other sectors can rise. There are particularly large increases in the outputs of food, rubber, and agriculture. This again is as one would expect; the demand for basic consumer necessities should rise if incomes are redistributed to the poor. These results, like those in SEN 3 and TRANS 2, support the structuralist arguments that a more egal-

Table 9-22. Changes from the Base Levels of Output, by Sector, as a Result of Income Redistribution in DIST 2

Sector	Output change (percent)
1. Crop agriculture	1.92
2. Animal agriculture	1.22
3. Commerce	0.99
4. Electricity	0.51
5. Services	0.03
6. Mining	0.43
7. Nonmetallic minerals	0.06
8. Metallurgy	0.17
9. Machine tools	−0.05
10. Electrical goods	1.56
11. Transport goods	−1.75
12. Wood and furniture	0.59
13. Paper	0.87
14. Rubber	2.43
15. Leather	−0.11
16. Chemicals	1.26
17. Textiles	0.72
18. Clothing	0.15
19. Food	3.76
20. Beverages	0.10
21. Tobacco	1.28
22. Publishing	0.77
23. Miscellaneous	0.47
24. Construction	0.11
25. Domestic servants	−11.55

itarian income structure would necessitate significant shifts in output patterns away from a luxury-goods orientation.

With labor released from the low-productivity sector of domestic servants, the output of other sectors can rise. Indeed, it can rise by much more than the fall in output of the domestic servants sector, since labor is more productive in the other sectors. This leads to the Cr$18 million rise in GNP, a result opposite what most would expect from an income redistribution when capital stocks are fixed by sector.

As a result of all the above changes, income distribution as measured by aggregate distribution measures generally improves. After-tax measures in DIST 1 got a little better in three of four cases, despite the inflation (which normally worsens distribution) and despite the fact that the actual GNP share being shifted (0.82 percent) was small. In DIST 2 three of the four measures were very much better, the Gini by an enormous (for it) 11 percent, and the Theil measure by 40 percent. Paradoxically, the variance of log incomes worsened. This measure is relatively insensitive to movements in the upper end of the income distribution, and in the middle reaches distribution probably got a little worse. Profits were redistributed to type 3, 4, and 5 workers according to their wages, thus accentuating the spread between these three groups of workers.

To summarize, profit redistribution can have strong impacts nationally when significant shares of GNP are being redistributed. A redistribution of only agricultural profits is not significant nationally, since they represent only 1.65 percent of GNP. Nevertheless, even when the national effects are small, profit redistributions do have major effects on the groups directly involved: those that are gaining or losing the profits. Therefore, even limited profit redistributions, if specifically targeted, can have significant impacts on the incomes of the poor.

Suppression of Intersectoral Wage Differentials: DIST 3

In equation (7.12) the wages paid for the same type of labor in different sectors are not the same, but are related to an economy-wide wage index by factors of proportionality, $\overline{w_{mi}}(\tau)$. For all the experiments reported in this chapter, except this one, these proportionality factors were kept at the same level as those for 1959. They are implicit in table 8-4. Neoclassical economics provides no good explanation why such intersectoral differences should persist, but all empirical evidence shows that they do exist and that they are fairly constant over time.

What would happen, in a neoclassical model of the Brazilian economy, if all such intersectoral differences were somehow mandated away? This is done in DIST 3. As seen in table 8-4, it is generally the labor-surplus sectors that pay lower than average wages for each type of labor. Manufacturing generally pays higher than average wages. An exception is the heterogeneous service sector. There the wages of the lower skilled workers (such as shoeshine boys) are less than the average they would get elsewhere, while the wages of the highly educated workers (such as bankers) are above their average.

Since we assume that labor markets operate in a neoclassical way, wages are always equated to marginal products. When the

Table 9-23. DIST 3 Employment as a Proportion of Base-run Employment

Sector	Labor types						
	Family farm workers (1)	*Sharecroppers* (2)	*Uneducated* (3)	*Primary-educated* (4)	*Secondary-educated* (5)	*Highly educated* (6)	*All, in man-units*
1. Crop agriculture	1.0101	1.0199	0.8036	1.1486	—	—	1.0281
2. Animal agriculture	0.9056	0.9133	0.7413	1.0134	—	—	0.9395
3. Commerce	—	—	1.0153	1.2694	1.0866	0.9455	1.1386
5. Services	—	—	0.1029	0.1316	0.1109	3.5696	0.3717
4, 6–23. Manufacturing	—	—	1.2110	1.2188	1.3799	0.1751	1.1950
24. Construction	—	—	0.7749	0.9697	2.0650	0.5253	1.0781
25. Domestic servants	—	—	2.8304	0.6585	0.1415	—	0.8690

— Not applicable.

intersectoral differences in wages paid to the same labor type are smoothed, wages are lowered in sectors that paid above the average for a particular labor type and are raised in those that paid below the average. Since the wage of each labor type equaled its marginal product, at base-run sectoral employment levels the marginal product must have been above average if the wage were above average, and it must have been below average if the wage were below average. With the above average wages for certain types of labor lowered in DIST 3, the sector will hire more of that labor until its marginal product falls to the new wage, and again the converse is true. Mainly, only substitution between labor types will occur, since the sector will hire more or less labor in total (measured in efficiency units as a CES aggregate) only if the demand for its product changes. Remember that capital stocks are fixed by sector, and that the total demand for sectoral outputs is not very price responsive.

The actual shifts in labor employment by sector are given in table 9-23, where DIST 3 employment is given as a proportion of base-run employments. Many of the shifts are enormous, and they move in the direction expected. For example, in services, which paid above average wages for the highly educated (labor type 6) and below average for the other three labor types it employs, a proportionately large amount of type 6 substitutes for types 3, 4, and 5. The marginal product of type 6 was high in services in the base run, so that when the wage paid for this type is lowered, much more of this labor is hired.

The type 6 that services hired came from manufacturing and construction. These two sectors must therefore hire more types of 3, 4, and 5 in the aggregate to make up for the loss of type 6, if they are to produce as much output as is demanded.

Types 1 and 2 are tied to the agricultural sectors, and only types 3 and 4 can substitute for them. With the wage equalization, the wages of types 3 and 4 are raised in the agricultural sectors, since they had been below average there. The agricultural sectors would therefore want to get rid of some of types 3 and 4, but they cannot since there is no more of types 1 and 2 to replace them. The wages of 1 and 2 therefore get bid up, until the agricultural sectors no longer wish to get rid of types 3 and 4.

The results of all these shifts in the labor force on the average wages of the six labor types are given in table 9-19. The actual average wage levels across sectors are given there for the base run and DIST 3. Since the intersectoral wage structure is not the same in the base and DIST 3, we cannot use our usual wage index (the wages of labor in sector 1). The average wage is more appropriate in DIST 3, since there each labor type is paid its average wage. As the table shows, the wages of labor types 1 and 2 rise the most, and the wage increase for the other labor types declines steadily with the ascending levels of skill.

Aggregate GNP supply rises by a great deal because labor shifts out of the initially low-wage labor-surplus sectors. Sector 25, domestic servants, provides the best example, since it is the only one which does not use any fixed capital, and since its output demand is very price responsive (it sells only to consumers). It also paid wages which were much below average. When wage rates for domestic servants are raised, the price of their output rises, but this price rise cannot be passed on to the consumer as easily as in other sectors. The demand for, and therefore the supply of, the sectoral output falls, releasing labor to work in more productive sectors. The output of the domestic servants sector in DIST 3 is 20 percent below its output in the base run. Although this is the most dramatic demonstration of why GNP supply will rise with a wage equalization, the general bias will operate in all other sectors. In those that formerly paid below average wages the output demands fall, to the extent that demand is price responsive, and in those that had paid above average wages output demands rise.

Because the per unit price of labor to the high-wage sectors (generally, the modern industrial sectors) is lowered in DIST 3, the price such sectors charge for their output (under competition) is lowered. In addition, the capital stock they employ would become superfluous, as they try to substitute the now cheaper labor for the capital, unless the profit rate on their capital is lowered. Since the capital stock is fixed by sector, the profit (rental) rate will have to fall. Conversely, in those sectors that have their wages raised, the price they can charge and their profit rates rise. This is shown in table 9-24, where the producers' prices and profit rates in DIST 3 are shown as a proportion of their base-run values. In what may superficially appear to be a paradox, those sectors in which the price of labor was raised enjoy a huge rise in their profit rates, and those in which the price of labor was lowered experience a sharp fall in their profit rates.

Overall the experiment was mildly inflationary, with the GNP deflator rising almost 25 percent (despite an increase in total

Table 9-24. DIST 3 Producers' Prices and Profit Rates as a Proportion of Their Base-run Values

Sector	*Price*	*Profit rate*
1. Crop agriculture	1.68	1.60
2. Animal agriculture	1.56	1.39
3. Commerce	1.26	1.64
4. Electricity	1.25	1.37
5. Services	1.38	1.38
6. Mining	0.77	0.53
7. Nonmetallic minerals	0.90	0.83
8. Metallurgy	0.86	0.85
9. Machine tools	0.80	0.62
10. Electrical goods	0.91	0.90
11. Transport goods	0.81	0.66
12. Wood and furniture	1.08	0.84
13. Paper	0.92	0.85
14. Rubber	1.10	0.48
15. Leather	1.07	0.77
16. Chemicals	0.99	0.83
17. Textiles	1.09	0.88
18. Clothing	1.04	1.04
19. Food	1.37	0.87
20. Beverages	0.94	0.65
21. Tobacco	0.83	0.90
22. Publishing	0.97	1.09
23. Miscellaneous	0.98	1.02
24. Construction	1.17	1.60
25. Domestic servants	1.77	—

— Not applicable.

supply). Prices *dropped* in sectors producing investment and government consumption goods, bringing nominal expenditures on these items down also. In the final solution, their share of nominal GNP decreases by 15 percent from the base levels, even though in real terms their demand was constant. Despite all this, there was general price inflation, resulting from saving's decreasing even more than nominal investment. There were three major reasons: a decrease in depreciation allowances along with investment goods prices; falling profits in manufacturing, the main source of retained earnings; and decreased government profits and wage tax receipts from these sectors.

As a result of these movements the GNP share of all labor types increased, with that of the poorer labor groups rising the most.

The share of labor types 1 and 2 rose by over 42 percent, that of labor type 6 by only 5 percent. The proprietors lost in their share of GNP because of the modest inflation. The share of profits falls overall, but this masks the wide variation in sectoral changes in profits. The GNP share of agricultural capitalists rose by 48 percent, while that of manufacturing capitalists (the biggest single group of capitalists) fell by 32 percent.

The income distribution shifts in a complicated way with some poor groups (proprietors) losing and some rich groups (capitalists in commerce and services) gaining, but generally the shift is toward equality. The confusion is reflected in the aggregate income distribution measures: two of them improve (the Gini and Theil) and two of them worsen (the variance of log incomes and Atkinson's measure). Given the relative sensitivities of these measures, one might subjectively say that the Gini and Theil improved more than the variance of log incomes and the Atkinson measure deteriorated. The improvement in the Gini, which is sensitive to the middle ranges, reflects the greater equality in the middle ranges of the distribution (the incomes of the various labor types across sectors moving toward each other). The worsening of the variance of log incomes, which is sensitive to the bottom ranges, reflects the fall in real income of agricultural proprietors, who are at the very bottom of the income distribution.

Maintain the 1965 Wages in 1968 and 1971: DIST 4

There has been a great deal of controversy in Brazil on what the effects would be of maintaining the wage structure of the mid-1960s into later years. As discussed in chapter 8, wage differentials across skill groups narrow in the later years of the general equilibrium model solutions because of the neoclassical modeling of the labor market and the large increases in the relative supplies of the higher skill groups. In DIST 4 we study the effects, in a neoclassical model, of maintaining the 1965 wage levels in the model solutions of 1968 and 1971.

The 1971 results are given in table 9.27. Remember that 1971 was a year of high aggregate demand, and 1965 and 1968 (in the model solution) were years of low demand. This is reflected in the levels of wages in 1968 and 1971 as a proportion of 1965 wages (see table 9-25). In the base-run solution for 1968 the average wage declined a little, but in 1971 wages rose by a factor

Table 9-25. Base-run Values of Wages in 1968 and 1971 as a Proportion of 1965 Wages

Labor type	1968 wage/1965 wage	1971 wage/1965 wage
1. Family farm workers	1.0052	3.1802
2. Sharecroppers	0.9906	3.0970
3. Uneducated	1.0059	3.3047
4. Primary-educated	0.9229	2.6826
5. Secondary-educated	0.8586	2.2640
6. Highly educated	0.7932	1.9583

of 2 to 3 (in nominal terms; prices rose by the same amount). Relative wages changed a great deal. In order to remain fully employed in the face of large increases in their relative supplies, the higher skilled workers had to lower their relative wages.

With wages maintained at their 1965 levels, the employment demands are predictable for neoclassical markets: the demand for the rapidly increasing labor types will fall in relation to their supply. The 1971 results are given in table 9-27. With 1965 wages, the demands for labor types 5 and 6 do not keep up with their increased supplies, while for labor types 1, 2, and 3 there is a great deal of excess demand. The 1968 results show the same pattern.

All these figures are in relation to the new, generally higher supplies of labor available in 1968 and 1971. The demand for all types of labor did increase in these years even when 1965 wages were maintained. This is shown in table 9-26, which gives the DIST 4 employment demands in 1968 and 1971 as a proportion of the 1965 demands. The first and most obvious point is that demands for all labor types did increase between 1965 and the later

Table 9-26. DIST 4 Employment Demands in 1968 and 1971 as a Proportion of 1965 Demands

Labor type	1968/1965	1971/1965
1. Family farm workers	1.2793	1.7492
2. Sharecroppers	1.2661	1.7257
3. Uneducated	1.2721	1.7951
4. Primary-educated	1.3039	1.9207
5. Secondary-educated	1.3970	1.8353
6. Highly educated	1.4690	1.8864

years. In 1971, a year of high aggregate demand, the labor demands had risen by 70 to 90 percent in the six years since 1965. The second point is that in light of the growth patterns of sectoral demands and of sectoral capital stocks, the demand for higher skilled workers grew at a somewhat faster rate when the wage structure was maintained.

Because wages were kept at their 1965 levels, which were one-half to one-third their 1971 levels in the base run, the price level was 52 percent lower in DIST 4 than in the base. This follows because, as has repeatedly been pointed out, capital is valued at its current reproduction cost, and the price level will therefore fall by almost as much as the cost of labor falls. In addition, the GNP supply rises by a very large amount, as a reflection of the aggregate excess demand for labor, which we assume is made available. In the base run this leads, of course, to the doubling and tripling of money wages.

In interpreting the other figures of tables 9-27, 9-28, and 9-29 one must keep in mind that figures such as the GNP shares of labor and the aggregate distribution coefficients are computed on the basis of the *employed* labor force. Unemployed workers are not counted. Therefore the GNP shares of higher skilled workers fall, even though their wages have been kept at a high level, since the number employed falls. At the same time, the GNP shares of lower skilled workers rises. As a result, in three cases out of four, the aggregate distribution measures show improvement in distribution among employed workers, capitalists, and proprietors.

Many have argued that the Brazilian government has followed a policy of fixing the wage structure at mid-1960s levels and then increasing aggregate demand. As we see in DIST 4, this would keep up the wages of higher skilled workers when neoclassical labor markets would make them fall. Such a policy would increase employment demand by 70 to 90 percent in our model in six years, with the demand for higher skilled workers increasing at a slightly faster pace than that for lower skilled workers.

Export Effects on Employment

In a final set of simulations with the model, we compute the possible effects on employment in 1971 from changes in exports, assuming that nominal wages remain constant. Tables 9-27 to 9-29 give the full set of results from EXP 1, where all exports were

Table 9-27. DIST 4 and EXP 1 Solutions—Output, Price, Expenditure, and Employment Variations: 1971, Wages Fixed

Item	Base level	DIST 4 Absolute change	DIST 4 Ratio to base	EXP 1 Absolute change	EXP 1 Ratio to base
Output and prices					
GNP (millions of 1959 cruzeiros)	4,185	249	1.0596	−51	0.9878
GNP deflator	2.7106	−1.4033	0.4823	−0.0442	0.9837
Final demands					
Personal consumption/GNP	0.6466	0.0165	1.0255	0.0004	1.0006
Government					
Purchases of goods/GNP	0.1045	−0.0037	0.9642	0.0004	1.0042
Labor payments/GNP	0.0679	−0.0112	0.8348	0.0020	1.0294
Investment					
New capital formation/GNP	0.1335	0.0028	1.0213	0.0012	1.0089
Capital replacement/GNP	0.0548	0.0047	1.0855	0.0004	1.0072
Foreign trade					
Exports/GNP	0.0447	0.0427	1.9554	−0.0033	0.9255
Less imports/GNP	0.0521	0.0517	1.9914	0.0009	1.0181
Transfers/GNP	0.0531	0.0493	1.9293	0.0006	1.0116
Employment levels (tens of thousands)					
Family farm workers	301	258	1.8576	−7	0.9775
Sharecroppers	91	47	1.5233	−2	0.9771
Uneducated	440	852	2.9351	−10	0.9777
Primary-educated	1,500	4	1.0026	−32	0.9787
Secondary-educated	385	−71	0.8161	−8	0.9787
Highly educated	99	−48	0.5144	−2	0.9821

Table 9-28. DIST 4 and EXP 1 Solutions—Functional Income Distribution Measures: 1971, Wages Fixed

			DIST 4		EXP 1	
Item	*Base level (1959 cruzeiros)*	*Base share in GNP*	*Change in GNP share from base*	*Ratio of GNP share to base*	*Change in GNP share from base*	*Ratio of GNP share to base*
Wages and salaries	4,458,694	0.3931	−0.0622	0.8418	0.0023	1.0060
Family farm workers	129,616	0.0114	0.0017	1.1460	0.0001	1.0083
Sharecroppers	89,518	0.0079	−0.0003	0.9615	0.0000	1.0045
Uneducated	447,741	0.0395	0.0313	1.7923	0.0002	1.0038
Primary-educated	2,003,687	0.1766	−0.0365	0.7934	0.0010	1.0059
Secondary-educated	1,091,394	0.0962	−0.0288	0.7008	0.0006	1.0059
Highly educated	696,739	0.0614	−0.0295	0.5199	0.0006	1.0091
Entrepreneurial income	442,541	0.0390	0.0425	2.0904	0.0006	1.0157
Profits and depreciation allowance	3,532,975	0.3115	−0.0175	0.9440	−0.0047	0.9848
Distributed profits	2,012,077	0.1774	−0.0143	0.9196	−0.0034	0.9810
Agricultural capitalists	187,036	0.0165	−0.0049	0.7012	−0.0000	0.9986
Manufacturing capitalists	862,356	0.0760	−0.0063	0.9178	−0.0028	0.9628
Commerce capitalists	231,202	0.0204	−0.0030	0.8548	0.0003	1.0134
Services capitalists	576,084	0.0508	0.0003	1.0065	−0.0005	0.9903
Highly educated labor	155,401	0.0137	−0.0005	0.9671	−0.0003	0.9781
Other workers	0	0.0000	0.0000	1.0000	0.0000	1.0000
Retained profits	899,056	0.0793	−0.0079	0.9007	−0.0018	0.9777
Depreciation allowance	621,842	0.0548	0.0047	1.0855	0.0004	1.0072
Taxes	2,908,891	0.2564	0.0371	1.1448	0.0018	1.0070
Value added tax	1,901,678	0.1677	−0.0059	0.9648	−0.0014	0.9914
Labor wage tax	578,725	0.0510	−0.0074	0.8546	0.0003	1.0067
Profit tax	636,241	0.0561	−0.0033	0.9405	−0.0013	0.9760
Net tariffs	−207,751	−0.0183	0.0537	−1.9332	0.0041	0.7741
Gross national product	11,343,101					

Table 9-29. DIST 4 and EXP 1 Solutions—Saving, Taxes, and Size Distribution Measures: 1971, Wages Fixed

Item	Base level	DIST 4		EXP 1	
		Change in portion from base	*Ratio of portion to base*	*Change in portion from base*	*Ratio of portion to base*
Savings ratios					
Total saving/GNP	0.1884	0.0074	1.0395	0.0015	1.0079
Depreciation allowance/saving	0.2910	0.0126	1.0435	−0.0004	0.9986
Retained corporate earnings/saving	0.4208	−0.0561	0.8667	−0.0125	0.9703
Personal saving/saving	0.0534	−0.0039	0.9279	−0.0006	0.9894
Balance of payments deficit/saving	0.0394	0.0441	2.1182	0.0221	1.5602
Government saving/saving	0.1954	0.0031	1.0160	−0.0087	0.9555
Tax ratios					
Total government taxes/GNP	0.2880	−0.0101	0.9648	−0.0024	0.9918
Labor tax/total taxes	0.1772	−0.0203	0.8852	0.0026	1.0144
Profit tax/total taxes	0.1948	−0.0049	0.9747	−0.0031	0.9841
Value added tax/total taxes	0.5822	0.0000	1.0001	−0.0001	0.9998
Tariffs/total taxes	0.0255	0.0267	2.0453	0.0006	1.0250
Income tax/total taxes	0.0203	−0.0014	0.9295	0.0001	1.0025
Size distribution before taxes and transfers					
Gini coefficient	0.5724	−0.0290	0.9494	−0.0035	0.9938
Theil measure	1.0921	0.0595	1.0544	−0.0262	0.9760
Variance log income	0.7111	−0.2023	0.7156	−0.0018	0.9975
Atkinson measure	0.5885	−0.0690	0.8827	−0.0035	0.9940
Size distribution after taxes and transfers					
Gini coefficient	0.5776	−0.0212	0.9634	−0.0030	0.9948
Theil measure	1.0692	0.0208	1.0195	−0.0241	0.9775
Variance log income	0.7367	−0.1347	0.8171	−0.0015	0.9980
Atkinson measure	0.5965	−0.0448	0.9250	−0.0031	0.9948

Table 9-30. Employment Elasticities from Changing Export Demands

Labor type	10 percent increase in all exports (EXP 1)	50 percent increase by sector: Crop agriculture (EXP 2)	Machine tools (EXP 3)	Chemicals (EXP 4)	Food (EXP 5)
1. Family farm workers	0.2250	0.0449	0.0072	0.0070	0.0842
2. Sharecroppers	0.2290	0.0435	0.0075	0.0070	0.0868
3. Uneducated	0.2233	0.0359	0.0086	0.0084	0.0712
4. Primary-educated	0.2130	0.0255	0.0102	0.0097	0.0596
5. Secondary-educated	0.2125	0.0108	0.0121	0.0108	0.0367
6. Highly educated	0.1791	0.0092	0.0105	0.0085	0.0284

reduced 10 percent. The employment consequences of EXP 1 are given in table 9-27 and, along with the results for EXP 2 through EXP 5, in table 9-30.

The evidence is hardly conclusive, but it does suggest that exports of relatively high-technology goods are likely to have minimal impact on Brazilian employment, particularly that of low-skill groups. Food and agricultural exports, however, may have fairly significant employment benefits. Since recent export promotion policy in Brazil has favored sectors such as machinery and chemicals, one can only conclude that its goals were not chiefly employment creation and income redistribution. The relationships among the magnitudes of the numbers in table 9-30 are obvious and eloquent.

Summary and Conclusions

The following conclusions are drawn from the simulations discussed in this chapter:

SEN 1: More difficult substitution among labor types equalizes earnings in the sense that it leads to a narrower wage structure, with smaller differences in favor of relatively plentiful high-skill workers. Overall, reduced labor substitutability reduces aggregate supply, leading to inflation and to real income losses for proprietors, thus increasing inequality.

SEN 2: Less flexible supply in the labor-surplus sectors of the economy reduces real output and makes the income distribution worse.

SEN 3: Growth under conditions of diverse demand patterns

will be unequalizing. Both this and the previous two simulations emphasize that structural rigidities in the economy are unequalizing.

INV 1: Macroeconomically, reduced investment demand will lead to an immediate fall in the price level, improving distribution as the economy is under less pressure to produce saving. Over time, however, the share of profits rises as the capital stock becomes smaller in relation to the demand for it. The sectors producing investment goods are the principal ones hurt by the fall in demand.

INV 2 and INV 3: Changes in the pattern of investment, even when the overall level of real investment remains the same, can lead to significant improvements in distribution. If the prices charged by investment-goods-producing sectors are lowered, as is done through reductions in the profit rates when investment is directed toward them in a neoclassical world, the nominal cost of investment falls, leading to deflation.

GOV 1 and GOV 2: Reductions in government spending lead to rises in government saving which must be offset, with given investment demands, by falls in retained corporate earnings. The model deflates, improving the income distribution.

TRANS 1 and TRANS 2: Simply reducing the nominal level of transfers leads to deflation and an improvement in aggregate distribution. Redirecting transfers from rich households to poor leads to significant improvements in distribution with no deflation. Sectoral output and employment levels must shift from luxury goods to necessities.

TAX 1, TAX 2, and TAX 3: Attempts to change sectoral labor demands through changes in the tax structure will be futile. It is not possible to change the relative cost of capital to labor in a sector by changing the profit tax rate, since there will be offsetting movements in profit rates. Nor will changes in the tax on wages matter, since the cost of capital will move in the same direction as the cost of labor. But significant improvements in the distribution of income will result from shifting from wage taxes to profit taxes.

RATE 1: Devaluation increases domestic saving, leading to deflation and an improvement in distribution.

EDUC 1, EDUC 2, and EDUC 3: Growth as well as equity considerations lead to the conclusion that Brazilian education programs should be directed to the illiterate rather than to the already highly educated.

Table 9-31. Summary Statistics: Ratios of Variable Wage Solutions to Base Solution, 1971

Item	*SEN 1*	*INV 1*	*GOV 1*	*TRANS 2*	*TAX 3*	*EDUC 3*	*DIST 2*	*DIST 3*
Real GNP	0.99	0.97	1.00	1.00	1.00	1.00	1.00	1.03
GNP deflator	1.17	0.70	0.51	0.99	0.89	0.92	0.91	1.25
Labor share of GNP								
Total	1.03	0.95	0.92	1.00	1.05	0.99	0.98	1.14
1. Family farm workers	1.10	0.95	0.94	1.01	1.05	0.99	0.99	1.43
2. Sharecroppers	1.09	0.95	0.94	1.00	1.05	0.99	0.98	1.42
3. Uneducated	1.09	0.95	0.93	1.00	1.05	0.58	0.98	1.29
4. Primary-educated	1.04	0.95	0.92	1.00	1.05	1.09	0.98	1.18
5. Secondary-educated	1.00	0.94	0.91	1.00	1.05	0.98	0.98	1.01
6. Highly educated	0.97	0.96	0.92	1.00	1.05	0.98	0.98	1.05
Capitalist share of GNP								
Total	1.01	0.97	0.87	1.00	0.90	0.99	0.99	0.99
Agriculture	1.06	0.92	0.90	1.01	1.04	0.99	1.00	1.48
Manufacturing	1.01	0.93	0.78	0.99	0.82	0.99	0.50	0.68
Commerce	1.01	0.94	0.85	1.00	0.97	0.98	0.50	1.21
Services	1.00	1.04	0.98	1.00	0.93	1.00	0.49	1.22
Highly educated labor	1.00	0.99	0.89	1.00	0.88	1.00	5.31	0.98
Proprietor share of GNP	0.86	1.43	1.95	1.01	1.12	1.08	1.11	0.81

Outputs								
1. Crop agriculture	0.99	0.98	1.01	1.01	1.01	1.01	1.02	1.04
2. Commerce	0.99	0.98	0.97	1.00	1.01	1.00	1.01	1.05
5. Services	0.99	0.96	1.01	1.00	1.00	1.01	1.00	1.03
11. Transport goods	0.99	0.94	0.99	0.99	1.00	1.00	0.98	1.06
16. Chemicals	0.99	0.98	0.97	1.00	1.01	1.00	1.01	1.06
19. Food	0.99	0.99	1.03	1.02	1.02	1.01	1.04	1.05
24. Construction	1.00	0.91	0.97	1.00	1.00	1.00	1.00	1.02
25. Domestic servants	0.94	1.04	1.07	0.96	0.95	1.02	0.88	0.80
Employment								
1. Crop agriculture	1.01	0.99	1.01	1.01	1.01	0.99	1.02	1.03
2. Animal agriculture	0.98	0.99	1.01	1.00	0.99	0.99	1.03	0.94
3. Commerce	1.00	1.01	0.93	1.00	1.01	1.02	1.02	1.14
5. Services	0.98	1.12	1.05	1.00	0.99	1.03	1.01	0.37
4, 6–23. Manufacturing	1.00	0.99	0.95	0.99	1.02	1.01	1.02	1.19
24. Construction	1.03	0.90	0.94	1.00	1.00	1.00	1.00	1.08
25. Domestic servants	0.96	1.04	1.07	0.96	0.95	1.03	0.88	0.87
Distribution measures								
Gini	1.00	0.97	0.93	0.96	0.97	0.99	0.89	0.91
Theil	0.99	0.97	0.88	0.94	0.89	0.99	0.61	0.88
Variance log incomes	1.07	0.84	0.77	0.89	0.96	0.95	1.03	1.13
Atkinson	1.03	0.92	0.87	0.94	0.96	0.98	0.93	1.04

Table 9-32. Summary Statistics: Ratios of Fixed Wage Solutions to Base Solution, 1971

Item	SEN 1	INV 1	GOV 1	TRANS 2	TAX 3	DIST 2	DIST 3	DIST 4[a]
Real GNP	1.00	0.95	0.95	1.00	1.00	1.00	1.07	1.06
GNP deflator	1.01	0.99	0.92	1.00	0.94	1.00	0.88	0.48
Labor share of GNP								
Total	1.00	1.01	1.04	1.00	1.06	1.00	1.06	0.84
1. Family farm workers	1.25	1.01	1.08	1.02	1.07	1.02	1.20	1.15
2. Sharecroppers	1.20	1.01	1.07	1.02	1.06	1.02	1.20	0.96
3. Uneducated	1.27	1.01	1.06	1.01	1.06	1.00	1.51	1.80
4. Primary-educated	0.99	1.01	1.05	1.00	1.06	0.99	1.34	0.80
5. Secondary-educated	0.96	1.01	1.02	1.00	1.06	1.00	0.42	0.70
6. Highly educated	0.87	1.01	1.03	1.00	1.06	1.00	0.91	0.52
Capitalist share of GNP								
Total	1.00	1.00	0.93	1.00	0.90	1.00	0.99	0.92
Agriculture	1.00	1.00	1.05	1.01	1.06	1.02	1.24	0.70
Manufacturing	1.00	0.97	0.86	0.99	0.83	0.51	0.66	0.92
Commerce	1.00	1.04	1.04	1.00	0.99	0.51	1.24	0.85
Services	1.00	1.03	0.97	1.00	0.93	0.49	1.30	1.01
Highly educated labor	1.00	1.00	0.92	1.00	0.88	6.36	1.02	0.97
Proprietor share of GNP	0.99	1.00	1.09	1.01	1.06	1.01	1.15	2.09

Output								
1. Crop agriculture	1.00	0.95	0.95	1.01	1.01	1.01	1.12	1.10
3. Commerce	1.00	0.95	0.92	1.00	1.00	1.00	1.09	1.06
5. Services	0.99	0.94	0.96	1.00	0.99	0.99	1.04	1.05
11. Transport goods	1.00	0.92	0.95	0.99	1.00	0.98	1.09	1.06
16. Chemicals	1.00	0.95	0.92	1.00	1.01	1.01	1.09	1.05
19. Food	1.01	0.96	0.96	1.02	1.01	1.03	1.16	1.14
24. Construction	1.00	0.90	0.95	1.00	1.00	1.00	1.03	1.02
25. Domestic servants	0.96	0.94	0.89	0.96	0.94	0.87	0.95	1.18
Employment								
1. Crop agriculture	1.07	0.95	0.94	1.02	1.01	1.01	1.13	1.32
2. Animal agriculture	1.04	0.93	0.90	1.00	0.98	1.02	1.11	1.41
3. Commerce	1.07	0.97	0.86	1.00	1.01	1.01	2.06	1.50
5. Services	1.12	0.97	0.80	1.00	0.97	0.97	0.66	2.25
4, 6–23. Manufacturing	1.05	0.93	0.86	1.00	1.01	1.00	1.78	1.40
24. Construction	1.13	0.89	0.94	1.00	1.00	1.00	1.88	1.62
25. Domestic servants	0.99	0.94	0.89	0.96	0.94	0.87	0.92	1.25
Distribution measures								
Gini	0.99	1.00	0.98	0.96	0.97	0.90	0.86	0.96
Theil	1.00	0.98	0.91	0.95	0.89	0.61	0.95	1.02
Variance log incomes	0.97	1.00	0.99	0.89	0.99	1.09	0.70	0.82
Atkinson	0.99	1.00	0.98	0.94	0.97	0.96	0.85	0.93

a. DIST 4 has wages set at 1965 base levels.

DIST 1 and DIST 2: Profit redistribution can lead to significant improvements in overall distribution. The redistributions affect the GNP shares of only the groups directly involved: there is little spillover to other groups. With a more egalitarian income distribution, real GNP grows as less labor is wasted in low-productivity sectors such as domestic servants.

DIST 3: Elimination of wage differentials across sectors leads to massive labor shifts, from initially low-wage to high-wage industries. This increases aggregate GNP supply a great deal. Profit rates fall in those sectors that before redistribution paid higher wages, and rise in the initial low-wage sectors.

DIST 4: Maintenance of 1965 wages into 1968 and 1971 leads to uniform increases in demands for the six labor types. This is not enough to keep up with the rapidly increasing supplies of the higher skilled workers and leads to their unemployment.

EXP 1 through EXP 5: Low-skill groups benefit much more from expansions in exports of agricultural goods and processed foods than do high-skill groups, while the opposite holds for the exports of modern technology and industrial goods.

Our remaining task is to put into perspective the magnitudes of these responses of the general equilibrium model to policy changes. Tables 9-31 and 9-32 give the ratio changes of important variables from the base run to selected other simulations for the variable wage and fixed wage variants. Table 9-1 summarizes the policy shifts underlying each solution.

It is a truism that general equilibrium models are rather unresponsive to policy shifts, and this appears to be borne out in tables 9-31 and 9-32. The ratios of the values of most variables in the policy simulations to their values in the base range between 0.90 and 1.10, the main exceptions being the price level and some of the distributive shares (especially that of proprietors). This stability is more apparent than real, however, when the model responses are compared in magnitude with the shocks imposed on the base solution by policy shifts. For example, in GOV 1 government purchases of goods and services is lowered by only 3.3 percent of GNP, but as a result, prices fall 49 percent, the GNP share of proprietors rises by 95 percent, the GNP shares of various capitalists fall by between 10 and 22 percent, sector outputs shift by up to 7 percent, sector employment levels vary by 7 percent, the Gini coefficient improves by 7 percent, and the variance of log incomes improves by 23 percent.

Other experiments, such as TRANS 2, TAX 3, and DIST 2, lead to improvements in the aggregate distribution of income even when other variables, such as the price level, remain unchanged. Similar comments can be made about other solutions and serve to illustrate that the general equilibrium model *is* responsive to policy shifts. The magnitude of its responses is muted only because the policy changes imposed are not radical.

Of course, the income distribution improvements resulting from these policy changes are not radical either, and their magnitude suggests that tinkering with tax rates, profit redistributions, and wage structures will not move the Brazilian economy very far toward egalitarianism. The general equilibrium model results may provide some sort of guide for taking small equalizing steps, but they say very little indeed about the design of larger political and economic changes in Brazil.

References

Bacha, Edmar L., Milton da Mata, and Rui Lyrio Modenesi. 1972. *Encargos trabalhistas e absorção de mão-de-obra*. Coleção relatorios de pesquisa no. 12. Rio de Janeiro: Instituto de Planejamento Econômico e Social/Instituto de Pesquisas (IPEA/INPES).

Fishlow, Albert. 1973. Brazilian income size distribution: Another look. Berkeley: University of California, Department of Economics; processed. Published in Portuguese as: Distribuição da renda no Brasil: Um novo exame. *Dados* 11 (1973):10–80. (Published by Instituto Universitario de Pesquisas, Rio de Janeiro.)

Kelley, Allen C., Jeffrey G. Williamson, and Russell J. Cheetham. 1972. *Dualistic economic development: Theory and history*. Chicago: University of Chicago Press.

Langoni, Carlos Geraldo. 1974. *As causes do crescimento econômico do Brasil*. Rio de Janeiro: Apec Editora.

Sen, Amartya. 1973. *On economic inequality*. New York: W. W. Norton.

Taylor, Lance, and Edmar L. Bacha. 1976. The unequalizing spiral: A first growth model for Belindia. *Quarterly journal of economics* 90:197–218.

10

Brazilian Income Distribution in the 1960s: "Facts," Model Results, and the Controversy

Edmar L. Bacha and Lance Taylor

ATTEMPTS AT EXPLAINING CHANGES in the Brazilian income distribution during the 1960s can be grouped conveniently into six hypotheses. Five accept that there was deterioration in distributional equity. One denies that any such thing occurred.[1]

The five positive explanations of increasing inequality further split into two groups, emphasizing microeconomic market adjustments on the one hand, and institutional and macro phenomena on the other. The micro stories emphasize, first, certain statistical regularities of the development process, which we label "Kuznets effects"; second, they stress the importance of unequalizing Marshallian wage responses to sudden increases in excess demand for skilled labor as growth accelerates, in a skill differentials hypothesis.

1. Most of the discussion about Brazilian inequality is focused on the 1960–70 period because demographic censuses taken at the beginning and end of the decade are by far the most important sources of information about distributional trends. Differing interpretations of the census data, however, underlie many polemical positions. For a brief review of the numbers available, see the appendix to this chapter.

More historically oriented scholars point out the negative impact on the income distribution of the post-1964 wage squeeze, which forced labor payments down during the 1964–67 period. When rapid growth of output resumed after 1967, the wage compression at the bottom of the distribution allowed bigger profit margins and remunerations at the top (in both the public and private sectors) giving rise to a wage spread. Both these lines of analysis fit naturally with the formal models of this volume, which are built around assumptions that make income concentration with growth the likely outcome. Finally, recent papers by American economists contend that the wrong measurements were used, and try to dispose of the debate by claiming that on relevant welfare scales income distribution did not in fact deteriorate in the 1960s.

Six Hypotheses of Brazilian Income Distribution

In this section we try to pass along some of the polemical flavor of the six interpretations of income distribution in Brazil and state their principal assumptions more fully. Thereafter, we discuss the extent to which each is supported by economic reasoning and the "facts," insofar as they are known. Our conclusions will be agnostic, but predisposed toward the hypotheses of the wage squeeze, wage spread, and income concentration. It is only fair to warn the reader in advance that we are counted among the authors of papers arguing these points of view.

Kuznets Effects

The hypothesis of Kuznets effects stresses that changes in the structure of employment accompanying the intermediate stages of modern economic growth can easily lead to increases in income inequality. It is favored by Langoni (1973), in a book widely cited in the Brazilian debate, and by Fields (1977).

The original idea is from Kuznets (1955), who conjectured that as labor moved from rural to urban occupations, income distribution would deteriorate because income is less concentrated in rural communities. Kuznets also thought that this rise in inequality would be temporary, largely restricted to an intermediate phase of capitalist development when there are substantial intersectoral movements of the population. Afterward, equalizing factors would prevail, allowing for a decrease in inequality with further economic growth.

This hypothesis of an inverse U-shaped relation between income concentration and per capita income has been tested by a number of econometricians, using cross-section international data. The cross-country evidence is broadly consistent with Kuznets's conjecture, although large deviations from the regression curve stand out (Ahluwalia 1976; Bacha 1978).

In his polemical chapters Langoni (1973) emphasizes general structural shifts of the Kuznets type, but his statistical work focuses mainly on the unequalizing impact of the expansion of education between 1960 and 1970. Despite a substantial decline in illiteracy rates, the distribution of educational attainment became more unequal, largely because of a marked expansion in the number of university and secondary-school graduates in relation to primary-school graduates. As shown below, income is more equally distributed among the less educated, so that the overall distribution was worse. Perhaps more important, narrowing of income differences by educational levels—which could offset such an increase in inequality—was not observed in Brazil in the 1960s.

This restatement of Kuznets's ideas gained easy acceptance in Brazilian government circles. For example, Antonio Delfim Netto (serving as minister of finance but identifying himself as a university professor) wrote in a foreword to Langoni's book:

> Langoni proves that the observed increase in inequality is a direct consequence of market disequilibria accompanying the development process. Thus, the behavior of relative incomes reflects, mostly, the intense process of differentiation of the labor force caused by the rapid expansion of modern sectors. In these sectors, however, workers are very productive and, because of this, receive relatively high earnings even when the variance is larger. In this context, it makes no sense to use the increase in inequality as an index of welfare deterioration. (Langoni 1973, p. 14.)

Skill Differentials

The explanation based on skill differentials was proposed as part of Langoni's (1973) study and maintains that short-run Marshallian adjustment processes in the labor market are responsible for the observed stretching of wage differentials in the 1960s. The idea is that the labor supply is structured by well-defined skill levels, and this structure is constantly changing as a result of the educational process. The wage structure is anchored at the bottom by the elastic supply of the unskilled, but elasticities of substitution between skill groups are assumed to be low and rapidly declining at higher rungs along the educational ladder. Growth in labor demand is supposed to be biased toward higher skill types because physical capital and advanced skill are complementary. The sectoral mix of aggregate demand is shifting toward skill-intensive industries and technical progress is skill-using.

According to this set of assumptions, GDP growth in Brazil during the 1960s could not help but drive up demand for skilled workers at a faster pace than they were being produced by the educational system. As a consequence, wage differentials by years of schooling widened—though perhaps only temporarily. This alleged market response partially explains the rising Gini coefficient over the decade.

The skill differentials hypothesis is clearly compatible with emphasis on Kuznets effects, and it was also adopted by the government as part of the official interpretation of rising inequality. For example, at the height of the distribution debate in 1975 Minister of Finance Mario Simonsen asserted that "In fact, the main reason for worsening income distribution seems to have been an inadequate profile of labor qualifications vis-à-vis the needs of the market" (Simonsen 1975, p. 18). The implicit technological assumption that the wage response to faster growth in the skilled labor supply would be highly equalizing is taken up in detail below.

Wage Squeeze

Economists not directly associated with the Brazilian government take other tacks. One was independently suggested by Fishlow (1972) and Hoffmann and Duarte (1972) and further developed by Hoffmann (1973). It stresses that the repressive wage policy that figured in the economic stabilization program following the 1964 military coup was a factor in producing the increase in income inequality.

More precisely, the cited authors observe that the earnings of unskilled and semiskilled urban laborers place them in three intermediate deciles (fifth to seventh) of the income distribution.

These three deciles are the ones for which average real income grew least between 1960 and 1970. Minimum wage control and the lagging wage formula for collective bargaining hit exactly these income strata the hardest and are asserted to have caused their observed low real growth. Rural workers were only indirectly affected by urban minimum wage requirements, and upper-income groups in the city escaped the wage squeeze because their salaries were not determined through collective bargaining.

Wage Spread

An explanation related to that of the wage squeeze was originally suggested in an unpublished paper by Tavares (1969), further explored by Bacha (1976, Essay no. 2.4), and favorably discussed by Wells (1974) and Fishlow (1973*b*). It starts with the observation that in the modern sector both production and government service activities are organized along hierarchical lines. The relative levels of wages parallel the structure of command and influence within organizations, with market processes guaranteeing rough comparability of remunerations across management units. The average wage differential between managers and workers widens as gross profits increase, and it is influenced by the level of payments received by upper-level government technocrats. If the market at the top end of the wage spectrum tightens, vacancies are more likely to be filled by accelerated on-the-job training and downgrading of ascriptive job characteristics than to be wiped out by wage adjustments.[2]

Applied to Brazil, these ideas suggest that broadening earnings differentials in the 1960s will not be explained by scarcities of skilled labor, as maintained by the official spokespersons. Rather, wage repression after 1964, combined with demand-boosting policies after 1967, allowed firms to achieve much higher profit rates than before. These filtered through the organizational hierarchy, allowing increasing pay rates to administrative and professional positions. The wage squeeze at the bottom of the scale and rising government salaries for technocrats moving back and forth from the private sector helped keep the whole structure stable.

2. See Doeringer and Piore (1971) for an initial statement of theories of the dual labor market, and Cain (1976) for a review of the burgeoning literature. The analysis of manpower and wage policies of São Paulo firms by Barbosa, Morley, and Souza (1976) is consistent with the job-rationing process sketched in the text.

Income Concentration with Growth

For many years Latin American economists of structuralist persuasion have stressed that rapid economic growth is likely to be associated with increasing income inequality, for a variety of reasons. Much of their argument transcends economics as usually construed and cannot easily be captured by mathematical or statistical reasoning. Some flavor of structuralist analysis shows up, however, in models such as those in this volume that stress macroeconomic adjustments via forced saving. For example, the results of chapter 4 demonstrate in a macro model without an important monetary sector that during the 1960s saving adjusted to the current value of investment via shifts in the real values of private, foreign, and government saving brought about by changes in the inflation rate. Subsequent monetary analysis (Cardoso 1978) develops this line of thought to show that the observed decrease in the government budget deficit and the growth spurt after 1967 were consistent with an increase in wage repression, reducing the need to rely on inflationary finance. Such macroeconomic reasoning is consistent with micro wage squeeze and wage spread, and the three hypotheses fit together as a consistent alternative to the government's rationalizations of increasing inequality.

Wrong Measurement

Some analysts (on the whole not Brazilian) suggest that the whole inequality debate is pointless because of inadequate data and faulty methodology. Morley and Williamson (1975) observe that Langoni's data for the income-earning population yields a Lorenz curve for 1970 lying strictly below the corresponding curve for 1960. For income earners, the increase in inequality is unambiguous. If labor force participants with zero income are included, however, the Lorenz curve for 1960 crosses the 1970 curve from below, implying that the poorest groups became relatively better off in 1970.

In a similar though independent analysis, Fields (1977) bases his comparison on equivalent real income intervals rather than on income deciles. He concludes that the Brazilian "poor" (those earning up to Cr$2.10 a month in 1960 and up to Cr$99.00 in 1970) increased their average income by more than 60 percent over the decade, whereas the nonpoor (all others in the labor force) raised their income by only 25 to 30 percent during the same period.

Both the Morley-Williamson and Fields arguments can be criticized on methodological and statistical grounds. We take up this task in the following section, as a prelude to more quantitative discussion of the other hypotheses.

Wrong Measurement Dismissed

The reliance of all analysts on the 1960 and 1970 Brazilian demographic censuses has forced them to adopt all kinds of extrapolation techniques to try to get at the "true" income distribution. The census data give information only about cash incomes received by samples of individuals in the economically active population. These data must necessarily be supplemented by inferences about income in kind, underreporting at the top of the distribution, closure of open-ended income brackets, and so forth before they can be useful.

The results of such manipulations presented by Langoni (1973) have received closest attention since he had access to large samples from both censuses as opposed to other economists such as Fishlow (1972) and Hoffmann and Duarte (1972) who had to rely on summary 1970 census tabulations. Langoni's overall distribution estimates are reproduced in table 10-1.[3]

Morley and Williamson (1975) take exception to Langoni's choice of income *earners* as the population of reference and compare the distributions for all individuals in the economically active population, including zero-income recipients. The latter, for the most part, are unpaid family workers in the rural sector (Fishlow and Meesook 1972; Langoni 1973). Fishlow (1972) developed a technique to estimate how much of the money in-

3. Langoni's data manipulations have at least one important drawback: he continuously emphasizes the fact that he did not need to guess the mean income of the upper open-ended income interval for 1970 because he had access to individual census data. It is now known, however, that the census bureau tabulated all individuals with monthly incomes higher than Cr$9,997 (approximately US$2,150) as earning exactly Cr$9,998 (Costa 1975). In a footnote to table 4-5 in the preliminary version of his book, Langoni (1972) seems to be aware of this fact, but it is not mentioned in the published version of his work (Langoni 1973). By treating the upper open-ended income class as if it were closed, Langoni underestimates the degree of income concentration by at least 2.7 percent in the very insensitive Gini scale (Costa 1975).

come of rural family heads was redistributed to these zero-income recipients in 1960. Langoni (1973) found Fishlow's procedures too subjective and did not do the same for 1970: his solution was to exclude these workers from the analysis. Morley and Williamson's proposal is to put them back in the picture with zero-income levels and identify them as unemployed. The proportion of zero-income recipients falls from 14.7 to 9.6 percent of the labor force between 1960 and 1970. As a consequence, the 1970 Lorenz curve of the distribution of cash income for the labor force crosses the corresponding curve for 1960 from above—unequivocal welfare judgments on the two distributions can be made no longer.[4]

Morley and Williamson's point is a reminder of the inadequacy of using cash income as a basis for welfare judgments. The problem is not solved, however, by calling the zero-income recipients "unemployed," for this they certainly are not.[5] Rather, one should consider a broader income concept including payments in kind, or compare family instead of individual incomes, because the proportion of zero-income families is minimal in both 1960 and 1970. Since these alternatives are unfortunately not available, the only practical solution is to restrict attention to the income-earning population.

This leads to Fields's (1977) first point, that in absolute scale the Brazilian poor were better off in 1970 than in 1960. The effective basis for this conclusion is the 18.3 percent gain in average incomes of the poorest 40 percent of the income-earning population shown in table 10-1. This result might not be maintained, however, if comparisons included income in kind, because market-related processes became increasingly important in Brazilian agriculture between 1960 and 1970. The proportion of unpaid family workers, resident laborers, and sharecroppers fell, while that of wage earners soared. Under changing agricultural labor market conditions such as these, cash income comparisons alone clearly overstate the real income growth of the rural poor.

4. Morley and Williamson attempt to estimate the value for Atkinson's inequality aversion coefficient beyond which the 1970 distribution is "better" than the 1960 one. As shown by Hoffmann (1976) this cannot be done with zero-income earners in the sample, because Atkinson's measure requires the existence of the logarithm of all income levels.

5. The openly unemployed represented only 1.3 percent of the labor force in 1970. A comparable figure is not available for 1960, but indirect evidence suggests that it would not be much larger. See Wells (1976).

Proper evaluation of Fields's contention would require data on changes in income in kind, which do not exist.

Fields also stresses absolute income changes, although most of the debate has been about relative income shifts. He oversteps the bounds of the data, however, when he asserts that "average real incomes among families defined as poor by Brazilian standards increased by as much as 60 percent while the comparable figure for nonpoor families is around 25 percent" (Fields 1977, p. 570). Fields compares the average monthly incomes in equivalent real income intervals in the two census years, say, between 0.0 and 2.1, or 2.1 and 3.3 1960 cruzeiros (as well as other pairs of end points). The average income in each such interval will of course change with both the number of income recipients it contains and the income per head they receive. Population movements among intervals are at least as important as income growth itself in changing the distribution by size, and Fields's procedure of scaling up average incomes within fixed intervals leaves them out completely.

In addition, Fields's estimates of the real income growth of the poor are vitiated by faulty statistical procedures. He defines the "poor" as those earning up to 2.1 1960 cruzeiros a month both in 1960 and 1970. In his equation (4) he imputes to this group an income share equal to 6 percent in 1970, up from 5.2 percent in 1960 (Fields 1977, p. 575). Since the proportion of the "poor" in the labor force declined from 37 percent in 1960 to 35.5 percent in 1970, he concludes that the "poor" experienced a much higher growth rate of income than the "nonpoor." Using Langoni's data (Langoni 1973, table 3-2, p. 61), we can draw an approximate Lorenz curve for the income distribution in 1970. From this curve we estimate that the income share of the lowest 35.5 percent of the population was in fact 4.35 percent rather than 6.0 percent as described by Fields. Hence, in proportion to the total population, the "poor" were 4.1 percent fewer than in 1960, but their income share in 1970 was 16.3 percent lower. In relative terms, in 1970 the "poor" were worse off than in 1960. The picture is bleaker if we exclude from the "poor" the zero-income earners (this is what we should do since we do not know what happened to the real income of these people between 1960 and 1970). In this case, the proportion of the "poor" increases from 22.3 to 23.8 percent of the population between 1960 and 1970. But their income share drops as before, from 5.2 to 4.5 percent of the total.

These computations of course depend on our construction of a Lorenz curve by interpolation between Langoni's discrete data points. In a more refined analysis, Ahluwalia and others (1978) use the available data to put upper and lower bounds on income growth of the "rich" and the "poor" in Brazil. Again, they find that Fields's strong conclusions are not justified and further question his use of a single price deflator to compute 1960–70 "real" income changes for different population groups.

The way not to fall into Fields's trap is quite traditional—one simply compares distributional changes by looking at time-invariant population percentiles, ordered according to income level. Using this yardstick, we verify in table 10-1 that the cash income of the poor (say, the lowest 40 percent of the distribution) proportionately increased by much less than the cash income of the rich (say, the highest 20 percent of the distribution) between 1960 and 1970.

Table 10-1. Comparison of Income Distribution by Income Deciles, 1960 and 1970

Income-earning population deciles	*Percentage of total income*			*Average income (in 1970 cruzeiros per month)*		
	1960	*1970*	*Percent change*	*1960*	*1970*	*Percent change*
Lowest 10 percent	1.17	1.11	−5.1	25	32	+28.0
10	2.32	2.05	−11.6	48	58	+20.8
10	3.42	2.97	−13.2	71	84	+18.3
10	4.65	3.88	−16.6	96	110	+14.6
10	6.15	4.90	−20.3	127	139	+9.5
10	7.66	5.91	−22.8	158	168	+6.3
10	9.41	7.37	−21.7	195	210	+7.7
10	10.85	9.57	−11.8	225	272	+20.9
10	14.69	14.45	−1.6	305	411	+34.8
Highest 10 percent	39.66	47.79	+20.5	815	1,360	+66.9
Highest 5 percent	27.69	34.86	+25.9	1,131	1,984	+75.4
Highest 1 percent	12.11	14.57	+20.3	2,389	4,147	+73.6
Lowest 40 percent	11.57	10.00	−13.6	60	71	+18.3
40	34.08	27.80	−18.5	176	197	+11.9
Highest 20 percent	54.35	62.20	+14.5	560	886	+58.2
Total income-earning population	100.00	100.00		206	282	+36.9

Source: Langoni (1973), table 3-5, p. 64.

In summary, both Morley and Williamson and Fields substitute computation for common sense in asserting that the Brazilian size distribution became more egalitarian over the 1960s. Both approaches amount to misinterpretation of the available data and are best dismissed as red herrings.

Kuznets Effects

The income distribution study by Langoni (1973) apparently was undertaken with both polemic and scholarly intent. Happily for the author, he could make his two objectives compatible by focusing on structural changes of the type discussed by Kuznets: "a substantial fraction of the increase in inequality observed in the period is associated with the educational improvement of the labor force, the transfer of workers from the primary sector to the urban sector, and a larger participation of youth and women in the labor market" (Langoni 1973, p. 15).

These assertions are based on decompositions of the shifts in the variance of logarithms of payments received by members of the income-earning population between 1960 and 1970. Suppose that income recipients are stratified into G groups according to some relevant characteristic such as sector of activity or educational level. Take the variance of logs of income as the measure of income inequality and consider the changes in this measure between two points in time. Apart from interaction effects, movements in the variance of log incomes can be decomposed in three terms. The first, which we call "composition changes" (or Kuznets effects), represents the variations caused by people shifting from one group to another—as long as log variances differ between groups, this will affect the overall log variance. The second component, which we name "relative income changes," captures variations in the relative incomes of the different groups (for example, the overall variance goes up when the average income of college graduates increases more than the average income of illiterates). Finally, the third component, "within-group variance changes," takes into account the impact on the overall variance of changes in the variances within groups. In symbols, let

V = overall variance of log income
x^i = proportion of total population in group i; $i = 1, ..., G$

w^i = ratio between the geometric mean of incomes in group i and the overall geometric mean of incomes[6]

v^i = variance of logs of incomes in group i.

As shown by Theil (1967, pp. 123–24), the overall variance can be written as

$$V = \sum_{i=1}^{G} x^i \left(\log^2 w^i + v^i\right). \qquad (10.1)$$

Let Δ stand for changes in the variables between two periods (say, between 1960 and 1970). Then $\Delta V = \Delta V^* +$ higher-order terms, where

$$\Delta V^* = \sum_{i=1}^{G} \left[(\log^2 w^i + v^i)\Delta x^i + x^i \Delta \log^2 w^i + x^i \Delta v^i\right]. \qquad (10.2)$$

ΔV is the estimated change in the variance of logs, and its first order approximation, ΔV^*, is the explained change in the variance of logs. The terms within brackets in (10.2) are, respectively, the composition change, the relative income change, and the within-group variance change.

ΔV, ΔV^*, and their components can be estimated from Langoni's computations of the structural characteristics of the income-earning population for the 1960 and 1970 census data; these are reproduced in table 10-2. The decomposition results are summarized in table 10-3 with alternative 1960 and 1970 weightings on the Δx^i, $\Delta \log^2 w^i$, and Δv^i terms appearing in (10.2).

Our findings and the parallel results reported by Fishlow (1973*b*) are rather surprising in view of Langoni's insistence upon the importance of compositional changes in explaining the increase in the variance of log income in the period. Population movements between regions and between sectors of activity had an *equalizing* influence on the overall variance, in spite of the

6. In the computations, we use the ratio of arithmetic means as a proxy for the w^i since the geometric means are not published by Langoni. We have not been able to determine if this substitution introduces a systematic bias in our results. As a matter of arithmetic, estimated changes in the variance of log incomes should be identical for all classifications. For reasons we do not understand, this principle of accounting is *not* satisfied by the numbers in Langoni's summary tables. Hence, we cannot explain the differences in estimated variances appearing in the first column of table 10-3.

Table 10-2. Structural Characteristics of the Income-earning Population, 1960 and 1970

Classification	x^i_{70}	x^i_{60}	w^i_{70}	w^i_{60}	v^i_{70}	v^i_{60}
Education						
Uneducated	0.2975	0.3905	0.3972	0.5415	0.5304	0.4755
Primary school	0.5447	0.5171	0.8511	1.0293	0.7282	0.6262
Junior high	0.0803	0.0516	1.7092	2.1463	0.8525	0.6084
Senior high	0.0524	0.0265	2.4397	2.6145	0.7405	0.5167
College	0.0251	0.0140	6.0496	5.4780	0.8572	0.5916
Sex						
Male	0.7925	0.8322	1.0851	1.0728	0.9273	0.7429
Female	0.2048	0.1687	0.6595	0.6504	1.0493	0.7035
Sector						
Primary	0.4005	0.4656	0.4894	0.5874	0.5474	0.5110
Secondary	0.1974	0.1524	1.2730	1.2427	0.7411	0.5580
Tertiary	0.4021	0.3820	1.3723	1.3592	1.1725	0.8852
Age						
10–19	0.1425	0.1245	0.3481	0.4412	0.5468	0.4374
20–24	0.1581	0.1489	0.7021	0.7864	0.6746	0.5899
25–29	0.1371	0.1421	0.9894	1.0048	0.8324	0.6756
30–39	0.2303	0.2422	1.2092	1.1796	0.9405	0.7704
40–49	0.1718	0.1736	1.3652	1.2184	1.0606	0.8180
50–59	0.1005	0.1029	1.2589	1.2087	1.0968	0.8527
60–69	0.0449	0.0492	1.0638	1.0534	1.1087	0.8458
70+	0.0130	0.0166	0.8085	0.8398	0.9948	0.7518
Region or state						
Rio de Janeiro	0.1058	0.1036	1.5887	1.6214	0.8423	0.7027
São Paulo	0.2278	0.2086	1.5107	1.3738	0.8663	0.6346
South	0.1677	0.1472	0.9610	1.1068	0.7329	0.5304
Minas Gerais and Espirito Santo	0.1351	0.1595	0.7270	0.8204	0.8962	0.7484
Northeast	0.2763	0.3066	0.5568	0.5680	0.8128	0.5296
North and Center-West	0.0872	0.0744	0.8440	1.0486	0.6385	0.5887

Note: x^i = share of individuals of group i in total income-earning population; w^i = ratio between the mean of incomes of group i and the mean of incomes of all individuals; v^i = variance of logs of incomes of individuals in group i. The subscripts 60 or 70 denote the year of reference for the above variables.

Source: Langoni (1973), tables 4-1 and 4-2, pp. 81 and 86.

substantial migrations from the rural sector to urban activities and from poorer to richer regions between 1960 and 1970. This result seems to contradict the original version of Kuznets's hypothesis for the Brazilian case. In two other population dimensions, sex and age, the compositional changes contributed to increasing the overall variance, but only slightly so. No more than 1.2 to 3.1 percent of the total change in variance is explained by shifts in age composition of the population, and only 2.4 to 4.7

percent by changing sex composition.[7] The results in table 10-3 also indicate that changes in the educational composition of the labor force account for at most 14.6 percent of the increase in the variance of log incomes with 1960 weights, but with 1970 weights this contribution could be as little as 3.9 percent. This finding clashes with Langoni's contention, apparently based on the same data and methodology, that "the changes in relative incomes explain 23 percent of the total increase observed in the period, whereas *changes in composition explain 35 percent*, and the increase in inequality within groups represents 42 percent" (Langoni 1973, p. 93, emphasis added). According to the results reported in table 10.3, relative income changes were responsible for no less than 52.7 percent of the explained change in variance of log incomes, with within-group variance accounting for from 29.2 (with 1960 weights) to 43.4 percent (with 1970 weights) of the total. We convinced ourselves that our results were consistent with Langoni's basic data (except as noted in note 6) but could not find the reasons our final results differ from his. Similar skepticism by Malan and Wells (1973) and Fishlow (1973*b*) leads us to conclude that Kuznets effects were not important in shaping trends in the Brazilian size distribution in the 1960s.

Skill Differentials

Simonsen summarized the hypothesis of skill differentials as follows: "Only 10.34 percent of the economically active population had at least a high school diploma [in 1960], and college graduates represented only 1.6 percent of the labor force. Hence, vis-à-vis the needs of the market, unskilled laborers were overabundant, meanwhile skilled labor types were rather scarce"

7. Of course these decompositions are conditional on our (and Langoni's) choice of the variance of log incomes as a measure of inequality. In (10.2) since population changes Δ_x^i (which must sum to zero) are weighted by a term in the *square* of ratio incomes ($\log^2 w^i$), movements in and out of groups at the extremes of the size distribution are weighted highly. Even so, the composition changes in table 10-3 are not large and might indeed have their signs reversed under other decompositions of overall inequality, such as the entropy measure proposed by Theil (1967). In mathematical terms table 10-3 shows small composition changes because in (10.2) the v^i will be more or less equal across groups, and despite their overweighting of the extremes of the distribution the $\log^2 w^i$ terms will not differ greatly from one. An essentially similar point is made by Fishlow (1973*b*).

Table 10-3. Decomposition of the Change in the Variance of Logs of Incomes, 1960 and 1970

Classification[a]	Estimated change in variance of logs (ΔV)	Explained change in variance of logs (ΔV^*)	Proportional contributions to explained change (percent): Composition change	Relative income change	Within-group variance change
Education					
1960 weights	0.2916	0.3296	14.6	56.2	29.2
1970 weights	0.2916	0.2534	3.9	52.7	43.4
Sex					
1960 weights	0.2218	0.2162	2.4	−0.2	97.8
1970 weights	0.2218	0.2270	4.7	−0.4	95.7
Sector					
1960 weights	0.2573	0.2596	−1.8	42.3	59.5
1970 weights	0.2573	0.2547	−2.9	37.6	62.3
Age					
1960 weights	0.2642	0.2592	1.2	31.8	67.0
1970 weights	0.2642	0.2704	3.1	33.7	63.2
Region					
1960 weights	0.2232	0.2269	−4.5	13.4	91.1
1970 weights	0.2232	0.2199	−6.2	13.4	92.8

Note:

$$\Delta V = \sum_i x_{70}^i (\log^2 w_{70}^i + v_{70}^i) - \sum_i x_{60}^i (\log^2 w_{60}^i + v_{60}^i)$$

$$\Delta V^* \text{ (1960 weights)} = \sum_i [(\log^2 w_{60}^i + v_{60}^i)(x_{70}^i - x_{60}^i) + x_{60}^i(\log^2 w_{70}^i - \log^2 w_{60}^i) + x_{60}^i(v_{70}^i - v_{60}^i)]$$

$$\Delta V^* \text{ (1970 weights)} = \sum_i [(\log^2 w_{70}^i + v_{70}^i)(x_{70}^i - x_{60}^i) + x_{70}^i(\log^2 w_{70}^i - \log^2 w_{60}^i) + x_{70}^i(v_{70}^i - v_{60}^i)].$$

The composition change is $(\log^2 w_{60}^i + v_{60}^i)(x_{70}^i - x_{60}^i)$; the relative income change is $x_{60}^i (\log^2 w_{70}^i - \log^2 w_{60}^i)$; and the within-group variance change is $x_{60}^i(v_{70}^i - v_{60}^i)$. See table 10-2 for the meaning of the symbols.

a. Classifications include the groups listed in table 10-2.

Source: Estimated from Langoni (1973), tables 4-1 and 4-2, pp. 81 and 86.

(Simonsen 1975, p. 19). Though the polemic intent of this ministerial observation is clear, its static analysis rather misses the point. In looking at *changes* in the income distribution by skill types over 1960–70, one would have to work with shifts in labor force composition over the period. Table 10-4 shows that the population share of college graduates increased by 80 percent, while their per capita income increase (51.9 percent) was greater than any other educational group. In contrast, the population share of the uneducated fell by a quarter, and their per capita income stayed constant. Any theory of competitive labor markets would suggest that average payments to the college-educated should have fallen under this sort of shift, while payments to the depleted ranks of illiterates should have gone up. Widening skill differentials in the face of increasing numbers of the skilled during the 1960s make up the real puzzle in table 10-4. It is not resolved by observations about labor force composition in 1960.

To delve deeper and test whether the results in table 10-4 can be explained by some sort of bias favoring the highly educated in the growth of Brazilian labor demand, one would have to construct a model of the economy during the 1960s in which producing sectors demand different types of labor skill. Four groups of authors have in fact undertaken exercises of this nature—Morley and Williamson (1975), Fishlow (1973*b*), Cardoso in chapter 4 and Lysy and Taylor in chapters 6 through 9 of this volume. We review their results seriatim.

Morley and Williamson construct a demand-determined dynamic input-output model so calibrated that sectoral output levels track historical growth paths closely (see their table 1B). Total employment growth in each sector is related to output growth by an elasticity set to the observed ratio of these respective growth rates (their equation 7). Employment of each type of labor by sector is determined from a set of coefficients reflecting the 1960 composition of "skills," which are identified with eight income fractiles from the 1960 demographic census. A previous paper (Morley and Williamson 1974, table 2) indicated that this appa-

Table 10-4. Comparison of Income Distribution by Educational Level for the Income-earning Population, 1960 and 1970

Educational level	Population share (percent)		Average monthly income (1970 cruzeiros)		Percentage change, 1960–70	
	1960	1970	1960	1970	Population	Income
Uneducated	39.05	29.75	111	112	2.2	0.0
Primary school	51.71	54.47	211	240	41.3	13.7
Junior high	5.16	8.03	440	482	108.9	9.5
Senior high	2.67	5.24	536	688	163.4	28.4
College	1.40	2.51	1,123	1,706	140.8	51.9
Total	100.00	100.00	206	282	34.2	36.9

Source: Langoni (1973), table 4-2, p. 86; the income-earning population in 1960 is calculated from data in Fishlow and Meesook (1972).

ratus could by used to track *total* employment growth in the 1949–62 period rather accurately. It did not, however, verify how well the model performs with respect to employment growth during the 1960s.

From their simulations, Morley and Williamson (1975) conclude that estimated demand (*not* known supply) for their highest skill group grew by 4.8 percent annually between 1960 and 1970, whereas the growth rate in demand for the lowest skill group was 3.2 percent. In effect, they are asserting that the composition of demand shifted in favor of industries intensive in the employment of high-income workers in 1960.

Was this differential in simulated hiring patterns sufficient to explain the observed stretching of wages? Naturally, the answer depends on the elasticities and the actual growth rates of supply. Having preempted the obvious candidates for supply growth, namely, 4.8 percent a year for the highly skilled and 3.2 percent for low-skilled workers, they set supply growth equal to 2.6 percent a year for *both* labor types. This number has nothing to do with actual employment growth by skill type (compare Langoni's estimates of changes in the shares of the economically active population by educational level in table 10-4). Nonetheless, Morley and Williamson use it together with arbitrary estimates of supply and demand elasticities for each skill to conclude that observed wage changes can be "explained" by demand and supply considerations alone. Given their assumptions, the conclusion looks like a non sequitur.

Despite their unrealistic model, Morley and Williamson do have hold of a real problem in economic analysis, but they go at it from the wrong angle. Fishlow (1973*b*) adopts a more realistic, though partial equilibrium, point of view. His question is, How biased would demand growth for higher skill levels have to be to achieve consistency with observed trends in payments, given that relative growth rates of supply were working in the opposite direction? This bias in supply growth is of course extreme—according to table 10-4 the number of college graduates grew by 141 percent over the decade, whereas the combined supply of the uneducated and primary-school graduates went up by only 25 percent. Distinguishing three educational classes, Fishlow writes labor demand functions of the form

$$\Delta \log L_{it}/L_{ot} = \sigma_i \, \Delta \log w_{it}/w_{ot} + r_i \, \Delta t \qquad (10.3)$$

where L_{it} = demand for skill i; L_{ot} = demand for unskilled labor;

σ_i = elasticity of substitution between labor types i and 0; w_{it} = wage of skill i; w_{0t} = wage of unskilled labor; r_i = difference between the rate of labor-using technical progress for skill class i and that for unskilled workers; Δ = difference operator; i = medium-skilled or highly skilled; t = time.

Assuming changes in demand equal to observed changes in supply, Fishlow estimates the r_i's which would be consistent with the observed wage variations between 1960 and 1970, with elasticities of substitution in the range between 1 and 4. His conclusion is that the r_i's would have to be between 6.1 and 11.9 percent a year for higher skills and between 4.0 and 5.2 percent a year for medium skills. These numbers Fishlow finds exceedingly high in view of the rate of growth of per capita GDP in the period, which was on the order of 3 percent a year. He concludes that supply and demand alone cannot explain the widening earnings differential observed over the period.

A partial explanation for Fishlow's paradox is provided by Cardoso in chapter 4. She observes that the Morley-Williamson model is not closed with respect to the savings-investment identity; that is, there is no assurance that the estimated changes in (real) money wages are consistent with the observed growth in personal saving. On the basis of actual growth rates in money wages and real investment, Cardoso's simulations in a closed macro model show that there must have been a substantial shift in the functional distribution during the 1960s, as profits rose to sustain saving. A large part of the income distribution shift toward richer Brazilians (many of whom are college-educated) resulted from this savings-investment interaction, which both Morley-Williamson and Fishlow ignore.

Similar conclusions are provided by Lysy and Taylor from simulations with the multisectoral, multiskill general equilibrium model of chapters 6–9, calibrated to Brazilian 1960–70 data. Without inclusion of skill-biased technical progress as in (10.3), their model predicts *narrowing* wage differentials but a rise in the profit share parallel to that of Cardoso. In addition, their results track observed employment growth by sector reasonably well.

The Lysy-Taylor results on narrowing wage differentials derive from the competitive labor market structure they assume. With elasticities of substitution among skill types of less than infinity (their values hover around 5), any supply increase as great as that for the college-educated in table 10-4 will inevitably lead to a decrease in its relative remuneration in competitive hiring. If the substitution elasticity between the skilled and the rest of the labor force is low, simple calculations show that an even larger wage reduction would be needed to accommodate the 80 percent increase in college-trained workers in table 10-4. But low substitution elasticities, or the "essential" nature of skilled workers, is precisely what proponents of the skill differentials hypothesis assert. To make their case under labor competition (which they also presuppose) they have to rely on unreasonably high rates of biased technical change, as pointed out by Fishlow. Such assumptions are best shaved away by Occam's razor, and for that reason we conclude that the skill differentials hypothesis is not a useful explanation of Brazilian distributional change.

Wage Squeeze

The gist of the wage squeeze argument has been sketched above: the restriction on money wage increases imposed as part of the post-1964 stabilization program sharply reduced real income growth rates in the middle deciles of the size distribution and produced the rise in inequality documented in table 10-1. To analyze this hypothesis fully requires familiarity with the institutional character of the Brazilian labor market and numerical inferences based on scattered and inadequate data. We first discuss institutions and numbers, and then go on to somewhat more formalized hypothesis testing.

Patterns of Wage Settlements

Since 1940 Brazil has had a system of regional minimum wages which are periodically readjusted, lately on May 1 of each year. Collective wage negotiations involving both the labor union for a given regional industrial grouping and the corresponding firms have also been conducted regularly, under the supervision of government bodies and labor courts, since the early 1930s when the so-called Consolidation of Labor Laws was put into effect. The right to strike under prescribed conditions was legally guaranteed until the military takeover in 1964. At that time the right-to-strike law became a dead letter, and the most important labor unions in the country were subject to police intervention. New rules for collective wage negotiations were also drawn: the bilateral negotiation system was maintained, but mandatory wage guidelines were specified.

A complicated wage readjustment formula conceived by Mario Simonsen was put forward; periodically, the government specified the values of each of the variables entering the formula. The wage readjustment itself, however, had to be ratified for each labor negotiation by the Wage Department of the Ministry of Labor, either directly (in cases of undisputed agreements between unions and managers) or through the regional labor courts. Given the bureaucratic red tape, some margin of variation in wage negotiations always prevailed, despite the government's attempt to enforce homogeneity in wage increases. Starting in 1974, the government came up with a new simplified formula allowing it to decree monthly the yearly rate of wage readjustments to be followed in the ongoing negotiations.

In table 10-5 different legal wage indexes are presented. In the first two columns are the average yearly minimum wage indexes for the city of Rio de Janeiro and all state capitals. The third column gives yearly averages of the monthly rate of wage readjustments calculated by the Wage Department since 1966 (the deflator is the yearly average of the Rio cost of living index). The fourth column (eighteen unions) is a real wage index for unionized workers in the state of São Paulo.

There are a number of interesting contrasts between the minimum wage index and the eighteen-unions index: both rise in value from 1957 through 1961, when the minimum wage index loses momentum. The unions index, however, continues to increase until 1963, the last year of the "populist" Goulart government. In the 1960s as a whole there is very little change in the unions index: the 1970 value is 5 percent below that of 1960, but the 1969 value is the same as in 1959. By contrast, real minimum wages in 1970 are 30 percent lower than in 1960.

In view of this evidence, two questions emerge. First, how effective are the government wage guidelines in constraining market wage rates? Second, if effective, what are the likely impacts of government wage policy on the level and structure of employment? These questions are at the heart of the polemics on income distribution in Brazil. Much of the critical literature has been directed at exploring the negative impact of wage policy on

Table 10-5. Guideline Indexes of Real Wages, 1957–74

Year	Minimum wage indexes: City of Rio de Janeiro (1960 = 100)	Minimum wage indexes: State capitals	Average union index (1965 = 98)	Eighteen-unions index (1960 = 100)
	(1)	(2)	(3)	(4)
1957	114	98	—	98[a]
1958	99	85	—	103[b]
1959	113	99	—	94[c]
1960	100	88	—	100
1961	115	101	—	105
1962	96	84	—	105
1963	89	81	—	107
1964	89	80	—	103
1965	82	74	98	98
1966	76	69	90	92
1967	73	66	83	89
1968	74	67	84	92
1969	71	64	86	94
1970	70	63	86	95
1971	69	63	88	98
1972	71	65	92	102
1973	74	67	96	107
1974	69	64	94	107[c]

— Not applicable.
a. Eight unions.
b. Ten unions.
c. Fifteen unions.

Sources: Column (1): Yearly average of the monthly value of the minimum wage for Rio de Janeiro deflated by the Rio cost of living. Sources: Suplicy (1974) and Hoffman (1976).

Column (2): Ratio between the weighted average of the minimum wages in the state capitals (excluding Brasília, and with weights given by the population of each capital in 1960) and the minimum wage in the city of Rio, multiplied by the index in column (1).

Column (3): Calculated from the yearly average rate of wage settlements authorized by the Ministry of Labor (deflated by the yearly average of the cost of living index for Rio). Sources: Ministry of Labor, Wage Department; and Simonsen (1975).

Column (4): Calculated from the unweighted average of the yearly rate of wage settlements of the following unions in São Paulo: bank workers, joiners, graphic workers, metal workers, textile workers, theater workers (not available for 1957 and 1958), journalists (not available for 1957), newspaper graphic workers (not available for 1957 and 1958), glass workers (not available for 1974), paper workers (not available for 1957), plastic material workers, toy workers (not available for 1957, 1958, and 1959), interior metal workers (not available for 1957 and 1959), real estate brokers (not available for 1957, 1958, 1959, and 1974), and brokerage house employees (not available for 1957, 1958, 1959, and 1974); and the bank workers union of Paraná (not available for 1957 and 1958). Deflated by the average cost of living index for Rio for the first or second half of the year, according to the timing of the settlement. *Source:* DIEESE (1975).

the distribution of income and the welfare of the poor.[8] On the other side, economists associated with the government and a few others contend that wage restraint either did not influence the income distribution or acted to improve it through beneficial employment effects.[9]

Effects of Minimum Wage Policy

Arguments regarding wage policy were critically surveyed by Macedo (1977). With respect to minimum wages (the series cited most frequently by all participants in the debate) he makes three main points:

1. Minimum wages apply only in the formal market and, for example, do not cover urban and rural workers without regular jobs, the poor self-employed, and domestic servants. Even in the parts of the labor market they do cover, minimum wage requirements are in some cases known to be evaded. As we have already noted, the minimum wage does not affect people in the lower deciles of the size distribution and in no way represents an income floor. Macedo cites survey evidence to the effect that over a quarter of Brazilian income recipients gained less than *half* the minimum wage in 1972. Over half the income recipients had earnings below the legal minimum.

2. "While the level of real minimum wages has decreased since 1964, the proportion of workers receiving minimum wages in the urban formal market has also apparently decreased ... The fact that the minimum wage has been losing importance is due both to the decline in its real value over time and to the diminished importance of institutional wages in a tightening labor market" (Macedo 1977, pp. 119–20).

3. Since there is evidence (Macedo 1974; Barbosa, Morley, and Souza 1976) showing the importance of internal labor markets and occupational ladders in the Brazilian manufacturing sector, "it is difficult to believe that in the formal sector covered by the minimum wage law the people receiving minimum wages

8. The critical literature is scattered and often not formally published. A partial sampling would include Fishlow (1972, 1973*a*, 1973*b*), Hoffmann and Duarte (1972), Malan and Wells (1973), Carvalho (1973), Wells (1974), Suplicy (1974), Serra (1975), Singer (1975), DIEESE (1975), and Hoffman (1976).

9. See, for example, Langoni (1973), Simonsen (1975), Velloso (1975), and Morley and Williamson (1975).

in 1970 are the same as those who received minimum wages in 1960. Moreover, there is no guarantee that those employed at the minimum wage levels of 1970 would be employed if the minimum wages were higher. Therefore, the loss caused by the drop in the real value of the minimum wage cannot be unambiguously determined" (Macedo 1977, pp. 120–21).

Macedo's third point is another version of our criticisms above of Fields's work—in discussing relative inequality it makes no sense to consider changes in real income of either the "poor" or "those receiving the minimum wage." We can add structure to the discussion if we assume that manufacturing workers tend to enter internal labor markets at the minimum wage and progress steadily up a real wage ladder with stable income increments between the rungs. If these assumptions hold, then the drop in real minimum wages between 1960 and 1970 is equivalent to a downward shift in the whole wage ladder, and workers at all rungs lost absolutely. A repressed wage ladder may be a good simile for the outcome of the confrontation between labor and the military after 1964, but Macedo is right in asserting that it provides little direct evidence about what happened to relative inequality in the size distribution.

Macedo's second observation about wage drift requires more careful scrutiny. The phenomenon certainly occurred, at least in connection with minimum wages. The clearest evidence comes from Bacha, Mata, and Modenesi (1972), reproduced here in table 10-6. For Brazil as a whole, they show that the index of the real value of the minimum wage declines by 9.7 percent from April 1965 to April 1968. In the same period the number of workers receiving minimum monthly wages up to 1.05–1.07 falls from 43.2 to 36.1 percent of the manufacturing labor force; for both São Paulo and Rio de Janeiro the fall is much more pronounced. Between April 1968 and April 1969, when the minimum wage held constant in nominal terms and fell 19.7 percent in real terms, the proportion of all Brazilian industrial workers near the minimum wage fell from 36.1 to 28.4 percent of the total. The trend reversed subsequently, with the share rising to 29.7 percent in 1971. Wage drift away from the minimum is suggested by these figures, though possibly in exaggerated form since they are not corrected for a probable increase in hours of work as the growth rate accelerated in the late 1960s. The rise in the proportion in 1969–71 may have been due to low-skill people entering the labor force at or below the minimum wage during the boom.

Table 10-6. Share of Workers in the Industrial Sector with Monthly Earnings in the Neighborhood of the Highest Minimum Wage, 1965–71
(percent)

Date	*Monthly earnings in minimum wage units*	*São Paulo (state)*	*Rio de Janeiro*	*Brazil*	*Real minimum wage index (1965–67 = 100)*
April 1965	Up to 1.05	35.6	42.2	43.2	97.7
April 1968	Up to 1.07	24.3	27.2	36.1	88.2
April 1969	Up to 1.07	16.7	17.1	28.4	70.8
April 1971	Up to 1.06	19.3	17.2	29.7	68.3

Note: Calculated from the Two-thirds Law data of the Serviço de Estatística da Previdencia do Trabalho and the Centro de Documentação e Informatica of the Ministry of Labor. The minimum wages are for Rio de Janeiro and São Paulo, deflated by the Rio cost of living (Suplicy 1974). The Two-thirds Law earnings distributions for the intervening years and for 1972 and 1973 are organized in income intervals not allowing the direct computation of the share of workers in the neighborhood of the highest minimum wage.

Source: Bacha, Mata, and Modenesi (1972).

Other evidence for wage drift is also available. In table 10-7, for example, the yearly growth rates from 1966 to 1972 of real wages of unskilled, skilled, and managerial positions in a group of large industrial Brazilian firms are compared. The real wages of unskilled positions definitely went down; for skilled positions the story is mixed. On the average skilled workers managed to get some moderate increases in real wages, but those on top reaped most of the gains with a 7.2 percent real salary growth annually in that period. In the rural areas the poor apparently did not have better luck than in the cities. Rural wages outside the state of São Paulo did not rise in relation to minimum urban wages until late in 1973, as illustrated by the data in table 10-8. In São Paulo rapid agricultural modernization together with stricter enforcement of the rural labor legislation enacted in 1963 speeded up the process of change in modes of agricultural employment. A progressive approximation of the rural wage to the minimum standard as shown in table 10-9 was possible, even under the loose labor market conditions prevailing from 1963 to the end of the decade.

Insofar as wage drift occurred, it demonstrates that the government could not completely control market wages through its minimum wage guidelines. But one should not jump from the position that the short-run elasticity of the money market wage with respect to the official minimum is equal to one (a position apparently taken by the critical literature) to its opposite extreme,

Table 10-7. Behavior of Workers' and Managerial Earnings in a Group of Large Industrial Firms, 1966–72

Occupation	Average number of observations	Monthly average earnings, April 1972 (cruzeiros)	Annual growth rate of real earnings[a] (percent) 1966–68	1969–72	1966–72
Workers					
Servant[b]	1,615	385	−0.06	−3.1	−1.4
Helper[b]	1,852	512	−2.8	−1.8	−1.2
Industrial car operator	152	714	−4.4	−1.4	−0.7
Welder	110	826	−0.1	3.0	3.4
Painter	112	766	4.8	1.3	0.9
Blacksmith	18	970	0.5	5.7	3.4
Mason for refractory	74	1,066	0.2	3.4	3.7
Plumber	60	784	−4.2	9.7	−1.5
Electrician	270	1,220	8.5	1.4	4.6
Mechanic	306	1,167	3.8	1.8	3.7
Laboratory analyst	67	1,494	6.4	6.5	7.4
Machine tool operator	469	1,171	0.0	−0.2	2.5
Industrial designer	78	1,769	1.5	9.5	4.7
Managers					
Head of personnel division	7	3,301	17.8	3.9	10.2
Head of production division (high school level)	39	3,300	−0.3	6.5	3.4
Head of department	15	6,437	0.6	6.1	8.3
Head of production division (college level)	20	4,963	3.6	7.7	10.9
Head of maintenance division (college level)	16	5,225	2.5	11.8	7.1
Head of quality control department	11	7,027	3.5	11.2	9.1
Head of production department	20	7,235	6.9	4.3	7.1
Head of maintenance department	13	7,360	4.0	12.0	8.7

a. All data are for the month of April.
b. Unskilled workers.
Source: Wage surveys of Companhia Siderúrgica Nacional; reproduced from Bacha (1976), Essay no. 2.4.

that this elasticity is equal to zero. In fact, *median* wages in the manufacturing sector do seem to respond to the minimum wage, as shown by the regressions of table 10-10.

These regressions use as dependent variables transforms of the median wage in the manufacturing sector of Rio de Janeiro city from 1952 through 1975, and as independent variables transforms of the minimum wage in Rio, the cost of living index for this city,

Table 10-8. Brazil: Rural Wages Outside São Paulo and Highest Minimum Urban Wage, 1966–73
(cruzeiros per month)

Month	*Rural wage*[a]	*Minimum urban wage in Rio*	*Rural-urban wage ratio*
June 1966	45.96	84.00	0.55
Dec. 1966	51.48		0.61
June 1967	61.84	105.00	0.59
Dec. 1967	66.71		0.64
June 1968	73.61	129.60	0.57
Dec. 1968	76.82		0.59
June 1969	84.78	156.00	0.54
Dec. 1969	91.06		0.58
June 1970	99.82	187.20	0.53
Dec. 1970	114.10		0.61
June 1971	130.34	225.60	0.58
Dec. 1971	141.19		0.63
June 1972	156.99	268.80	0.58
Dec. 1972	170.77		0.64
June 1973	204.10	312.00	0.65
Dec. 1973	241.47		0.77

a. Average monthly earnings of permanent rural workers, Brazil except São Paulo.
Source: Conjuntura Econômica, vol. 28, no. 6 (1974), and vol. 29, no. 1 (1975).

Table 10-9. São Paulo: Rural Wages and Minimum Urban Wages, 1962–74
(cruzeiros per day)

Month or period	*Daily wage of resident rural worker*	*Minimum wage in São Paulo (city)*	*Rural-urban wage ratio*
June 1962	0.21	0.44	0.48
June 1963	0.32	0.76	0.42
June 1964	0.56	1.52	0.37
June 1965	1.08	2.38	0.45
June 1966	1.44	3.03	0.48
June 1967	2.22	3.79	0.59
November 1968	3.40	4.68	0.73
March 1969	3.45	4.68	0.74
November 1969	4.49	5.63	0.80
March 1970	4.62	5.63	0.82
November 1970	5.65	6.76	0.84
March 1971	5.68	6.76	0.84
November 1971	7.21	8.14	0.89
March–November 1972	8.38	8.24	1.02
March–November 1973	11.35	9.68	1.17
March–November 1974	13.40	11.48	1.17

Note: Multiply the wages by 30 to obtain monthly rates for comparison with table 10-8.
Source: Institute of Agricultural Economics, Secretariat of Agriculture, State of São Paulo, subjective mail survey of local agricultural stations.

Table 10-10. Rio de Janeiro City Manufacturing Sector: Results of Regressions of Median Wages on Selected Variables, 1952–73

Regression	Coefficients of independent variables (t ratios in parentheses)					
	Minimum wage[a]	Cost of living[b]	GDP per capita[c]	Constant	R^2	DW
1. All variables deflated by a time index[d]	0.390 (2.683)	5.705 (3.735)	3.256 (4.351)	5.375 (0.686)	0.99	2.7
2. All variables in natural logs deflated	0.476 (6.874)	0.228 (1.855)	0.280 (3.133)	1.589 (8.737)	0.99	1.8
3. All variables deflated by a price index[e]	0.662 (9.180)	n.a.	3.164 (2.850)	3.724 (2.815)	0.80	1.7
4. All variables in natural logs deflated by a price index[e]	0.519 (8.604)	n.a.	0.218 (2.941)	1.424 (11.630)	0.78	1.6

n.a. Not available.

Note: Median wages are for Rio de Janeiro manufacturing sector, in centavos of cruzeiros. Observations for March 1952, June 1954, March 1955, June 1955, March 1956, December 1956, April 1957, November 1957, April 1958, November 1958, April 1959, November 1959, April 1961, November 1961, April 1962, November 1962, and April 1963 from Bacha, Mata, and Modenesi (1972, p. 97); original sources: *Conjuntura Econômica* (1958), and *Anuario Estatístico do Brasil, 1965.* Observations for April of 1965, 1966, 1967, 1968, and 1969 calculated from Bacha, Mata, and Modenesi (1971, p. 69); original source: Ministry of Labor, Two-thirds Law. Observations for April of 1971, 1972, and 1973 calculated from Ministry of Labor, Two-thirds Law, 1972 (26 tabulations), 1973 (32 tabulations), and 1974 (38 tabulations).

a. Minimum wages for Rio de Janeiro, in centavos of cruzeiros, from *Anuario Estatístico do Brasil,* 1974.

b. Cost of living index for Rio de Janeiro, with 1965–67 = 100; data from *Conjuntura Econômica* (1975).

c. GDP per capita in current ten centavos of cruzeiros. Interpolated from series in *Conjuntura Econômica* (1971), and Vargas Foundation, *Sistema de Contas Nacionais*, 1974. The new GDP series was scaled down to be made compatible with the old series, using as a deflator the ratio of the respective GDP estimates for 1970.

d. Time index: number of months elapsing since the first observation in March 1952.

e. Price index: cost of living in Rio de Janeiro, with 1965–67 = 10,000. Deflation is used to counteract heteroscedasticity in the monetary series.

and the GDP per capita for the country as a whole. The results show the significance of the minimum wage as a determinant of the median wage after taking into account the independent effects of inflation and GDP growth on market wages. In fact, according to regressions 2 and 4, the elasticity of the median wage with respect to the minimum wage is approximately one-half—a sizable ratio in light of the fact that, at least since 1965, workers earning up to the minimum wage make up less than 40 percent of the labor force in the manufacturing sector of Rio. According to regressions 1 and 3, subtracting one cruzeiro from the minimum wage means subtracting between 48 and 66 centavos from the median wage.

The wage drift is indicated by the statistical significance of the coefficients of nominal GDP per capita and the cost of living in regressions 1 and 2, and by the coefficients of deflated GDP per capita in regressions 3 and 4. According to regression 2, for each 10 percent rise in the cost of living index (with constant minimum wages and nominal GDP per capita) the median wage increases by only 2.3 percent. This suggests that workers *are* hurt by inflation if the legal minimum wages are not properly readjusted. From regression 4, a 10 percent increase in deflated GDP, with constant real minimum wages, results in an increase of only 2.2 percent in median wages. This result is consistent with the idea that, under Brazilian conditions, workers will not get their fair share of productivity gains if legal minimum wage limits are not adequately increased.

The decline in unskilled urban wages was paralleled by a deterioration in living conditions of the poor in the largest Brazilian urban centers. *Favelas* (squatter settlements) were removed from downtown working areas, and water and sewerage facilities were inadequate. Diarrhea and malnutrition followed, while infant mortality increased substantially in the 1960s. The association between infant mortality trends in the Center-South and living conditions of the urban poor in the 1950s and 1960s is brought out by the data in table 10-11. We estimate correlation coefficients of −0.80 and −0.75 for the series of infant mortality and real minimum wages in São Paulo city and Belo Horizonte, respectively. The minimum wage plays two roles in this relationship: first, as a proximate index for the purchasing power of the urban poor; second, as a proxy for the urban poor's access to public goods such as clean water and medical facilities. In an unpublished manuscript, Dr. Walter Leser, from the Escola Paulista de Medicina in São Paulo, shows that the proportion of the population with access to clean water supplies in greater São Paulo declined throughout the 1960s. According to Leser's statistical results, the minimum wage is a significant explanatory variable in regression equations where the share of the population with access to clean water in São Paulo is included as an additional variable to explain the trends of infant mortality in that city in the postwar period.

Table 10-11. São Paulo and Belo Horizonte: Infant Mortality and Minimum Wages, 1952–73

<table>
<tr><th></th><th colspan="2">Infant mortality rate (per 1,000 born alive)</th><th colspan="2">Minimum wage index (São Paulo 1952 = 100)</th></tr>
<tr><th>Year</th><th>São Paulo</th><th>Belo Horizonte</th><th>São Paulo</th><th>Belo Horizonte</th></tr>
<tr><td>1952</td><td>71.0</td><td>n.a.</td><td>100</td><td>n.a.</td></tr>
<tr><td>1953</td><td>79.2</td><td>n.a.</td><td>88.2</td><td>n.a.</td></tr>
<tr><td>1954</td><td>79.7</td><td>n.a.</td><td>107.3</td><td>n.a.</td></tr>
<tr><td>1955</td><td>86.5</td><td>101.3</td><td>116.1</td><td>111.1</td></tr>
<tr><td>1956</td><td>86.4</td><td>104.6</td><td>119.4</td><td>111.0</td></tr>
<tr><td>1957</td><td>75.5</td><td>92.1</td><td>131.2</td><td>117.0</td></tr>
<tr><td>1958</td><td>70.2</td><td>95.8</td><td>114.0</td><td>101.6</td></tr>
<tr><td>1959</td><td>65.4</td><td>96.1</td><td>130.1</td><td>116.8</td></tr>
<tr><td>1960</td><td>62.9</td><td>74.2</td><td>115.1</td><td>103.4</td></tr>
<tr><td>1961</td><td>60.2</td><td>86.4</td><td>132.0</td><td>118.5</td></tr>
<tr><td>1962</td><td>64.4</td><td>76.7</td><td>120.4</td><td>108.1</td></tr>
<tr><td>1963</td><td>69.9</td><td>99.8</td><td colspan="2">109.7</td></tr>
<tr><td>1964</td><td>67.7</td><td>86.3</td><td colspan="2">110.8</td></tr>
<tr><td>1965</td><td>69.4</td><td>92.3</td><td colspan="2">103.2</td></tr>
<tr><td>1966</td><td>73.8</td><td>87.2</td><td colspan="2">94.6</td></tr>
<tr><td>1967</td><td>74.3</td><td>98.3</td><td colspan="2">91.4</td></tr>
<tr><td>1968</td><td>76.6</td><td>102.3</td><td colspan="2">92.5</td></tr>
<tr><td>1969</td><td>84.3</td><td>107.3</td><td colspan="2">89.3</td></tr>
<tr><td>1970</td><td>88.3</td><td>107.7</td><td colspan="2">86.0</td></tr>
<tr><td>1971</td><td>85.4</td><td>102.0</td><td colspan="2">87.1</td></tr>
<tr><td>1972</td><td>85.7</td><td>105.3</td><td colspan="2">89.3</td></tr>
<tr><td>1973</td><td>93.5</td><td>124.8</td><td colspan="2">82.1</td></tr>
</table>

n.a. Not available.

Sources: Average yearly minimum real wages for São Paulo (including extra monthly salary after 1962) from Suplicy (1974). Wages for Belo Horizonte were calculated by applying to the São Paulo data the average yearly differential between the nominal minimum wages in the two cities. Infant mortality rates from Instituto Brasileiro de Geografia e Estatística (IBGE), *Anuario Estatístico*, various issues, and from the Department of Statistics, State of São Paulo. The price deflator for wage data is the Vargas Foundation cost of living index for Rio de Janeiro, except for 1973 when the nongovernment-controlled Curitiba cost of living index is applied.

The results reported by Costa (1975), based on a population sample of the 1970 demographic census, are also relevant here: he finds that the life expectancy of the children of rural-urban migrants is lower than that of the children of rural inhabitants. It is not migration as such, but the deteriorating living conditions in the cities that explain the increase in infant mortality reported in table 10-11.

These results point strongly toward the conclusion that the minimum wage is not a meaningless index of real incomes of the urban poor. Similarly, even if table 10-9 shows that rural wages in São Paulo state drift past legal minimum wages in the capital, the average rural wage for the rest of the country follows very closely the behavior of minimum urban wages in the 1966–72 period, as shown in table 10-8. This last pattern *is* consistent with the idea that a causal relation between minimum wages and agricultural wages may hold for rural Brazil outside São Paulo.

This leads us to an inference often drawn about wage floors, that "higher minimum wage levels could have caused adverse employment effects for those at the bottom of the income distribution" (Macedo 1977, p. 119). Macedo himself remains uncommitted on the issue of whether higher minimum wages would protect only workers in formal urban markets, actually harming the working poor in the informal sector and the countryside by closing off modern sector job openings. Government-related economists have strongly asserted that this is the case, and their argument should be analyzed.

The anti-minimum wage argument really has separate micro- and macroeconomic strands. The micro variant emphasizes the negative effect of increases in (sectoral) real labor costs on (sectoral) employment levels. The macro argument asserts that high wages are likely to reduce aggregate saving, and therefore investment and output growth in the long run. We consider these assertions in turn.

The major piece of evidence supporting the hypothesis that labor cost increases may have had negative effects on employment in Brazil is from Bacha, Mata, and Modenesi (1971). They show that the elasticity of employment with respect to labor costs in the manufacturing sector is about 0.43 for the 1949–69 period. This is the average value of the elasticities in regressions for two-digit manufacturing sectors, weighted by their 1959 employment levels. In his Ph.D. dissertation, however, Macedo (1974) argued convincingly that these results are not robust. He relies on the observation that average wages (measured as the yearly wage bill divided by average monthly employment) can be expected to move cyclically opposite to employment. Such would be the case if both hirings and firings are concentrated at the low end of the pay scale, as predicted by the Doeringer and Piore (1971) internal labor market hypothesis and verified for Brazilian manufacturing by Macedo. In addition, the existence of internal labor markets suggests that the relevant variables to analyze are the minimum (or entrance) wage and employment of the unskilled, as opposed to the averages Bacha, Mata, and Modenesi used.

Because of the opposite cyclical movements of wages and employment, Macedo's argument suggests that an elasticity of employment with respect to wage costs of 0.43 overestimates the "true" capital-labor substitution response, if it even exists. Hence, the negative employment effect of minimum wages is not likely to be severe. Moreover, there are macro considerations suggesting that it may be further attenuated or even reversed.

Macro Effects of Nominal Wage Changes

We take it as likely from table 10-10 that government control of minimum wages (and other policy instruments) substantially influences the nominal level of wages received by different classes of workers. Our question is, What are the distributional and employment effects of government manipulation of the money wage?

This kind of question is most naturally answered by looking at shifts in the functional income distribution. After 1964 two plausible generalizations about the operation of the "modern" part of the Brazilian economy are: (1) firms could easily pass along increases in money labor costs by increasing output prices; and (2) profit or markup rates rose in response to greater pressure on available saving to satisfy rapidly growing investment demand.

The first observation means that employment responses to lagging money wages must have been quite weak, even if capital-labor substitution possibilities existed. Of importance for substitution are the changing *real* labor costs (the growth rate of money wages less the growth rate of output prices). Though real wages fell, the macro model simulations in chapter 4 show that the change was not enough to generate much new employment, even if an improbably strong substitution response is assumed. Conversely, more rapidly growing money wages might have led to higher real wages and a higher labor share, if the overall growth pattern of the 1960s had not been disturbed.

But is it admissible to describe the rest of the post-1964 growth story as though other elements remained unaltered? Probably not, for the second observation means that the functional distribution must have shifted toward capitalists during the growth spurt after 1965, given the modest growth in the balance of payments deficit and the fiscal cash surplus as alternative sources of saving. Here, the money wage lag *permitted* less reliance on deficit government finance and forced saving as an engine of growth, allowing capitalists' saving to come to the fore (Cardoso 1978). Wage repression and a declining labor share were inevitable counterparts to the military government's success in slowing inflation and stepping up the rate of output growth. The implications of the functional distribution changes for the income distribution by size are taken up under "Profits and Wage Spread" below.

Many of these same results reappear in more disaggregated form in the simulations of the general equilibrium model in chapter 9. In these, certain payments flows are fixed in nominal terms, and money wage increases are largely passed along in price increases in relation to these payments.[10] Under these circumstances, the elasticities of employment of different skill groups with respect to labor costs are both small and of uncertain sign. A related point is that precisely because they do not strongly affect employment patterns, shifts in relative payments to labor and capital induced by government policy (minimum wages, social security levies, profit taxes) can substantially affect the income distribution, as shown in detail in chapter 9.

All these macro arguments point to clear conflicts between the classes over wage policy. To put the issue bluntly, why should workers—rather than the middle classes or the rich themselves—have to pay through lagging nominal wages for the investment of the rich or of the state? In the models just described, different savings patterns among classes may explain *why* workers pay under current government policy, but they scarcely justify the existing arrangements. In fact, under other socioeconomic policies, ranging from a more humane tax structure up through outright expropriation, growth could be maintained or accelerated without making the workers worse off.[11]

10. That such price movements are at the heart of Keynes's view of capitalist macroeconomics is amply verified in chapters 2 and 19 of his *General Theory of Employment, Interest and Money* (1st ed., London, New York: Macmillan, 1936). His ideas are interpreted for planning models by Taylor and Lysy (1977).

11. These explosive social issues may help explain why economists linked to the Brazilian government have refrained from using forced-saving arguments to analyze the growth pattern of the 1960s. In fact, discussion of whether income concentration has furthered growth has been restricted to economists who are

Other Wage Policy Issues

Most students of the Brazilian labor market—such as Macedo (1977), Bacha (1976, Essay no. 2.4), Mata and Bacha (1973)—point to the importance of wage drift. Nonetheless, Mata and Bacha also emphasize that market phenomena alone do not seem able to explain the divergent behavior of blue-collar wages in the 1949–58 and the 1958–69 subperiods: measured as a percentage of productivity gains, real wage growth for production workers was equal to 0.56 in the second period, down from 0.79 in the first period. Although econometric evidence is not available, it is quite likely that this difference can be attributed to the fact that labor unions had a say about wages during 1948–59, whereas government fiat determined them during most of the second period.

In the 1960s there arises a hotly debated question of the *timing* of the income concentration process. As discussed in chapter 2, GDP growth over the decade can be divided into three subperiods: the first, 1960–62, when real output grew at 7.7 percent a year; the second, 1962–67, when the growth rate was down to 3.4 percent; and the last, 1967–70, with growth rates of GDP equal to 9.3 percent a year. There seems to be a tacit agreement that income distribution did not deteriorate between 1960 and 1962. Fishlow (1973*b*), Wells (1974), and Hoffmann (1973) argue that the deterioration occurred during the 1964–67 period, when the real minimum wage losses were sharper, whereas Langoni's argument of skilled labor scarcity is fitted for the years of high growth under military command since 1967. Unfortunately, there is no evidence on income distribution for the 1960–65 period, and the available data on earnings in the manufacturing sector since 1966 do not allow a clear distinction between the alternative hypotheses. This is because, for purposes of comparing income distributions, the ratio between the minimum wage and the GDP per capita clearly is a more satisfactory index of the wage compression policy than is the real value of the minimum wage, which is used by Fishlow, Wells, and Hoffmann. That ratio falls throughout the 1966–72 period and is highly negatively corre-

---

critical of the economic policies of the military regime. See, for example, Furtado (1968 and 1972), Serra (1972), Oliveira (1972), Fishlow (1973*a*, 1973*b*), Tavares and Serra (1973), Wells (1974, 1976), Tavares (1974), and Bacha (1976, Essay no. 1.3).

lated with the available indexes of industrial growth (table 10-12.).

In table 10-13 are results from several regressions attempting to explain Hoffmann's estimates of Gini coefficients in the manufacturing sector (from column 1 of table 10-12) with variables relating to wage policy and economic growth during 1966–72.[12] It turns out that the Gini coefficients in manufacturing are negatively related to the wage ratio in a statistically significant way, regardless of specification of the regression equation (regressions 2 through 4). When the value of industrial output and its growth rate enter the regression without the wage ratio (regression 1), they increase income concentration, but these effects become insignificant when the wage ratio is also included (regressions 2–4). Wage policy does appear to have some influence on income concentration within industry. The applicability of this finding to other sectors of the economy or to the 1960–65 period remains a moot point, however, since no data are available to test the competing hypotheses.

Profits and Wage Spread

Labor-surplus conditions and repressive labor policies help explain why Brazilian workers near the median of the size distribution benefited little if any from economic growth in the 1960s. Still lacking, however, is an explanation for the substantial real income increments enjoyed by those at the top of the income distribution.

The macroeconomic work by Cardoso (1978) suggests that rising profit shares are consistent with the character of the Brazilian growth process after 1964. Her profit numbers, however, are *derived*—though from models that otherwise fit available Brazilian data well. Unfortunately, information from primary sources about changes in the functional income distribution is extremely limited. The Vargas Foundation has published estimates of the labor share in urban income for 1949, 1959, and 1970–75

12. All equations include a dummy variable, IBGE, which separates the observations for the concentration ratios calculated from the Two-thirds Law (IBGE = 0) from the observations from the Instituto Brasileiro de Geografia e Estatística industrial surveys (IBGE = 1). For more information on data sources, see Hoffmann (1973).

Table 10-12. Concentration Ratios in Manufacturing Industry and Explanatory Variables, 1966–72

Data type and period	*Gini coefficient (1)*	*Real minimum wage (1966 = 100) (2)*	*Real* GDP *per capita (1966 = 100) (3)*	*Minimum wage ratio (4)*	*Growth rate of industry (5)*	*Industrial output (1966 = 100) (6)*
Two-thirds Law						
April 1967	0.370	95.5	101.9	93.9	6.9	101.7
April 1968	0.370	95.5	107.6	88.9	9.0	118.9
April 1969	0.407	80.3	113.9	70.4	13.6	131.3
April 1970	0.411	80.3	121.2	66.4	10.4	145.0
April 1971	0.410	79.4	130.8	60.7	10.2	159.6
April 1972	0.426	80.5	141.5	56.8	11.5	180.3
Instituto Brasileiro de Geografía e Estatística (IBGE)						
April 1966	0.356	100.0	100.0	100.0	3.5	100.0
November 1968	0.417	84.9	111.3	76.4	16.9	125.1
November 1969	0.425	84.6	118.1	71.8	10.4	138.2
November 1970	0.439	85.8	126.6	67.8	10.4	152.3

Sources: Column (1): Gini coefficients for 1966–71 from Hoffmann (1973); for 1972 from Wells (1974).

Column (2): Real minimum wages calculated from highest nominal minimum wage deflated by the general price index for domestic use, from Hoffmann (1973).

Column (3): Real GDP per capita interpolated from annual data in reports of the Central Bank of Brazil, 1973 and 1974.

Columns (5) and (6): Growth rate of industry and industrial output interpolated from annual data in Suzigan and others (1974, p. 127).

Table 10-13. Manufacturing Industry Gini Coefficients, 1966–72: Regression Coefficients and Standard Errors
(ten observations)

	Variables (standard errors in parentheses)						
Regression	*Constant*	*IBGE*	*Wage ratio*	*Industrial output*	*Growth rate of industry*	R^2	*Se*
1	0.259	0.0185	—	0.000790	0.00291	0.89	0.0111
	(12.07)	(2.50)		(4.74)	(2.53)		
2	0.534	0.0206	−0.00184	−0.0000879	0.00109	0.94	0.0094
	(3.54)	(3.24)	(−1.84)	(−0.18)	(0.78)		
3	0.619	0.0216	−0.00240	−0.000320	—	0.93	0.0091
	(6.06)	(3.60)	(−3.54)	(−0.83)			
4	5.35	0.0217	−0.00187	—	—	0.92	0.0089
	(33.92)	(3.70)	(−8.87)				

Source: Data from Hoffmann (1973).

(*Conjuntura Econômica* [1977], no. 8). These figures suggest that factoral income distribution was unchanged between 1949 and 1959 (with the wage share in both years equal to 56 percent), and that it shifted toward profit earners in the following decade (with the wage share roughly constant at 51 percent between 1970 and 1975). Data on profits in the manufacturing sector in Bacha, Mata, and Modenesi (1971), reproduced in table 10-14, suggest an increase in the share of profits in value added, especially since 1968. Some of this profit increase may have spilled over into the personal income estimates of the 1970 demographic census, which unfortunately are not disaggregated by income types. Profits tend to be reinvested during cyclical upturns, however, and nonearned incomes are not captured effectively by simple census questionnaires. Profit-related gains may account for only a small part of the income changes observed between the two census years.

What then does explain the substantial increase in earnings at the top of the census-based income distributions? We have already concluded that supply and demand for labor skill types would not alone explain the wage spread observed in the 1960s.

Table 10-14. Breakdown of Gross Value Added in Manufacturing, 1939–72

		Percentage share of gross value added		
Year	Gross value added (thousands of current cruzeiros)	Gross profits	Earnings plus labor tax	Earnings
1939	7.05	0.66	0.34	0.31
1949	41.00	0.64	0.36	0.33
1959	365.40	0.55	0.45	0.42
1966	10,255	0.54	0.46	0.37
1967	14,471	0.57	0.43	0.34
1968	24,178	0.64	0.36	0.28
1969	28,150	0.60	0.40	0.32
1970	43,200	0.63	0.37	0.29
1972	62,700	0.58	0.42	0.34

Note: Gross value added is equal to IBGE's "value of industrial transformation" minus "other indirect taxes" and "other expenditures" (excluding social security–related expenses). It is net of indirect taxes but gross of profit taxes and depreciation allowances. Labor tax includes severance pay but excludes employees' contribution to social security. Earnings are gross of employees' contribution to social security.

Sources: IBGE, Industrial Census 1939, 1949, 1959, and 1970; IBGE, Produção Industrial 1966, 1967, 1968, and 1969; and IBGE, Pesquisa Industrial 1972.

An alternative, non-neoclassical interpretation emphasizes the explanatory power of widening, hierarchy-related income differentials. According to this view, the labor market is segmented into two noncompeting groups, managers and laborers, with managers sharing in the residual income left over after workers are paid their wages. In this case, it is hierarchical position rather than qualification, or span of influence rather than marginal productivity, that determines a person's earnings. This statement obviously expresses an extreme view, since the empirical evidence reviewed below indicates that both qualification (as measured by years of education, age, and experience) and hierarchy (as measured by an index of functional importance of positions) are important determinants of individuals' earnings.

Bacha (1976, Essay no. 2.4) produced evidence—partially presented in table 10-7—that the earnings of managers (at the level of division and department heads) in a group of large Brazilian manufacturing firms increased on the average by 7.2 percent a year from 1966 to 1972, whereas the wages of semiskilled and skilled workers grew at 2.9 percent, and the wages of unskilled occupations declined by 1.3 percent a year in the same period. Skills proved to be important determinants of workers' wage increases, but even so these lagged the growth in payments to those occupying positions higher in the firms' hierarchy. A difficulty in Bacha's data is that all occupations requiring college education are labeled "managerial," hence qualification is not really given a fair test. Langoni (1973) includes a set of occupational dummies in regressions explaining income levels in 1970, but he distinguishes only between "employer," "employee," and "self-employed." If noncontractual incomes were adequately recorded, which certainly is not the case in Langoni's census figures, these dummies might provide a reasonable test of naive Marxist theories of income determination. Even then, they would fail to do justice to the hierarchy hypothesis. In any case, Langoni finds the coefficients of the occupational dummies statistically significant but with marginal contributions to the explanation of income inequality much smaller than education, age, sector, or region. Fishlow (1973*b*), working with 1960 census data, partially reverses Langoni's findings by allocating a fraction of the money income of rural family heads to the working members of the family who do not receive cash payments. In this case, occupation has the highest marginal contribution to the explanation of income followed by education, age, sector, and region. Fishlow's findings are a reminder of the pervasive importance of ownership patterns as a determinant of income distribution in rural settings, when sensible data corrections are made.[13]

Relevant results for the hierarchy hypothesis are reported in Pastore, Haller, and Gomez-Buendia (1975), who investigated a sample of more than 22,000 specialized workers in nearly 700 private industrial firms in São Paulo in 1970–71. They ran standardized multiple regressions of wages on variables representing occupational influence levels (in rank-order scores), job experience (in year-equivalents), and seniority (years with the firm). The two most important explanatory variables for wages are occupational influence level and education, the partial correlations of which with wages are, respectively, 0.33 and 0.32. Even in such a large sample, however, these two independent variables display a correlation coefficient as high as 0.40, hence their separate effects on wages are hardly distinguishable. This is borne out by the fact that the hierarchy variable alone explains 23 percent of the variance in wages, whereas all five explanatory variables together manage to explain no more than 36 percent. The unexplained portion of wage dispersion remains large even after including all reasonable socioeconomic variables in the analysis, as much in Langoni's census-based regressions as in Pastore's sample survey results.

In contrast to Pastore's large sample procedures, da Silva and Perez (1975) have done a detailed study of a single firm in the manufacturing sector of São Paulo. For each employee, they obtained data on wages, sex, age, education (eight levels), seniority and hierarchical position (unskilled worker, skilled worker, supervisor, white-collar employee, head of department, manager-director). They conclude that wage levels can be explained either by education or hierarchy. When both variables are included in the regression, hierarchy fares better than education. Multicollinearity is a serious problem, however, and the construction of the hierarchy variable is questionable. Consequently, the empirical results are difficult to interpret.

13. Sayad (1977) has called attention to the income concentration effect of subsidized credit programs, especially in the rural areas. Farms with over 200 hectares, accounting for 60 percent of total crop area, received 70 percent of total rural credit in 1970, with implicit subsidies estimated as equal to 12 percent of total federal government fiscal revenues.

The sociological and organizational considerations underlying the hierarchy hypotheses can be given more economic content by centering attention on the behavior of the public sector. Hard data are not available, but perhaps 15 percent is a reasonably good guess for the proportion of the Brazilian labor force working for the government (including public enterprises). This figure doubles if the agricultural sector is ignored. Outside the agricultural sector, the public sector probably absorbs more than 50 percent of total white-collar employment, a proportion which may have increased moderately between 1960 and 1970.

Macedo (1974) argues that the post-1964 wage crunch hit particularly hard on public functionaries in general government service (but not necessarily employees in public enterprises, for which he had no data). According to the national accounts, expenditures for wages and salaries in general government activities (again not public enterprises) remained roughly constant as a share of GDP. This gives credence to casual empirical observation that salaries paid to "supergrade" public employees rose substantially after 1964.

Similar evidence regarding remunerations to managers in public enterprise is provided by Bacha (1976, Essay no. 2.4), where it is shown that between 1966 and 1973 managers' salaries grew much faster in a sample of firms heavily weighted with public enterprises than in a second sample in which private firms prevailed. According to Mata and Bacha (1973), in 1966–69 white-collar salaries in the manufacturing sector grew fastest in the group of industries where public enterprises are dominant. These pieces and bits of evidence suggest that the public sector may have been the leading agent of wage spread since 1964. At least in part the higher salaries at the top were made possible by increases in taxes, public enterprise prices, and public utility rates. These could take place without reducing private profit rates because, at the same time, the wage policy was squeezing the remunerations of lower-paid occupations both in the public and private sectors.

The hierarchy hypothesis dovetails neatly with the Keynesian orientation of many of the ideas advanced previously about Brazilian income distribution. By providing a natural explanation of wage scales, it complements analyses of distributional responses to shifts in the money wage (as in chapters 4 and 5) or to changes in employment patterns (as in chapter 9).

Mutual consistency of a set of partial explanations for something as complex as the size distribution of income does not guarantee that they are correct. At least it does indicate, however, that they have to be met with something better than the non-critical analysts of income distribution in Brazil have so far produced.

Appendix: Brazilian Distributional Data

The process of discriminating between alternative hypotheses in the debate on Brazilian income distribution is made particularly difficult by the lack of an adequate data basis. The following is a very brief review of the availability of data on wages and income distribution in the country.[14]

The available sources of data on wage behavior are as follows:

1. Average wages on a yearly basis can be constructed for the manufacturing sector since 1949 from the surveys and census of the Instituto Brasileiro de Geografía e Estatística (IBGE). For most years, a breakdown by blue-collar and white-collar workers, by state, and by two-digit subsectors can be made. These wage data are subject to limitations derived from the mode of calculation as the ratio between the wage bill and average monthly employment. Other problems include missing observations and differing coverages of the yearly surveys.

2. Occupational wage series for the urban sector are available in private wage surveys of a restricted number of firms, as reported in Bacha (1976, Essay no. 2.4). At least one of these surveys starts in 1964 (GRUPISA), but the most systematic of them, by Companhia Siderúrgica Nacional, is available from 1966. At a very high level of aggregation, comparable occupational wage data can be obtained from the IBGE National Household Survey (PNAD) for the four quarters of 1968 and 1969, the first quarter of 1970, and the fourth quarters of 1972 and 1973. Monthly wages in the construction industry in five state capitals are available in special IBGE publications since 1969.

3. Finally, biannual wage data for rural occupation are available for the state of São Paulo in roughly comparable form with some missing observations since 1948 (Sendin 1971). For other

14. For additional details about data, see Fishlow and Meesook (1972), Bacha, Mata, and Modenesi (1972), Langoni (1973), and Werneck (1975).

states, the same information has been published from 1966 through 1973 in *Conjuntura Econômica* by the Vargas Foundation.

Factor shares information is harder to obtain. The Vargas Foundation used to publish an estimate of national income by factor types running from 1947 through 1962, but the series was discontinued because of its low reliability even by the standards of the Brazilian national accounts. Gross value added for the manufacturing sector can be obtained from the decennial industrial census and, by interpolation, from the yearly industrial surveys. Adjustment procedures are tricky, as Bonelli (1975) explains, but an approximate series for the share of wages in value added can be constructed for the manufacturing sector for most years after 1949; for no other productive sector can this be done with a reasonable degree of accuracy.

Size distributions of income are available from the demographic census of 1960 and 1970 and from the National Household Surveys. These data do not include income in kind (which is very important in the rural sector), direct tax payments, and, naturally, capital gains (obtained by accumulation of undistributed profits or otherwise). For the formal urban sector, earnings distributions are published by the Ministry of Labor annually since 1965, with an increasing degree of coverage and accuracy: this is the so-called Two-thirds Law data. Income tax returns also provide an alternative source of data for more recent years, as discussed by Langoni (1973). Different authors have had access to individual sample data from each of the sources above; at present, however, only aggregate data are available for general use, although IBGE has plans to produce a sample of the 1970 census for public use.

References

Ahluwalia, Montek S. 1976. Inequality, poverty and development. *Journal of development economics* 3(4) December: 307–42.

Ahluwalia, Montek S., John H. Duloy, Graham Pyatt, and T. N. Srinivasan. 1978. Who benefits from economic growth—An examination of Fields' reexamination for Brazil. Washington, D.C.: Development Research Center, World Bank; restricted circulation document.

Bacha, Edmar L. 1976. *Os mitos de uma década: Ensaios de economia brasileira.* Rio de Janeiro: Paz e Terra.

———. 1978. The Kuznets curve and beyond: Growth and changes in inequality. In Edmond Malinvaud, ed. *Economic Growth and Resources*. New York: St. Martin's Press, 1979.

Bacha, Edmar L., Milton da Mata, and Rui Lyrio Modenesi. 1972. *Encargos trabalhistas e absorção de mao-de-obra.* Coleção relatorios de pesquisa no. 12. Rio de Janeiro: Instituto de Planejamento Econômico e Social/Instituto de Pesquisas (IPEA/INPES).

Barbosa, M., S. Morley, and M. Souza. 1976. Evidencias sobre o mercado interno de trabalho en um processo de crescimento rapido. Brasilia: CNRH / Instituto de Planejamento Econômico e Social.

Bonelli, Regis. 1975. Growth and technological change in Brazilian manufacturing industries during the sixties. Ph.D. dissertation, University of California at Berkeley.

Cain, Glen. 1976. The challenge of segmented labor market theories to orthodox theory: A survey. *Journal of economic literature* 14(4):1215–57.

Cardoso, Eliana A. 1978. Growth and real wages: Modelling the Brazilian economic miracle. Cambridge: Massachusetts Institute of Technology, Department of Economics; processed.

Carvalho, Livio. 1973. Princípios e aplicação da política salarial pos-1964. Ensaios para discussao no. 8. Brasília: University of Brasília, Department of Economics.

Costa, R. 1975. Size income distribution of Brazil in 1970: A cross-section analysis of income distribution by occupations. Ph.D. dissertation, Vanderbilt University.

DIEESE (Departmento Intersindical de Estatística e Estudos Sócio-Econômicos). 1975. *10 Anos de politica salarial*. São Paulo; processed.

Doeringer, Peter, and Michael Piore. 1971. *Internal Labor Markets and Manpower Analysis*. Lexington: D. C. Heath.

Fields, Gary S. 1977. Who benefits from economic development? A reexamination of Brazilian growth in the 1960's. *American economic review* 67(4):570–82.

Fishlow, Albert. 1972. Brazilian size distribution of income. *American economic review* 62(2):391–402.

———. 1973*a*. Some reflections on post-1964 Brazilian economic policy. In A. Stepan, ed. *Authoritarian Brazil*. New Haven: Yale University Press.

———. 1973*b*. Brazilian income size distribution: Another look. Berkeley: University of California, Department of Economics; processed. Published in Portuguese as: Distribuição da renda no Brasil: Um novo exame. *Dados* 11(1973):10–80. (Published by Instituto Universitario de Pesquisas, Rio de Janeiro.)

Fishlow, Albert, and Astra Meesook. 1972. Technical appendix: Brazilian size distribution of income, 1960. Berkeley: University of California, Department of Economics; processed.

Furtado, Celso. 1968. *Um projeto para o Brasil*. Rio de Janeiro: Civilização Brasileira.

———. 1972. *Análise do 'modelo' brasileiro*. Rio de Janeiro: Civilização Brasileira.

Hoffman, Helga. 1976. Wage indexation and anti-inflationary incomes policy in Brazil. *Bulletin of the Society for Latin American Studies*. University of Leicester.

Hoffmann, Rudolfo. 1973. Consideracoes sobre a evolução recente da distribuição da renda no Brasil. *Revista de administração de empresas* 13(4):7–17.

———. 1976. Distribuição da renda no Brasil: Uma adendo e uma correção a um artigo de Morley e Williamson. *Estudos econômicos*. São Paulo: FIPE/USP.

Hoffmann, Rudolfo, and J. C. Duarte. 1972. A distribuição da renda no Brasil. *Revista de administração de empresas* 12(2):46–66.

Kuznets, Simon. 1955. Economic growth and income inequality. *American economic review* 45(March):1–28.

Langoni, Carlos Geraldo. 1972. Distribuição da renda e desenvolvimento econômico do Brasil: Uma analise da década 1960–70. São Paulo: Instituto de Pesquisas Econômicas and Ministerio da Fazenda; processed.

———. 1973. *Distribuição da renda e desenvolvimento econômico do Brasil*. Rio de Janeiro: Editora Expressão e Cultura.

Macedo, Roberto Bras Matos. 1974. Models of the demand for labor and the problem of labor absorption in the Brazilian manufacturing sector. Ph.D. dissertation, Harvard University.

———. 1977. A critical review of the relation between post-1964 wage policy and the worsening of Brazil's size income distribution in the 1960's. *Explorations in economic research* 4(1):117–40.

Malan, Pedro, and John Wells. 1973. Distribuição da renda e desenvolvimento econômico do Brasil. *Pesquisa e planejamento econômico,* 3(4):1103–24. Reproduced in R. Tolipan, and A. C. Tinelli. *A controversia sobre distribuição da renda e desenvolvimento.* Rio de Janeiro: Zahar Editores, 1975.

Mata, Milton da, and Edmar L. Bacha. 1973. Emprego e salarios na industria de transformação, 1949–69. *Pesquisa e planejamento econômico* 3(4). Reproduced as Essay no. 2.3 in Bacha (1976).

Morley, Samuel A., and Jeffrey G. Williamson. 1974. Demand, distribution and employment: The case of Brazil. *Economic development and cultural change* 23(1):33–60.

———. 1975. Growth, wage policy and inequality: Brazil in the 1960s. Social Systems Research Institute Workshop Series no. 7519. Madison, Wis.: University of Wisconsin; processed.

Oliveira, Francisco. 1972. A economia brasileira: Critica a razao dualistica. *Estudos Cebrap* 2:3–82 (São Paulo).

Pastore, J., A. Haller, and H. Gomez-Buendia. 1975. Wage differentials in São Paulo's labor force. *Industrial relations* 14(3):345–57.

Sayad, J. 1977. Planejamento, credito e distribuição da renda. *Estudos econômicos* (São Paulo, April).

Sendin, P. 1971. Elaboração de um indice de salarios rurais para o Estado de São Paulo. Institute of Agricultural Economics, Secretariat of Agriculture, State of São Paulo.

Serra, José. 1972. El milagro econômico brasileno: Realidad o mito? *Revista Latino Americana de ciencias sociales* 3(June): 171–216 (Santiago, Chile).

———. 1975. A reconcentracão da renda: Justificacoes, explicacoes, duvidas. In R. Tolipan and A. C. Tinelli. *A controversia sobre distribuição da renda e desenvolvimento.* Rio de Janeiro: Zahar Editores, 1975.

Silva, J. G., and M. Perez, 1975. A importancia da educação e da hierarquia na diferenciação dos salarios: Um estudo de caso. *Revista de administração de empresas* 15(5):52–61.

Simonsen, Mario H. 1975. A politica salarial dos governos da revolução. Brasília: House of Representatives Committee on Wage Policy, November 18; processed.

Singer, P. 1975. Desenvolvimento e repartição da renda no Brasil. In R. Tolipan and A. C. Tinelli. *A controversia sobre distribuição da renda e desenvolvimento.* Rio de Janeiro: Zahar Editores, 1975.

Suplicy, E. M. 1974. Alguns aspectos da politica salarial. *Revista de administração de empresas* 14(5):32–45.

Suzigan, W., and others. 1974. *Crescimento industrial no Brasil: Incentivos e desempenho recente.* Relatório de pesquisa no. 26. Rio de Janeiro: Instituto de Planejamento Econômica e Social (IPEA).

Tavares, Maria Conceição. 1969. Caracteristicas da distribuição da renda no Brasil. Rio de Janeiro: Escritorio CEPAL/ILPES; processed.

———. 1974. *Acumulação de capital e industrialização no Brasil.* Rio de Janeiro: Tese de Livre Docencia, Faculdade de Economia e Administração, Universidade Federal do Rio de Janeiro.

Tavares, Maria Conceição, and J. Serra. 1973. Beyond stagnation: A discussion on the nature of recent development in Brazil. In James F. Petras, ed. *Latin America: From dependence to revolution.* New York: John Wiley.

Taylor, Lance, and Frank J. Lysy. 1979. Vanishing income redistribution: Keynesian clues about model surprises in the short run. *Journal of development economics* 6(March):11–30.

Theil, H. 1967. *Economics and information theory.* Amsterdam: North-Holland.

Velloso, J. P. 1975. Brasil social. Depoimento na Comissão Parlamentar de Inquerito sobre Political Salarial, Camara dos Deputados, September 24. Rio de Janeiro: Serviços Gráficos, Instituto Brasileiro de Geografía e Estatística.

Wells, John. 1974. Distribution of earnings, growth and the structure of demand in Brazil during the 1960s. *World Development* 2(1). Published in Portuguese in R. Tolipan and A. C. Tinelli. *A controversia sobre distribuição da renda e desenvolvimento.* Rio de Janeiro: Zahar Editores, 1975.

———. 1976. The distribution of personal income in Brazil during the 'sixties': A critical note on a recent paper by Morley and

Williamson. Cambridge: University of Cambridge, Faculty of Economics and Politics; processed. Published in Portuguese in *Estudos econômicos* (FIPE/UPS).

Werneck, D. 1975. As estimativas sobre emprego na indústria de construção. *Pesquisa e planajamento econômico*, 5(2):577–92.

INDEX

(*Page numbers in italics designate tables.*)

The full range of World Bank publications, both free and for sale, is described in the *Catalog of World Bank Publications;* the continuing research program is outlined in *World Bank Research Program: Abstracts of Current Studies.* Both booklets are updated annually; the most recent edition of each is available without charge from the Publications Unit, World Bank, 1818 H Street, N.W., Washington, D.C. 20433, U.S.A.

Lance Taylor is professor of nutrition economics at the Center for International Studies, Massachusetts Institute of Technology. Edmar L. Bacha is professor of economics at the Catholic University of Rio de Janeiro. Eliana A. Cardoso is assistant professor of economics at Boston University. Frank J. Lysy is assistant professor of political economy at Johns Hopkins University. All have been consultants to the World Bank Development Research Center.